Out&About

in Rochester & Southeastern Minnesota

Adventure Publications, Inc.
Cambridge, Minnesota

Dedication

For my husband, Jay,
and my son, Evan,
who bring joy to my journey.

Acknowledgments

It is with deep appreciation, love, and gratitude that I honor my husband, Jay, for the gifts of time and encouragement he so generously gave me during the writing of this book. His unconditional love, support, and faith in me made it possible for me to pursue my aspirations of becoming a published author. Jay, you are an extraordinary man, and I love you.

I especially appreciate the help I received from my eight-year-old son, Evan, who traveled with me on many hot summer days instead of spending an afternoon at the pool or playground. Evan's "eagle eyes" and keen observation skills lead to many delightful discoveries and made our journey throughout southeastern Minnesota lots of fun. Thank you, Evan, for being such a patient, well-behaved boy. Always remember, I love you.

To my sister, Victoria Bowman; my parents, Paul and Pamela Onori; my grandmother, Florence Onori; and my grandparents William and Norah Calligan, thank you for always believing in me. I love you.

To my dear friends, Cathy Dillon, Lisa Ganser, Gloria Jensen, Sue Kosharek, Kristin Limberg, Lynda Pietruszka, Tami Ramirez, Kris Ulsh, and Linda Wenner, I am so blessed to have you all in my life. Thank you for celebrating my successes and sharing my sorrows. Your friendship, prayers, support, and words of encouragement are so precious to me. Also, many thanks to my friend, Carol Tamminga, who gave me the idea for this book.

To my forever friends, Patricia Aurenz, Laura Dubato, Lori Hudson, and Brenda Stoeckmann, you are so dear to me. I miss you all very much.

To Gordon and Gerri Slabaugh of Adventure Publications, thank you so much for giving me the opportunity to write and publish my first book. It has been a challenging and rewarding experience.

Most importantly, I thank the Lord, our God, for bestowing all these blessings and gifts upon me.

Note

Please use good common sense while traveling out & about. Neither Adventure Publications nor the author can be held liable for any injury or damage resulting from the use of this guide. The author has made every attempt to verify contact information, cost and hours for the sites in this guide, but please call ahead to verify.

Copyright 2003 by Nicole Onori Hansen
Published by Adventure Publications, Inc.
820 Cleveland Street South
Cambridge, MN 55008
Printed in the United States of America
ISBN 1-59193-004-9

Table of Contents

Introduction **5**

Part I: Arts & Entertainment **7**
Chapter 1: Art Centers & Galleries 8
Chapter 2: Performing Arts & Music 18
Chapter 3: Coffeehouses & Tea Rooms 36
Chapter 4: Story Telling 47

Part II: Tours & Excursions **49**
Chapter 5: Attractions & Points of Interest 50
Chapter 6: Historic Sites 58
Chapter 7: Museums 66

Part III: Seasonal Events **73**
Chapter 8: Seasonal Events: Winter 74
Chapter 9: Seasonal Events: Spring 82
Chapter 10: Seasonal Events: Summer 89
Chapter 11: Seasonal Events: Fall 105

Part IV: Outdoor Activities **112**
Chapter 12: Campgrounds 113
Chapter 13: Horseback Riding, Hay & Sleigh Rides 130
Chapter 14: Nature Centers 134
Chapter 15: Farmers' Markets, Gardening, Orchards,
   Berry Picking & Christmas Tree Farms 139
Chapter 16: Parks 147
Chapter 17: Zoos & Wildlife 161

Part V: Sports & Recreation **170**
Chapter 18: Recreational Sports 171
Chapter 19: Spectator Sports 239
Chapter 20: Winter Recreation 244

Part VI: Bits & Pieces **257**
Chapter 21: Birthday Party Places 258
Chapter 22: Health, Wellness & Spiritual Resources 262
Chapter 23: Special Interest Groups & Clubs 267
Chapter 24: Unique Shopping 283

Part VII: Appendices **290**
Appendix 1: Rochester City Map 291
Appendix 2: Rochester Downtown Map, Subway & Skyway 292
Appendix 3: Rochester Park & Recreation Map .293
Appendix 4: Seating Charts to Area Theaters & Arenas 294
Appendix 5: Chambers of Commerce 301
Appendix 6: Visitor Information & Tourist Centers 302
Appendix 7: Historical Societies 304

Index **306**

Cost Key

The dollar symbol is used throughout the book as a general guideline for the approximate cost of an activity. It is recommended that you contact an establishment directly for specific price information.

$–Inexpensive
$$
$$$–Moderate
$$$$
$$$$$–Very Expensive

It's always a good idea to call ahead before making a visit to any of the sites and events within this guide. For some of the organizations and clubs, the contact information provided is for the director, coach or organizer. Please keep in mind that you might be calling a person's home phone or place of business.

Seating charts for area theaters and arenas are for reference only. Seating may vary based on performances. Special thanks to the Rochester Convention and Visitors Bureau and the Rochester Civic Center for providing maps and charts.

INTRODUCTION

The distinction of Most Livable Small City in America was earned by Rochester, Minnesota in *Money* magazine's 13th annual Best Places to Live Survey in its November 1999 issue. Rochester also received the honor of Most Livable City in America by the *Money* magazine survey in 1993, and was rated the Most Livable Small Midwestern City in 1998. Furthermore, *Redbook* magazine named Rochester one of the ten best cities for working mothers in June, 1996.

Rochester was an undiscovered treasure until the *Money* magazine survey bestowed its praises on the city as one of the top three places to live for five consecutive years, from 1993–1997. Although *Money* changed its survey method in 1998 by comparing cities according to size, Rochester has continued to receive exemplary honors in the small city category. More impressively, these remarkable achievements have been unprecedented by any other large or small city included in the survey since its inception in 1986.

The big city amenities that Rochester provides to both visitors and residents within the safe and convenient environment of a smaller city exemplifies its unique atmosphere. Moreover, this mid-sized, Midwestern hub (Olmsted County population 124,000-plus) exudes a distinct cosmopolitan flavor largely due to the consistent influx of foreign visitors to the city. International visitors who seek medical care at Rochester's world-famous Mayo Clinic comprise approximately 2.5% of its annual 1.1 million outpatient visits. In fact, it is common to see people from around the world adorned in their customary ethnic attire and speaking their native tongues in this locale that borders the heart of rural America. In fact, the Mayo Clinic accommodates these international visitors by providing interpreters for approximately 32 different languages, and more than 50 languages are spoken within the student body of the Rochester Public Schools.

Rochester "officially" became the third largest city in Minnesota in 2002 when the State Demographic Center indicated its population had grown to 89,000-plus citizens. Although the trend in this southeastern Minnesota community is growth, according to Phil Wheeler, Olmsted County Planner, the city of Rochester and Olmsted County have maintained control of Rochester's growth by remaining committed to its land use plans. Rochester currently ranks 87th on the nation's list of fastest-growing metropolitan areas based upon data from the 2000 census. In addition to this, the Rochester Public School System exceeded an enrollment of 16,000 students for the first time in its history during the fall of 1999, and boasts the third highest high school graduation rate as compared to 300 similarly sized cities by a *Rochester Profile and Business Reference Guide, 1999–2000 Edition*, published by the Rochester Area Chamber of Commerce. It is interesting to note that 27% of Olmsted County's population was comprised of children and youth 18 years of age and younger according to information gathered by the United States Census Bureau in 2000.

One look at Rochester's booming growth in population, home construction, school enrollment and commercial development indicates that more people are relocating to Rochester, Minnesota, to take advantage of the quality of life its residents have enjoyed for years.

What makes Rochester such a grand place to live and raise a family? It is the low crime rate, clean air and water, outstanding health care, a great public school system, extraordinary parks, and a well-balanced, diverse selection of social, cultural, and recreational activities for all ages that makes Rochester an awesome place to live! Better yet, all this is available within 10–20 minutes of one's doorstep. Newcomers and long time residents of this upper Midwestern city are attracted to these amenities despite the bone-chilling winters. Perhaps it is the 200-plus sunny days per year that make the cold not only tolerable, but enjoyable for both lovers of winter recreation and those who prefer the warmth of indoor activities.

Although Rochester continues to be a thriving community primarily due to the traditional work ethic and spirit of volunteerism embraced by its citizens, the national media attention it has received from *Money* magazine's Best Places to Live Survey has sparked the interest of many Americans eager to find a wholesome place to raise their families. As a result of the *Money* survey, the Rochester Area Chamber of Commerce receives hundreds of inquiries per year from prospective residents, and the city hosts approximately 1.5 million visitors annually.

Out & About in Rochester & Southeastern Minnesota is the first comprehensive guidebook for residents and visitors of Rochester that features the city as a place to live, work, visit, and play. It is not always necessary to look 80 miles north to the Twin Cities of Minneapolis and Saint Paul to find a multitude of things to do. Social, cultural, recreational, and civic opportunities are abundant in Rochester and southeastern Minnesota. Visitors, residents, and newcomers no longer need to rely upon word-of-mouth recommendations to become familiar with Rochester because *Out & About in Rochester & Southeastern Minnesota* makes it easy to locate arts and entertainment, outdoor activities, seasonal events, sports and recreation, tours and excursions, historic sites, and commonly requested community information. The guidebook is a useful tool and practical resource for singles, couples, families with children, youth, and teens as well as teachers, youth leaders, or other persons in a position to plan and implement trips, activities, or outings for small or large groups. Organized into seven, easy-to-read sections, readers of *Out & About in Rochester & Southeastern Minnesota* will be pleasantly surprised to discover the wealth of opportunities available throughout the region. May you have a safe and enjoyable journey as you go out and about in Rochester and southeastern Minnesota.

Part I:
Arts & Entertainment

Chapter 1: Art Centers & Galleries presents a guide to a wide variety of local and regional art centers and retail galleries.

Chapter 2: Performing Arts & Music has information about theaters, musical groups, magicians, and children's music organizations and classes.

Chapter 3: Coffeehouses & Tea Rooms covers places to grab a cup of coffee to go as well as those that offer regularly scheduled entertainment.

Chapter 4: Story Telling provides information about places that regularly schedule story telling events for children.

Chapter 1: Art Centers & Galleries

ROCHESTER
Art in the Sky
skyway of 1ˢᵗ Street parking ramp, downtown Rochester
For more information contact the Youth Commission of Olmsted County, (507) 287-2135

The Youth Commission of Olmsted County has sponsored Art in the Sky since 1996. This unique gallery, located in the public skyways of the 1ˢᵗ Street Parking Ramp, showcases the artwork of area students. The skyway gallery has exhibited more than 3,000 pieces of student artwork. Rotating displays include an interesting variety of art forms and mediums.

Artistic Framers
16 3ʳᵈ Street SW, Rochester, MN 55902, (507) 281-4890

Artistic Framers, located on Historic 3ʳᵈ Street, offers creative framing by a certified framer as well as a large selection of framed and unframed original and fine art and a tasteful collection of seasonal gifts and home decor. The works of renowned artists such as Thomas Kinkade, Guy Buffet, Trisha Romance, Simon Bull, Danielle Deplan, Greg Olsen, and others may be found at Artistic Framers.

Cost: varies by purchase
Hours: Monday, Tuesday, Wednesday, Friday, 9 a.m.–5:30 p.m.; Thursday, 9 a.m.–8
    p.m.; Saturday, 9 a.m.–3 p.m.

Callaway Gallery
101 1ˢᵗ Avenue SW, Rochester, MN 55902, (507) 287-6525
Located on the subway level of the Marriott Hotel.

A variety of contemporary art forms are available for viewing or purchase at Callaway Gallery. The gallery features the work of artists from Rochester, North America, and Mexico with a large selection of wearable art in the form of fabric, jewelry, and leather. There are also many pieces of "functional artwork" made from wood, metal, and glass such as lamps, clocks, vases, and jewelry boxes as well as the more traditional wall art and sculpture. The highly sought after Oaxacan woodcarvings of Mexico are also available at Callaway Gallery.

Cost: varies by purchase
Hours: Monday–Friday, 9:30 a.m.–5:30 p.m.; Saturday, 10 a.m.–4 p.m.

The Gilded Star Gallery
324 South Broadway, Rochester, MN 55904, (507) 535-7572

A love of art inspired owner, Barbara Gentling Truax of Rochester, to open The Gilded Star Gallery in downtown Rochester. The gallery is located in a historic building (circa 1910) that was originally a bakery and in recent years was the home of Broadway Antiques. Newly opened in December 2001, the three-story gallery has exposed brick walls and rich hardwood floors, which not only provide a distinctive space for the display of artwork, but also a warm atmosphere for visitors. Displays at The Gilded Star Gallery include the original work of local, regional, national, and international artists in a variety of mediums and styles. Unique to The Gilded Star is the opportunity for artists to have Premier Openings at the gallery as well as a bridal registry, art classes for youth and adults, art appreciation workshops, and Hang It Again, a consignment service for fine artwork. Studio space may be rented for special events and receptions. Please inquire at the gallery.

Cost: varies by purchase
Hours: Monday–Friday, 11 a.m.–6 p.m.; Saturday, 10 a.m.–2 p.m.; or by appointment

Herring Art and Frame

5500 Hwy. 63 South, Rochester, MN 55904, (507) 288-4339, 800-950-2293, www.herringart.com, e-mail: vinceherring@aol.com

Rochester's premier retail art gallery and frame shop, Herring Art and Frame, was established by Vince and Mary Herring more than 30 years ago. As certified picture framers, the Herrings have been nationally and internationally recognized with awards by the Professional Picture Framers Association and induction into the National Picture Framers Hall of Fame for their outstanding work in creative framing. As an authorized Wild Wings Dealer and Signature Dealer for Thomas Kinkade, the gallery at Herring Art and Frame offers customers a distinctive selection of quality artwork. Visitors browsing through the warm and peaceful atmosphere of the gallery will find a complete collection of Terry Redlin prints, a large selection of artwork by nationally published artists as well as local and regional favorites such as Marc Hanson, Michael Sieve, and Charlotte Wiskow. Art-related giftware available at Herring Art includes collectible plates and figurines, notecards, heirloom ornaments, and decorative boxes imbedded with tile replicas of printed art.

Cost: varies by purchase
Hours: Monday–Saturday, 9 a.m.–5:30 p.m. or by appointment

James Krom Natural Images

20 2nd Avenue SW, Rochester, MN 55902, (507) 281-2827, 800-747-1458, e-mail: jimkrom@aol.com
Second location at 101 1st Street SW, Rochester, MN 55902, in the subway level of the Marriott Plaza Hotel, (507) 281-2827

James Krom Natural Images is located in the subway level of the Marriott Plaza Hotel. The gallery sells both decorative and functional artwork by approximately 27 artists, most from Minnesota. The art collection at Natural Images includes a variety of paintings, still life, wildlife, and landscapes by James Krom and others in watercolor, acrylic, and oils. The medley of artwork available also includes, but is not limited to, delicate blown glass sculptures, wood turned bowls, vases, and candleholders as well as wearable art in the form of silk painted scarves, pant suits, jackets, and tee shirts by Mary Elizabeth Sheehan, and dichroic glass jewelry by Betty Devine and Judy David.

Cost: varies by purchase
Hours: Monday–Friday, 10 a.m.–5 p.m., both locations

L'Atelier

9 1st Street NW, Rochester, MN 55901, (507) 281-9176

L'Atelier has been the gallery and studio of Rochester artist, Claire Jane Schulz, for more than sixteen years. This L'Atelier or "working studio" is described by the artist as an off-beat gallery that displays and sells fine art. Her artistic endeavors include more than 25 years experience with watercolor and oil painting as well as teaching these mediums to adults through Rochester's Community Education program. Ms. Schulz is a member of the Twin Cities WaterColor Society. She also accepts commissioned work.

Cost: varies by purchase
Hours: by chance or appointment

Mayo Medical Center Art Collection

Hilton, Mayo and Siebens Buildings, 200 1st Street SW, Rochester, MN 55905, (507) 284-2511 or (507) 538-1091, www.mayo.edu or www.mayoclinic.org/becomingpat-rst/tours.html

The Mayo Medical Center Art Collection may be viewed by taking the guided Mayo Clinic Art Tour or browsing through the artwork displays at your own pace. The guided, one-hour tour begins at the information booth adjacent to Judd Auditorium in the subway level of the Mayo building. Although the tour may change from time to time due to the rotation of exhibits, visitors will experience the work of renowned national and international artists that is displayed throughout the Mayo, Hilton, Siebens, Plummer, and Gonda Buildings. Highlights of the Mayo collection located in the Gonda Building include Dale Chihuly's "Untitled" blown glass chandeliers, Ivan Mestrovic's "Man and Freedom" sculpture, Yaacov Agam's "Welcome," a rotating triangular monolith that intrigues viewers with its metamorphosis of color, and a photographic mural entitled "My Brother and I," which honors the Mayo brothers, Dr. William J. Mayo and Dr. Charles H. Mayo. Some other interesting exhibits displayed throughout the Clinic are samples of Andy Warhol's "Pop Art" (located across from the Patient and Visitor Cafeteria in the Mayo Clinic subway), terra cotta panels from the exterior of the original Mayo Clinic Building mounted onto the walls of the Siebens subway, and the stunning architecture of the Plummer Building. Although it involves a great deal of walking through many Mayo Medical Center buildings, it is well worth your time to view this truly impressive art collection.

Cost: free
Hours: tour: Monday–Friday, 1:30 p.m.
  Mayo Medical Center: 8 a.m.–5 p.m.

The Peace Fountain and Charles Eugene Gagnon

Peace Plaza in downtown Rochester
Gagnon Sculpture Gallery (private tours only), (507) 282-5202

The "Peace Fountain," a twelve-foot-high bronze sculpture created by the sculptor for the City of Rochester, was unveiled in 1989 and has become a historic landmark in downtown Rochester's Peace Plaza. "The fifty-seven peace doves uplift the human spirit in an unending quest for global peace and symbolize the fifty states and seven major continents of the world." The graceful sculpture embraces and communicates the values that have come to reflect the sculptor's work. In fact, the United Nations Educational Scientific and Cultural Organization in Paris, France, honored Charles E. Gagnon in 1991 for the "Peace Fountain" sculpture by selecting it to be featured in the UNESCO Courier, a publication printed in 35 languages and distributed to 120 countries throughout the world.

Charles Eugene Gagnon, an internationally renowned sculptor, has been a Rochester resident for more than 40 years. As a sculptor, Mr. Gagnon strives to "bring a sense of hope, joy, and intrinsic dignity to mankind" through his artistic contributions, which have been commissioned, exhibited and honored throughout the world in the United States, Canada, Japan, South America, the United Kingdom, and Europe. His work has been influenced by the Baroque period, nineteenth century French sculpture as well as the objective and figurative sculptures from the early and mid-twentieth century.

Mr. Gagnon's artistic accomplishments have earned him honors by the Smithsonian Institution (1998), The Mayor's Gold Medal of Honor for Artistic and Cultural Achievement (Rochester, 1987), inclusion in a Vatican Collection (1984), the Dictionary of International Biography (1977), Who's Who in American Art, Who's Who in the Midwest, and Who's Who in America (1976), and an Exhibition and Purchase Award at the Madison Avenue Gallery in New York City (1962).

In addition to the "Peace Fountain," Rochester residents and visitors may view sculptures that have been commissioned and created by Charles E. Gagnon at Saint Mary's Hospital, "Saint Francis" (1969); Mayo Clinic, "Dancer Stretching" (1969) and "Bust of Conrad N. Hilton"; and Zumbro Lutheran Church, "Crucifixion" (1969). Currently, Charles Gagnon along with his wife Arlyn continue to make Rochester their home. He maintains a working studio in Rochester and is highly sought after by public institutions and private collectors throughout the world for the commission and creation of new sculptures.

The Gagnon Sculpture Gallery, located in Rochester, is open to private tours only. For more information, please call (507) 282-5202.

Rochester Art Center
320 East Center Street, Rochester, MN 55904, (507) 282-8629, www.rochesterusa.com/artcenter

The Rochester Art Center, originally established in 1946 as a nonprofit organization, continues to provide the community with year-round exhibitions of local, regional, national, and international artists. Exhibition openings are open to the public and offer art enthusiasts the chance to meet the exhibiting artist. Rotating exhibits may include displays of traditional or contemporary forms of painting, drawing, sculpture, photography, clay works, textiles, and other media. The innovative programs also offered by the Rochester Art Center are a reflection of the organization's commitment to bring art into the community for people of all ages. Programs such as artist workshops in the schools, organizing public outdoor art projects, arranging gallery tours, film presentations, and lectures as well as providing hands-on art classes for children, youth, and adults are just some of the opportunities available through the Rochester Art Center.

Currently, the Rochester Art Center has plans to become the premier center for the visual arts in the region with the construction of a new 36,000-square-foot facility. The updated art center will have a Grand Lobby, an art wing overlooking the river with exhibition galleries, classroom studios, and a café. Its relocation within the Mayo Civic Center Complex will make it a more integral part of Rochester's conference and entertainment venues by providing visitors easy access to the Art Center via downtown skyways and building connections to the Civic Center.

Cost: free
Hours: Tuesday, Wednesday, Friday & Saturday, 10 a.m.–5 p.m.; Thursday, 10 a.m.– 5 p.m.; Sunday, noon–5 p.m.; Monday, closed

SEMVA—Southeastern Minnesota Visual Artists Gallery

16 1st Street SW, Rochester, MN 55902, (507) 281-4920, www.semva.com
Located on the Peace Plaza in downtown Rochester.

SEMVA is a nonprofit, cooperative gallery that was created in 1989 by local and regional visual artists. This unique gallery provides a gathering place for artists as well as a community venue to support and appreciate the visual arts. The SEMVA Gallery boasts Rochester's largest selection of original fine arts and crafts. Exhibits include an eclectic selection of paintings, drawings, beadwork, woodcarving, fiber arts, sculpture, pottery, photography, folk art, Hardanger, jewelry, batik, and more. As you browse through the gallery, it is especially interesting to read the artist biographies that are located adjacent to their work. You may even have the opportunity to meet your favorite artist since they staff the gallery on a rotating basis.

Cost: varies by purchase
Hours: Monday, Tuesday, Wednesday & Friday, 10 a.m.–6 p.m.; Thursday, 10 a.m.–
    9 p.m.; Saturday, 10 a.m.–6 p.m.; Sunday, noon–4 p.m.

The Silver Pear at the Fast Frame Gallery

324 1st Avenue SW, Rochester, MN 55902, (507) 287-8488

The Silver Pear, located within the Fast Frame Gallery, is a quality gift shop that prides itself on offering customers an exclusive selection of artwork including many one-of-a-kind pieces in all types of media. Whether you're looking for wall art, ornamental glass, fountains, handmade soaps, or sculpture, browse the Silver Pear to find a your special treasure.

Cost: varies by purchase
Hours: Monday–Thursday, 9:30 a.m.–6 p.m.; Friday, 9 a.m.–5 p.m.; Saturday,
    9:30 a.m.–4 p.m.

The Studio Academy Gallery

33 7th Street NE, Rochester, MN 55906, (507) 529-1662

The Studio Academy, a Rochester Charter School, is designed to provide secondary students with a rigorous academic curriculum that is integrated with a foundation in the visual and performing arts. The Studio Academy Gallery primarily displays the artwork of students and faculty; however, the work of local artists is occasionally presented. Exhibits are rotated seasonally and represent a wide variety of artistic mediums including pencil and charcoal drawings, watercolor, oil and acrylic paintings, photography, stained glass, clay, silverwork, costuming, digital artwork, mixed media and more. Please call to confirm hours and public access to the gallery.

Cost: free
Hours: Monday–Friday, 9 a.m.–3 p.m.

University Center Art Gallery

855 30th Street SE, Rochester, MN 55904, (507) 529-2728 or (507) 285-7210

A permanent collection of artwork is displayed throughout the corridors of Rochester's University Center and in the quiet lounge located adjacent to the college's Hill Theater. A showcase of digital artwork may be viewed in the university atrium or the online digital gallery at www.roch.edu/digiart

Val Webb Gallery
315A Apache Mall, Rochester, MN 55902, (507) 289-3995

Val Webb Gallery, an authorized Wild Wings dealer, is located in Rochester's Apache Mall. The gallery predominantly displays artwork that depicts wildlife, outdoor, and family/child themes. Well-known artists featured throughout the gallery include Terry Redlin, Thomas Kinkade, Charles Peterson, Steve Hanks, and others. The original artwork of local artists, such as Mike Schad of Oronoco, is also displayed and sold at the gallery. In addition to this, the gallery has a fine selection of collector plates, ornaments, decorated boxes, notecards, and clocks.

Cost: varies by purchase
Hours: Monday–Friday, 10 a.m.–9 p.m.; Saturday, 10 a.m.–8 p.m.; Sunday,
    11 a.m.–6 p.m.

Watercolors for Lita's Children
Rochester, MN, (507) 285-0184

Rochester watercolor artist, Barb Agerter, originally opened her studio in 1996 as a tribute to her mother, Lita, who has 10 children and 32 grandchildren. The water-color paintings that she creates embrace the spirit of childhood and have been described as delightful, charming, and timeless. As a self-published artist, Barb Ageter has had success distributing her work nationwide at galleries, fine gift shops, and children's stores. Her work has also been featured in major sales catalogs by Sak's, Folio, and Seasons. Ms. Ageter welcomes inquiries by those interested in viewing her work or visiting her studio.

CHATFIELD
Country Art Gallery
13913 Hwy. 30, Chatfield, MN 55923, (507) 867-4016, 888-500-3600, www.bernardcountryart.com

Experience the nostalgia of an authentic 1892 one-room country schoolhouse while visiting Harvey Bernard's Country Art Gallery. With separate entryways for boys and girls, slate blackboards, and the original bell and teacher's desk, the school-house provides a fitting atmosphere to display Mr. Bernard's silhouette farm art. The pen and ink silhouette art depicts country life on the farm in the 1930s and 1940s during the transition from horse power to tractors. In addition to silhouette art, Mr. Bernard's creations also include full-color pen and ink prints and oil paintings. Stop by the Country Art Gallery during your travels to southeastern Minnesota and visit with Mr. Bernard. Not only will he share his artwork with you, but his boyhood memories of attending the schoolhouse as well.

Cost: varies by purchase
Hours: Monday–Friday, 9 a.m.–5 p.m.; Saturday, by chance; call for winter hours

HARMONY
Clover Art Gallery
35 Center Street East, Harmony, MN 55939, (507) 886-3313, www.clovergallery.com or
e-mail: bergen@means.net

The Clover Art Gallery's open and contemporary atmosphere invites browsing among the collection of artwork representing local and regional artists. There is something for everyone at this gallery that has an eclectic selection of "functional" artwork such as pottery, basketry, jewelry, woodwork, and metal work as well as decorative paintings, folk art, sculpture, photographs, and mixed media designs. Visit the Clover Art Gallery during your next trip to Harmony. You may just find that one-of-a-kind piece of art that you can't live without.

Cost: varies by purchase
Hours: Monday–Saturday, 9 a.m.–6 p.m.; Fridays until 8:00 p.m.; Sundays,
    10 a.m.–4 p.m.

HOUSTON
Our Front Porch Gallery & Gathering Place
110 North Grant Street, Houston, MN 55943, (507) 896-2787, avila@acegroup.cc

Our Front Porch Gallery & Gathering Place is situated just a block from the Root River State Trailhead in Houston. The gallery, owned by Kelley Stanage, features the original work of local and regional artists.

Gallery visitors will find an interesting variety of art forms on display including oil paintings, drawings, pottery, sculpture, fiber art, jewelry, collage, and mixed media. If the weather is warm and the time is right, you may find yourself listening to Kelley's band, Blues Overdue, during one of their occasional performances on the Front Porch.

Cost: varies by purchase
Hours: summer: Tuesday–Saturday, 11 a.m.–6 p.m., or by appointment
    winter: Thursday–Saturday, noon–6 p.m., or by appointment
    closed during January and February

LAKE CITY
Wild Wings Gallery
2101 South U.S. Hwy. 61, Box 100, Lake City, MN 55041, (651) 345-5355, 800-248-7312, www.wildwings.com

Walk into a world of wildlife art at the Wild Wings Gallery Catalog Showroom in Lake City. Although the gallery is prized among collectors of nature and wildlife-themed art, Wild Wings has also been a publishing firm of limited edition prints since 1968. The gallery is known for its display and sales of quality paintings, prints, sculptures, and wood carvings by renowned wildlife artists. Wild Wings also carries a large selection of fine furniture and home decor with nature-related themes. Nature lovers will find a wide variety of collector plates, stained glass items, dishes, clocks, lamps, glassware, and linens to suit their taste and beautify their homes. Just to the south of the gallery, visitors will notice several rows of towering trees. These trees were planted about 60 years ago by the Boy Scouts in remembrance of local soldiers who died in World War II.

Cost: varies by purchase
Hours: Monday–Saturday, 9 a.m.–6 p.m.; Sunday, 11 a.m.–5 p.m.

LANESBORO
Cornucopia Art Center
103 Parkway Avenue North, Box 152, Lanesboro, MN 55949, (507) 467-2446, www.lanesboro.com

In 1996, Lanesboro received the distinction of being named one of The 100 Best Small Art Towns in America. The Cornucopia Art Center, a nonprofit, professional organization, strives to serve the community by "providing meaningful art experiences for people of all ages" through workshops and school programs while also maintaining a high quality sales gallery that exhibits and the work of local, regional, national and international artists. Moreover, Cornucopia supports the art community by providing exhibition space, opening receptions, an artist-in-residence program, and employment opportunities in teaching, mentorship, and curator positions for both emerging and established artists. Additional programs sponsored by the art center include musical performances and literary readings. Of course, it's a refreshing experience just to visit the gallery and view the exhibits, which feature a wide variety of contemporary art forms and mediums such as painting, metal working, woodcarving, silk screen, stained glass, and cast metal sculpture. Whether you're searching for an aesthetically pleasing addition for your art collection or a piece of wearable art, you are likely to find it at the Cornucopia Art Center.

Cost: varies by purchase

Hours: winter: Monday, by appointment; Tuesday–Saturday, 10 a.m.–5 p.m.; Sunday, noon–5 p.m.

summer: Monday, by appointment; Tuesday–Saturday, 10 a.m.–6 p.m.; Sunday, noon–6 p.m.

OWATONNA
Owatonna Arts Center & Sculpture Garden
435 Garden View Lane, Owatonna, MN 55060, (507) 451-0533, www.owatonna.org
Located in the West Hills Complex.

A sculpture garden representing the works of four Minnesota artists greets visitors to the Owatonna Arts Center (OAC). The Arts Center, known for its unique Christmas displays, features year-round rotating exhibits that illustrate a wide variety of art mediums and a permanent collection of Marianne Young costumes. OAC also offers a variety of art classes for children, youth, and adults. Please contact OAC for a current schedule of classes, gallery exhibits, and events.

Cost: free admission; fee varies by classes

Hours: Tuesday–Sunday, 1 p.m.–5 p.m., or by appointment

WINONA
Center Gallery at Saint Mary's University of Minnesota
Toner Student Center, 700 Terrace Heights, Winona, MN 55987, (507) 457-1652, 800-635-5987, www.smumn.edu

The Center Gallery of Saint Mary's University of Minnesota is located on campus in the Toner Student Center. The University's Art and Design Department annually presents four professional exhibits and two student exhibits at the gallery. Please call for information about current exhibits and showings. Displays of student artwork may be viewed in the Student Gallery, which is located in St. Joseph's Hall.

Cost: free

Hours: Sunday–Saturday, 9 a.m.–8 p.m., during exhibitions

Paul Watkin's Art Gallery
Watkin's Hall, Winona State University, King and Winona Streets, Winona, MN 55987, (507) 457-5395, 800-342-5978, www.winona.edu

The Paul Watkin's Art Gallery, located in Watkin's Hall on the campus of Winona State University, features the work of local, regional, and national artists. The gallery also presents art shows every three to four weeks with the display of rotating exhibits. The second floor of Watkin's Hall is home to the WSU Student Art Gallery, which not only features student exhibitions, but selections from the Watkin's Gallery as well. Please call the gallery for a current schedule of art shows and receptions.

Cost: free
Hours: Monday–Friday, 8 a.m.–4 p.m.

Winona Arts Center
5th and Franklin Streets, Winona, MN 55987, (507) 453-9959, www.winonaartscenter.org or www.winonafilmsociety.org

The Winona Arts Center has been in existence since the mid-1960s. It is currently a private organization that is supported solely by its members. The arts center has a gallery with a small permanent collection and rotating exhibits, which showcase the work of local high school and college students as well as professional works by regional and national artists. Additional offerings include art classes for children, youth, and adults, a Film Series held every other weekend from April through October, and other special programs such as poetry readings and musical performances. The Winona Arts Center hosts an Annual Holiday Sale the first weekend in December that provides visitors with the opportunity to browse and purchase fine arts and crafts. Please call the arts center for information about classes, gallery events, the film series, special programs, or to obtain a brochure with a list of current events and activities.

Cost: gallery: free; classes: $–$$$$; admission to films: $
Hours: call for current hours
  films, showings: Fridays–Saturdays, 8 p.m.; Sundays, 7 p.m. (every other weekend from April–October)

ZUMBROTA
Crossings at Carnegie
320 East Avenue, Zumbrota, MN 55992, (507) 732-7616, www.crossingsatcarnegie.com

Crossings at Carnegie is located in the 1907 Zumbrota Library, which has been beautifully restored by owner Marie Louise. Its mission is "connecting people with the process of creating, striving for an organic holistic approach to the arts, and enriching the lives of all who enter our doors." Crossings at Carnegie is not only an art center but a community gathering place as well. In addition to a gallery that features the work of regional artists, the center also offers coffeehouse-style concerts on Saturday evenings and Sunday afternoons, fitness classes, art and writing classes, community potluck dinners, dances of universal peace, community recitals, and more. The artwork displayed throughout the gallery and in the gift shop is available for purchase. So pay a visit to Crossings at Carnegie, and experience just how Marie Louise has transformed an old library into "a place that makes you feel good." Call Crossings or check their website for class and concert schedules. Registration is required for some classes, and reservations are suggested for concerts.

Cost: free admission; classes and concerts: fees vary

Hours: gallery and gift shop: Monday, Tuesday, Wednesday, & Friday, 10 a.m.–5 p.m.;
Thursday, 10 a.m.–8 p.m.; Saturday, 10 a.m.–4 p.m.
concerts: Saturdays, 8 p.m.; Sundays, 2 p.m.
classes: times vary

Chapter 2: Performing Arts & Music

Performing Arts: Theater

ROCHESTER
Children's Dance Theater
P.O. Box 6655, Rochester, MN 55903, (507) 281-2810

Children's Dance Theater (CDT) is a nonprofit, incorporated dance theater company that was founded in 1987 for "the purpose of creating high-quality theatrical dance performances as well as providing young dancers with an enriching learning environment by offering them the opportunity to explore different styles of dance and experience the creative process that goes into a production." Auditions are open to dancers with varying levels of dance training and experience. Young dancers who perform in CDT productions typically represent a variety of area studios, schools, and communities. The CDT usually produces one show per year. Previous productions have included *The Lion King*, *Beauty and the Beast*, *The Wizard of Oz*, *Cinderella*, *Peter Pan*, and *A Christmas Carol*. The yearly spring performance is well publicized and information may be found via public notices on posters, flyers, and in newspaper ads. Dancers interested in auditioning for a CDT production may call Lou Ellen Wolfe at the above number.

Hill Theater at Rochester Community & Technical College (RCTC)
851 30th Avenue SE, Rochester, MN 55904, (507) 285-7200, www.roch.edu

Theater performances by student thespians are held in the spring and fall at Hill Theater of Rochester Community and Technical College. Auditions are not open to the public. Please call RCTC Theater Department or check the college's website for information about upcoming performances.

The Masque Youth Theatre and School, Inc.
P.O. Box 5932, Rochester, MN 55903, theater address: 14 4th Street SW, Rochester, MN 55902, (507) 287-0704, www.masque.org or e-mail: go2masque@aol.com

The Masque Youth Theatre and School is an extraordinary organization that has been an essential element of Rochester's theater scene since 1987. Masque's mission is "to develop the creative potential of the young people of Southeastern Minnesota through active participation in a youth theater which recognizes, respects, and nurtures their growth and encourages the development of social relationships with all age groups through theater arts." This is accomplished by promoting student participation not only as actors but in all aspects of the theater such as play selection, serving on of the Board of Directors, stage managers, assistant directors and directors, design and construction of sets and costumes, play writing, and sound and light controls.

The Masque has maintained three troupes, the Masque Storytellers, Masque Mimes, and Masque Puppeteers since it originated 16 years ago. In addition to this, they offer a wide variety of theater classes including Beginning, Intermediate, and Advanced Creative Dramatics, Creative Movement, Improvisation, Mime, Juggling and Clowning, The Plays of Shakespeare, The Art of Storytelling, and more. Classes are available for children as young as five and some are open to adults.

As a performing arts venue, The Masque Theatre produces about five shows per year. Auditions for these shows are open to the public. Please call The Masque or visit their website for more information about Masque Troupes, classes, performance schedules, auditions, ticket information, or other questions.

Mayo Stage Door Drama Club
1420 11th Avenue SE, Rochester, MN 55904, (507) 285-8820

The Mayo Stage Door Drama Club of Rochester's Mayo High School presents annual fall and spring theatrical performances. The cast members are selected by audition from the Mayo student body, which represents grades 9–12. Please call the ticket information hotline for details about the next show.

Pyramid Theater Alliance
Rochester, MN, (507) 437-7527, e-mail: spkinney@smig.net

The Pyramid Theater Alliance is a small nonprofit theater company that was organized in the early 1990s. The company has primarily produced dinner theater shows at select Rochester hotels, including the long-running musical *Forever Christmas*, at the Best Western Apache, (507) 289-8866. They have also performed in the Rochester Playwright Festival. Auditions are typically by invitation, but producers Steve and Penny Kinney welcome inquiries from interested actors. Please call the Pyramid Theater Alliance for more information about auditions or a performance schedule. Reservations may be arranged for large travel groups or bus tours interested in booking a show.

Rochester Civic Theater
220 East Center Street, Rochester, MN 55904, (507) 282-8481

Rochester Civic Theater (RCT) has been a mainstay of the community theater scene since its opening season in 1951. Since it celebrated its 50th Anniversary during the 2001–2002 season, the RCT staff and volunteers continue the theater's tradition of artistic excellence by staging high quality productions for Rochester and southeastern Minnesota. This rich heritage includes the presentation of two musicals, four nonmusicals and two shows by the Young People's Theater. In addition to this, RCT serves the community by providing diverse outreach programs such as Touch Continuum, No Easy Answers, The Inside-Out Players, Showstoppers, Summer Theater Institute, and Youth and Adult Theater Classes. Touch Continuum and No Easy Answers, nationally recognized sexual abuse and prevention programs developed by RCT, have been presented to public and private school students in Rochester and the surrounding communities since the early 1980s. The Inside-Out Players and Showstoppers are both traveling troupes of young actors. The Inside-Out Players primarily perform plays, while the Showstoppers focus on the presentation of musical revues. The Summer Theater Institute provides children in grades 3–8 with the opportunity to participate in a two-week "theater camp." A wide variety of theater classes are also available for children (grades 3 and up), youth, and adults. Class topics range from Beginning Acting to Sword Fighting to Behind the Scenes to Directing. As Minnesota's largest community theater, RCT remains a "theater of the community" and welcomes newcomers to volunteer or sign up for classes. In fall 2002, patrons and participants of RCT welcomed the theater's unveiling of a shared entry with Mayo Civic Center, a spacious lobby and expanded facilities. For further information about these programs, a season schedule, reservations, and ticket information, call RCT or check out their website.

Rochester Radio Theater Guild
Rochester, MN, (507) 288-3082 or (507) 282-0941, www.rrtg.org

The Rochester Radio Theater Guild (RRTG) evolved from a group that originally gathered to perform an old-time radio show as a fundraiser for the Rochester Civic Theater. Due to the popularity of the performance, another show was presented and eventually the troupe now known as the RRTG was born. The troupe continues to "promote the replication and enjoyment of old-time radio" by re-creating a variety of science fiction, comedy, drama, suspense and musical radio shows as they were produced in the 1930s and 1940s. The RRTG typically stages three public perform-ances a year as well as "road shows" for private organizations. The troupe welcomes auditions for speaking parts, singers, musicians, and technical crew. Please call the RRTG or check out their website for more information about auditions and upcoming shows.

Rochester Repertory Theater Company
314½ South Broadway, Rochester, MN 55904, (507) 289-7800, www.rochesterrep.org, e-mail: BoxOffice@RochesterRep.org

The "Rep," an intimate 90-seat theater located in a historic building on Broadway Avenue in downtown Rochester, was originally established in 1984. The theater continues to provide Rochester with a venue for controversial shows that examine the struggles and meaning of ordinary life in plays such as *Agnes of God*, *The Ice Fishing Play*, *Wonderful Tennessee*, and *Crossing Delancy* along with big name shows like *Evita* and *MacBeth*. The Rep primarily produces shows that are suitable for teen and adult audiences. Auditions are open to the public. Please contact the Rep or check out their website for a season schedule, audition dates, and ticket information. Please note that patrons must climb a steep set of stairs in order to reach the theater. No handicapped access is available.

Special Performances at Rochester Public Library
101 2ⁿᵈ Street SE, Rochester, MN 55904, (507) 285-8000

Special programs and events at the Rochester Public Library often feature perform-ances by theater troupes, musical groups, magicians and puppeteers. Please call the library or check their website for a schedule of current events.

Vertigo Theatre Factory
c/o 1105 7ᵗʰ Avenue NE, Rochester, MN 55906, (507) 288-2867, www.vertigotheatrefactory.org or e-mail: vertigo@chartermi.net

The Vertigo Theatre Factory describes itself as "a loosely organized nonprofit theater company that produces alternative theater, often with mature content, while culti-vating and fostering burgeoning theatrical talents." Vertigo seeks to perform both original and established plays that would not otherwise be staged in Rochester. Vertigo often performs at theater festivals and regional competitions. Please call the Vertigo Theatre Factory or check out their website for information about auditions and upcoming performances.

LANESBORO
Commonweal Theater Company & Lanesboro
Radio Company at the St. Mane Theater
P.O. Box 15, 206 Parkway North, Lanesboro, MN 55949, (507) 467-2525, 800-657-7025, www.commonwealtheatre.org, or e-mail: info@CommonwealTheatre.org

Situated in the heart of southeastern Minnesota, Lanesboro is a small town (population 850) that has become known as one of the "Best Small Art Towns in America." The Commonweal Theater Company has undoubtedly contributed to this recognition. The nonprofit professional theater company was started on a shoestring budget by Eric Bunge in 1989 and has matured into an organization "dedicated to delighting and challenging the audiences of our region." The staff of professional theatrical artists accomplishes this mission by remaining committed to community diversity, artistic integrity, providing educational programs, and making live theater accessible to as many people as possible. The Commonweal's year-round season offers a tasteful selection of shows. Productions have included *Twelfth Night*, *A Christmas Carol*, *Quilters*, *The Merchant of Venice*, and *Our Town*. Please call the Commonweal Theater or check out their website for a current season schedule and ticket information. Reservations are encouraged.

The Lanesboro Radio Company, an offshoot of the Commonweal Theatre Company, produces live radio shows from mid–May–Labor Day on Sunday evenings at 7:00. The shows are broadcast live from the St. Mane Theater and may be attended or heard on KFIL radio (103.1 FM and 1060 AM). Tickets for the radio show are purchased on a first come, first served basis. No reservations are available.

MANTORVILLE
The Mantorville Theater Company
Mantorville, MN 55955, (507) 635-5420, www.mantorvillain.com or www.mantorville.com

Mantorville's rich architectural heritage earned it a place on the National Register of Historic Places in 1975. This charming town is also home to the Mantorville Theater Company, a little theater with a lot of pizzazz. Although the little theater maintains an active schedule of full length shows and musicals, it is probably best known for its melodramas, which are staged from June through August. This unique form of theater encourages the audience to create a cacophony of boos and hisses for the villain(ess) and enthusiastic cheers for the hero(ine). It's definitely an experience you don't want to miss! Please call for a season schedule, show times, ticket information, or reservations.

PLAINVIEW
The Jon Hassler Theater
412 West Broadway, Plainview, MN 55964, (507) 534-2900, www.jonhasslertheater.org

In an effort to preserve the history and culture of rural America, the Rural America Arts Partnership has sponsored the development and opening of The Jon Hassler Theater in Plainview. The theater, located in the Center for Rural America Arts, was formerly an International Harvester implement building. Jon Hassler is a renowned Minnesota author who spent his growing-up years in Plainview. As an author, Jon Hassler has penned several novels, short stories, plays, and books for young people. His works are known for their accurate portrayal of life in small town America. The

225-seat theater, which boasts state-of-the-art lighting and sound systems and a 3,000-square-foot lobby, opened its first full season of plays during the summer of 2000. It has established an affiliation with the Lyric Theater of Minneapolis to stage year-round productions by professional actors. Jon Hassler's childhood home was moved adjacent to the theater in 1999, and plans are underway for its renovation and establishment as a writers' center. Please call the theater or check out the website for more information about the theater's current and upcoming performance schedules.

SPRING VALLEY
The Brave Community Theater
Mailing address: 424 North Broadway, Spring Valley, MN 55975, (507) 346-7407, (507) 346-7367 (Spring Valley City Clerk)

The Brave Community Theater of Spring Valley has been presenting plays for Fillmore County for more than 25 years. The community theater performs three shows per year, which are usually held in the late winter, summer, and early fall at the Spring Valley Community Center. Previous performances have included *Hello Dolly*, *Annie Get Your Gun*, *Camelot*, and *Fiddler on the Roof*. Auditions are open to the public. Although the shows are primarily publicized throughout Fillmore County, information about upcoming performances may be obtained by calling the above numbers.

STEWARTVILLE
Stewartville Performing Arts Center
Performing Arts Center at Stewartville High School, Stewartville Community Education, 500 4ᵗʰ Street, Stewartville, MN 55976, (507) 533-1650, (507) 533-1432 (ticket information), www.ssd.k12.mn.us or www.stewartvillemn.com

The Stewartville Department of Community Education along with interested members of the community established the Stewartville Community Theater in 1996. The theater group had performed one annual show during its first three years. However, since the opening of the 500 seat Performing Arts Center at the Stewartville High School in 1999, the group has been able to produce two shows per year, a comedy or drama in late winter and a musical in August. Auditions are open to the public. Youth and teens are often cast in the musical. Please contact Stewartville Community Education for more information about auditions, a current performance schedule, or ticket information.

WINONA
Theatre du Mississippi
111 Riverfront, Suite 205, Winona, MN 55987, (507) 457-0844, www.TheatreDuMississippi.org or e-mail: info@TheatreDuMississippi.org

Winona's Theatre du Mississippi (TdM) was established in 1998 as a nonprofit professional theatre "dedicated to producing high quality artistic activities that address important contemporary issues." Performances by TdM are held at a variety of indoor and outdoor venues including a turn-of-the-century Masonic Theater. The theatre company has supported local talent by producing and staging the premiere performances of original scripts by regional playwrights. Besides presenting plays, TdM has produced two feature length films. Its first feature film, *Greta's Song*, an award winning drama about domestic abuse written by Scott Thompson of

Whitehall, Wisconsin, was produced in 1999. As part of its mission to encourage education and artistic development for people of all ages, TdM offers "Actors Studio" classes for children, youth, and adults as well as the nationally recognized Kindermusic program for very young children. Please contact TdM or visit their website for more information about their current and upcoming performances, purchasing tickets or signing up for classes.

Magical Shows and Magicians

ROCHESTER
All Star Magic Gala

Don't miss the annual All Star Magic Gala produced by the Rochester Mystic 13 Magic Club. The Gala is a benefit for local charities and features magicians of all skill levels including members of the Society of Young Magicians, professional magicians as well as those who pursue magic as an avocation. The All Star Magic Gala is usually held sometime between mid-October and early November. Contact the Mayo Civic Center at (507) 287-2222 for dates and ticket information.

Bob Miller Comedy Magic
Rochester, MN, (507) 281-2213, 800-566-9931, www.bobmillermagic.com

Bob Miller is a full-time professional magician who performs tableside magic at local restaurants, offers magic shows for children's birthday parties, presents comedy magic stage shows for adults, and walk-around magic at picnics, carnivals, and receptions. The Comedy Head Cutter, The Powers of Darkness, and The Burned Bill Barbecue are just a few of his adult routines. If it's balloon magic that you're after, Bob has a "Balloon Booth" available for parties and events. A trained balloon artist will perform balloon magic by creating balloon animals, hats, and toys. Call Bob Miller Magic or check out his website for a current performance schedule and more detailed information about his magic shows.

Brent W. Coggins—Magic by Sin'gee'
Rochester, MN, (507) 289-5155, 888-289-5155, www.singee.com

Audiences of all ages are fascinated with the creative and innovative Magic by Sin'gee' (a.k.a. Brent W. Coggins). He has become known as Sin'gee' because the element of fire is used in many of his magic performances. Brent has been a leader in the local magic arena by organizing The Young Magicians of Southeast Minnesota in 1992 and reorganizing the Mystic 13 Magic Club of Southeast Minnesota in 1983. If you're looking for a "Fiery Entertainer with the Personal Touch," contact Magic by Sin'gee' or visit his website for more information and a current performance schedule.

Magical Entertainer—Alan Skogerbo
Rochester, MN, (507) 287-6069, www.magicalan.com or e-mail: mago@rconnect.com

Magical entertainer Alan Skogerbo has captivated audiences of all ages for more than 30 years with his delightful blend of magic and humor. As a full-time professional magician, Alan provides family-oriented magical entertainment for schools, churches, corporations, clubs, and festivals. His shows inspire people of all ages to find the kid inside themselves through the wonder and mystery of magic. Alan has developed a special program for elementary school students, the "Magic of the Rainforest," which he performs to educate children about the destruction of the rainforest through a dynamic show of magic, puppets, music, and other surprises. As a member of the Fellowship of Christian Magicians for more than 25 years, Alan's experience also includes performances at international conventions and television appearances. Please call Alan or visit his website for more information about his magical entertainment.

Mr. & Mrs. Magic—Magical Michael & Terri McKay
Rochester, MN, (507) 529-7777, magicalmichael7777@juno.com

Mid-America's Most Amazing Magicians, Michael and Terri McKay hail from Rochester, Minnesota. The duo known as Mr. and Mrs. Magic produce full-scale productions for large venues such as casinos, schools, churches, and corporate meetings. Their extravagant show features stage illusions along with music, comedy, and show girls. Magical Michael has even entertained audiences as an opening act for David Copperfield. As full-time, professional magicians, Magical Michael and Terri perform locally, regionally and throughout the United States. For more information, please call the Mr. & Mrs. Magic Hotline at (507) 529-7777.

Rochester Mystic 13 Magic Club
Don Campbell, (507) 288-6892; Brent Coggins, (507) 289-5155; Alan Skogerbo, (507) 287-6069

The magic club that formed in Rochester about 50 years ago was originally known as Mystic 13. The club, now known as the Rochester Mystic 13 Magic Club, was reorganized in 1984 and became formally chartered as Assembly # 205 of the Society of American Magicians. More recently, the club was incorporated as a non-profit organization in 1999. Several prominent magicians in the Rochester area are actively involved in the club, which is "dedicated to promoting magic as a performing art." The Mystic 13 Magic Club also supports The Society of Young Magicians, a club open to youth (ages 7–17) who are interested in learning the art of magic. Mystic 13 Magic supports the Society of Young Magicians by providing the youth with instruction and guidance in a supportive atmosphere. Parents are always welcome to attend the meetings with their children. Please contact one of magicians listed above if you're interested in becoming a member of the Mystic 13 Magic Club or the Society of Young Magicians.

Performing Arts: Music

ROCHESTER
Arts on Fifth Avenue
Christ United Methodist Church, 400 5th Avenue SW, Rochester, MN 55902, (507) 289-4019

Arts on Fifth Avenue was founded in 1998 by Stephen Distad, former Music Director of Christ United Methodist Church in 1998. As an arts program affiliated with the church, its mission is "to offer the people in the communities of southeastern Minnesota a unique arts outreach program that promotes a vital connection to God through creative forms of music, drama, and the arts." The Arts on Fifth program presents an annual season of four to eight performances that include concerts, dramas and dances that reflect styles ranging from classical to contemporary. The Philadelphia

Organ Quartet, The Minnesota Boychoir, and Moore By Four are just a few of the distinguished groups that have performed on the Arts on Fifth stage. Season memberships are available. Please call for a current schedule and ticket information.

Choral Arts Ensemble of Rochester
Assisi Heights, Suite 900, 1001 14th Street NW, Rochester, MN 55901, (507) 252-8427, www.choralartsensemble.org or e-mail: cae@millcom.com

The 40-voice Choral Arts Ensemble, founded by Music Director Dr. Rick Kvam in 1985, evolved from two local groups, the Rochester Men's Capella and the Rochester Chamber Chorale. Dr. Kvam's credentials include degrees in Music and Choral Conducting from both Harvard College and the University of Cincinnati College–Conservatory of Music. In addition to this, he received the U.S. Bank Sally Ordway Irvine Award for Arts Initiative (1999) and was awarded the Mayor's Medal of Honor (1998) for artistic and cultural service to the City of Rochester. Under the guidance of Dr. Kvam's artistic leadership, the Ensemble has become known for its outstanding performances of choral-orchestral masterworks by composers such as Mozart, Bach, and Haydn as well as presentations of unaccompanied choral music from the Renaissance period to the 20th century. In October 2001, the Ensemble was invited to perform a world premiere by American composer, Stephen Paulus, with the St. Paul Chamber Orchestra at the Ordway Center for Performing Arts in St. Paul. Moreover, the organization is devoted to the commissioning and performance of new works. Please call to obtain more information about the Ensemble's current performance schedule and ticket information.

Festival of Music Series
First Presbyterian Church, 512 3rd St. SW, Rochester, MN 55902, (507) 282-1618

First Presbyterian Church of Rochester has presented its Festival of Music series since 1991 in order to provide concerts for people of all ages that "focus on the musical traditions that seek to articulate humanity's understanding of the divine." The concerts feature a variety of vocal and instrumental performances by local artists as well as renowned artists from throughout the United States and the world.

Festival of Music concerts are free and open to the public. All concerts are held on Sunday afternoons throughout the church year. A Lenten Organ Recital Series is also presented at First Presbyterian Church on Wednesdays from 12:15–12:45 during the Lenten season. Please call the First Presbyterian Church for specific concert dates and times.

Harmony for Mayo Concerts
Mayo Medical Center, 200 1st Street SW, Rochester, MN 55905, (507) 266-3378, Mayo Life & Leisure Programs, (507) 284-4480

The Mayo Center for the Humanities in Medicine in conjunction with the Chorale Arts Ensemble of Rochester presents a series of weekly concerts held on the Mayo Clinic Campus. The noontime concerts feature vocal and instrumental performances in a wide variety of musical styles including jazz, blues, classical, bluegrass, and country. The Harmony for Mayo concerts are just one way that the Center for the Humanities strives to achieve its goal of "fostering compassion, sensitivity, and insight in patient-caregiver relationships and to support professional collegiality." The year-round concerts are held on Mondays from 12:10 p.m.–12:55 p.m. Performance locations vary throughout the Mayo Medical Center Campus, and summer concerts are held outdoors, weather permitting. All concerts are free and open to the public, and audience members are invited to bring a lunch to the noontime concerts. Occasionally, the Harmony for Mayo concert series presents special evening performances. A current concert schedule may be found in Mayo publications and flyers distributed throughout Mayo Medical Center or by contacting the Mayo Life & Leisure Program at (507) 284-4480. Musicians interested in performing at a Harmony for Mayo concert should contact the Choral Arts Ensemble at (507) 252-8427.

The Lyra Concert Baroque Orchestra

P.O. Box 112, Rochester, MN 55903, (507) 254-1235, (651) 523-2459, www.lyraconcert.org

The Lyra Concert is a Baroque period orchestra based in the Twin Cities that regularly performs a concert series in Rochester. Artistic Directors for the Lyra Orchestra, Jacques Ogg and David Douglass, are both musicians of international acclaim and considered to be among the world's finest early music performers. The orchestra is dedicated to the performance of music from the 17th and 18th centuries. Please call (507) 282-7418 for information about the Lyra Concert series.

Mayo Clinic Chamber Symphony

Mayo Medical Center, 200 1st Street SW, Rochester, MN 55905, Mayo Life & Leisure Programs, (507) 284-4480; Symphony Director, (507) 284-2673

The Mayo Clinic Chamber Symphony is a nonprofessional ensemble of Mayo Medical Center employees and persons who are related to a Mayo employee. The orchestral group was originally formed in the early 1980s and currently has about 35 members. The Chamber Symphony may be heard three times per year at their fall, Christmas, and late winter/early spring concerts. Performance dates are typically posted in Mayo Clinic publications and in the Rochester Post-Bulletin or may be obtained by calling the Mayo Clinic Life & Leisure programs. The group welcomes new members, and musicians interested in joining the group should contact Symphony Director, John Schultz at (507) 284-2673.

Oasis Courtyard Programs at Calvary Episcopal Church

Calvary Episcopal Church, 3rd Avenue & 2nd Street SW, Rochester, MN 55902, (507) 282-9429, www.calvary-rochester.org

Calvary Episcopal Church was originally built during the Civil War between 1862–1863. As Rochester's oldest church, it is now surrounded by the Mayo Clinic campus in the heart of downtown Rochester. In 1987, Calvary Episcopal began to view its presence as spiritual oasis amid the hustle and bustle of the city and started an outreach program, the Oasis Courtyard Series, for residents and visitors of the area. The Oasis Courtyard Series features two summer programs that take place outdoors in a lush grassy area surrounded by colorful gardens. Tuesdays in the Courtyard focus on a program of meditative arts and relaxation. Participants are provided with the opportunity to partake in meditative and relaxation exercises such as yoga, Qi-gong, Tai Chi, Rieke, and guided imagery. On Thursdays, the Courtyard series offers noontime vocal and instrumental concerts, storytelling, theatrical performances, poetry readings, and more. The program presents a wide variety of musical styles from folk to classical to jazz and everything in between. The summer programs are held in the Calvary Episcopal Church Courtyard on Tuesdays and Thursdays at noon. In the event of inclement weather, events are held inside the church. All programs are free and open to the public, and audience members are invited to bring a lunch. Please note that the church sanctuary is open daily from 8 a.m.–9 p.m. for meditation, prayer, rest, and reflection. Call the church or visit their website for a current schedule of programs.

Rochester Aria Group

Music Director, (507) 282-3208, www.rochesterariagroup.org or e-mail: tengeo@aol.com

The Rochester Aria Group was formed by Artistic Director, George Smith, in 1999 to provide performance opportunities for opera singers who are serious amateurs or aspiring professionals and to promote the live performance of classical singing in Rochester. The nonprofit organization strives to bring quality performances to established opera fans and attract listeners who may not be familiar with this type of singing. The group often invites prominent guest artists to perform with local singers at their concerts, which number about two to three per year. Recitals are usually held at the Unitarian Universalist Church in southwest Rochester. Please call the music director or visit the Rochester Aria Group's website for more information about joining the group or to obtain a concert schedule.

Rochester Carillon

Plummer Building, 2nd Street SW, Mayo Medical Center, Rochester, MN 55905, (507) 284-8294, (507) 282-3730

Rochester is fortunate to have a 56-bell carillon with a four and one-half octave range housed in the tower of Mayo's Plummer Building. A carillon is an outdoor musical instrument with 23 or more bronze, cup-shaped bells that are rigidly fixed to supporting beams and do not swing when played. A carillonneur plays the instrument from a clavier, a keyboard console with a double row of batons (oak keys) and a pedal board. The smallest bell weighs 19 pounds, and the largest bell, almost six feet tall, weighs 7,840 pounds. In the 1920s, a medical trip to Belgium sparked Dr. William J. Mayo's interest in carillons. Although construction of the Plummer Building was already underway, the architectural plans were revised to include a carillon tower. The original 23 bell carillon, a gift from the Mayo brothers, was erected in the Plummer Tower during the 1920s, and its inaugural recital was held on September 16, 1928. Thirty-three new bronze bells, a clavier, practice console, and a playing cabin were added to the Rochester Carillon in the summer of 1977 due to generous gifts from Frances G. Sheets and Isabella Gooding Sanders, descendants of Rochester pioneer settler, Alphonso Gooding. Current carillonneur, Dean Robinson is only the second bellmaster in the history of the Rochester Carillon. He has been playing the Rochester Carillon since the spring of 1958. Tours of the Rochester Carillon may be arranged by calling (507) 284-8294 or (507) 282-3730. Carillon performances may regularly be heard on Mondays at 7 p.m. and Wednesdays & Fridays at noon. Special recitals are also performed on Memorial Day, the Fourth of July, and Christmas Eve. Carillon concerts are about 20 to 25 minutes in length and are best heard in an open area at least 500 feet downwind from the tower. The bells are heard most clearly during cold, crisp weather.

Rochester Civic Music

City Hall, 201 4th Street SE, Suite 170, Rochester, MN 55904, (507) 281-6005, ticket information: (507) 285-8076, www.ci.rochester.mn.us/music or e-mail: dcarr@ci.rochester.mn.us

Rochester Civic Music (RCM) is an organizational department of the City of

Rochester that serves the community by providing residents with a diverse selection of high quality musical and educational programs as well as performance opportunities for musicians. RCM ensembles include the Rochester Civic Music Concert Band, Rochester Civic Music Community Band, Rochester Civic Music Concert Choir, and Jazz Ensemble. In addition to performances by these ensembles, RCM sponsors a complete concert schedule representing a broad range of musical genres such as blues, Celtic, rock, reggae, jazz, and salsa. YuleFest, an annual Christmas celebration, and Down by the Riverside, a seven-week series of outdoor concerts during July and August are also sponsored by RCM. Additional educational and outreach programs available through RCM include an Artist-in-Residence Program, Annual Youth Concert Program, Concert Previews Program, Behind the Scenes Program, and Master Classes and Clinics Program. Please contact RCM for more information about concerts and educational programs.

Rochester Civic Music Community Band

The mission of the Rochester Civic Music Community Band is "to provide personal enrichment for avocational or novice musicians" who seek to play as part of an ensemble. No auditions are required to join the 50-piece band, which also serves as a place for experienced musicians to hone their instrumental skills if they have not played for a significant amount of time. The motto of the Rochester Civic Music Community Band is "Having Fun Through Music," so whether you're a musician interested in joining the band or a music lover who just wants to attend one of the Community Band's concerts, you're sure to have a good time. All concerts are free and open to the public. Please call Rochester Civic Music for more information about joining the band or to obtain a current performance schedule.

Rochester Civic Music Concert Band

The Rochester Civic Music Concert Band is a professional ensemble whose mission is to "preserve, advance, and foster in the community an appreciation of, and promote as a professional artistic endeavor, the art of concert band music." In order to maintain a high degree of artistic excellence within the Concert Band, musicians are selected by competitive audition and receive compensation for their performances. The Concert Band maintains a year-round schedule including performances with the Rochester Civic Music Concert Choir, and at YuleFest and the Down by the Riverside concerts. Please call Rochester Civic Music for more information about auditioning for the Concert Band or to obtain a current performance schedule including ticket prices and reservations.

Rochester Civic Music Concert Choir

The Concert Choir ensemble is open to vocal musicians by competitive audition only. The mission of the Rochester Civic Music Concert Choir is to "preserve, advance, and foster in the community an appreciation of, and promote as a professional artistic endeavor, the art of choral singing." Performances by the Concert Choir usually include accompaniment by the Rochester Civic Music Concert Band. Please call Rochester Civic Music for more information about auditioning for the Concert Choir or to obtain a current performance schedule including ticket prices and reservations.

Down by the Riverside Concerts

A popular seven-week series of outdoor concerts, is sponsored by Rochester Civic

Music. These free, summertime concerts take place on Sunday evenings during July and August in Mayo Park, located behind the Rochester Civic Center. Rochester Civic Music supports the careers of local and regional artists by featuring them as opening acts at the Down by the Riverside concerts. The concert series features "artists of merit" as headliner acts so that it may reach a broader audience and provide the community with exposure to a wide variety of musical genres. Headliner acts have included well-known artists such as Jonny Lang, The Dixie Chicks, and Herman's Hermits. Rochester's Down by the Riverside concerts have become a much anticipated community event where hundreds, sometimes thousands of people come together with friends, families, and neighbors to enjoy the simple pleasures of life—socializing, picnicking, and listening to music. So grab your lawn chair, picnic blanket, and cooler, and join the community gathering where you'll more than likely run into a friend. Concessions are available at all concerts. All concerts begin at 7 p.m. and end at approximately 9:30 p.m. Opening acts typically perform for about 45 minutes. In the event of inclement weather, concerts are held inside the Civic Center. Please call Rochester Civic Music for more information about the Down by the Riverside concerts.

Rochester Male Chorus

Box 6254, Rochester, MN 55903, (507) 282-1538, www.rochmalechorus.freeservers.com or e-mail: rochmalechorus@mail.com

The Rochester Male Chorus (RMC) was originally founded in January 1930 by Harold Cooke. In addition to performing at major cities throughout the Upper Midwest, the group has become known as Rochester's Ambassadors of Music after performing at such venues as the Sugar Bowl (New Orleans), the Cotton Bowl (Dallas), the 1976 NFL playoff game in Minneapolis, the World's Fair in Seattle, and at the White House on Palm Sunday in 1973. Local performances include annual Christmas and Spring Concerts with guest appearances by the Rochester Boychoir, which is sponsored by the RMC. Through its membership in the Associated Male Choruses of America, the RMC also participates in Big Sings nationally and internationally with other male choruses. Membership in the Rochester Male Chorus is open to men of all ages who love to sing and desire to perform for the community. Although no formal singing experience is necessary, auditions are required and held twice a year for those interested in joining the chorus. The RMC also invites inquiries for performances at special events such as dinner or office parties. Please contact the Rochester Male Chorus for concert and audition information or if you want to hire them for your special event.

Rochester Music Guild

P.O. Box 5802, Rochester, MN 55903

The Rochester Music Guild is an organization that supports the Rochester Orchestra and Chorale as well as young musicians in the southeastern Minnesota region through financial contributions and volunteer assistance. The Guild sponsors an Annual Scholarship Competition for vocal, instrumental, piano, and string musicians in 8th through 12th grades. Scholarship applications are due in mid-January followed by a music competition in February. A Winner's Recital is held in March. Please contact the Guild if you are interested in joining the organization as a volunteer or to obtain a scholarship application.

Rochester Music Men

(507) 367-2485, www.rochestermusicmen.org or e-mail: chorusContact@rochestermusicmen.org

The Rochester Music Men, a barbershop-style chorus, is the Rochester, Minnesota, chapter of the Society for the Preservation and Encouragement of BarberShop Quartet Singing in America (SPEBSQSA). The 38,000 member SPEBSQSA is the largest, all-male singing society in the world. Although the Rochester Music Men began in the late 1950s, the group officially became an SPEBSQSA chapter in 1960. The barbershop chorus and quartets from within the singing group perform an annual show for the Rochester community. In addition to this, the Rochester Music Men host the SPEBSQSA District chorus competition every other year and may be heard at several parades throughout the region during the summer months. Visitors are always welcome at rehearsals. The barbershop chorus is open to men of all ages who enjoy singing. Although men interested in joining do not need a "trained" voice, potential members will be voice-placed within the group and must meet qualifications of the music team. Call the Rochester Music Men or visit their website for more information about a current performance schedule, joining the chorus, or to hire them for your special event.

Rochester Orchestra and Chorale

P.O. Box 302, Rochester, MN 55903, (507) 286-8742, 877-286-8742, www.ROandC.org or e-mail: office@ROandC.org

The Rochester Orchestra and Chorale evolved from the Rochester Civic Orchestra and Chorale (1919–1995), the only semi-professional ensemble in America that was administered by a city. As the Rochester Civic Music Department began to shift its emphasis from classical concerts to popular music performances, the musicians of the ensemble along with Maestro Jere Lantz, sought a way to secure the future of the high-quality ensemble. Under the leadership of Maestro Jere Lantz, the ensemble separated from Rochester Civic Music to form an independent organization now known as the Rochester Orchestra and Chorale. The organization's first independent season was produced and presented in 1996–1997. Today, the Rochester Orchestra and Chorale "aspires to serve our community and region by preserving, nurturing, and advancing the art of music through education and high-quality performances that seek to touch the soul." Maestro Jere Lantz has provided artistic leadership for the Orchestra and Chorale for more than 20 years. In addition to his enthusiasm and extensive experience, nationally and internationally, Maestro Lantz has distinguished himself as a dynamic conductor by his keen ability to connect with audiences by telling them the story behind the music. The Rochester Orchestra and Chorale also sponsors HoNk★SQuEAk★ScRaTcH★BOOM! This educational program helps fourth through sixth graders in the area choose the instrument they would like and best be suited to play. Please contact the Rochester Orchestra and Chorale or visit their website to find out more about their history, Maestro Jere Lantz, the current performance schedule, special activities, and ticket information.

Sweet Adelines

(507) 367-2485, www.sweetadelineintl.org

The Zumbro Valley Chorus, a chapter of Sweet Adelines International, is a women's barbershop-style singing group that strives to preserve and perfect the art of barbershop singing while also enjoying the friendships formed throughout the years of performing the harmonic hobby. The chorus has been entertaining audiences with their song and dance shows for more than 30 years. In May 2000, the Zumbro Valley Chorus won the Can-Am Region 6 First Place Small Chorus and was awarded Fourth Place Overall. The chorus typically performs once a month and shows range from full-scale productions to smaller events such as singing at nursing homes or the county fair. Nevertheless, the highlight performance of the year for the Zumbro Valley Chorus is during the spring convention when they compete with choruses from throughout the region for the regional championship. The Zumbro Valley Chorus is open to women of all ages. Call the group or visit their website for more information about a current performance schedule, joining the chorus, or to hire them for your special event.

Trombones Anonymous
Rochester, MN, (507) 289-3141, e-mail: willsr@mcleodusa.net

Trombones Anonymous is a unique ensemble! Organized in 1987 by Dr. Moses Rodriguez, the trombone choir first performed at Rochester's Apache Mall in 1990. The origin of the name, Trombones Anonymous, came about when the group was still loosely organized, and an open rehearsal schedule was held for anyone who could make it. Annual performances held by the 8–14 member ensemble include a show for the Cancer Survivors Picnic in June at Assisi Heights, a spring and fall concert, and 4–5 appearances during the Christmas season at nursing homes and events such as the Festival of Trees and The Rescue of Santa in downtown Rochester. Their repertoire of music includes a mix of jazz, easy listening and marches. Please call or e-mail Steve Williams for more information about joining Trombones Anonymous, a current performance schedule, or to hire the group to perform at your special event.

CHATFIELD
Chatfield Brass Band and Chatfield Music Lending Library
P.O. Box 578, 81 Library Lane, Chatfield, MN 55923, (507) 867-3275, chatbandselco.lib.mn.us or www.rochestermn.com/community/chatfieldbrass/

The Chatfield Brass Band was assembled in 1969 by Jim Perkins. It evolved from the original Chatfield Town Band that was organized in 1882, but later dissolved. When the band found it difficult to obtain challenging sheet music, Mr. Perkins requested unneeded sheet music from high schools throughout the United States. Eventually, this simple request led to the construction of the Chatfield Music Lending Library after the band received thousands of pieces of sheet music. As a result, Chatfield has become known as "Bandtown USA," and bands from around the globe have borrowed sheet music from the Chatfield Music Lending Library. In 1982, the Chatfield Brass Band traveled to Washington D.C. to play for President Jimmy Carter and perform at the John Phillip Sousa Memorial Concert. The Chatfield Brass Band plays at community events throughout the region and may be heard in many summer parades. Please call the Chatfield Brass Band or Chatfield Music Lending Library, if you're interested in joining the band or want more information about the band's performance schedule.

KASSON
Southeastern Winds Community Band
Kasson, MN 55944, Band Director: (507) 634-7650, Kasson-Mantorville Community Education: (507) 634-4464

The Southeastern Winds Community Band was originally established in the late 1970s and is sponsored by the Kasson-Mantorville Community Education program. Its mission is to "provide an ensemble in which adult musicians can play for their own enjoyment." The band plays a variety of music including concert overtures, show tunes, and marches at local fairs and festivals as well as senior centers, nursing homes, and other private gatherings. Anyone is welcome to join the band, and no auditions are required. Please contact Band Director, Mike O'Neill, for more information about joining the band, a concert schedule, or to hire the band for your gathering.

Stewartville Community Band

Stewartville Community Education, 500 4th Street, Stewartville, MN 55976, (507) 533-1650, (507) 536-0826 (Music Director), www.stewartvillemn.com

The Stewartville Community Band was formed in the early 1980s to provide adult musicians of all skill levels with an opportunity to play their instrument for their own pleasure. The band plays a variety of music including marches, big band, pop, and contemporary for a handful of area parades and performs a few concerts during the year. The band traditionally plays a Fourth of July concert and a concert at the Stewartville Community Progressive Dinner (first weekend in November). No auditions are required and newcomers who have a love to play their instruments are invited to join the band. Concerts are usually publicized via public notices on posters, flyers, and in the Stewartville Star and Rochester Post-Bulletin newspapers. Please contact Band Director, Jerry Spencer, for more information about joining the band, a performance schedule, or to hire the band for your event.

Children's Music Events & Organizations

"HoNK*SQuEAK*ScRaTcH*BOOM!"

Rochester Orchestra & Chorale, P.O. Box 302, Rochester, MN 55903, (507) 286-8742, 800-286-8742, www.ROandC.org, e-mail: office@ROandC.org

HoNK*SQuEAK*ScRaTcH*BOOM! is a unique educational program sponsored by the Rochester Orchestra and Chorale for area students in fourth through sixth grades. Under the guidance of accomplished musicians, the students are given the opportunity to have a hands-on experience with instruments they are interested in playing. When they are able to try out a wide variety of instruments, students may find that the experience confirms their original choice or learn that they are better suited for or interested in another instrument. This annual event is held at the beginning of the school year in September. Please contact the Rochester Orchestra and Chorale for more information.

Honors Choirs of Southeastern Minnesota

Assisi Heights, Suite 920, 1001 14th Street NW, Rochester, MN 55901, (507) 252-0505, www.honorschoirs.org or e-mail smhc@rconnect.com, honorschoirs@qwest.net

Founded in 1992 by Artistic Director, Rick Kvam, The Southeastern Minnesota Honors Choirs is a nonprofit organization for area youth in grades 3–12. The purpose of the organization "is to promote the highest standard of excellence in the performance of choral music for the education and enjoyment of the youth and the community at large." Weekly rehearsals challenge choir members to grow as they practice voice training techniques, learn about music history and theory, and prepare a repertoire of challenging choral music. The organization consists of five choirs including: the Children's Choir (grades 3–5), Treble Choir (grades 5–6), Honors Chorale (grades 7–9), Honors Concert Choir (grades 10–12), and the Lyric Singers (grades 8–12, women only). The Choirs are open to all students by audition, except the Children's Choir, which is nonauditioned but requires an entrance interview. The Honors Choirs maintain an active performance schedule at local and regional venues during the school year. The Concert Choir, Chorale Choir, and Lyric Singers are on a three-year touring cycle for post-season performance trips. Choir tours are typically involve travel to international destinations and include performances at choir festivals and competitions. In fact, the Honors Concert Choir won first place in the mixed choir division at the Vienna Youth and Music Festival in July 1998 and earned two second place awards at the International Choir Festival in Arnhem, Netherlands in the youth choir and school choir divisions. In addition to this, the Honors Concert Choir recorded its fourth CD and the Honors Chorale its first CD in the summer of 2001. Please call the Honors Choirs office or visit their website for more information about the individual choirs, brief biographies of the choir directors, auditions, performance schedules, or to obtain tickets.

Music Together®

Rochester, MN, (507) 252-8689, www.rochmusictogether.com or e-mail: Rochfamilymusic@aol.com

Music Together was originally conceived by Kenneth K. Guilmartin of the Center for Music and Young Children (CMYC) in Princeton, New Jersey, and developed in collaboration with Lili M. Levinowitz, Ph.D., an expert on early childhood music education. The Music Together curriculum provides young children (birth–age 6) with developmentally appropriate music experiences that emphasize and facilitate parent/caregiver involvement. Based on research from the fields of early childhood education and music learning theories, the Music Together program has become nationally recognized and is now taught in 36 states and several countries around the world. In September 2000, Karen Edmonds of Rochester, the local Music Together Director, began offering the classes for southeastern Minnesota. The 45 minute, mixed age classes engage children and adults in songs, chants, movement activities, and instrument play so that they have an opportunity to explore and create rhythm patterns, movement, and songs. YogaKids® and Kindermusik® programs are also available at the studio. Please contact Director Karen Edmonds for more information about programs, a class schedule, or to sign-up for a Music Together class.

Music with Connie Jelatis Hoke

512 3ʳᵈ Street SW, Rochester, MN 55902, (507) 287-8111, (507) 534-2290, www.musicwithconnie.com or e-mail: musiconnie@mindspring.com

Music with Connie is a dynamic, whole-arts music program with a curriculum based on the teachings of Carl Orff and Anton Kodaly, which has been offered in Rochester since the fall of 1992. Connie Jelatis Hoke, Director of the Music with Connie program, developed the whole-arts curriculum, which is a unique approach to music education that "fosters a comfort with and love of music" by providing children with the opportunity to explore musical concepts through singing, listening, movement, literature, dance, visual arts, musical games, drama, and instrument exploration. She is a master at providing the children with a nurturing environment and actively engaging them in age-appropriate programs that are both fun and exciting.

Her outstanding programs include: Musical Whimsy (ages 2½–3½), Musical Wonder (ages 4–6), Musical Journeys (ages 6–7), Musical Magic (ages 7–11), and the Musical Magic Performance Troupe (for students who have completed one year of Musical Magic or by invitation). Please call Music with Connie or visit the website for more information about Connie's qualifications, class descriptions, and registration.

Rochester Area Girls' Choir
Rochester, MN, (507) 289-6644, www.rochesterareagirlschoir.org

The Rochester Area Girls' Choir was founded in 1978 by Diane Toogood and her late husband, Roger. The mission of the nonprofit, volunteer organization is "to promote the love of singing, music, and the abilities of young girls to cooperate and work together in a group" as well as to learn more about the Rochester community and perform a variety of musical styles. The Girls' Choir consists of three groups including the Cherub Choir (kindergarten–grade 3), Choristers Choir (grades 4–6), and the Carolers Choir (grades 7–12). In addition to singing at concerts in the community, the Choristers and Carolers Choirs have the opportunity to perform on a tour of the Upper Midwest. Please call Director Diane Toogood, for more information about auditions, a concert schedule, or to make arrangements for the Girls' Choir to sing at your special event.

Rochester Boychoir
First Presbyterian Church of Rochester, 512 3rd Street SW, Rochester, MN 55902, (507) 282-1618, www.rochestermn.com/community/boychoir

The Rochester Boychoir is an auditioned choir open to boys aged 8–14 years old. The Boychoir receives musical training from Mr. Lee Afdahl, organist and Director of Music at the First Presbyterian Church of Rochester. Mr. Lee Afdahl is well-known internationally for his creative leadership in conducting handbells and children's choir festivals. Boys in the choir also have the opportunity to perform a repertoire of both sacred and secular music in the community and throughout the region. Please call Mr. Afdahl for information about auditions, a current performance schedule, or to arrange a performance by the Rochester Boychoir at your special event.

Southeastern Minnesota Suzuki Association—SEMSA
c/o Heidi Miksanek, P.O. Box 755, Rochester, MN 55903

The Southeastern Minnesota Suzuki Association (SEMSA) is an organizational group that provides opportunities and support for young people and their parents as they pursue instrumental lessons via the Suzuki method. Shinichi Suzuki, founder of Suzuki Talent Education, believed that "all children are born with great talent," and they learn music the same way they learn language. Suzuki Talent Education enables the child to develop a high level of musical ability and self-confidence by providing them with an enriched learning environment along with the close involvement of the mother or father. SEMSA members receive newsletters, instrument exchange lists, and the opportunity to participate in group lessons, recitals, educational workshops, and more. Contact SEMSA if you're interested in learning more about the Suzuki method of music instruction or want to find a Suzuki-trained teacher.

Southeastern Minnesota Youth Orchestra—SEMYO

Assisi Heights, Suite 450, 1001 14th Street NW, Rochester, MN 55901, (507) 282-1718, www.semyo.org or e-mail: SEMYO@rconnect.com

The Southeastern Minnesota Youth Orchestra (SEMYO) is an auditioned orchestra for elementary and secondary students from fifth through twelfth grades. SEMYO's is "dedicated to the artistic and personal development of young instrumental musicians." The organization consists of two major orchestras, the Philharmonic Orchestra and the Concert Orchestra as well as several small ensembles known as Chamber groups. As a general guideline, the Philharmonic Orchestra primarily consists of musicians in grades 5–9, and the Concert Orchestra consists of more experienced musicians in grades 9–12. However, orchestral placement is primarily determined by the musician's ability and the needs of the orchestras rather than age alone. The Philharmonic and Concert Orchestras perform a concert before a paying audience at the end of each trimester. SEMYO also sponsors a Concerto Competition that provides young musicians with the opportunity "to prepare a challenging piece, perform that piece for judges, and receive constructive feedback on their performances." Winners of the Concerto Competition have the opportunity to play as a soloist with the orchestra. Please contact SEMYO or visit their website for more information about the orchestras, auditions, concerts, competitions, and artistic directors.

Chapter 3: Coffeehouses & Tea Rooms

ROCHESTER
Bravo Espresso and Gourmet Coffee
550 Apache Mall, Rochester, MN 55902, (507) 281-4076

This kiosk café is located in the heart of Rochester's Apache Mall. Several bistro style tables nestled around the kiosk are available as an informal gathering spot for the local coffee klatch, mothers with young children, mall walkers or anyone browsing the mall. There is a good selection of specialty coffees, tea, Italian sodas and hot chocolate. Muffins, biscotti, and shortbread cookies are available for sale as is coffee paraphernalia.

Cost: $
Hours: Monday–Friday, 8:45 a.m.–9 p.m.; Saturday, 8:45 a.m.–8 p.m.; Sunday, 9:45 a.m.–6 p.m.

Bravo Espresso
Galleria Mall, 111 South Broadway, Rochester, MN 55902, (507) 252-9420

A kiosk located on third floor of downtown Rochester's Galleria Mall offers a small selection of specialty coffees, tea, and baked goodies. Seating in the food court area is a busy and loud place during the lunch hour.

Cost: $
Hours: Monday–Friday, 7 a.m.–7 p.m.; Saturday–Sunday, 10 a.m.–5 p.m.

Caribou Coffee
3938 Marketplace Drive NW, Rochester, MN 55901, (507) 252-0066, www.caribaucoffee.com

Escape to a log cabin in the city at Caribou Coffee. Customers will be warmed by the delicious blends of coffee and tea as well as the down home atmosphere, which has comfortable seating, a double fireplace, and a small children's area with a kid-sized table and chalkboard. The selection of coffees includes Coffee of the Day, Classic Coffees, a variety of light and dark roasts, Wild Coffees such as Turtle Mocha, Mint Condition, and Hot Apple Blast as well as several iced coffee drinks. Tea lover's will find a choice of green, black, blended black, and herbal teas, and children will love the hot cocoa, reindeer drinks, and silly soda. Accompany your beverage with one of the delicious muffins, scones, quick breads, croissants, reindeer cookies, brownies or other sweet treats. A limited selection of sandwiches is also available. Caribou Coffee also sells bulk coffee, insulated coffee mugs, chocolate covered espresso beans, hoof mints, carabiner key chains, and other goodies. Caribou Coffee is also located at Rochester's Apache Mall (507) 288-5117, and will soon be opening at the Subway level of the Rochester Marriot in downtown Rochester.

Cost: $$
Hours: Monday–Thursday, 6 a.m.–10 p.m.; Friday, 6 a.m.–10 p.m.; Saturday, 6:30 a.m.–10 p.m.; Sunday, 6:30 a.m.–9 p.m.

The Coffee Mouse Café at the House of the Crafty Mouse
116 17th Avenue NW, mini-mall at Miracle Mile Shopping Center, Rochester, MN 55901, (507) 282-7711, www.craftymouse.com

The Coffee Mouse Café adjoins the House of the Crafty Mouse Gift Shop and is also accessible through the Miracle Mile's mini-mall area. Step into the country kitchen atmosphere of the café—"with sugar and spice and everything mice," it's easy to relax at one of the white gingerbread style tables or high top tables while you wait for the House of the Crafty Mouse to open, or take a break from shopping at the Mouse and other shops at The Miracle Mile. The Café features a House Mouse Coffee Blend, which along with its other custom blends, is roasted daily. Other beverages on the menu include flavored coffees, lattes, espresso, cappuccino, mocha, a house tea latte, and the Mouse's special blends of hot chocolate and apple cider. In addition to assorted pastries, cookies, fudge, jumbo turtles, and English toffee, the Café serves its signature Heart pocket sandwich of the day, soups, a savory cheesy mouse muffin, and chicken or tuna salad sandwiches. Flavored waters, milk, juices, iced tea, and soda are also available.

Cost: $

Hours: Monday–Friday, 9:30 a.m.–8 p.m., Saturday, 9:30 a.m.–5 p.m.; Sunday, 11:30 a.m.–5 p.m.

Daube's Bakery

1310 5th Place NW, Rochester, MN 55901, (507) 289-3095

A Rochester original. Daube's is a local from scratch bakery with a loyal following. A cozy atmosphere welcomes singles, couples, and families to relax and savor its aromas and flavors away from the hustle and bustle of the typical franchise coffeehouse bakery. Specialties include muffins, pastries, cheesecake, carrot cake & a variety of crusty breads. Delicious homemade sandwiches, soups, and salads are also available for lunch.

Cost: $–$$

Hours: Monday–Saturday, 6 a.m.–6 p.m.; Sunday, 7:30 a.m.–2 p.m.

Daube's Konditorei & German Restaurant

14 Historic 3rd Street SW, Rochester, MN 55902, (507) 280-6446

Daube's third location is a quiet haven tucked into Historic 3rd Street of downtown Rochester that attracts the mature customer. An antique red brick wall embedded with decorative stepping stones provides the backdrop for the dining area. Daube's signature pastries, gourmet coffees, and specialty lunch sandwiches are available. The coffeehouse/bakery is transformed into Rochester's only authentic German restaurant in the evening. Reservations are recommended for the German restaurant.

Cost: $–$$$

Hours: bakery/konditorei: Monday–Saturday, 7 a.m.–5 p.m.
  German restaurant: 5 p.m.–9 p.m.

Daube's Pastry Pavilion

Marriott Hotel, subway level, 155 1st Avenue SW, Rochester, MN 55902, (507) 252-8878

Amid the hustle and bustle of the Marriott Hotel subway, Daube's provides a convenient place for downtown employees, visitors, and Mayo Clinic patients to tempt their taste buds with sumptuous baked goods, a variety of coffees or a savory bistro-style lunch. Nosh in the casual, out-of-the-way pavilion or take your food to go.

Cost: $–$$

Hours: Monday–Friday, 7 a.m.–5 p.m.; Saturday–Sunday, closed

Java Café and Salad Brothers

1239 2nd Street SW, Rochester, MN 55902, (507) 280-6319

A clean, cafeteria-style coffeehouse located across from Saint Mary's Hospital offers a quiet refuge from the hustle and bustle of the medical center. Choose from an assortment of beverages including hot and iced coffees. Accompany your drink with a low-fat muffin, cinnamon roll, quiche, or breakfast sandwich. Selections from the lunch menu include a special of the day, baked potatoes, sandwiches, and soups.

Cost: $
Hours: Monday–Saturday, 6:15 a.m.–8:30 p.m.; Saturday–Sunday, 8 a.m.–7 p.m.

Java Café Coffee and Espresso

120 Elton Hills Drive NW, Rochester, MN 55901, (507) 285-4991

Java Café is an upbeat place to hang out after skating at the recreation center across the street or a long stretch on the bike trail. Customers also come to read the newspaper and meet for conversation in the casual atmosphere while enjoying a variety of homemade soups, sandwiches, pastries, gourmet coffees, and Bridgeman's ice cream. A great place for families.

Cost: $
Hours: Monday–Friday, 6:30 a.m.–8:30 p.m.; Saturday–Sunday, 7 a.m.–8:30 p.m.;
   Sunday–Saturday, 6:30 a.m.–9:30 p.m. (summer)

Loveugly Cabaret Bar & Coffee Lounge

320 1st Avenue SW, Rochester, MN 55902, (507) 529-3880, www.loveugly.com

The Loveugly, a coffee lounge by day and bar and cabaret by night, opened its doors to Rochester in September 2002. This alternative entertainment venue, founded by Mike Savage, was once an underground gathering place for the creative community. A hip atmosphere greets patrons who may sit at one of several cabaret-style tables or the coffee bar. Patrons are welcome to browse the small art gallery in the rear of the club and have access to free wireless internet service. The entertainment schedule typically includes a local or touring band on Friday and Saturday nights and an open mike night on Mondays. The Loveugly boasts variety in its musical lineup with performances of rock, country, jazz and everything in between. A selection of fine coffees, teas, smoothies, organic beverages, spirits and a few light snacks are available. Alcoholic beverages are not served until 4 p.m.

Cost: $, cover charge for live entertainment
Hours: Monday–Friday, 6 a.m.–1 a.m.; Saturday, 9 a.m.–1 a.m.; Sunday
   10 a.m.–1 a.m.

Marcelli's Espresso and Gourmet Coffee

1111 2nd Street SW, Rochester, MN 55902, (507) 287-9250

A Mediterranean atmosphere greets you in this tiny café located across from Saint Mary's Hospital. The menu features espresso, a variety of iced and hot coffees, smoothies, granitas, and Italian sodas. A limited pastry selection is also available. A small smoking section is available in the rear of the restaurant.

Cost: $
Hours: Monday–Friday, 6 a.m.–5 p.m.; Saturday, 9:30 a.m.–5 p.m.; Sunday, closed

Panera Bread

460 Crossroads Drive SW, Rochester, MN 55902, (507) 285-5800, www.panerabread.com

Panera is a popular gathering place for families and friends to break bread together. The urban contemporary atmosphere invites you to relax near the cozy fireplace or share a more private booth area. Accompany your espresso, specialty coffee drink, tea, fresh-squeezed orange juice or lemonade with a decadent pastry, danish, bagel, croissant, muffin, biscotti or cookie. For lunch or dinner, feast on soup in a bread bowl, a hot panini sandwich or one of the sandwiches or salads made with a unique medley of ingredients. Peanut butter and jelly is available for the little ones. One taste of Panera Bread will have you coming back again and again.

Cost: $–$$
Hours: Monday–Saturday, 6 a.m.–9 p.m.; Sunday, 7 a.m.–8 p.m.

Starbucks at Barnes & Noble—Historic Chateau Theatre

15 1ˢᵗ Street SW, Rochester, MN 55902, (507) 288-3848, www.bn.com

Contemporary meets historic at Rochester's Starbucks, which is located on the second level of Barnes & Noble in the restored Chateau Theatre. The ceiling is illuminated with "stars in the night sky" that overlook interior balconies and an ornamental "French Village" decor. Starbucks is a community gathering place with great appeal for all ages. Entertainment, poetry readings, book signings, discussion groups, book clubs, and chess night are just some of the organized events scheduled for the café. The café menu features a large variety of specialty coffees, teas, and Italian sodas as well as luscious pastries, cheesecake, and biscotti. Prepared sandwiches and a soup of the day rounds out the menu.

Cost: $–$$
Hours: Monday–Friday, 7 a.m.–10 p.m.; Saturdays, 9 a.m.–10 p.m.; Sundays, 10 a.m.–9 p.m.

Starbucks at Barnes & Noble

425 Apache Mall, Rochester, MN 55902, (507) 281-7950, www.bn.com

Starbucks, located in Barnes & Noble at Rochester's Apache Mall, offers customers a quiet escape from the harried atmosphere of the mall. The café's casual setting is a great place to kick back and relax while you sip one of Starbucks specialty coffees, teas, or Italian sodas. A selection of luscious pastries, cheesecake, biscotti, and prepared sandwiches is also available.

Cost: $–$$
Hours: open daily, 9 a.m.–11 p.m.

LA CRESCENT

Apple on Main Tea Room & Gifts

329 Main Street, La Crescent, MN 55947, (507) 895-1995

The Apple on Main Tea Room is located in the southeastern Minnesota city of La Crescent, also known as the "Apple Capital of Minnesota." The cozy tea room celebrates this heritage with apple decor in a cottage style atmosphere. Seating is available in two rooms or a small screened porch, but reservations are strongly recommended due to the popularity of the Tea Room with both locals and visitors.

Enjoy morning coffee, tea and pastries from 9:30 a.m.–11 a.m. or stop by for lunch. Lunch is served from 11 a.m.–2 p.m. and features a daily "blackboard entree," quiche, salads, homemade soups, and sandwiches. Afternoon tea and dessert, which includes a variety of cheesecakes, pies and other sweet treats, is available from 2 p.m.–3:30 p.m. After a relaxing cup of tea or savory lunch, don't forget to browse the gift shop area that has Ashby's tea, cookbooks, gourmet mustards and honey products, porcelain tea sets, and other apple-related items for sale.

Cost: $
Hours: Monday–Saturday, 9:30 a.m.–4 p.m.

LAKE CITY
Chickadee Cottage Tea Room and Restaurant
317 Lakeshore Drive North (Hwy. 61), Lake City, MN 55041, (651) 345-5155, 888-321-5177, www.chickadeecottagetearoom.com or e-mail: teatime@rconnect.com

The Chickadee Cottage invites you to "Step Back to Homemade and Leisurely" in their early 1900s home that is surrounded by gardens, paths, and a gazebo. The restored home is located on The Great River Road as it passes through Lake City. It is a lovely place to spend time in the company of friends or family as you savor selections from the "always made-from-scratch" menu. Breakfast, lunch, and English Afternoon Tea is served six days per week. Breakfast is served from 7:30 a.m.– 11 a.m., except on Sundays. On Sundays, the Chickadee Cottage rolls out its "Fabulous Sunday Family Breakfast" from 8 a.m.–2 p.m. with bountiful platters of sweet rolls, fruit, eggs, sausages, and cheesy potatoes. Lunch is served from 11 a.m.–4:30 p.m. Choose from a delicious selection of soups, sandwiches, salads, and regional entrees. A traditional English-style afternoon tea begins at 2:30 p.m. and includes fresh fruit, tea sandwiches, scones with devonshire cream, dessert, and a pot of tea. A Londonberry tea, featuring English biscuits, white cheddar, apples and grapes, and a glass of wine or sherry is also offered.

After relaxing awhile, take time to browse through the distinctive collection of gift items displayed throughout the cottage. Tea sets, dolls, cookbooks, picture frames, chickadee art prints, garden accessories and flags, teapot covers, and T-shirts are just a sample of the items for sale. Don't forget to pick up a loaf of fresh-baked bread, shortbread, scones, or cookies from the bakery counter.

As a final note, autumn is celebrated at the Chickadee Cottage during the month of October with special Minnesota Festive Fall Dinners on Friday evenings. This annual tradition is popular and requires advance reservations.

Cost: $–$$$
Hours: open seasonally from April–November: Tuesday–Saturday, 7:30 a.m.– 4:30 p.m.; Sunday, 8 a.m.–2 p.m.; Monday, closed

Oak Center General Store
mailing address: Route 1, Box 52BB, Lake City, MN 55041
physical address: 260 Hwy. 63, Zumbro Falls, MN 55991, (507) 753-2080
Located on U.S. Hwy. 63 between Zumbro Falls and Lake City.

An earthy and organic experience awaits you at the Oak Center General Store. This turn-of-the-century General Store attracts a wide variety of people from families to farmers to physicians and everyone in between. The organic grocery market provides a unique venue for Saturday night Folk Forum Concerts that are held upstairs in a community gathering area/coffeehouse. Before heading upstairs for the concert, help yourself to a cup of coffee or tea in the community kitchen—a place where water is still heated on a cast iron stove. Once upstairs, you will find wholesome snacks such as popcorn, huge chocolate chip and oatmeal raisin cookies, and bottled juices and beverages for sale. Settle into your seat, but be prepared to listen to a bit of a social-political soapbox before being introduced to the performers. A variety of regional, national, and international artists take the stage at Oak Center to perform the Folk Forum concerts, which typically feature an evening of folk, ethnic, Celtic, jazz, gospel, or blues music. The Folk Forum schedule runs from late September to April. Reservations are suggested. Call the Store for a current entertainment schedule or to make concert reservations. Concerts begin at 8 p.m.

Cost: sliding scale admission fees
Hours: store: Monday–Saturday, 9 a.m.–6 p.m.

Rhythmn & Brew
220 East Chestnut Street, Lake City, MN 55041, (651) 345-5335

Take a stroll on Lake City's Riverwalk, overlooking Lake Pepin, before heading to Rhythm & Brew. The combination coffeehouse/ice cream shop is typically packed on warm summer evenings as folks gather to share wholesome entertainment on Friday and Saturday nights. This community living room attracts a hodgepodge of singles, couples, families, and seniors to its informal atmosphere. Ice cream, shakes, malts, cookies, sundaes and specialty sodas such as ginger beer and sarsaparilla mingle with the cappuccino, latte, and espresso coffee selections on the menu. Breakfast sandwiches are served in the morning until 11 a.m.

Cost: $
Hours: Monday–Saturday, 7 a.m.–4:30 p.m.; Saturday, 7 a.m.–10 p.m.; Sunday, closed; call for summer hours

LANESBORO
Sojourner Café
204 Parkway Avenue North, Lanesboro, MN 55949, (507) 467-3057

The Sojourner Café is located next to the Commonweal Theater on Lanesboro's award-winning Main Street. Theater patrons, tourists and locals alike enjoy the casual and friendly environment of the Sojourner. The lunch menu includes delicious homemade soups, sandwiches, salads, and desserts. The friendly staff is especially accommodating for those with young children who just want a hot dog or peanut butter and jelly sandwich for lunch. Nightly dinner entrees are planned on a weekly basis and feature home-cooked selections such as manicotti, pot roast, baked chicken breast, beef stew, and shrimp stir fry. Friday evenings usually feature an Italian entree, and prime rib is typically served on Saturday evenings. A variety of hot and iced coffee and tea drinks as well as Italian sodas, wine and specialty beers are also available. Entertainment is often scheduled for Saturday nights. Call for current schedule and times.

Cost: $–$$
Hours: Monday, closed; Tuesday–Saturdays, 11 a.m.–8 p.m.; Sunday, 11 a.m.–5 p.m.; summer: call for hours

PLAINVIEW
Rebekah's
330 West Broadway, Plainview, MN 55964, (507) 534-4065
Located just ½ block from the Jon Hassler Theater in Plainview.

Rebekah's welcomes you to Plainview with its small-town charm and a warm and homey atmosphere. The coffeehouse and restaurant is tastefully decorated with memorabilia that reflect its roots as the former home of the Odd Fellows organization. Rebekah's lunch menu features a Farmers' Market Deli with a diverse selection of beverages as well as made-from-scratch soups, sandwiches, salads, and baked goods prepared with organic ingredients whenever possible. Vegetarian and vegan items are also available. During the evening, Rebekah's offers its patrons either a fine dining experience or a casual meal at the Pizza Tratorria in the lower level, a former antique cellar. Family-style Sunday dinners are a special treat with selections reminiscent of Grandma's kitchen. Live entertainment is regularly scheduled on Friday and Saturday evenings at 7 p.m. Call to check the current entertainment schedule or to make dinner reservations.

Cost: $–$$$, small cover charge for entertainment
Hours: Lunch: Tuesday–Saturday, 11 a.m.–2 p.m.
  fine dining and Pizza Tratorria: Thursday–Saturday, 5:30 p.m.–11 p.m.
  Sunday Dinner: 11 a.m.–6 p.m.
  closed Monday

PRESTON
Brick House on Main Coffeehouse and Gift Shop
104 East Main Street, Preston, MN 55965, (507) 765-9820, www.bluffcountry.com/brickhouse.htm

An 1800s home is the setting for this peaceful coffeehouse in rural southeastern Minnesota, located just three blocks from the junction of the Root River State Bike Trail and Preston-Harmony Bike Trail. Unwind in the front room of the Brick House near the fireplace, escape upstairs to a quiet room filled with board games, or bask in the sunshine of the spacious modern seating area in the rear of the house. Cappuccino, espresso, lattes, smoothies, and Italian sodas are served along with lunch selections that include hot and cold sandwiches, soups, and salads. Root beer or strawberry floats, ice cream and fresh baked cookies, scones, and muffins are some of the sweet treats available. Regional gift items for sale are tastefully displayed throughout the house. Choose from a diverse selection of Minnesota and Amish gifts, books, cards, T-shirts, Red Wing pottery, and locally hand-crafted jewelry. The Brick House is also the home of Send Me Minnesota—a mail order basket company that exclusively features Minnesota products. Bike rentals are available.

Cost: $
Hours: Monday–Friday, 8:30 a.m.–5 p.m.; Saturday, 9 a.m.–5 p.m.; Sunday,
  9 a.m.–5 p.m. (mid-May–summer only)

ST. CHARLES
Victorian Lace Inn B & B, Tea Room & Gift Shop
1512 Whitewater Avenue, St. Charles, MN 55972, (507) 932-4496, e-mail: viclaceskv@prodigy.net

A medley of teacup place settings uniquely adorns the plants and flowers of the garden walkway to the Victorian Lace Tea Room. As you step up onto the grand porch and crank the old-fashioned doorbell of this 1860s vintage Victorian home, you step into the peaceful surroundings of a different era. The Tea Room seats 17–20 people and has an atmosphere that invites quiet reflection and conversation. Victorian Lace serves both lunch and English style Afternoon Tea/High Tea. The lunch menu is presented verbally and typically offers a choice of three or four entrees. Afternoon Tea/High Tea begins at 2 p.m. and includes a seasonal assortment of finger sandwiches, hot savories, scones, desserts, and, of course, tea. Cream Tea, which simply features tea and dessert, is also offered in the afternoon. Reservations are strongly recommended and are required for Afternoon Tea.

The Victorian Lace Tea Room is also home to The Victorian Tea Club and The Red Hats and Pearls Tea Group. The Victorian Tea Club meets the third Friday of every other month at 1 p.m. and features speakers or presentations related to the Victorian era. The Red Hats and Pearls Tea Group, an official member of the National Red Hat Tea Society, is primarily a social club for those aged 50 and over (although "50-something wannabes" are also welcome). Both clubs welcome new members. The Tea Room can accommodate larger groups for card clubs, birthdays, bridal showers, baby showers, children's tea parties or other events with advance notice and reservations. Tea classes, "themed" tea days, holiday teas, and children's tea parties may also be arranged.

A small gift shop is located within the tea room as well as At the Garden Gate, a carriage house behind the inn. Call (507) 932-4916 for hours At the Garden Gate.

Cost: $–$$
Hours: Tuesday–Saturday, 11:30 a.m.–4 p.m.; Sunday and Monday, closed

WABASHA
Eagle's Nest
330 2nd Street, Wabasha, MN 55981, (651) 565-2077

A very modern and spacious atmosphere welcomes both children and adults to this coffeehouse, which was renovated from an early 1900s restored automobile dealership and garage. A large gnome collection greets visitors to the Eagle's Nest. Street lanterns illuminate the restaurant, and an abundant supply of magazines available for perusal encourages patrons to linger over coffee or lunch. The menu features sandwiches served on a cro-bagel, a cross between a bagel and croissant. Other selections include baked goods, ice cream, cold drinks, juices, beer and wine, and a creative array of coffee drinks such as the Avalanche, Betty Boop, and Snickermocha. The huge deck, with outdoor seating, is a great place to enjoy an ice cream cone on a warm summer afternoon. Music is usually scheduled for Saturday nights. Please call to check the current entertainment schedule. The Eagle's Nest also has a small selection of locally-made and regional gift items for sale.

Cost: $
Hours: Monday–Friday, 6 a.m.–6 p.m.; Saturday, 6 a.m.–7 p.m.; Sunday, 6 a.m.–5 p.m.
   summer: Monday–Friday, 6 a.m.–7 p.m.; Saturday, 6 a.m.–8 p.m. (10 p.m., if entertainment); Sunday, 6 a.m.–5 p.m.

WINONA
Acoustic Café
77 Lafayette, Winona, MN 55987, (507) 453-0394

The Acoustic Café, just one block from the Mississippi riverfront, has a warm and inviting ambiance. The red-brick walls, and worn, but well-maintained wooden floors and wooden booths give this coffeehouse a cozy and comfortable feel. A coffee bean roaster is prominently displayed in the café and is used to freshly roast the coffee beans in small batches. Soups, sandwiches, pita sandwiches, chili, nachos, and a large dessert menu with ice cream, cheesecake, cookies, scones, and muffins accompany the gourmet coffees, teas, hot chocolate, Italian and French sodas, and chai on the menu. The Acoustic Café has an active entertainment schedule with live music on Friday and Saturday nights from 8:30–11 p.m. Local and regional musical talent regularly take the stage at the Acoustic Café, and local artisans are supported through the display of their original artwork. Stop by the Café to pick up an entertainment schedule or call for more information.

Cost: $–$$
Hours: Monday–Thursday, 7:30 a.m.–10 p.m.; Friday, 7:30–midnight; Saturday, 9:30–midnight; Sunday, 9:30 a.m.–9 p.m.

Blue Heron Coffeehouse
451 Huff Street, Winona, MN 55987, (507) 452-7020

Located across the street from Winona State University, the Blue Heron is a typical college town coffeehouse. The coffeehouse itself is small and seats about 18 with a few additional tables outside but is also connected to the Lutheran Campus Center (LCC) with seating for another 30 people. Amid the hustle and bustle of the morning crowd, you will find a quiet place to sit in the LCC. The LCC offers a bright, sunny room that feels like home. With sofas, a bubbling fountain, piano, and wall of used paperback books for sale, it's a great place to enjoy a specialty coffee, espresso, chai, Italian soda or tea from the Blue Heron. The Blue Heron has a limited deli and bakery menu with sandwiches, soups, salads and desserts that are homemade from organic ingredients whenever possible. Entertainment is occasionally sponsored by the LCC. Call the Lutheran Campus Center at (507) 452-8316, or visit their website at www3.Winona.msus.edu/lcc for more information about scheduled events.

Cost: $
Hours: Monday–Friday, 7 a.m.–10 p.m.; Saturday, 8 a.m.–10 p.m.; Sunday, 9 a.m.–5 p.m.

The Green Lantern Coffeehouse
571 East 3rd Street, Winona, MN 55987, (507) 453-9520

Pull up at stool at The Green Lantern Coffeehouse. Formerly a neighborhood bar and a speakeasy during the prohibition, The Green Lantern is a fun place to mingle with local Winona residents. The original character of the 100-year-old building is retained by the green checkerboard floor, coffee bar, and hodgepodge of tables. Gourmet coffees, smoothies, and exotic teas are served along with a small selection of soups, sandwiches, and desserts. Weekend entertainment hosted by The Green Lantern includes live music, puppet theater, poetry readings, art shows, and an open mike night on Sundays. Please call for current entertainment schedule.

Cost: $
Hours: Wednesday–Sunday, 9 a.m.–9 p.m.; Monday and Tuesday, closed

WYKOFF
The Bank Gift Haus and Tea Room
P.O. Box 205,105 Gold Street, Wykoff, MN 55990, (507) 352-4205, www.bluffcountry.com

The oldest building in Wykoff, a former bank, is now home to The Bank Gift Haus and Tea Room. Constructed of brick, it was the only building to remain standing on the west side of Gold Street after a devastating fire in 1895. In fact, charred roof beams are still visible near a small section of the ceiling. The Bank Gift Haus and Tea Room commemorates its history as a bank with beautiful mahogany and marble teller windows where visitors purchase their gifts. An old safe, safety deposit boxes, and a wallpaper trimmer are among the interesting antiques to view while you browse the shop. You will be delighted to find a tasteful selection of seasonal home decor and gift items as well as crystal, china tea sets, Heritage Lace products, collectibles, inspirational books, garden flags, Ty Beanie Babies, and a large assortment of greeting cards. Wander downstairs to the Kinderhaus and year-round Christmas Shop, and you will discover a collection of high-quality children's toys, books, Gotz dolls as well as Christmas ornaments, giftware, candles, and decor. Homemade fudge, made on site, is also available for purchase.

The Bank Haus Tea Room is a quiet and relaxing place to enjoy conversation and company. Located in the back of the Gift Haus, it has a seating capacity of 20. The menu features a limited choice of homemade soups, salads and desserts that changes every day or two. Special entrees may occasionally be made. Reservations are strongly recommended. Groups are welcome, but advance notice is preferred.

Cost: $
Hours: tea room: 11:30 a.m.–4 p.m., closed Sundays
  gift shop: Monday–Saturday, 10 a.m.–5 p.m.

Historic Wykoff Jail Haus Bed & Breakfast
Looking for a unique experience while visiting? Try an overnight stay in Wykoff's Historic Jail Haus, which was built in 1913. The two-room jail house can comfortably accommodate four people. Two bunk beds are located in the original cell block, and a small living area with a TV is furnished with a queen-sized sofa sleeper. The Jail Haus is open year-round and has air-conditioning and a modern, handicapped-accessible bathroom. For more information or to make reservations, please contact the Bank Gift Haus and Tea Room at (507) 352-4205.

ZUMBROTA
Aromas
218 Main Street, Zumbrota, MN 55992, (507) 732-7600, www.zumbrota.com

A small town hangout that is comfortable and welcoming to both teens and adults. Suitable for children during daytime hours. Aromas features an active music schedule with performances every Friday and Saturday night. Style of music varies. Call for information about current musical venues. The reasonably priced menu includes: deli sandwiches, soups, baked goods, and ice cream along with a variety of hot and cold drinks.

Cost: $
Hours: Monday–Friday, 7 a.m.–4 p.m.; Saturday, 7 a.m.–9 p.m.; Sunday,
   9 a.m.–noon

Crossings at Carnegie

320 East Avenue, Zumbrota, MN 55992, (507) 732-7616, www.crossingsatcarnegie.com

Crossings at Carnegie is located in the 1907 Zumbrota Library, which has been beautifully restored by owner Marie Louise. Its mission is "connecting people with the process of creating, striving for an organic holistic approach to the arts, and enriching the lives of all who enter our doors." Crossings at Carnegie is not only an art center, but a community gathering place as well. In addition to a gallery, which features the work of regional artists, the center also offers coffeehouse-style concerts on Saturday evenings and Sunday afternoons, fitness classes, art and writing classes, community potluck dinners, dances of universal peace, community recitals, and more. The artwork displayed throughout the gallery and in the gift shop is available for purchase. So pay a visit to Crossings at Carnegie, and experience just how Marie Louise has transformed an old library into "a place that makes you feel good." Call Crossings or check their website for class and concert schedules. Registration is required for some classes, and reservations are suggested for concerts.

Cost: free admission; classes and concerts: fees vary
Hours: gallery and gift shop: Monday, Tuesday, Wednesday, & Friday, 10 a.m.–5 p.m.;
   Thursday, 10 a.m.–8 p.m.; Saturday, 10 a.m.–4 p.m.
   concerts: Saturdays, 8 p.m.; Sundays, 2 p.m.
   classes: times vary

Chapter 4: Story Telling

Barnes & Noble Booksellers at the Historic Chateau Theatre
15 1ˢᵗ Street SW, Rochester, MN 55902, (507) 288-3848, www.bn.com

Weekly story time is available for toddlers and preschoolers on Friday mornings at 10 a.m. Call the store or check the monthly newsletter for story theme of the week. Occasionally, a costumed storybook character visits with the children. Parents must remain with children during the 30–60 minute story time, which is located in the children's area on the first floor.

Cost: free
Hours: book store: Monday–Friday, 9 a.m.–10 p.m.; Saturdays, 9 a.m.–10 p.m.;
   Sundays, 10 a.m.–9 p.m.
   café: Monday–Friday, 7 a.m.–10 p.m.; Saturdays, 9 a.m.–10 p.m.; Sundays, 10
   a.m.–9 p.m.

Barnes & Noble Booksellers
425 Apache Mall, Rochester, MN 55902, (507) 281-7950, www.bn.com

Story time at Barnes & Noble in Apache Mall is an "event" for local children who gather on small benches around a stage adorned with a make-believe forest and Winnie the Pooh characters. Children and their parents are invited to join in the fun on Mondays and Wednesdays at 11 a.m. and 7 p.m. Call the store or check the monthly newsletter for story theme of the week. Occasionally, a costumed story-book character visits with the children.

Cost: free
Hours: open daily, 9 a.m.–11 p.m.

Pied Piper Children's Books & Music
Miracle Mile Shopping Center, 8 17ᵗʰ Avenue NW, Rochester, MN 55902, (507) 281-1890,
e-mail: thepiper@earthlink.net

The Pied Piper warmly welcomes toddlers and preschoolers to story time Wednesday mornings at 10:30 a.m. The small play area with a cozy sofa invites children and their parents to snuggle up for 30 minutes of literary adventure. Saturday events vary weekly and may include book signings, entertainment, and/or fun classes for children. After story time, browse leisurely through the rich literary environment. Selections include books, music and videos for children of all ages. Parenting books and a limited selection of fiction and poetry for adults is also available.

Cost: free
Hours: Monday–Friday, 10 a.m.–7 p.m.; Saturday, 10 a.m.–5 p.m.

Rochester Public Library
101 2ⁿᵈ Street SE, Rochester, MN 55904, (507) 285-8000; www.rochesterpubliclibrary.org

The library offers a weekly 30 minute story time for preschoolers and kindergarten-ers during the school year on Wednesday and Thursday mornings and Thursday afternoons. Registration is required for the fall, winter, and spring sessions. Activities include stories, fingerplays, songs, puppets, and a short film at the end of each session. This program is intended for children (age 3–5) who are ready to attend story time independently. Parents are asked to wait in the Children's area while story time is in session.

A Bedtime Story Hour for Families is available on Tuesdays at 7 p.m. during the school year. Stories, puppets, and films often relate to seasonal themes. No registration is required. Parents are invited to stay with their children during this story hour.

Family Funfest is available at the library on Saturday mornings at 10:30 a.m. Programs include special theater or musical performances, magic shows, animal demonstrations, and films.

The library is a community treasure. Enrichment services for adults and young adults include book discussion groups such as the Armchair Travelers, Mystery Book Club, Notable Nonfiction, Newberry Award Book Club, and Plain Readers Group. Regularly scheduled events include a lecture series, the coffeehouse author series, poetry readings, literature-into-film discussions, a writer's group, and computer classes such as Internet Basics and Genealogy Research. Homework assistance for teens is available two nights per week.

A summer reading program is open to both children and young adults ages 12–18. Children are awarded prizes for completion of the reading program. Young adults are eligible to win prizes by entering their name in a drawing every time they have read a book. To participate, pick up forms at the library.

Cost: free
Hours: Monday–Thursday, 9 a.m.–9 p.m.; Friday, 9:30 a.m.–5:30 p.m.; Saturday (during school year), 9:30 a.m.–5:30 p.m.; Sunday (during school year), 1:30 p.m.–5:30 p.m.; Saturday (summer), 9:30 a.m.–1:30 p.m.; Sunday (summer), closed

Visitor Privileges at the Rochester Public Library

Minnesota residents may use their home library card to borrow books, magazines, and audiovisual materials. Other visitors may obtain the same privileges by purchasing a temporary library card for $5. All visitors are welcome to read, browse, or attend library programs. The library is conveniently located in downtown Rochester across from the Mayo Civic Center and is a short walk from Mayo Medical Center and most downtown hotels.

Part II:
Tours & Excursions

Chapter 5: Attractions & Points of Interest highlights cave tours, Amish tours, farm tours, hospital tours, and riverboat cruises.

Chapter 6: Historic Sites provides information about significant historic buildings and sites in the region such as houses, mills, villages, and downtown historic districts.

Chapter 7: Museums provides a guide to a variety of regional museums such as wildlife, carriage, woodcarving, steam engine, and orphanage museums.

Chapter 5: Attractions & Points of Interest

ROCHESTER
Historic Chateau Theatre Barnes & Noble
15 1st Street SW, Rochester, MN 55902, (507) 288-3848, www.nationalregisterofhistoricplaces.com

The Historic Chateau Theatre, located off the Peace Plaza in downtown Rochester, was originally built in 1927. The ornately decorated theater served as a movie house until its closing curtain in 1983. The Chateau was refurbished in 1994 and is now home to Barnes & Noble Booksellers and Starbucks Café. The exterior marquee features a sunburst design with 636 lightbulbs, and the interior resembles a French village with "stars in the night sky" that overlook interior balconies and ornamental decor.

Cost: free admission
Hours: book store: Monday–Friday, 9 a.m.–10 p.m.; Saturdays, 9 a.m.–10 p.m.;
    Sundays, 10 a.m.–9 p.m.
    café: Monday–Friday, 7 a.m.–10 p.m.; Saturdays, 9 a.m.–10 p.m.; Sundays,
    10 a.m.–9 p.m.

Peace Plaza
1st Street SW, Rochester, MN 55902
The Peace Plaza is located next to the Historic Chateau Theatre/Barnes & Noble and the Galleria Mall in downtown Rochester. Rochester Convention & Visitor's Bureau, (507) 288-4331, 800-634-8277, www.rochestercvb.org

The Peace Plaza, an outdoor courtyard in downtown Rochester, serves as a gathering place for community events as well as a place to meet friends for coffee and conversation. The focal point of the Peace Plaza is the "Peace Fountain," a twelve foot high bronze sculpture that was created by Rochester resident and internationally renowned sculptor, Charles E. Gagnon, for the City of Rochester. The sculpture has become a historic landmark in downtown Rochester since its unveiling in 1989. It eloquently speaks the language of peace to all cultures as described by its creator: "The fifty-seven peace doves uplift the human spirit in an unending quest for global peace and symbolize the fifty states and seven major continents of the world." Take time to visit the Peace Plaza on your next trip to downtown Rochester.

Rochester Methodist Hospital
201 West Center Street, Rochester, MN 55902, (507) 266-7890, www.mayo.edu

Rochester Methodist Hospital is one of two Mayo Foundation hospitals in Rochester. The 700-plus bed hospital is located in the heart of Mayo Medical Center in downtown Rochester. Visitors are welcome to take a self-guided tour of the three-building hospital from 8 a.m.–8:30 p.m. Tour brochures are available at the hospital information desk. Please call the hospital for more information. Free.

Saint Mary's Hospital
1216 2nd Avenue SW, Rochester, MN 55902, (507) 255-5123, www.mayo.edu

Saint Mary's Hospital, a 1,000-plus bed hospital, is one of two Mayo Foundation hospitals in Rochester. The Mayo Eugenio Litta Children's Hospital, an 85-bed hospital within Saint Mary's Hospital, is a unique feature of the six-building facility.

Visitors are welcome to take a self-guided tour of the hospital from 8 a.m.–
8:30 p.m. Tour brochures are available at the hospital's information desks. Please call
the hospital for more information. Guided tours are also available by appointment
and require one month advance notice. Please call (507) 284-9258 to arrange a special tour. Free.

ELBA
Elba Fire Tower

State Hwy. 74, Elba, MN, www.firetower.org
Located a few miles north of Whitewater State Park off State Hwy. 74.

The Elba Fire Tower, situated high atop a bluff in Elba, is a National Historic
Lookout. The lookout was restored in recent years and opened to the public in July,
1997. The fire tower serves as an educational resource as well as sightseeing attraction.
Informational displays provide visitors with the opportunity to learn about the history
of the Whitewater Valley and the effects that erosion has had in the region over the
past 100 years. A challenge awaits those who come to gaze at the landscape from the
top of the tower, since the base of the tower may only be reached by hiking a trail on
the north side of the bluff, which has 634 wooden steps, or driving to the bluff top
and walking about one mile on a dirt road. Once at the fire tower, a climb of about
100 steps will reward you with magnificent views of the Whitewater River Valley.

Cost: free
Hours: April–October: open daily, sunrise to sunset

ELGIN
Country Heritage Adventures

5209 County Road 21 NE, Elgin, MN 55932, (507) 282-6604, www.mnfarmtours.com

Country Heritage Adventures (CHA) promotes agriculture and an understanding of
different rural lifestyles by providing first hand farm experiences through tours of
rural southeastern Minnesota farms and orchards. A variety of adventures, from
turn-of-the-century to modern farming operations, await those ready to tour one
or many of the nine CHA sites. Farm and orchard tours may be arranged for small
or large groups by either contacting Country Heritage Adventures directly or calling the individual member farms listed below. Whether it's a family outing to one
farm or a group bus tour to multiple farms, Country Heritage Adventures can assist
you with making arrangements to meet the needs of your group. Upon request,
CHA will also help your group with lunch plans or reservations.

Country Heritage Adventures Farm Tour Sites include:

Apple Ridge Orchard
Mazeppa, MN 55956, (507) 843-3033, www.appleridgeorchard.com

Bluff Breeze Farm
Cannon Falls, MN 55009, (507) 263-5441

Dis & Dat Country Mall
RR 1, Box 124, Plainview, MN 55964, (507) 534-4248

Ellison Sheep Farm
15775 Hwy. 60 Boulevard, Zumbrota, MN 55992, (507) 732-5281

Ewe Name It Ranch
Located a few minutes west of Kellogg on County Road 18, (507) 767-4498

Hadley Valley Enterprises
3330 Hadley Valley Road NE, Rochester, MN 55906, (507) 282-9845

Land of a Thousand Winds
68617 150th Avenue, Dodge Center, MN 55927, (507) 374-6892, (507) 374-2317

Lynnhaven Farm and Antiques
5209 County Road 21 NE, Elgin, MN 55932, (507) 282-6604

Picket Fence Garden & Gifts
7904 College View Road East, Eyota, MN 55934, (507) 289-6093

Sekapp Orchard and Farms
3415 Collegeview Road East, Rochester, MN 55904, (507) 282-4544

HARMONY
The Amish Community of Southeastern Minnesota
Amish Country Tours and Michel's Amish Tours offer knowledgeable tour guides who accompany visitors through Harmony's Amish colony. Tour guides travel along with you in your own car or bus and provide visitors with insight into the Amish culture and lifestyle. As you travel through areas of the "Old Order" Amish community, you will have the opportunity to visit one or more Amish homesteads. This up close and personal experience will allow you to get a glimpse of the Amish way of dress, Amish farmers working the fields with horse-drawn equipment, and the tools used in an Amish woodworking shop. Visitors also have the chance to purchase handmade crafts, furniture, and food at some of the homesteads.

Tours may include stops at other local sites of interest. Tours are available on weekdays and Saturdays. Please call Amish Country Tours or Michel's Amish Tours for more information or to reserve a tour.

Amish Country Tours
P.O. Box 906, Harmony, MN 55939, (507) 886-2303, (507) 886-2577, www.shawcorp.com/amish

Tours depart from the Village Depot & Antique Shop on North Main Street. Mini-buses are also available for tours.

Cost: $$–$$$$

Michel's Amish Tours
P.O. Box 156, 45 North Main Street, Harmony, MN 55939, (507) 886-5392, 800-752-6474, www.bluffcountry.com/michel.htm
Tours depart from Michel's office and Gift Shop at the above address. Year-round tours are available.

Cost: $$–$$$$

Niagara Cave
P.O. Box 444, Harmony, MN 55939, (507) 886-6606, 800-837-6606, www.niagaracave.com
From Harmony, take Hwy. 139 south for 2½ miles, turn west on County Road 30, drive about 2½ miles and follow the signs.

Niagara Cave, an expansive cave system in the Harmony area, was discovered in 1924 when a few pigs fell into a hole in the ground. After further exploration and development, the cave was opened to the public in 1934. Visitors who take the guided, one-hour cave tour witness unique geological formations including calcite flowstone, fossils, stalactites, limestone deposits that are over 400 million years old, and a 60 foot high waterfall. Believe it or not, there is also a wedding chapel within the cave and more than 300 weddings have been performed in Niagara Cave throughout the years. Upon their ascent from the cave, visitors have the opportunity to mine for gemstones and fossils, hike on a short nature trail, or enjoy a picnic lunch on the grounds. Visitors must bring their own picnic lunch. The 10-acre picnic grounds has a shelter with seating for over 100 people. Since Niagara Cave remains a temperature of 48°F year-round, a light jacket and comfortable walking shoes are recommended for tours. Private tours are available by appointment.

Cost: $
Hours: April: Saturday–Sunday, 10 a.m.–4:30 p.m.
  May–September: open daily, 9:30 a.m.–5:30 p.m.
  October: Saturday–Sunday, 10 a.m.–4:30 p.m.

LA CRESCENT
Apple Blossom Scenic Drive
La Crescent, MN 55947, (507) 895-2800

La Crescent, Minnesota, is also known as the "Apple Capital of Minnesota" and is the "Gateway to Apple Blossom Scenic Drive." Apple Blossom Scenic Drive runs north from La Crescent for approximately seven miles and will take you on an ascent to the some of the most spectacular views of the Upper Mississippi River Valley from southeastern Minnesota's blufflands. In addition to magnificent scenery, you will see charming homes and farms along the way as well as the opportunity to stop by an orchard or two. To access Apple Blossom Scenic Drive, go to Main Street in La Crescent and follow the apple-shaped signs for the scenic drive. As you head north on Apple Blossom Drive the road will be renamed Winona County Road 1 at the county line. After completing the seven mile scenic drive you may turn right on Winona County Road 12 for a steep descent into Dakota. Interstate 90 may be accessed from Dakota. Another option is to turn left on Winona County Road 12 to Nodine and drive north to Interstate 90 and Great River Bluffs State Park. Please contact the La Crescent Chamber of Commerce, P.O. Box 132, La Crescent, MN 55947, (507) 895-2800, 800-926-9480 or check out www.lacrescent.com for more information about Apple Blossom Scenic Drive or apple orchards in the La Crescent area.

Mississippi River Lock & Dam #7
300 South 1st Street, La Crescent, MN 55947, (507) 895-2170, www.lacrescent.com

The Mississippi River Lock and Dam #7 is located about one mile north of La Crescent, adjacent to the Minnesota Dresbach Tourist Information Center, off Interstate 90. An observation platform and visitor's center, which is housed in the dam's old control house is open to the public. Visitors may have the opportunity to watch boats of all sizes "lock through" during a trip to the lock and dam. This amazing structure is engineered to provide eight feet of vertical lift for watercraft ranging from canoes to barges. Please call the lock and dam for more information.

Cost: free
Hours: observation platform: open 24 hours, daily
  visitor's center: call for hours

LA CROSSE, WI
The Great River Steamboat Company
227 Main Street, La Crosse, WI 54601, (608) 784-4882, 800-815-1005, www.juliabelle.com

The Great River Steamboat Company offers a variety of cruises on the Julia Belle Swain, an authentic steam-powered, passenger vessel that was built in 1971. An excursion on the Julia Belle is like stepping back in time. A variety of cruises are available on the 21-foot paddlewheeler including ½ day sightseeing tours with or without lunch, evening dinner cruises with musical entertainment, and multiple-day adventures. Tours depart from docks in the La Crosse, Wisconsin area. For more information and reservations or visit their website.

Cost: varies by excursion
Hours: departure times vary

LANESBORO
Das Wurst Haus
117 Parkway Avenue North, Lanesboro, MN 55949, (507) 467-2902, www.lanesboro.com

A trip to historic Lanesboro isn't complete without a visit to Das Wurst Haus, a casual German-style eatery with homemade sausages, mustards, freshly baked breads, ice cream, milkshakes, and root beer floats. The menu features bratwurst, sauerkraut, German potato salad, Haus Root Beer, and Schell's Beer brewed in New Ulm, Minnesota. What really makes a visit to Das Wurst Haus special is the warm, family atmosphere and the Das Wurst Haus Band, an accordion and tuba duo that entertains customers with their impromptu performances.

Cost: $
Hours: April: Saturday–Sunday, 11 a.m.–5 p.m.
  May–October: Monday–Friday, 11 a.m.–5 p.m.; Saturday, 11 a.m.–6 p.m.; Sunday, 11 a.m.–5 p.m.

R & M Amish Touring
Route 2, Box 202, Lanesboro, MN 55949, (507) 467-2128, www.bluffcountry.com/rmamish.htm
Tours leave from the R & M office in Lanesboro, located next door to the American Legion, across the street from Mrs. B's Bed and Breakfast.

The 2½-hour guided tour offered by R & M Amish Touring of Lanesboro allows visitors to experience life as it was in the 1900s when they visit Amish farms in the area. Learn about the "Old Order" and "New Order" Amish as you tour an Amish woodworking factory, quilt shop, a buggy and covered wagon factory, a sawmill and harness shop, and a one-room school house. Visitors also have the opportunity to purchase Amish made baskets, quilts, furniture, and food along the way. Tours also include stops at other local sites of interest. R & M provides van transportation for the tours, which are held on weekdays and Saturday. Overnight tour packages and fall and winter tours are also available. Call R & M Amish Touring for reservations and a current tour schedule.

Cost: $$ (per person)
Hours: Monday–Saturday, call for a current schedule

Scenic Valley Winery
P.O. Box 395, 100 East Coffee Street, Lanesboro, MN 55949, (507) 467-2958, 888-965-0250

Sip on fruit wines made from Minnesota-grown fruits at the Scenic Valley Winery in downtown Lanesboro. Located in an old creamery, the Scenic Valley Winery showroom offers a cool place to sample a variety of wines such as apple, raspberry, rhubarb, and wild plum. The winery also sells a unique selection of vegetable-based cooking wines. Bottled wine, wine-related products, and other gifts items are available for purchase. Shipping is only available within the state of Minnesota.

Cost: varies by purchase
Hours: April–December: Monday–Saturday, 10 a.m.–5 p.m.; Sunday, noon–5 p.m.
  January: closed
  February–March: Friday–Saturday, 10 a.m.–4:30 p.m.; please call to confirm fall and winter hours

MANTORVILLE
Mantorville Brewing Company
East 5th Street, Mantorville, MN 55955, (507) 635-5404, www.mantorville.com

Mantorville Brewing Company is a microbrewery based in historic Mantorville that distributes its Stagecoach Ale to the Austin, Rochester, and Winona areas. The brewery was opened in the mid-1990s and produces Stagecoach Ale, an American Pale Ale that is brewed from a variety of Minnesota and Wisconsin malts and barrel aged. The ale was named after the stagecoach line that once ran through Mantorville and southeastern Minnesota. Tours of the Mantorville Brewing Company are available by appointment.

OWATONNA
Wells Fargo Bank
101 North Cedar, Owatonna, MN 55060, (507) 451-5670, www.ci.owatonna.mn.us or www.owatonna.org

Wells Fargo Bank of Owatonna, formerly known as National Farmer's Bank, was designed by renowned architect, Louis Sullivan. Originally constructed from 1906 to 1908, the bank is now listed on the National Register of Historic Places and is considered an architectural masterpiece by architects throughout the world. Highlights of the building include gold leaf arches, terra cotta tiles, colossal chandeliers, impressive stained glass windows, and murals by artist Oskar Gross. Self-guided tours of this historical landmark are available Monday through Saturday during bank hours.

Cost: free
Hours: Monday–Friday, 8 a.m.–5:30 p.m.; Saturday, 8 a.m.–noon

PRESTON
Mystery Cave at Forestville State Park
Route 2, Box 128, Preston, MN 55965, Main Office: (507) 352-5111, Cave Office: (507) 937-3251, www.dnr.state.mn.us

Located 4 miles south of State Hwy. 14 on Fillmore County Road 5, then 2 miles east on Fillmore County Road 118.

Joseph Petty discovered Mystery Cave in February 1937 when he noticed melting snow while walking along the South Branch of the Root River. The melting snow was caused by escaping 48°F air from the cave. Upon further investigation, he discovered the cave's main entrance, and later a secondary entrance known as Mystery II. In 1988, the cave was purchased by the State of Minnesota and is now part of Forestville State Park. Mystery Cave was formed by floodwaters and glacial meltwaters and is estimated to be approximately 500,000 to 1 million years old. Its 13 miles of natural passages make it the longest cave in Minnesota. Much of the cave is composed of sea dwelling plants and animals that have been cemented into limestone over the past 450 million years. The cave has two passage levels with many unique geological formations including flowstone, stalagmites, stalactites and fossils as well as dripping water and clear blue water pools. Mystery Cave offers both one hour and two hour guided tours. The short tour is accessible to wheelchairs and strollers. It requires ½ mile of walking on a ramped concrete walkway with modern lighting. The tour brings visitors to Turquoise Lake, which is 130 feet below ground. The two hour tour is only available on summer weekends and involves ¾ mile of walking on steps and gravel paths with lighting by handheld lanterns. There are fewer formations but larger passages on this tour, which is not recommended for small children. Mystery Cave remains a constant temperature of 48°F year-round, so a light jacket and comfortable walking shoes are recommended for tours. Take time before or after your tour to look at the interesting display of cephalopods, brachiopods, gastropods, trilobites and crinoids at the visitor's center. Picnic areas are available on the grounds.

Cost: park entrance: $; cave entrance: $–$$
Hours: spring and fall (weekends only): first tour, 11 a.m.; last tour, 4 p.m.
   summer weekends: first tour 10:30 a.m.; last tour, 5 p.m.
   summer weekdays (early June): first tour, 11 a.m.; last tour, 3 p.m.
   summer weekdays (mid-June on): first tour, 11 a.m.; last tour, 5 p.m.

WABASHA
Delta Queen Steamboat Docking
Wabasha Area Chamber of Commerce: P.O. Box 105, Wabasha, MN 55981, (651) 565-4158, 800-565-4158, www.wabashamn.org
Winona Visitor's Center: Hwys. 14/16 and Huff Street, Winona, MN 55987, (507) 452-2278, (507) 452-2272, 800-657-4972, www.visitwinona.com
American Queen Steamboat Company: www.deltaqueen.com

Experience the majesty and grandeur of a steamboat docking as the Delta Queen makes its scheduled stops in Wabasha and Winona. The Delta Queen regularly stops at these Mississippi River towns during its excursions to and from St. Paul. Call the Wabasha Visitor's Center, Winona Visitor's Center, or the American Queen Steamboat Company for a schedule of summer and fall dockings.

WINONA
Delta Queen Steamboat Docking
Wabasha Area Chamber of Commerce: P.O. Box 105, Wabasha, MN 55981, (651) 565-4158, 800-565-4158, www.wabashamn.org
Winona Visitor's Center: Hwys. 14/16 and Huff Street, Winona, MN 55987, (507) 452-2278,

(507) 452-2272, 800-657-4972, www.visitwinona.com
American Queen Steamboat Company: www.deltaqueen.com

Experience the majesty and grandeur of a steamboat docking as the Delta Queen makes its scheduled stops in Wabasha and Winona. The Delta Queen regularly stops at these Mississippi River towns during its excursions to and from St. Paul. Call the Wabasha Visitor's Center, Winona Visitor's Center, or the American Queen Steamboat Company for a schedule of summer and fall dockings.

Julius C. Wilkie Steamboat Center at Levee Park

P.O. Box 733, Winona, MN 55987, (507) 454-1254, (507) 457-8258, www.visitwinona.com
Located between Walnut and Johnson Streets on the Mississippi River in Winona.

The Julius C. Wilkie Steamboat Center is housed in an actual size steamboat replica, located in Winona's Levee Park. When visitors climb aboard the Julius C. Wilkie, they travel back in time to the Victorian era and find themselves in luxurious surroundings. The elegant decor onboard includes a grand staircase, ornate posts, brass chandeliers, stained glass windows and other furnishings. A museum with artifacts of river history and miniature steamboat models is located on the first deck. The Adele Wilkie Grande Salon on the second deck depicts the lifestyle of the 1800s aboard a steamboat. The upper deck offers spectacular views of the Mississippi River, Winona, and its surrounding bluffs. The steamboat center is open for tours from Memorial Day through Labor Day. Please call for more information.

Cost: $
Hours: Memorial Day–Labor Day: Wednesday–Sunday, 10 a.m.–4 p.m.

Sugar Loaf Bluff

Sugar Loaf Bluff, once a navigational landmark for early river pilots, is the remnant of a local quarry that was mined for limestone, dolomite, and stone until about 1887. The towering column of stone is a stunning backdrop to Winona's landscape. Winona puts the spotlight on Sugar Loaf at night by lighting the bluff, which is located in east Winona above the junction of highways 14/61 and 43.

WYKOFF

Historic Wykoff Jail Haus Bed & Breakfast

Wykoff, MN 55990
Reservations may be made by calling the Bank Gift Haus and Tea Room, (507) 352-4205.

Looking for a unique experience while visiting southeastern Minnesota? How about an overnight stay in Wykoff's Historic Jail Haus, which was built in 1913. The two-room jail house can comfortably accommodate four people. Two bunk beds are located in the original cell block, and a small living area with a TV is furnished with a queen-sized sofa sleeper. The Jail Haus is open year-round and has air-conditioning and a modern, handicapped-accessible bathroom. For more information or to make reservations, please contact the Bank Gift Haus and Tea Room.

Chapter 6: Historic Sites

ROCHESTER
Assisi Heights Convent
1001 14th Street NW, Rochester, MN 55901, (507) 280-2180, (507) 282-7441, www.RochesterFranciscan.org

Assisi Heights, the congregational center for Rochester's Franciscan Order, is situated on a 100-acre landscape of rolling hills overlooking the city of Rochester. The Italian Romanesque architecture of the seven-building convent strongly resembles the Basilica of Saint Francis of Assisi in Italy. Construction of Assisi Heights began in 1952 and the building was finished and dedicated in 1955. The convent's exterior was fashioned from Mankato stone, Spanish roof tiles, and granite trim from Norway, Sweden, Minnesota, and Texas. Imported marble from Italy, France, Morocco, Portugal, Yugoslavia and Belgium as well as Maryland and Tennessee was used to create the elaborate interior, which has several residential wings, administrative offices, a large chapel, kitchen, health care, retirement, and educational facilities, and the Chapel of Our Lady of Lourdes, which can accommodate 600 people. Due to declining numbers in the Franciscan Order, Assisi Heights is now shared by other religious denominations and community groups. Assisi Community Center (ACC), a nonprofit retreat, conference, and healing center is also housed at the convent. ACC offers a variety of programs, retreats, and conferences for the community for people of all faiths. Guided tours of Assisi Heights are available on the days listed below.

More information about ACC may be found in Chapter 22.

Cost: by donation
Hours: tours: Monday, Wednesday, Friday, Saturday, 2 p.m.

Heritage House
225 1st Avenue NW, Rochester, MN 55901, (507) 288-4331, 800-634-8277
Located behind Rochester Methodist Hospital.

Heritage House was built in 1875 by Rochester merchant, Timothy Whiting. It was originally located in what was known as Rochester's "Lower Town," but was relocated to Rochester's Central Park in 1972. The restored residence depicts a typical middle class, Midwestern Victorian-style home of the late 1800s. The authentically furnished house has a kitchen, dining room, library, nursery, two parlors, and master bedroom. Quilts, dolls, and other period collections are displayed throughout the house. Tours are available during the summer months.

Cost: $
Hours: May–October: Sunday, Tuesday, and Thursday, 1 p.m.–3:30 p.m., or by appointment

Mayo Clinic Art & Architectural Tour
Mayo Clinic, 200 1st Street SW, Hilton, Mayo and Siebens Buildings, Rochester, MN 55905, (507) 284-2511, (507) 538-1091, www.mayo.edu or www.mayoclinic.org/becomingpat-rst/tours.html
Tours depart from Judd Auditorium on the subway level of the Mayo Clinic building.

The Mayo Medical Center Art Collection may be viewed by taking the guided Mayo Clinic Art Tour or browsing through the artwork displays at your own pace. The guided, one-hour tour begins at the information booth adjacent to Judd Auditorium in the subway level of the Mayo building. Although the tour may change from time to time due to the rotation of exhibits, visitors will experience the work of renowned national and international artists that is displayed throughout the Mayo, Hilton, Siebens, Plummer, and Gonda Buildings. Highlights of the Mayo collection located in the Gonda Building include Dale Chihuly's "Untitled" blown glass chandeliers, Ivan Mestrovic's "Man and Freedom" sculpture, Yaacov Agam's "Welcome," a rotating triangular monolith that intrigues viewers with its metamorphosis of color, and a photographic mural entitled "My Brother and I," which honors the Mayo brothers, Dr. William J. Mayo and Dr. Charles H. Mayo. Some other interesting exhibits displayed throughout the Clinic are samples of Andy Warhol's "Pop Art" (located across from the Patient and Visitor Cafeteria in the Mayo Clinic subway), terra cotta panels from the exterior of the original Mayo Clinic Building mounted onto the walls of the Siebens subway, and the stunning architecture of the Plummer Building. Although it involves a great deal of walking through many Mayo Medical Center buildings, it is well worth your time to view this truly impressive art collection.

Cost: free
Hours: tour: Monday–Friday, 1:30 p.m.
  Mayo Medical Center: 8 a.m.–5 p.m.

Mayo Clinic General Tour

Mayo Clinic, 200 1st Street SW, Rochester, MN 55905, (507) 284-2511, (507) 284-2511, (507) 538-1091, www.mayo.edu or www.mayoclinic.org/becomingpat-rst/tours.html
Tours depart from Judd Auditorium on the subway level of the Mayo Clinic building.

Learn about the historical origins of Rochester's world-famous Mayo Clinic on a guided tour through the medical center. The 1½ hour tour begins with a brief historical movie followed by the opportunity to see historical displays, artwork, and several Mayo Clinic buildings.

Cost: free
Hours: tour: Monday–Friday, 10 a.m.
  Mayo Medical Center: 8 a.m.–5 p.m.

Mayowood Mansion

Olmsted County History Center, 1195 West Circle Drive SW, Rochester, MN 55902, (507) 282-9447, www.olmstedhistory.com
The Mayowood Mansion is located at 3720 Mayowood Road SW, Rochester, MN 55902.

Dr. Charles H. Mayo built the Mayowood Mansion on a 3,000-acre estate in southwest Rochester from 1910 to 1911. Mayowood, a 23,000-square-foot, 48-room residence, was home to three generations of the Mayo family. The interior is furnished with a large collection of the Mayo family's personal effects as well as a variety of English, French, American, Spanish, and German antiques. Guided tours of the historic estate provide a fascinating look at Mayo family life. After touring the mansion, take time to stroll the grounds, which are beautifully landscaped with gardens, fountains, and ponds. Mayowood may be rented for special events and meetings. Please contact the Olmsted County History Center for more information.

Cost: $

Hours: call the History Center for a tour schedule or reservations

Plummer House of Arts and Gardens

1091 Plummer Lane SW, Rochester, MN 55902, (507) 281-6160

Dr. Henry S. Plummer and his wife Daisy began construction of their English Tudor-style home in 1917. Dr. Plummer was a Mayo Clinic physician as well as an architect, tool and die maker, and inventor. He designed the Plummer House, which included many innovations that were advanced for their time, such as a central vacuum system, garage door openers, a dumb waiter, intercom system, electricity, and the first gas fireplace in Rochester. The mansion, greenhouse, water tower, garage, and gazebo are part of the estate that was once located on 65 acres. The grounds currently occupy 11 acres with beautifully landscaped gardens, a bird trail, quarry, and water tower. The five-story house has 49 rooms including nine bedrooms, ten bathrooms, five fireplaces, and a ballroom. The grounds are open to the public year-round, and the house is open for self-guided tours during the summer months. Group tours and rental of the house for special events may be arranged by calling Rochester Park and Recreation Department at the above number.

Cost: $

Hours: June–August: Wednesdays, 1 p.m.–5 p.m.; first and third Sundays of the
month, 1 p.m.–5 p.m.

Rochester Carillon

Tower of the Plummer Building, 2ⁿᵈ Street SW, Mayo Medical Center, Rochester, MN 55905, (507) 282-3730, (507) 284-8294

Rochester is fortunate to have a 56-bell carillon with a four and one-half octave range housed in the tower of Mayo's Plummer Building. A carillon is an outdoor musical instrument with 23 or more bronze, cup-shaped bells that are rigidly fixed to supporting beams and do not swing when played. A carillonneur plays the instrument from a clavier, a keyboard console with a double row of batons (oak keys) and a pedal board. The smallest bell weighs 19 pounds, and the largest bell, almost six feet tall, weighs 7,840 pounds. In the 1920s, a medical trip to Belgium sparked Dr. William J. Mayo's interest in carillons. Although construction of the Plummer Building was already underway, the architectural plans were revised to include a carillon tower. The original 23 bell carillon, a gift from the Mayo brothers, was erected in the Plummer Tower during the 1920s, and its inaugural recital was held on September 16, 1928. Thirty-three new bronze bells, a clavier, practice console, and a playing cabin were added to the Rochester Carillon in the summer of 1977 due to generous gifts from Frances G. Sheets and Isabella Gooding Sanders, descendants of Rochester pioneer settler, Alphonso Gooding. Current carillonneur, Dean Robinson is only the second bellmaster in the history of the Rochester Carillon. He has been playing the Rochester Carillon since the spring of 1958. Tours of the Rochester Carillon may be arranged by calling (507) 284-8294 or (507) 282-3730. Carillon performances may regularly be heard on Mondays at 7 p.m. and Wednesdays & Fridays at noon. Special recitals are also performed on Memorial Day, the Fourth of July, and Christmas Eve. Carillon concerts are about 20 to 25 minutes in length and are best heard in an open area at least 500 feet downwind from the tower. The bells are heard most clearly during cold, crisp weather.

Soldiers Field Veterans' Memorial
Soldiers Field Memorial Park, 7th Street and 2nd Avenue SW, Rochester, MN 55902

The Soldiers Field Veterans' Memorial was dedicated on June 25, 2000, and its inscription reads, "Let us not forget these veterans for they have shown the world that freedom is never free." The idea for a veterans' memorial in Rochester was born during a June 1995 reunion of the 173rd Airborne Brigade, which was held in Rochester because the brigade was adopted by the Rochester Jaycees during the Vietnam War. The awesome memorial, composed of granite, features a Wall of Remembrance, Circular Memorial Walls on the east and west sides, and a Walk of Remembrance. The Wall of Remembrance is engraved with the names of southeastern Minnesota Veterans who died in service to their country. The semi-circular walls present a pictorial and written depiction of military history from the Civil War to the present time, and memorial pavers encircling the monument form the Walk of Remembrance. The United States flag, Minnesota state flag, flags from all branches of the service, and the POW/MIA flags are all flown at the memorial.

Town Bell Clock and Alarm
Mayo Civic Center, Civic Center Drive, Rochester, MN 55902

The old Town Bell Clock and Alarm, Rochester's original city clock, was located atop an old fire station until about 1930. After its first restoration, it was housed in a tower at US Bank on 4th Street Southwest. In recent years, the clock was refurbished and relocated to the Mayo Civic Center Complex on Civic Center Drive in downtown Rochester. The authentic, four-faced clock is housed in a tower with glass panels that surround its gears and has a brass bell that hangs below its face. The clock is a noteworthy landmark because it is one of only 3,600 weight driven clocks that were manufactured by the Seth Thomas Company. The clock is driven by 250 pounds of cast iron weights and strikes every hour and half-hour.

CALEDONIA
Schech's Water Powered Mill
Caledonia, MN 55921, (507) 896-3481
Schech's Mill is located south of Houston and north of Caledonia on Houston County Road 10, just outside the small town of Sheldon. County Road 10 may be accessed from State Hwy. 76.

Schech's Mill, a three-story, water powered mill that was built of native limestone in 1876, is located in rural Caledonia. Ivan and Eleanor Krugmire, local farmers who live nearby, are caretakers of the grist mill, a historic site listed on the National Register of Historic Places. Schech's is the only operational grist mill in Minnesota and functions with its original equipment including the millstone and four stone burrs. Visitors who tour the mill are fascinated by its design and mechanics, especially when the wooden gears are set into motion and ground corn starts to flow from the machinery. Tours are available on weekends from April through October. Please call ahead to arrange a tour.

Cost: $
Hours: April–October: Saturday–Sunday

ELBA
Historic Marnach House
Elba, MN, Whitewater State Park, RR 1, Box 256, Altura, MN 55910, (507) 932-3007

Drive north on Hwy. 74 past Whitewater State Park and through the town of Elba. Continue on Hwy. 74 (turns into a gravel road) until you reach the Wildlife Management Headquarters. Park at the Wildlife Headquarters and follow the one-mile walking trail to the house.

Rollingstone is now a typical small town in rural southeastern Minnesota, yet its rich Luxembourg heritage is reflected by the older, European style homes on its streets and the names that can be found on local mailboxes and tombstones. Approximately 300 Luxembourg families immigrated to the community and Whitewater River Valley between 1855 and 1900. The Historic Marnach House in nearby in Elba was built by Luxembourger Nicholas Marnach in 1857. The house was restored in the early 1990s by volunteers from the United States and Luxembourg and serves as a reminder of pioneer times and the impact of land use practices on the Whitewater Watershed. Tours of the house are scheduled periodically throughout the year, and horse-drawn sleigh rides to the house are offered during the winter. Call Whitewater State Park for a tour schedule.

Cost: $
Hours: call for a tour schedule

HOMER
Historic Bunnell House

Homer, MN 55942, (507) 452-7575, (507) 454-2723, www.visitwinona.com
The Bunnell House is about 5 miles south of Winona, just off Hwys.14/61 in the town of Homer.

The first permanent residents of Winona County, fur trader Willard Bunnell and his wife Matilda Desnoyer Bunnell, built this three-story house overlooking the Mississippi River in the 1850s. The Historic Bunnell House has been restored to its original "Steamboat Gothic" architecture and is listed on the National Register of Historic Places. Guided tours of the house give visitors the opportunity to experience the sights, sounds, and smells of pioneer life. The Carriage House Gift Shop features traditional handicrafts, folk art, souvenirs, books, and historical reproductions.

Cost: $
Hours: Memorial Day–Labor Day: Wednesday–Saturday, 10 a.m.–5 p.m.; Sunday,
    1 p.m.–5 p.m.
    September–mid-October: Saturday, 10 a.m.–5 p.m.; Sunday, 1 p.m.–5 p.m.

MANTORVILLE
Historic Mantorville

Mantorville Chamber of Commerce, Riverside Gifts, P.O. Box 358, 420 Main Street NE, Mantorville, MN 55955, (507) 635-5464, www.mantorville.com

Mantorville, a small but quaint town located 17 miles northwest of Rochester, is situated in a valley along the north branch and middle fork of the Zumbro River. The town was settled by the Mantor brothers, Peter and Riley, in 1853. In 1975, the entire 12 block downtown area was listed on the National Register of Historic Places. It received this recognition largely due to the architectural heritage of its historic buildings, which are primarily constructed of "Mantorville Limestone." Quarried in Mantorville, this stone was in high demand throughout the country because it was easy to work with, but became increasingly harder as it endured the elements. The Grand Old Mansion, a bed and breakfast inn; the Opera House, a theater that stages old-fashioned melodramas and plays; the Dodge County

Courthouse, a county administration building, and the Hubbell House, a world-famous restaurant that was once a hotel are just a few of the historic buildings in town. Contact the Mantorville Chamber of Commerce or visit their website for more information about the Mantorville walking tour and the town's historic sites.

OWATONNA
Village of Yesteryear
1448 Austin Road, Owatonna, MN 55060, (507) 451-1420
Located on the Steele County Fairgrounds, 1525 South Cedar Avenue, Owatonna, MN 55060,
(507) 451-5305, www.ci.owatonna.mn.us or www.owatonna.org

The Village of Yesteryear, located on the Steele County Fairgrounds, features several buildings that date back to the 1800s. The buildings are furnished with 19th century decor and include two log cabins, a general store/post office, blacksmith shop, fire station, country school, railroad station, and a caboose dating back to the 1850s. The Dunnell Mansion, built in 1868, and the St. Wenceslaus of Moravia Church, built in 1876, are also located on the grounds. A good time to visit the Village of Yesteryear is during the Owatonna Extravaganza, a festival that commemorates the days of yesteryear with handcrafted demonstrations, blacksmithing, wagon rides, horse exhibitions, musical entertainment, an ice cream social and more. This one day event is held on a weekend in mid-July. Please call the Village of Yesteryear for more information. Guided tours are available with advance notice.

Cost: $
Hours: May–September: Tuesday–Sunday, 1 p.m.–5 p.m.

PICKWICK
Pickwick Mill
Route 4, Box 219, Pickwick, MN, (507) 457-0499, (507) 452-9658, nrhp.mnhs.org or
www.visitwinona.com
From Winona, drive south on Hwy. 61 about 15 miles, turn onto County Road 7 and drive
2 miles into Pickwick.

Listed on the National Register of Historic Places, Pickwick Mill was built in 1854 by W.T. Grant and Wilson Davis. The six-story, water powered Grist Mill has a 4 by 20 foot waterwheel and 6 floors of original machinery, and remained in operation until it was flooded in 1980. During the Civil War, the mill ran 24 hours a day in order to produce 100 barrels of flour daily for the Union Army. In 1919, the owner began to mill feed for livestock after being told that he would need a license to continue milling flour. Tours of the limestone mill are available from spring through fall. Visitors may also picnick and fish for trout at Lake LaBelle, adjacent to the mill. Mill Day, an annual event at Pickwick, is held on the second Saturday in September.

Cost: $
Hours: May, September–mid-October, Saturday–Sunday, noon–5 p.m.
 June–August: open daily, 10 a.m.–5 p.m., or by appointment

PRESTON
Historic Forestville
Route 2, Box 126, Preston, MN 55965, (507) 765-2785, (507) 352-5111, www.mnhs.org
Located 4 miles south of State Hwy. 16 on Fillmore County Road 5, then 2 miles east on Fillmore
County Road 118 Preston, MN 55965.

Historic Forestville, an 1890s farm village and rural trade center that was owned by businessman Thomas Meighen, is now a Minnesota Historical Site that offers interpretive programs and tours to the public. Costumed guides lead visitors through a first person living history program that allows them to experience life as it was during the turn of the century. A tour of the village includes browsing among period merchandise at the Mercantile, visiting the Meighen residence, and helping the gardener with his chores. Interpretive trails guide visitors to other historic buildings throughout the village. A great time to visit Historic Forestville is during one of their old-fashioned Evenings of Leisure. These evenings, held on a Saturday evening in late July and late August, welcome visitors to participate in music, storytelling, and games reminiscent of the late 19th century, such as horseshoes, croquet, checkers and euchre. Refreshments are served. Please call Historic Forestville for more information.

Cost: daily park fee: $; Tour: free.
Hours: Memorial Day–Labor Day: Tuesday–Friday, 10 a.m.–5 p.m.; Saturday, 11 a.m.–6 p.m.; Sunday, noon–5 p.m.
   September–mid-October: Saturday, 10 a.m.-5 p.m.; Sunday, noon–5 p.m.

SPRING GROVE
Ballard House
163 West Main Street, Spring Grove, MN 55974, (507) 498-5434, www.springgrovemn.com

The Ballard House is a 100-year-old historic hotel located in downtown Spring Grove. The three-story hotel, built in 1893, is now a tourism center, museum, and antique shop. After browsing for a special treasure, stop by the parlor-style coffee shop in the lower level for refreshments.

Cost: free
Hours: April–November: Sunday–Saturday, 10 a.m.–5 p.m.

STEWARTVILLE
Sears House
Stewartville Area Historical Society, 305 North Main Street, Stewartville, MN 55976, (507) 533-6470, www.stewartvillemn.com

The birth home of Richard Sears, founder of the Sears Roebuck Company, is located on Stewartville's Main Street. Sears was born at the home in 1863 and lived there until about 1869. The home was originally built in 1857, and is currently maintained by the Stewartville Area Historical Society. The historical society hosts an annual Christmas program at the house, and guided tours and historical programs are available by appointment. Please call for more information or to arrange a tour.

Cost: $
Hours: by appointment

WINONA
Downtown Winona Historic District
Downtown Winona, 3rd Street and East 2nd Street. Winona Convention and Visitors Bureau, 67 Main Street, Winona, MN 55987, (507) 452-2272, 800-657-4972, www.visitwinona.com

There are more than 100 historic sites in Winona's Commercial Historic District and East 2nd Street Commercial Historic District that are listed on the National

Register of Historic Places. These buildings represent the largest collection of Victorian commercial architecture along the Mississippi River in Minnesota. The Italianate and Queen Anne style buildings were constructed from 1857 to 1916. A downtown walking tour brochure of these sites may be obtained at the Convention and Visitor's Bureau, Visitor's Center, or Winona County Historical Society.

Winona's Glorious Stained Glass Tour

Winona Convention and Visitors Bureau, 67 Main Street, Winona, MN 55987, (507) 452-2272, 800-657-4972, www.visitwinona.com

Winona was founded in 1851 by Steamboat Captain, Orrin Smith. Due to the city's location along the Mississippi River, its lumber, milling, and transportation industries thrived, and Winona became a wealthy area by the 1880s. As a result of this wealth, prominent architects were hired by city businesses and churches to design and construct extravagant buildings. Several of these structures are adorned with stained glass designs and murals. Self-guided tours of the following commercial buildings are permitted during business hours: The J.R. Watkins Company, 150 Liberty Street; Merchant's National Bank, 102 East 3rd Street; Winona National Bank 204 Main Street; County Courthouse, 3rd Street west of Johnson Street; and the County Historical Society, 160 Johnson Street. However, advance notice is required to tour the stained glass artwork at the following churches: Church of Saint Stanislaus Kostka, (507) 452-5430; Central United Methodist Church, (507) 452-6783; First Congregational Church, (507) 452-4829; Central Lutheran Church, (507) 452-5156; First Baptist Church, (507) 452-9133; and the Chapel of Saint Mary of the Angels, (507) 453-5552. Please call the Winona Convention and Visitor's Bureau for a self-guided tour brochure or to arrange a guided tour of any or all of these buildings, which is available for groups of fifteen or more people.

Several distinguished stained glass studios are also located in Winona. Two of these studios, Conway Universal Studios, 730 54th Avenue, (507) 452-9209; and Cathedral Studios, 503 Center Street, (507) 454-4079 conduct group tours with advance reservations.

ZUMBROTA
Zumbrota Covered Bridge

Covered Bridge Park, contact Zumbrota City Hall, 175 West Avenue, Zumbrota, MN 55992, (507) 732-7318, www.zumbrota.com
Covered Bridge Park is located on Hwy. 58 just past downtown Zumbrota.

The Zumbrota Covered Bridge, located in Covered Bridge Park, was built in 1869 and currently stands 116 feet from its original location. Not only is the bridge on the National Register of Historic Sites, but it is also the last standing covered bridge in Minnesota. Other historic sites at the park include a railway depot (circa 1878) and an old country school house. In addition to this, the park has modern recreational facilities including the Kids' Kingdom Playground, designed by local school children and constructed by over 1,000 community volunteers, shaded picnic areas, a picnic shelter, ball fields, sand volleyball courts, horseshoe pits, a municipal swimming pool, a campground, 5 miles of scenic walking trails, snowmobile trails, and an ice rink.

Chapter 7: Museums

A listing of southeastern Minnesota Historical Societies is listed in Appendix 6. Many of these organizations also have a museum that features exhibits of local history and community memorabilia. Please contact the historical societies directly for information about local museums.

ROCHESTER
Mayo Historical Suite
Mayo Medical Center, 3rd floor of the Plummer Building, 1st Street and 3rd Avenue SW, Rochester, MN 55902, (507) 284-2511, (507) 538-1091, www.mayo.edu or www.mayoclinic.org/becomingpat-rst/tours.html

The Mayo Historical Suite, a museum located on the third floor of Mayo Medical Center's Plummer Building, provides visitors with a historical account of Mayo Clinic's early years. Displays include several cornerstones of original Mayo buildings, a large exhibit of Mayo family photographs and memorabilia, surgical instruments, the last offices of William J. Mayo and Charles H. Mayo used from 1928–1939, and the original practice clavier for the 23 bell carillon. The historical suite is open to the public during regular building hours. Guided Mayo Clinic tours are available on weekdays and include a visit to the historical suite. Tours of the Mayo Clinic History of Medicine Library, located on the 15th floor of the Plummer Building, are also available by appointment only. Call (507) 284-3676 or (507) 284-5538 to schedule a tour of the library. Information about Mayo Clinic tours may be found in Chapter 6.

Cost: free
Hours: Monday–Friday, 8 a.m.–5 p.m.
   History of Medicine Library: Monday–Friday, 9 a.m.–3 p.m.

Olmsted County Historical Society & Museum
1195 County Road 22 West, Rochester, MN 55902, (507) 282-9447, www.olmstedhistory.com

The Olmsted County Historical Society is a private, nonprofit organization that was established in 1926 with the mission to collect, preserve, and interpret the history of Olmsted County. The first county museum was located in the basement of the Rochester Public Library when it was located at the corner of 2nd Street and 3rd Avenue Southwest. This building now houses Mayo Medical Schools' Student Center. The History Center is currently located in southwest Rochester and features a museum, gift shop, and library with archives for genealogical research. Additional points of interest on the grounds include the George Stoppel Farm, an 1850s homestead; the William Dee Log Cabin, an 1862 furnished pioneer home; and the Hadley Valley School House, a traditional 1880s one-room school. The Mayowood Mansion is also under the auspices of the historical center, but is located off-site in southwest Rochester. The Historical Society also provides the community with a wide variety of educational programs and special events such as Christmas at Mayowood, Family Fun Day, Rochester Rooster's 1800s Base Ball, Summer History Workshops for Kids, Days of Yesteryear, and more. Please note that the homestead, pioneer cabin, and school house are only open from Memorial Day to Labor Day.

Call the history center or visit their website for more information and a schedule of upcoming events.

Cost: $
Hours: Tuesday–Saturday, 9 a.m.–5 p.m.

ALTURA
Carriage Museum at the Lazy D Campground
RR 1, Box 252, Altura, MN 55910, (507) 932-3098, www.lazyd-camping-trailrides.com
Located 8 miles north of St. Charles on County Road 74.

The Carriage Museum at the Lazy D Campground is a unique place to stop during your travels through the Whitewater River Valley. Antique carriage displays from the 19th and early 20th centuries are exhibited throughout the museum. If you're looking for a little adventure after your tour, Lazy D offers carriage rides and covered wagon rides, pulled by a team of draft horses, in the scenic Whitewater River Valley. Covered wagon rides have a seating capacity of 16–17 people and are approximately 45–60 minutes in length. Hour-long antique carriage rides can accommodate 2–4 people and are available with or without a picnic lunch. All rides depart from the Lazy D Campground. Reservations are needed for covered wagon and carriage rides.

Cost: museum, free; carriage rides, $$$
Hours: by appointment or chance

CHATFIELD
Pease Wildlife Museum
Thurber Building, 21 2ⁿᵈ Street SE, Chatfield, MN 55923, (507) 867-3810

The William Pease Wildlife Museum opened in 1989 as a tribute to the late William Pease who was an avid Chatfield outdoorsman. The museum displays Pease's collection of animal mounts and skins. Full animal mounts on display include a great blue heron, bald eagle, badger, leopard, snowy, screech and great horned owls, a wild turkey, snapping and bog turtles, a hawk, as well as other waterfowl and native Minnesota fish. Visitors may also view a variety of animal skins such as black bear, raccoon, red fox, mink, otter, muskrat, rattlesnake, lynx, and mountain lion. An interesting exhibit is the two-headed baby pig that was born on the Pease Farm. Other memorabilia in the museum includes Pease's Model T, antique fishing and hunting gear, and soap box derby race cars.

Cost: free
Hours: open by appointment only

HARMONY
Harmony Toy Museum
30 Main Avenue South, Harmony, MN 55939, (507) 867-3380, www.harmony.mn.us

The Harmony Toy Museum, an interesting collection of more than 4,000 pieces, was opened in 1994. The display of antique toys will rekindle childhood memories and spark the interest of the younger generation. The museum collection also includes pictures, prints, farm implements, trains and dolls.

Cost: by donation
Hours: mid-April–mid-October: Monday–Saturday, 9 a.m.–5 p.m.; Sunday, noon–5 p.m.

Slim's Woodshed Woodcarving Museum

160 1st Street NW, Harmony, MN 55939, (507) 886-3114, www.slimswoodshed.com

Slim's Woodshed Woodcarving Museum, Gift Shop and Working Studio is "an enjoyable spot for at least an hour" according to Slim. The museum features Slim's private collection and is the largest woodcarving museum in the Midwest with more than 1700 pieces from around the world. Some of the wood carvings date back to the 1800s, but some of Slim's most prized possessions are the small carvings and wood working tools he received from the Bily Brothers, world famous clock carvers from Spillville, Iowa, who were his neighbors when he was a boy. The museum is also home to the completed 120-plus piece Caricature Carvers of America Circus. Visitors of all ages will enjoy viewing the whimsical circus carvings that were created by 23 caricature carvers from the United States and Canada. One hour guided tours of the museum are available for a nominal fee. Additional on-site attractions include a gift shop with a variety of wood and alabaster carvings, wood-carving tools and supplies, a working studio, and an antique loft. Woodcarving classes and private lessons are available.

Cost: $
Hours: Monday–Saturday, 9 a.m.–5 p.m.; Sundays, noon–4 p.m.

MABEL
Mabel Steam Engine Museum

Steam Engine Park, Mabel, MN 55954, (507) 493-5350, (507) 735-5803

The small town of Mabel, also known as "Rural America's Steam Engine Capital," is home of the Mabel Steam Engine Museum. The museum has an impressive collection of huge steam-powered workhorses, antique tractors and farm implements, threshing machines, early gasoline engines and more. Steam Engine Days, an annual event that has been held in Mabel for more than 40 years, celebrates the development and use of steam-powered machinery with displays and demonstrations of the equipment, a steam engine parade, arts and crafts show, carnival, and stage shows. This event is held the weekend following Labor Day. Please call the museum for more information.

Cost: $
Hours: by appointment

OWATONNA
Minnesota State Orphanage Museum

540 West Hills Circle, Owatonna, MN 55060, 800-423-6466, www.owatonna.org

The State Public School for Dependent and Neglected Children in Owatonna was created by the Minnesota Legislature in 1885 and opened in December 1886. The orphanage, now a National Historic Site, served almost 20,000 children from 1886 to 1945. Some children lived at the orphanage temporarily while others spent their childhood there. Unfortunately, indentured placement of children on farms was implemented on a limited basis until the practice was abolished in 1936. Exhibits at the museum include photographs, clothes, toys, personal memorabilia as well as informational displays about the school's buildings, classrooms, and extracurricular activities. Visitors are welcome to walk the grounds, which are now the site of city administrative offices, the museum, and a cemetery with graves of the children who died while at the orphanage. Guided tours are available with advanced reservations.

Cost: $
Hours: Monday–Friday, 8 a.m.–5 p.m.; Saturday–Sunday, 1 p.m.–5 p.m.

PETERSON
1877 Peterson Station Museum
Mill Street, Peterson, MN 55962, (507) 895-2551, www.peterson-mn.com, e-mail: Johndar@acegroup.cc

The Peterson Railroad Depot was relocated from its original site to Mill Street in 1973. After its restoration, it was opened as the 1877 Peterson Station Museum in 1974. Museum displays include a fascinating collection of memorabilia from the community that reflects its Norwegian heritage. A sample of artifacts includes a Hardanger fiddle, Norwegian sugar lump cutter, Kubbestol carvings, 1874 plattes of Peterson, a cadaver cooling board and embalming instruments, a telephone directory listing short and long signals for telephone numbers and more. In addition to this, visitors may view a replica of a small homestead and the original depot outhouse. In 2001, the museum's new addition was opened to the public. At first glance, the Norwegian Nisse carving in this area seems to be displayed much like the other artifacts, but upon closer inspection, visitors discover that the building was constructed around the stump. This area of the museum features military records, purple hearts, and uniforms of local servicemen from World War I to Vietnam as well as sports memorabilia and larger items such as a French Burr Feed Mill and the Peterson State Bank safe. A developing genealogy library located within the museum provides volumes of information about the Norwegian lineage of the Peterson and Houston communities and Fillmore County dating back to 1861.

Cost: by donation
Hours: Memorial Day–Labor Day: Saturday and Sunday, 10 a.m.–5 p.m.

RUSHFORD
Rushford Area Historic Depot Museum and Trail Center
Box 338, Rushford, MN 55971, (507) 864-7560, www.rushford.net

The Rushford Historic Depot, originally built in 1867 by the Southern Minnesota Railway, now serves as a museum and trail center at the Rushford trailhead of the Root River State Recreation Trail. It is the only two story Southern Minnesota Railway depot located on its original site and has been listed on the National Register of Historic Places. The Rushford Area Historical Society owns the depot as well as the restored 1867 Episcopal Chapel and the Grinde School House exhibits located on the grounds. The Depot's two-story museum has a variety of interesting displays including old typewriters, stoves and clocks, the dental cabinet of Dr. R. W. Hammer, arrowheads, photographs, immigration papers, an 1868 panoramic map of the United States, Norwegian artifacts, jewelry, and more. The second floor is set up like an 1800s home with period toys, baby carriages, an 1898 washing machine, and other home-related paraphernalia. Genealogy information is available at the museum. The trail center is housed in a separate section of the depot and provides rest rooms, a shady place to rest, and an information center for visitors.

Cost: by donation

Hours: May–October: open daily, 8:30 a.m.–4:30 p.m.
  November–April: Monday–Friday, call for hours

SPRING VALLEY
Methodist Church Museum: A Laura Ingalls Wilder Site
221 West Courtland Street, Spring Valley, MN 55975, (507) 346-7659, (507) 346-7476 (off season)

The Spring Valley Methodist Church Museum was built in 1876 and is now on the National Register of Historic Places. Although the Victorian Gothic-style architecture and church interior with twenty-one stained glass windows are stunning, visitors are primarily drawn to the museum because Almanzo and Laura Ingalls Wilder attended church there from 1890 to 1891. Museum exhibits in the church sanctuary and lower level of the building include a Wilder family photographic display, religious artifacts from area churches, Conley camera collection, an 1874 wooden fire wagon, local pioneer business artifacts, a Richard Sears exhibit, an old-time country store, Spring Valley High School graduation photos from 1886 to the present, a nostalgic kitchen, and more. Wilder family grave sites may also be visited in the city cemetery located on the southeast corner of town. Please ask museum staff for directions to the cemetery. A gift shop is available at the museum.

Cost: $
Hours: June–August: open daily, 10 a.m.–4 p.m.
  September and October: Saturday–Sunday, 10 a.m.–4 p.m.
  October–May: open by appointment for groups

Washburn-Zittleman Historic House
220 West Courtland Street, Spring Valley, MN 55975, (507) 346-7659, (507) 346-7476 (off season)

The Washburn-Zittleman Historic House is a 19th century, two-story home that is furnished with period furniture. The house is adorned with unique woodwork and features 10 exhibit areas, including a parlor, sunken bedroom, and costume room that depict life at the turn-of-the-century. An interesting display of clothing, toys, furniture, kitchen gadgets and appliances, and other essential household items are located throughout the house, which is located across the street from the Methodist Church Museum.

Cost: $
Hours: June–August: open daily, 10 a.m.–4 p.m.
  September and October: Saturday–Sunday, 10 a.m.–4 p.m.
  October–May: open by appointment for groups

WABASHA
Arrowhead Bluffs Museum
RR 3, Box 7, Wabasha, MN 55981, (651) 565-3829

Arrowhead Bluffs Museum was opened in 1986 by Les Behrens, and his son, John Behrens. Their privately owned collection of firearms, mounted North American birds and wildlife, local Indian artifacts, wildlife art, and pioneer implements is tastefully displayed. The gun enthusiast will be impressed with the expansive gun collection (Henry Rifle, Colt, and Smith-Wesson) that wraps around the museum's walls and includes one of every Winchester gun made from 1886–1982 including all commemorative models made before 1982. The diverse wildlife exhibit includes a polar bear, brown bear, caribou, moose, musk ox, turkey, arctic fox, snapping turtle, Texas longhorn, and features bighorn sheep displayed in a natural mountain setting. It is also fascinating to view the 12,000-year-old mammoth tusk that was found in a local sand pit. In addition to maintaining Arrowhead Bluffs, Mr. Behrens also provides hunting consultations as well as gun sales, service, and repair. A gift shop is located on the premises.

Cost: $
Hours: May 1ˢᵗ–December: Sunday–Saturday, 10 a.m.–6 p.m.
  winter: by appointment

WINONA
Arches Museum
U.S. Hwy. 14 East, Winona, MN 55987, (507) 454-2723, www.visitwinona.com
The museum is located 11 miles west of Winona on Hwy. 14 between Stockton and Lewiston.

The Arches Museum, named for the stone railway arches in the area, depicts life as it was in the pioneer days. Collector Walter Rahn (1902–1984) was dedicated to the establishment of the museum, which has a covered bridge, furnished log home and barn from the 1860s, an authentic one-room pioneer school, agricultural equipment, tools, and other household items.

Cost: $
Hours: May–October: Wednesday–Saturday, 10 a.m.–5 p.m.; Sunday, 1 p.m.–5 p.m.

Polish Cultural Institute
102 Liberty Street & 363 East 2ⁿᵈ Street, Winona, MN 55987

The Polish Cultural Institute of Winona, also known as the Polish Museum, provides historical displays and artifacts of Winona's Polish heritage and the immigrants who came from a troubled homeland to work in area sawmills and river docks. Located in the former Laird, Norton Lumber Company building, the institute has an outstanding collection of prayer books and religious articles, family heirlooms, photographs, folk art, genealogical records, clothing, handcrafted items. Special cultural events sponsored by the museum along with other local ethnic groups are held throughout the year. A museum gift shop with Polish books and cultural keepsakes is located on-site. Please call for more information.

Cost: by donation
Hours: May–November: Monday–Friday, 10 a.m.–3 p.m.; Saturday, 10 a.m.–noon; Sunday, 1 p.m.–3 p.m.

Watkins Museum
150 Liberty Street, Winona, MN 55987, (507) 457-6095, www.WatkinsOnline.com

J.R. Watkins pioneered the concept of the direct sales company and implemented this business strategy by founding the Watkins Company in 1868. The Watkins company became a successful business empire that is still in existence today and continues to sell spices, toiletry products, vitamin supplements, and home care products. The museum offers an interesting look at the company's development and expansion with photographs, product displays dating back to 1868, and models of early delivery trucks. The current line of Watkins products are available for purchase at the museum.

Cost: free
Hours: Monday–Friday, 10 a.m.–4 p.m.; Saturday, 10 a.m.–2 p.m.

WYKOFF
Ed's Museum
Wykoff, MN 55990, (507) 352-4205

Ed's Museum is housed in a building that was originally constructed in 1876 and has been the location of many Wykoff businesses including a brewery, saloon, general store, harness shop, and barbershop. Edwin and Lydia Krueger acquired the store in 1933 and opened its doors as a Jack Sprat Grocery Store. After Lydia's death in 1940, Ed used the store to display his collection of old grocery items, movie memorabilia, antiques, and other artifacts related to Wykoff's history. Ed's Museum was created after Mr. Krueger bequeathed the property, the store and its contents to the city of Wykoff in 1989. Although Ed's collection is displayed as he left it, the Wykoff Area Historical Society is currently in the process of restoring the museum so that it would be a re-creation of the 1930s era Jack Sprat Store. Visitors may tour the Krueger's living quarters, the store and its original contents, and a storage area in the lower level. Ed's collection gives visitors a peek into a bygone era with displays of old posters, an antique meat slicer, an icebox, food products in their original containers, a player piano with sheet music from 1900 to 1930, typewriters, a tobacco case, antique toys, and memorabilia from the local schools and more.

Cost: by donation
Hours: Memorial Day–September: Saturday and Sunday, 1 p.m.–4 p.m., or by appointment

Part III:
Seasonal Events

Chapter 8: Seasonal Events: Winter

Chapter 9: Seasonal Events: Spring

Chapter 10: Seasonal Events: Summer

Chapter 11: Seasonal Events: Fall

Chapter 8: Seasonal Events: Winter

December

ROCHESTER
Carillon Christmas Concert
Rochester Carillon, Plummer Building, 2nd Street SW, Mayo Medical Center, Rochester, MN 55905, (507) 284-8294, (507) 282-3730

Enjoy the majestic sounds of Rochester's 56-bell, 4½-octave carillon during a special recital performed on Christmas Eve. The performance may be heard at 4 p.m. and 10:30 p.m. and is about 20 to 25 minutes in length. Carillon concerts are best heard in an open area at least 500 feet downwind from the tower during cold, crisp weather. Please see Chapter 2 for more information about the Rochester Carillon.

Celebration of Lights
Rochester Post-Bulletin, 18 1st Avenue SE, Rochester, MN 55904, (507) 285-7600, www.postbulletin.com or e-mail: news@post-bulletin.com
Must be a subscriber to access parts of the website.

Rochester's Annual Celebration of Lights is a citywide contest that provides area residents with the opportunity to showcase their holiday light displays. The Rochester Post-Bulletin publishes a list of the entries, and a panel of judges selects winners for each quadrant of the city based upon excellence of appearance. Contestants register through the Post-Bulletin, and the entry deadline is typically in early December. Prizes are awarded. Rochester City Lines [(507) 288-4353] provides a bus tour of the lights in mid-December for a nominal fee. Call Rochester City Lines to reserve seats for the bus tour.

Forever Christmas
Best Western Apache,1517 16th Street SW, Rochester, MN 55902, (507) 289-8866 extension 330, 800-552-7224 extension 330; Pyramid Theater Alliance, (507) 437-7527, e-mail: spkinney@smig.net

Forever Christmas is an annual dinner theater show produced by the Pyramid Theater Alliance, a small, nonprofit theater company. The long running musical, now a Rochester tradition, has been performed in Rochester since 1990 and is currently staged at the Best Western Apache. The show runs from early December through mid-January. Call the Best Western Apache for information, reservations, and tickets.

Holiday Homes Tour
Olmsted County History Center, 1195 West Circle Drive SW, Rochester, MN 55902, (507) 282-9447, www.olmstedhistory.com

The Holiday Homes Tour, an annual fundraiser sponsored by the Friends of Mayowood Residence and Historic Sites, features approximately five to six local homes. Homes on the tour represent a variety of styles ranging from historic houses with traditional decor to elegant contemporary homes to middle-income residences adorned with family heirlooms and home-spun decorations. A daytime and candle-light tour is given on the first Saturday in December. Visitors are responsible for their own transportation to the homes. No young children or strollers are permitted. Please contact the Olmsted County History Center for more information.

Live Nativity Drive-Through

Crossroads College (formerly Minnesota Bible College), 920 Mayowood Road, Rochester, MN 55902, (507) 288-4563, 800-456-7651, www.crossroadscollege.edu
Mayowood Road is only open to one-way traffic during the hours of this event. Please enter Mayowood Road from the west, off of Bamber Valley Road (County Road 8) to view the live nativity.

Crossroads College is transformed into the City of Bethlehem with a live, eleven-scene nativity display portraying the events of Jesus Christ's birth. As visitors drive through the campus they experience the joy and majesty of the Christmas story. This annual event is held during the first weekend in December. Anticipate a long wait in line.

The Nutcracker Ballet

Allegro School of Dance, 14½ 4th Street SW, Rochester, MN 55902, (507) 288-0125

The Nutcracker Ballet, a studio production of Rochester's Allegro School of Dance, has become a holiday tradition in the Rochester community. The ballet is performed with nearly 100 dancers, and cast members range in age from grade schoolers to adults. Public performances are staged at one of Rochester's high schools during the first weekend in December. Please contact the Allegro School of Dance for more information.

Yulefest

Rochester Civic Music, City Hall, 201 4th Street SE, Suite 170, Rochester, MN 55904, (507) 281-6005, Ticket Information: (507) 285-8076, www.ci.rochester.mn.us/music

Yulefest, an annual Christmas tradition in Rochester, features performances by the Rochester Civic Music Band and Choir along with a variety of guest performers. Mr. and Mrs. Santa usually make an appearance at this family-friendly event held in early December. Tickets are available through Rochester Civic Music.

High School Sports Tournaments

Rochester hosts a handful of high school hockey and basketball tournaments during the last week of December. Boys' and girls' teams from throughout the state compete at different Rochester venues. Check the Rochester Post-Bulletin's sports section for a complete schedule. Single ticket admission or tournament passes are available.

BYRON

Christmas in the Country

Garten Marketplatz Perennial Farm, 5225 County Road 15 SW, Byron, MN 55920, (507) 281-1023, www.gartenmarketplatz.com
Located 6 miles SW of Rochester, take Salem Road (County 25) 3 miles to Olmsted County 15, drive south on County Road 15 for 3 miles.

Garten Marketplatz Perennial Farm hosts "Christmas in the Country" from early November through mid-December. A nostalgic atmosphere awaits visitors to the "Garten House," an 1860s brick home located on 10-acre Civil War era farm that is transformed into a Christmas wonderland. Customers enjoy the sights, sounds, and smells of Christmas as they shop in a pleasant atmosphere away from the hustle and bustle of the city. Seasonal home decor such as holiday wreaths, swags, centerpieces and a variety of gift items including fountains, gardening accessories, ornaments, candles, music, and more may be found at this Christmas gift show.

KENYON
Old-Fashioned Christmas at Gunderson House
109 Gunderson Boulevard, Kenyon, MN 55946, (507) 789-6415, (507) 789-6123

Experience Christmas as it was celebrated in the late 1800s at the Historic Gunderson House. Tour guides dressed in period costumes greet guests who receive a tour of the home and a buffet dinner followed by an evening of musical entertainment in the sitting room. No young children are permitted at this event, which is held in early December. Call for reservations and to purchase tickets.

MAZEPPA
O'Brien Christmas Wonderland
23525 453rd Street, Mazeppa, MN 55956

Visitors are welcome to drive by the Christmas Wonderland of Lights created by Dennis & Marilyn O'Brien. The O'Briens adorn their Mazeppa home with countless strings of lights to celebrate the season. Displays may vary from year to year and include many hand-crafted decorations. The first lighting is the day after Thanksgiving and continues every evening from about 4:30 p.m.–10:30 p.m. until January first.

MANTORVILLE
Olde-Fashioned Christmas in Mantorville
Contact: Riverside Gifts, 521 Main Street North, Mantorville, MN 55955, (507) 635-5464, www.mantorville.com

Mantorville, a small town on the National Register of Historic Places, welcomes visitors to experience the charm and traditions of an old-fashioned Christmas on the first Saturday in December. As you stroll through town and browse among the many gift shops, take time to visit with Santa, listen to the wandering carolers, enjoy a sleigh ride, or go on the Tour of Homes. Warm up by having lunch or dinner at the Historic Hubbell House. Small fee for the Tour of Homes and pictures with Santa. Receive discounts at local businesses when you buy a Mantorville button. Buttons and tickets for the Tour of Homes are available at local businesses.

RUSHFORD
Rushford's Parade of Lights
Signal Bank of Rushford, Rushford, MN 55971, (507) 864-7755

The Rushford Parade of Lights is an annual event that is a celebration of community as well as a fundraiser and food drive for the area. The parade includes lighted floats, carolers dressed in Victorian-era clothing, and visits with Santa. The parade is usually held the second Saturday in December at 7 p.m.

January

ROCHESTER
Martin Luther King Junior Celebration
NAACP, P.O. Box 6472, Rochester, MN 55902, (507) 288-5300
Diversity Council, 220 South Broadway, Rochester, MN 55904, (507) 282-9951, www.diversitycouncil.org

This weekend celebration commemorates the life of Dr. Martin Luther King Junior with a Prayer Breakfast, Multicultural Talent Show, Martin Luther King Junior Rally and Freedom March through downtown Rochester, traditional celebrations and other community activities. The events are held in late January during the weekend of Martin Luther King Junior's birthday. Please contact the NAACP or Diversity Council for more information.

Rochester Sports and Vacation Show

B & J Promotions, P.O. Box 1926, North Mankato, MN 56002, (507) 387-7469
This event is held at the Mayo Civic Center, 30 Civic Center Drive SE, Rochester, MN 55904, (507) 287-2222, www.mayociviccenter.com

The Rochester Sports and Vacation Show, held the last full weekend in January, features over 100 exhibitors from the upper Midwest and Canada. This cabin fever reliever showcases outdoor recreational equipment and vacation destinations as well as offering a variety of seminars on fishing, hunting, and other outdoor sports. Exhibits include boats and campers of all sizes, fishing and hunting gear, representatives from U.S. and Canadian resorts, convention and visitor's bureaus, and more. This event is held at the Mayo Civic Center in Rochester. Admission fee.

Wedding Extravaganza

Showcase Productions, Rochester, MN, (507) 282-9225, www.wedex.com
This event is held at the Mayo Civic Center, 30 Civic Center Drive SE, Rochester, MN 55904, (507) 287-2222, www.mayociviccenter.com

Brides-to-be gather at the Wedding Extravaganza, an annual one-stop shopping event complete with two fashion shows, to plan and dream about their special day. The extravaganza includes hundreds of displays by vendors who provide wedding related services and products. Representatives from bridal gown shops, reception halls, caterers, limousine services, invitations, photographers, bands, florists, hairstylists, gift registries, wedding planners, dance lessons, jewelers, party supplies, make-up, nail salons, and more are available to assist with wedding plans and reserve dates for their services. This event is held the first Saturday after the New Year. Admission fee.

CANNON FALLS
Cabin Fever Days

Cannon Falls Chamber of Commerce, Cannon Falls, MN 55009, (507) 263-2289, www.cannonfalls.org

Cabin Fever Days is an annual two-day festival celebrating cold weather. The festival features the Annual Cannon Valley Sled Dog Race with competitors from the United States and Canada, skijoring and snowshoeing demonstrations, and a horse drawn sleigh and cutter parade at Lake Byllesby Regional Park. Additional events include the Cabin Fever Fun Run and four-mile run in downtown Cannon Falls, the Cannon Falls High School Alumni Basketball Game, and more. Concessions are available at the park. This event is held during the last Saturday and Sunday in January. Admission fee for some activities.

Cannon Valley Classic Sled Dog Races

Cannon Falls Chamber of Commerce, Cannon Falls, MN 55009, (507) 263-2289, www.cannonfalls.org

This is the largest annual sled dog race in the United States south of Duluth, Minnesota. There are over 100 competitors from the United States and Canada including junior divisions. The races are a featured event of Cannon Falls' Cabin Fever Days, which is scheduled during the last Saturday and Sunday in January. Events are held at Lake Byllesby Regional Park. Concessions are available at the park. Entrance fee for race participants. Free for spectators.

HARMONY
Candlelight Ski
DNR Trail Center, (507) 467-2552; Harmony, 800-247-MINN (6466), www.harmony.mn.us; Preston, 888-845-2100

Cross-country ski by candlelight on the Harmony-Preston Valley State Trail. The 1.5 mile candlelight ski, held on the third Saturday in January, begins and ends in Preston. A campfire is ready to warm skiers at both the trailhead and turn-around point. Refreshments are available at local businesses. A Great Minnesota Ski Pass, available on site for a few dollars, must be purchased to ski on the trail. Ski rentals are not available at this event. Call the DNR Trail Center to confirm the date and time of event.

WABASHA
Eagle Watch at Riverfront
The National Eagle Center and EagleWatch Observation Deck,152 Main Street, Wabasha, MN 55981, (651) 565-4989, www.eaglewatch.org, or e-mail: 4eagles@wabasha.net

The EagleWatch Observation Deck offers breathtaking views from the banks of the Mississippi and is a prime spot for eagle watching. If you're unable to locate the 500-square-foot deck by the grand 17-foot wooden eagle statue carved by Jim Smit of Nelson, Wisconsin, just look for the deck at the intersection of Pembroke Avenue and Lawrence Boulevard. Volunteers from the National Eagle Center staff the deck on Saturdays and Sundays from 1 p.m. to 3 p.m. (early November through March) to answer questions and assist with eagle spotting. Visitors may use spotting scopes and binoculars provided by the National Eagle Center. Please note that volunteers are available when weather conditions are 10°F or above, and there is no rain. Free.

February

ROCHESTER
Kid Fest
Ronald McDonald House of Rochester, 850 2ⁿᵈ Street SW, Rochester, MN 55902, (507) 282-3955, www.ronhouserochmn.org
Event held at the Heintz Center of Rochester Community and Technical College, 1926 Collegeview Road SE, Rochester, MN 55904

Kid Fest is an annual indoor carnival sponsored by the Ronald McDonald House of Rochester. The event, held the second Sunday in February, provides an afternoon of fun for young families. Activities include a variety of games, crafts, and stage shows. Children win small prizes as they play carnival games and may take home their creations from the craft tables. Food is available for purchase at the event. Proceeds benefit the Rochester's Ronald McDonald House. Admission fee for children ages two and older. Free admission for parents and children under age two.

Rochester Area Builders' Home and Garden Show

Rochester Area Builders, 3400 East River Road NE, Rochester, MN 55906, (507) 282-7698, www.rochesterareabuilders.org
This event is held at the Mayo Civic Center, 30 Civic Center Drive SE, Rochester, MN 55904, (507) 287-2222, www.mayociviccenter.com

The Rochester Area Builders' Annual Home Show has been a Rochester event for more than 20 years. The event features hundreds of exhibitors and free seminars with a wealth of information and ideas for home construction, remodeling, and improvement. Exhibits include windows and siding, floor coverings, fireplaces, garage doors, building materials, heating and cooling systems, kitchen and bathroom cabinetry, whirlpools, water purification systems, closet organizers, landscaping and playground equipment, interior decorating, security systems, mortgages, and more. This event takes place at Mayo Civic Center in early February. Admission fee.

Skyway Golf Classic

PossAbilities of Southern Minnesota, 1808 3rd Avenue SE, Rochester, MN 55904, (507) 281-6116, www.possAbilities.org

PossAbilities of Southern Minnesota, a nonprofit agency that provides "meaningful work and community opportunities for adults with developmental disabilities," sponsors the Annual Skyway Golf Classic. Two 18-hole miniature golf courses are set up throughout the pedestrian skyway system adjacent to downtown Rochester's Centerplace Galleria. Singles, doubles, and foursomes may enter the golf tournament, which is a fundraiser for PossAbilities of Rochester. This event is usually held the weekend before or after Valentine's Day. Children and families are welcome to participate in this event. Admission Fee.

Youth Ice Fishing Contest

Foster-Arend Park, 37th Street and East River Road NE, Rochester, MN
Rochester Park and Recreation Department, (507) 281-6160, www.ci.rochester.mn.us/park

The Rochester '76 Lions Club, a member of Lion's Club International, sponsors an annual ice-fishing contest for youth ages 15 and under. Youth must supply their own tackle; however, bait is furnished and holes will be pre-drilled. Prizes are awarded in two age categories. Additional activities at this event have included wagon rides, hot air balloon liftoffs, sled dog demonstrations, and more. Parental supervision is required at this event, which is held the second Saturday in February at Foster-Arend Park in northeast Rochester. Refreshments are available on site. Small entry fee. Please call a Lion's Club representative at (507) 288-5425 or visit www.rochester76lions.org for more information about this event.

KENYON
Don Knopf Memorial Carriage and Cutter Parade

Kenyon, MN 55946, (507) 789-5399, (507) 789-6415, www.cityofkenyon.com

This annual parade features between 75 and 100 animal-drawn carriages and cutters. Additional events include a petting zoo, Newfoundland dog cart rides, pony rides, and stage coach rides. Events are held on Main Street and begin at 10 a.m. The parade starts at 1:30 p.m. Kenyon's Historic Gunderson House is open for tours, and local churches hold a bake sale and sell crafts from third world countries during this event, scheduled the last Saturday in February.

LAKE CITY
Winter Fest
Lake City Tourism Bureau, 1401 North Lakeshore Drive, Lake City, MN 55041, www.lakecity.org

Choose from a variety of both indoor and outdoor activities at Lake City's annual Winter Fest. Outdoor activities have included the Winter Fest Cross-Country Ski Race at Frontenac State Park, a candlelight ski, snow golf, softball on ice, snow sculpting, and a medallion hunt. An Arts & Crafts Show, Taste Fest, Business Expo, Chili Cook-Off, and Pancake Breakfast are some of the indoor events that are usually held during this festival, which takes place the first weekend in February. Admission fee for some activities.

LANESBORO
Candlelight Ski
DNR Trail Center, (507) 467-2552; Lanesboro, 800-944-2670, www.lanesboro.com

Cross-country ski by candlelight on the Root River State Trail. The 1.5 mile candlelight ski, held on the first Saturday in February, begins and ends in Whalan. A campfire is ready to warm skiers at both the trailhead and turn-around point. Refreshments are available in Whalan. A Great Minnesota Ski Pass, available on site for a few dollars, must be purchased to ski on the trail. Ski rentals are not available at this event. Call the DNR Trail Center to confirm the date and time of event.

Winter Weekend Getaway at Eagle Bluff Environmental Learning Center
Route 2, Box 156A, 1991 Brightsdale Road, Lanesboro, MN 55949, (507) 467-2437, 888-800-9558, www.eagle-bluff.org or e-mail: hello@eagle-bluff.org

Seeking a cabin fever reliever? Eagle Bluff Environmental Learning Center's Winter Weekend Getaway is a sure cure to your cabin fever blues. Singles, couples, and families are welcome to register for the entire weekend including an overnight stay or may choose to participate in one or more activities as a day guest. A typical weekend itinerary includes some type of winter recreation such as cross-country skiing or snowshoeing, indoor rock climbing, a banquet, and concert. Please contact Eagle Bluff for dates, cost, program information, and registration materials.

WABASHA
Eagle Watch at Riverfront
The National Eagle Center and EagleWatch Observation Deck, 152 Main Street, Wabasha, MN 55981, (651) 565-4989, www.eaglewatch.org or e-mail: 4eagles@wabasha.net

The EagleWatch Observation Deck offers breathtaking views from the banks of the Mississippi and is a prime spot for eagle watching. If you're unable to locate the 500-square-foot deck by the grand 17-foot wooden eagle statue carved by Jim Smit of Nelson, Wisconsin, just look for the deck at the intersection of Pembroke Avenue and Lawrence Boulevard. Volunteers from the National Eagle Center staff the deck on Saturdays and Sundays from 1 p.m. to 3 p.m. (early November through March) to answer questions and assist with eagle spotting. Visitors may use spotting scopes and binoculars provided by the National Eagle Center. Please note that volunteers are available when weather conditions are 10° F or above, and there is no rain. Free.

Grumpy Old Men Festival

Wabasha Chamber of Commerce, P.O. Box 105, Wabasha, MN 55981, 800-565-4158, www.wabashamn.org

This festival was inspired by the movie, Grumpy Old Men, which is set in Wabasha, Minnesota. The festival is held on the last Saturday in February and features an ice-fishing contest (weather permitting), Walter Mattheau, Jack Lemmon, Sophia Loren, and Ann-Margret Look-Alike contests, and a dinner at Slippery's Restaurant. Additional events vary from year to year, but have included wagon rides, cribbage tournaments, softball in the snow, and a live band with dancing. Food vendors are available. Admission fee for some events.

Chapter 9: Seasonal Events: Spring

March

ROCHESTER
American Red Cross Annual Neighbor Saver Saturday

310 14th Street SE, Rochester, MN 55904, (507) 287-2200, semn.redcross.org or
e-mail: chapter@redcross-semn.org

The Rochester Chapter of the American Red Cross has sponsored the Annual
Neighbor Savers Saturday since 1992. This free event provides instruction in adult
CPR, rescue breathing, the Heimlich maneuver, and use of an automatic external
defibrillator. The class is typically held the second or third Saturday in March.
Participants must be age 12 and older and may choose to attend a morning or after-
noon session. Call the Red Cross to register two to three weeks before the class.

Annual Spring Gardening Seminar

Rochester Community Education, 201 8th Street NW, Rochester, MN 55901, (507) 285-8350,
www.rochester.k12.mn.us/community-ed.

This annual event is cosponsored by Rochester Community Education and the
Olmsted County Master Gardeners in mid-March. The seminar includes a keynote
speaker and two, hour-long sessions, each with a few choices of different gardening
topics. Topics have included shade gardening, lawn care options, gardening with
children, wildlife in the urban garden, floral basics, and growing vegetables in a small
area. For more information or registration materials, call Rochester Community
Education or look for the Annual Spring Gardening Seminar in the Winter/Spring
Community Education catalog.

KROC Home and Vacation Show

KROC Radio, 122 4th Street SW, Rochester, MN 55902, (507) 286-1010, www.kroc.com
This event is held at the Graham Arena Complex of the Olmsted County Fairgrounds, 3rd Avenue &
16th Street SE, Rochester, MN 55904, (507) 281-6040

The KROC Home and Vacation Show, an annual event for more than 39 years,
reminds Minnesotans that spring is just around the corner. Area residents browse
among hundreds of vendor booths to gather information about home improvement
services and products as well as recreational equipment and vacation destinations
within Minnesota. Exhibits include displays and information about lawn equipment,
whirlpool spas, RVs, pop-up campers, sewing machines, satellite dishes, cookware,
audio equipment, windows and siding, investments, bicycles, campgrounds, resorts,
and more. This event is held at the Graham Arena Complex of the Olmsted County
Fairgrounds in mid-March. Free admission.

WABASHA
Annual Soar with the Eagles Weekend

National Eagle Center,152 Main Street, Wabasha, MN 55981, (651) 565-4989, www.eaglecenter.org
or e-mail: 4eagles@wabasha.net

The Annual Soar with the Eagles Weekend, a two-day event that offers opportunities for eagle spotting and watching as well as nature-related seminars, is a great way

to become acquainted with the beauty of the Mississippi River Valley. Visit the National Eagle Center and have your picture taken with Harriet the Bald Eagle, look for eagles from the Eagle Observation Deck, or attend one or more seminars. Topics of educational seminars previously presented have included Photographing Wildlife, Leave No Trace Outdoor Ethics, and Waterfowl Identification. Children's activities, entertainment by Native American Dancers, and a Brunch with the Eagles are some of the other programs that have also been held. Soar with the Eagles is usually scheduled for the second or third weekend in March. No fee for seminars or eagle spotting. Fee for photos with Harriet, boat tours, and brunch. Call to make reservations for seminars and brunch. Children are welcome.

Eagle Watch at Riverfront

The National Eagle Center and EagleWatch Observation Deck,152 Main Street, Wabasha, MN 55981, (651) 565-4989, www.eaglewatch.org or e-mail: 4eagles@wabasha.net

The EagleWatch Observation Deck offers breathtaking views from the banks of the Mississippi and is a prime spot for eagle watching. If you're unable to locate the 500-square-foot deck by the grand 17-foot wooden eagle statue carved by Jim Smit of Nelson, Wisconsin, just look for the deck at the intersection of Pembroke Avenue and Lawrence Boulevard. Volunteers from the National Eagle Center staff the deck on Saturdays and Sundays from 1 p.m. to 3 p.m. (early November through March) to answer questions and assist with eagle spotting. Visitors may use spotting scopes and binoculars provided by the National Eagle Center. Please note that volunteers are available when weather conditions are 10°F or above, and there is no rain.

April

ROCHESTER

Bear Creek Pow Wow

Armed Forces Armory, 1715 Marion Road, Rochester, MN 55904
The Marion Road exit is located off Hwy. 52, just south of Rochester. Exit on Marion Road and drive north, the armory will be a few miles down the road on the left.

The Annual Bear Creek Pow Wow in Rochester is sponsored by the Native American Center of Southeastern Minnesota. Different tribes, Ho-Chunk, Lakota, Oneida, and Ojibwa, gather at this traditional Pow Wow, which features a host drum, Native American arts and crafts, food, dancing, and ceremonies. This event, held at the Armed Forces Armory in Rochester in early spring, is well publicized throughout the community. Please call (507) 280-0174 or (507) 374-2607 for more information. Admission fee.

Family Fun Night

Graham Arena Complex of the Olmsted County Fairgrounds, 3rd Avenue & 16th Street SE, Rochester, MN 55904, (507) 281-6040

Family Fun Night is an annual event sponsored by Child Care Resource and Referral, Rochester Park and Recreation, and the Rochester Kiwanis Club. The event features entertainment, games, and crafts for families with young children as well as information about local child-related services. Concessions are available at this event, which is usually held in late April. Please contact Child Care Resource and Referral at (507) 287-2020 for more information. Family admission fee.

Kids' Sports Expo

Rochester Community Education, 201 8th Street NW, Rochester, MN 55901, (507) 285-8350, www.rochester.k12.mn.us/community-ed

Almost all of Rochester's youth sports and recreational organizations and agencies are represented at the Kids' Sports Expo. Parents and kids have the opportunity to learn about sports and recreation activities available in the community, gather information, and see sporting demonstrations by local youth. This event is held every other year in mid-April. Please contact Rochester Community Education for more information or to obtain the date and location of the next Sports Expo. Information about youth sports organizations may also be found in Chapter 18, Recreational Sports. Free.

Rochester Figure Skating Club Annual Ice Show

Rochester-Olmsted Recreation Center, 21 Elton Hills Drive, Rochester, MN 55901, (507) 288-7536, www.web-site.com/rfsc

The Rochester Figure Skating Club (RFSC) presents its Annual Ice Show during the third weekend in April. This spectacular production showcases artistic and athletic performances by local youth of all ages and skating abilities. The combination of delightful performances by RFSC's younger skaters and the outstanding talent of its junior and senior skaters provides an entertaining show that will take your breath away. Admission fee.

Rochester International Film Festival

The Rochester International Film Group, (507) 288-8990, www.rifg.org or Rochester International Association, 300 11th Avenue NW, Rochester, MN 55901, (507) 289-5960, ext. 24

The Rochester International Film Group, an organization with about 600 members, coordinates the Annual International Film Festival in Rochester during late April. The event is organized in cooperation with the University Film Society, which brings a variety of independent and foreign films to the festival from the Minneapolis/St. Paul Film Festival held earlier in the month. The weekend festival typically offers a selection of 12 to 17 films for viewing at a local cinema and is supported by local businesses, grants, and individual donations. Please contact the Film Group for more information or check the Rochester Post-Bulletin for the dates, time, and location of this event.

Rochester World Festival

Rochester International Association and Intercultural Mutual Assistance Association, 300 11th Avenue NW, Suite 110, Rochester, MN 55901, (507) 289-5960, ext. 24

The Rochester World Festival, a special event sponsored by the Rochester International Association, has been celebrated in Rochester for more than 25 years. The festival provides area residents with the opportunity to celebrate the richness of Rochester's cultural diversity by experiencing the ethnic dances, music, art, and food of many nations. More than 30 cultures are often represented at the festival, which also includes a stage show, international fashion show, cultural art displays and demonstrations, children's activities and games, a Parade of Nations and more. This event is usually held the third Friday and Saturday of April. Ethnic food is available for purchase, and there is a small admission fee for the stage show. Call the RIA or check the Rochester Post-Bulletin for the location and time of this event.

CHATFIELD
Chatfield Trout Classic
Thurber Community Center, 21 2nd Street SE, Chatfield, MN 55923, (507) 867-3810

The Chatfield Trout Classic, an annual event sponsored by Chatfield's firefighters, is open to children and adults. Winners are awarded for the largest brown, rainbow, and brook trout in both children's (ages 12 and under) and adult categories. There is also a non-trout category for children. The contest is held on the opening day of stream trout fishing, typically the Saturday closest to April 15th. Contest registration and a pancake breakfast is located at the Chatfield Fire Hall on Main Street. Prizes are awarded. Small entry fee.

HARMONY
Bluff Country Studio Art Tour
Southeastern Minnesota Historic Bluff Country, P.O. Box 609, Harmony, MN 55939, 800-428-2030, www.bluffcountry.com

The artists of southeastern Minnesota open their studios and galleries to the public during the Bluff Country Studio Art Tour. Visitors have the opportunity to meet the artists, view demonstrations, and purchase original artwork of various mediums including pottery, fiber arts, sculpture, painting, mixed media, stone work, wood carvings, blown glass, jewelry, metal work, blacksmiths, and more. Brochures and maps of the art tour, featuring more than 40 studios, are available to assist visitors with planning their excursion throughout the region. They may be obtained from participating artists or the Southeastern Minnesota Historic Bluff Country Office. This event is held during the last weekend in April.

May

85-Mile Garage Sale
Mississippi Valley Partners, 888-999-2619, www.mississippi-river.org
Lake City Chamber of Commerce, (651) 345-4123, www.lakecitymn.org
Wabasha Chamber of Commerce, (651) 565-4158, www.wabashamn.org
This event is located along Minnesota's Great River Road (Highway 61) between Red Wing and Kellogg and Wisconsin's Great River Road (Highway 35) between Alma and Bay City.

An 85-Mile Garage Sale? Unbelievable, but true! Mississippi Valley Partners sponsors this spectacular garage sale that takes place in thirteen historic Mississippi River towns in Minnesota and Wisconsin during the first weekend in May. The Minnesota communities of Red Wing, Frontenac, Lake City, Camp LaCupolis, Reads Landing, Wabasha, and Kellogg, and the Wisconsin communities of Alma, Nelson, Pepin, Stockholm, Maiden Rock, and Bay City participate in this event. Bargain hunters may begin anywhere along the route, which follows Highway 61 on the Minnesota side of Lake Pepin and Highway 35 on the Wisconsin side of the lake. A trail of colored ribbons identifies participating garage sales in the towns mentioned above. Garage sale maps are available in the participating towns. For more information contact the Lake City Chamber of Commerce, the Wabasha Chamber of Commerce, or Missississpi Valley Partners.

Bluff Country Bird Festival

Southeastern Minnesota Historic Bluff Country, P.O. Box 609, Harmony, MN 55939, 800-428-2030, www.bluffcountry.com

Novice and experienced birders gather for this weekend festival to explore a variety of bird habitats and lesser known bird hot spots in southeastern Minnesota. The event includes an orientation; day and dusk trips to places such as Forestville State Park, Beaver Creek Wildlife Management Area, and Good Earth Village; two breakfasts; and a Saturday evening dinner with a speaker. The annual Bird Fest is held in different communities and areas within southeastern Minnesota from year to year. Participants must supply their own binoculars. Please contact Historic Bluff Country for registration materials and current cost.

ROCHESTER
Mayo Clinic Bike Safety Fair

Sponsored by Mayo Clinic Department of Emergency Medicine and Mayo Eugenio Litta Children's Hospital and the Department of Pediatrics, (507) 255-4744, (507) 284-2511
This event is usually held at Mayo Civic Center Arena, 30 Civic Center Drive SE, Rochester, MN 55904, (507) 287-2222, www.mayociviccenter.com

The Mayo Clinic Bike Safety Fair is a hands–on seminar where children, ages 5 to 11, have the opportunity to learn bike safety and injury prevention skills. Activities at this event have included planning a safe bike ride, first aid on the bike trail, obstacle course skills, helmet education and fitting, and information about registering for a bicycle license. Helmets are available for purchase at discount prices. Children must be registered to participate in this event, and all participants are required to wear a helmet and be accompanied by an adult. This event is held during the spring. The date, time, and location of this event may be found in the Rochester Post-Bulletin or by calling the number listed above. Free admission.

Olmsted County Gold Rush Days

Olmsted County Fairgrounds, 16th Street and 3rd Avenue SE, Rochester, MN 55904, (507) 285-8231

Olmsted County Gold Rush Days, an annual antique show and flea market, draws thousands of people to the Rochester area in a search of special treasures and collectibles. Collectors flock to Gold Rush Days to peruse the wares of more than 1,000 vendors who sell everything from antique furniture, toys, vintage jewelry, books, paintings, china and whatever else you can imagine. This event is held during Mother's Day weekend at the Olmsted County Fairgrounds. Free admission.

Transportation Fair

Parents Are Important In Rochester(PAIIR), Northrop Education Center, 201 8th Street NW, Rochester, MN 55901, (507) 285-8033, www.rochester.k12.mn.us/paiir

The Transportation Fair, an annual event sponsored by Parents Are Important In Rochester (PAIIR) and Rochester Public Works, continues to be a hit with preschoolers and young grade school children. This hands–on event allows kids to look at and climb on vehicles of every shape and size. School buses, fire engines, police cars, mail trucks, humvees, cherry pickers, snow plows, cement trucks, and handicapped–accessible vans are just some of vehicles waiting to be explored. This free event is usually held on the third Saturday in May. Concessions are available. Please contact PAIIR to confirm date, location and time of the fair.

BYRON

Oxbow Park Annual Fun Fest and Art Show

Oxbow Park, 5731 County Road 105 NW (at Olmsted 4 & 5 intersection), Byron, MN 55920, (507) 775-2451, www.olmstedpublicworks.com, e-mail: oxbow@ventures.net

Oxbow Park's Annual Fun Fest and Art Show is a one-day event held during the third weekend of May. Festival activities include animal demonstrations, art exhibits, musical entertainment, children's activities, and a re-creation of the late 1700s trapping era by the Buckskinners, a rendezvous group. Food vendors are available on the grounds. Please call Oxbow Park to confirm the date and time of this event. Free admission.

HARMONY

Aldrich Memorial Nursery School Annual Carnival

855 Essex Parkway, Rochester, MN 55901, (507) 289-3097

This annual carnival is a really fun event that features a variety of games, crafts, and prizes suitable for young families with preschool aged children. Tickets are required for participation in carnival games and crafts. Tickets may be purchased at the door. Concessions with a lunch menu and a bake sale are also available at this event, which is held the first Saturday in May.

HOUSTON

Money Creek Junction Bluegrass Festival

Cushon's Peak Campground, RR 1 Box 257A, 18696 State Hwy. 16, Houston, MN 55943, (507) 896-7325, e-mail: camppeak@acegroup.cc
Located 2 miles west of Houston off Hwy. 16.

Cushon's Peak Campground, situated on 180 acres of farmland and woods between the towns of Houston and Rushford, is the site of the Money Creek Junction Bluegrass Festival. Families are welcome at this weekend event, which is held in mid-May and mid-August. The festival includes performances by bluegrass bands, workshops for young musicians or others interested in learning about bluegrass instruments and music, and open mike sessions. Camping is available at the campground, and the Root River State Trail runs adjacent to the campground. Please see Chapter 12 Campgrounds, for detailed information about Cushon's Peak Campground. Day and weekend passes are available for the festival.

LAKE CITY

Great River Birding Festival

Mississippi Valley Partners, 888-999-2619, www.mississippi-river.org
Lake City Chamber of Commerce, (651) 345-4123, www.lakecitymn.org

The Annual Great River Birding Festival is sponsored and organized by the Audubon Society and Mississippi Valley Partners. The two-day event celebrates spring and International Migratory Bird Day with a variety of special events and interpretive programs. Guided birding hikes, backwater birding tours, bird banding, butterfly walks, photo shows, and musical entertainment are some of the activities held on both the Minnesota and Wisconsin sides of Lake Pepin. This event is usually held during the second weekend of May. Further information may be obtained from the Lake City Chamber of Commerce or Mississippi Valley Partners.

LANESBORO
Bluff Country Gathering
Lanesboro, MN 55949, (507) 498-5452, www.lanesboro.com

The Bluff Country Gathering, a four-day event held the weekend following Mother's Day, celebrates the folk traditions of old-time fiddle, banjo, guitar, and singing through a variety of workshops, concerts, and dancing experiences. Nationally renowned artists present instrumental workshops for beginners to advanced musicians as well as open workshops in singing, dancing, folklore discussions, mini-concerts, and other related topics. There are a limited number of spaces available for this event. Registration is required and will be taken on a first come, first served basis. Participants must bring their own instruments. Please call for more information and registration materials.

Old-Fashioned Barn Dance
Sons of Norway Hall, Parkway Avenue South, Lanesboro, MN 55949, (507) 498-5452
Lanesboro Visitor's Center, (507) 467-2696, 800-944-2670, www.lanesboro.com

Kick up your heels and come for an evening of fun at Lanesboro's Old-Fashioned Barn Dances. The dances are a re-creation of old-style barn dances reminiscent of the early 20th century. They are held at the Sons of Norway Hall and feature square, circle, and couples dancing with live music and calling. All dances are taught, and partners are not needed. Dances are held once a month from March through September on a Saturday evening, usually late in the month, from 8 p.m.–11 p.m. Please note that the dance in May is held at the Lanesboro Community Center, not the Sons of Norway Hall. Contact the Lanesboro Visitor's Center or visit www.lanesboro.com to obtain exact dates of the dances. Admission fee.

PRESTON
Trout Days
Preston Area Tourism Office, Box 657, Preston, MN 55965, (507) 765-2100, 888-845-2100, www.prestonmn.org

Preston welcomes visitors to explore southeastern Minnesota during Trout Days, a weekend celebration with activities for everyone in the family. Events typically include adult and kids' fishing contests, a car show, book sales, sports tournaments, dances, Root River Artist Show, city-wide rummage sale, a pancake breakfast, a grand parade, barbeque dinners, and more. Visitors also have easy access to Forestville/Mystery Cave State Park, the Root River and Harmony-Preston Valley State Recreation Trails, and the Root River. This event is held during the third weekend in May. Contact the Preston Area Tourism Office for more information.

SPRING GROVE
Syttende Mai Celebration
Spring Grove, MN 55974, (507) 498-5434, www.springgrovemn.com

Spring Grove celebrates its Norwegian heritage with this annual three-day event. Norwegian foods, dancing, arts and crafts, live music, tours, a parade, children's activities, trolls and more may be experienced at this festive celebration, which is held on the weekend closest to May 17th. Please contact the city of Spring Grove or visit their website for more information.

Chapter 10: Seasonal Events: Summer

June

Small Town Festivals in June

Small towns in southeastern Minnesota typically celebrate summer with a community festival. Events commonly held at these festivals include parades, street dances, food vendors, local sports tournaments, tractor pulls, ice cream socials, family fun nights, pancake breakfasts, city-wide rummage sales, carnival games and rides, fireworks, concerts and more. Please call for specific dates and a schedule of events.

Adams Dairy Days
Adams, MN 55909, (507) 582-3601
Second full weekend in June

Centerfest
Dodge Center, MN 55927, (507) 374-2575
Held during Father's Day weekend, usually the second weekend in June

Elgin Cheese Days
Elgin, MN 55932, (507) 876-2291
Held during Father's Day weekend

Fountain Trail Days
Fountain, MN 55935, (507) 268-4415
Second weekend in June

Goodview Days
Goodview, MN 55987, (651) 923-4310
Second weekend in June

Meadowfest
Grand Meadow, MN 55936, (507) 754-5280
Last weekend of June

Olde Tyme Days
Mantorville, MN 55955, (507) 635-5464
Held on third or fourth Sunday of June

Pine Island Cheese Festival
Pine Island, MN 55963, (507) 356-2888
Second full weekend of June

Viola Gopher Count
Viola, MN 55934, (507) 876-2888
Held the third Wednesday evening and third Thursday of June

Volksfest
Goodhue, MN 55027, (651) 923-4310
Second weekend in June

ROCHESTER
Cemetery Walk
Oakwood Cemetery, 41 7th Avenue NE, Rochester, MN; Olmsted County History Center, (507) 282-9447, (507) 282-1608 (cemetery), www.olmstedhistory.com
Located on 7th Street NE, off East Center Street.

The Oakwood Cemetery Walk, an annual event sponsored by the Olmsted County Historical Society and Oakwood Cemetery, is a guided historical tour with costumed actors who portray historic Rochester figures. The one-hour tours begin at Oakwood Cemetery's Healy Chapel. This event takes place during RochesterFest, usually the first Saturday of the festival. Admission fee.

Classic Car Rally
Sandy Point Supper Club, 18 Sandy Point Court NE, Rochester, MN 55906, (507) 367-4983

Classic car owners are welcome to showcase their prized possessions at the Classic Car Rally at Sandy Point Supper Club on Wednesday evenings at 5:50 p.m. from June until about October first. Car lovers gather in the parking lot and on the restaurant deck for a casual party and lots of conversation about cars.

Mayowood Garden Tour and Private Garden Tour
1195 West Circle Drive, Rochester, MN 55902, 507-282-9447, www.olmstedhistory.com

Tour the first floor of the Historic Mayowood Mansion before strolling through the beautifully landscaped gardens of Dr. Charlie Mayo's estate. After your tour, enjoy refreshments at the Mayowood Teahouse, and browse among the displays of artisans who have their wares for sale. As an added bonus, Olmsted County Master Gardeners are on-site to answer your gardening questions, and your ticket includes the tour of about four private gardens. Held the last Saturday in June. Admission fee.

Midwest Lumberjack Show and Championships
Silver Lake Park, 7th Street NE, Rochester, MN 55906, (507) 285-8769, www.rochesterfest.com

The Midwest Lumberjack Show in Rochester has been ranked a "world-class" competition by the North American Lumberjacks Association. World records have been set at this event, which draws top Jack and Jill competitors from throughout the United States and several foreign countries. A sample of events includes One-Man Bucking, Two-Man Sawing, Jack and Jill Sawing, Open Modified Chainsaw, Men's, Women's, Masters, and Youth Underhand Chop, Axe Throw and more. This event is held during the first weekend of RochesterFest in mid-June. Admission fee.

Rochester Roosters Old Time Baseball
Olmsted County History Center's Schmitt Field, 1195 West Circle Drive SW, Rochester, MN 55902, (507) 282-9447, www.olmstedhistory.com

The Rochester Roosters is a vintage baseball team that plays the game of American baseball as it originated in the mid-1800s. Players dress in period uniforms and compete with other vintage teams using replica balls and bats in a league that plays by 1860s rules. Games and tournaments are played periodically throughout the summer. Please contact the Olmsted County History Center or visit their website for a schedule. Admission fee: two bits (25 cents).

RochesterFest
Rochester, MN, (507) 285-8769, www.rochesterfest.com

RochesterFest was originally organized as a one-time community celebration in 1982, but its overwhelming success lead community leaders to make it an annual event. Over twenty years later, more than 100,000 people attend the week-long festival, which is held during the third week of June. Although downtown Rochester serves as the festival's central location, many RochesterFest events are held at different venues throughout town. RochesterFest boasts something for everyone including Taste of Rochester (a selection nearly 30 food vendors), the Midwest Lumberjack Championships, Cemetery Walk, a Treasure Hunt, Million Dollar Golf Shoot-Out, Junior Achievement Duck Derby, Family Fun Night, Penny Carnival, Daily Noontime Entertainment, Water Ski Show, Country Breakfast on the Farm, Rochester Honker's Baseball games, United Way Kite Festival, Hot Air Balloon Races, a Giant Street Dance with three stages, the Grande Parade, and much more. Please call the RochesterFest office or visit their website for more information. RochesterFest buttons and schedules are available at many area businesses.

CANNON FALLS
Voices of the Valley
Cannon Valley Trail, City Hall, 306 West Mill Street, Cannon Falls, MN 55009, (507) 263-0508, www.cannonvalleytrail.com
The Red Wing trailhead is located on Old West Main Street and Bench Street, one block from Hwy. 61 with parking nearby. The Cannon Falls trailhead originates near 3rd Street in Cannon Falls. Parking at this trailhead is limited, but may be accessed across from the ballpark on East Stoughton Street. The Welch Station Access is located along County Road 7 between the Village of Welch and Welch Village Ski Area.

Voices of the Valley is an interpretive program held on the Cannon Valley Trail at the Welch Station Access, the approximate midpoint of the trail as it runs between Red Wing and Cannon Falls. The entertaining and educational programs are designed to acquaint trail users with the Cannon River Valley. Voices of the Valley is held on the first Saturday of every month from May through September from 11 a.m.–3 p.m. The 19.7-mile paved trail winds along side the Cannon River and passes through a variety of natural habitats including marshlands, pastures, and wooded areas. The trail is open to inline skaters, bicyclists, skateboarders, hikers, and cross-country skiers. A Wheel Pass is required for all adults, aged 18 and up, from April 1st through November 1st who are riding on wheeled vehicles. Wheel passes are available at self-purchase stations along the trail, local businesses, and from trail attendants on weekends during the summer months. Maps, directions, and additional information may be obtained by contacting the Cannon Valley Trail office.

LAKE CITY
Water Ski Days
Lake City, MN 55041, (651) 345-4123, 800-369-4123, www.lakecitymn.org

Lake City, the Birthplace of Water Skiing, is nestled in a valley along the shores of beautiful Lake Pepin. The natural beauty of Lake Pepin and its surrounding bluffs is so breathtaking that it has been called the "Lake Lucerne of America." Water Ski Days is an annual festival hosted by the city to honor Ralph Samuelson, the Father of Waterskiing, who discovered the sport from the shores of Lake Pepin in 1922. Festival events typically include a water ski show, food concessions, an arts and crafts fair, live music, sports tournaments, a classic car show, parade, petting zoo, Miss Lake City pageant, boat parade and more. This event is held during the last full weekend in June. Please call the Lake City Chamber of Commerce for more information.

LANESBORO
Art in the Park
Sylvan Park, Lanesboro, MN 55949, (507) 467-2696, www.lanesboro.com

Art in the Park, a juried art show in historic Lanesboro, is a family event that features an artists' market, food, and entertainment. Artisans of virtually all media including textiles, painting, stained glass, pottery, wood, metal, and more display and sell their work in Lanesboro's beautiful Sylvan Park. A limited number of art demonstrations may also be available. Professional and regional high school ensembles perform concerts in the park gazebo during the show. Held on Father's Day weekend. Free admission.

Summer Weekend Getaway at Eagle Bluff Environmental Learning Center
Route 2, Box 156A, 1991 Brightsdale Road, Lanesboro, MN 55949, (507) 467-2437, 888-800-9558, www.eagle-bluff.org or e-mail: hello@eagle-bluff.org

Eagle Bluff Environmental Learning Center's Summer Weekend Getaway is a wonderful way for families and friends to enjoy the great outdoors without all the work. Singles, couples, and families are welcome to register for the entire weekend including an overnight stay or may choose to participate in one or more activities as a day guest. A typical weekend itinerary features outdoor recreational activities such as canoeing, hiking, and the tree top high ropes course as well as a banquet and concert. Please contact Eagle Bluff for dates, cost, program information, and registration materials.

ORONOCO
Rochester Water Ski Club
Box 193, Oronoco, MN 55960, (507) 367-4485
Shows are held on Lake Zumbro at Fisherman's Inn Restaurant, 8 Fisherman Drive NW, Oronoco, MN 55960.

The Rochester Water Ski Club was established more than 40 years ago and is currently an award winning team that performs public shows on Wednesday evenings at 7 p.m. throughout the summer. Club members and performers are primarily area teens, but range in age from four to fifty. The hour and one-half long water ski shows are performed on Lake Zumbro at the Fisherman's Inn Restaurant in Oronoco. The weekly shows include a variety of stunts and tricks including a ballet water dance line, pyramids, doubles, barefoot skiing, jumps, and more. Special shows are usually performed for the RochesterFest, Fourth of July, and Labor Day celebrations. These shows are held at Silver Lake Park in Rochester. Please check the Rochester Post-Bulletin for dates and times of these special shows. Free.

PLAINVIEW
Migrant Festival
Area Migrant Council, P.O. Box 464, Plainview, MN 55964, (507) 534-9204
This event is held at Immanuel Lutheran Church, 45 West Broadway, Plainview, MN 55964, (507) 534-3700

The Plainview Area Migrant Council sponsors an annual Migrant Festival in early June. The festival welcomes migrant workers with food, games, music, and prizes. It also helps them make a smooth transition into the community by providing access to community agencies. Free.

STEWARTVILLE
Summer Saturday Nite Concerts
Ironwood Springs Christian Ranch, 7291 County Road 6 SW, Stewartville, MN 55976, (507) 533-4315, 888-533-4316, www.ironwoodsprings.com

Ironwood Springs Christian Ranch of Stewartville welcomes the public to their Saturday Nite Concerts from late May through Labor Day weekend. Christian musicians perform out on the Ranch in the Log Chapel at 7 p.m. Please call or check the website to confirm the concert schedule. Free.

WABASHA
Meet Me Under the Bridge Concerts
Wabasha, MN 55981, (651) 565-4158, 800-565-4158, www.wabashamn.org

Heritage Park, located under the Interstate Bridge in downtown Wabasha, is the site for a series of free outdoor concerts that feature a variety of musical genres throughout the summer. The concerts are held on Friday evenings at 7 p.m. from late June through mid-August.

WINONA
Steamboat Days Festival
Winona Visitor's Center, Hwys. 14/16 and Huff Street, Winona, MN 55987, (507) 452-2278, (507) 452-2272, 800-657-4972, www.visitwinona.com

The Steamboat Days Festival has been an annual tradition in Winona for more than 50 years. The week-long festival, held during the third week of June, features a wide variety of events and activities including the Miss Winona Pageant, Grande Parade, Kiddie Parade, a Midway with rides, musical entertainment, sports tournaments, a treasure hunt, carnival, fireworks, powerboat races and more. The purchase of a festival button is required for admission. Call the Winona Visitor's Center for more information.

ZUMBROTA
Zumbrota Covered Bridge Music and Arts Festival
Covered Bridge Park, Zumbrota City Hall, 175 West Avenue, Zumbrota, MN 55992 (507) 732-7318, www.zumbrota.com
Located on Hwy. 58 just past downtown Zumbrota.

A great time to visit Zumbrota's Covered Bridge Park is during the Annual Covered Bridge Music and Arts Festival, which is held on the third Saturday in June. The festival features arts and crafts, antiques, flea markets, food vendors, sports tournaments, a parade, and a street dance. Visitors will also enjoy the park's historic sites, the Zumbrota Covered Bridge, a railway depot (circa 1878), and an old country school house as well as modern recreational facilities including the Kids' Kingdom Playground, shaded picnic areas, a picnic shelter, ball fields, sand volleyball courts, horseshoe pits, a municipal swimming pool, a campground, and five miles of scenic walking trails. Please see Chapter 16, Parks, for more information about Zumbrota's Covered Bridge Park.

Independence Day Celebrations

Fireworks at Stewartville's Summerfest
Stewartville, MN 55976, (507) 533-6006, www.stewartvillemn.com

The Great Harmony Fourth of July
Harmony, MN 55939, (507) 886-2469, 800-247-6466, www.harmony.mn.us

Independence Day at Historic Forestville
Forestville State Park, Preston, MN 55965, (507) 765-2785, www.mnhs.org

Old-Fashioned Fourth of July
Wabasha, MN 55981, (651) 565-4158, 800-565-4158, www.wabashamn.org

Rochester's Fourth of July Fireworks and Community Concert
Silver Lake Park, 7th Street NE, Rochester, MN 55906, (507) 288-4331, 800-634-8277, www.rochestercvb.org

Small Town Festivals and County Fairs in July

Small towns in southeastern Minnesota typically celebrate summer with a community festival. Events commonly held at these festivals include parades, street dances, food vendors, local sports tournaments, family fun nights, pancake breakfasts, city-wide rummage sales, carnival games and rides, fireworks, concerts and more. Please call for specific dates and a schedule of events.

Cannon Valley Fair
Cannon Falls, MN 55009, (507) 263-2289
July 1st–July 4th

Dodge County Fair
Dodge County Fairgrounds, North Mantorville Avenue, Kasson, MN 55944, (507) 634-7736, www.mfcf.com
Held the second or third weekend in July

Eyota Days
Eyota, MN 55934, (507) 545-2135
Third week in July

Fillmore County Fair
Fillmore County Fairgrounds, 413 East Fillmore Street, Preston, MN 55965, (507) 765-2100, 888-845-2100, www.mfcf.com
Held the third or fourth week in July

Good Neighbor Days
Byron, MN 55920, (507) 775-2316
Third weekend in July

Hey Days
Hayfield, MN 55940, (507) 477-3535, 477-2727
Third weekend in July

Houston Hoedown

Houston, MN 55943, (507) 896-3010, www.houstonmn.com
Last full weekend in July

Olmsted County Fair

Olmsted County Fairgrounds, 16ᵗʰ Street and 3ʳᵈ Avenue SE, Rochester, MN 55904,
(507) 285-8231, (507) 282-9862 (during fair), www.mfcf.com
Begins the last Sunday or Monday of July

Summerfest

Le Roy, MN 55951, (507) 324-5707
Third weekend in July

Summerfest

Stewartville, MN 55976, (507) 533-6006
Held July 2ⁿᵈ–4ᵗʰ

Survival Days

West Concord, MN 55985, (507) 527-2668

Wabasha County Fair

Wabasha County Fairgrounds, P.O. Box 101, 99 Coulee Way, Wabasha, MN 55981,
(507) 753-2007, www.mfcf.com
Held in mid-July

Winona County Fair

Winona County Fairgrounds, Hwy. 14 East, St. Charles, MN 55972, (507) 932-3059,
www.mfcf.com
Held during the first week in July

ROCHESTER

Annual Butterfly Count

Quarry Hill Nature Center, 701 Silver Creek Road, Rochester, MN 55906, (507) 281-6114,
www.rochester.k12.mn.us/quarryhill or www.monarchwatch.org
Accessible from County Road 22, also called East Circle Drive.

Quarry Hill Nature Center and the Zumbro Valley Audubon Society sponsor an
Annual Butterfly Count in July or August. The count is open to any school-aged
children and adults who are interested in butterflies. Participants assist nature center
staff with catching, identifying, tagging, counting, and releasing butterflies at Quarry
Hill Park and other sites within the Rochester area. No experience is necessary and
a practice count is usually held for prospective participants. Bring binoculars and a
butterfly guidebook if you have them. Please call Quarry Hill Nature Center for
more information.

Down by the Riverside Concerts

Mayo Park, Rochester, MN
Mayo Park is located behind Mayo Civic Center on Civic Center Drive in downtown Rochester. For
more information, contact Rochester Civic Music, City Hall, 201 4ᵗʰ Street SE, Suite 170, Rochester,
MN 55904, (507) 281-6005, www.ci.rochester.mn.us/music.

Down by the Riverside, a popular seven-week series of outdoor concerts, is
sponsored by Rochester Civic Music. These free, summertime concerts take
place on Sunday evenings during July and August in Mayo Park, located behind
the Rochester Civic Center. Rochester Civic Music supports the careers of local

and regional artists by featuring them as opening acts at the Down by the Riverside concerts. The concert series features "artists of merit" as headliner acts so that it may reach a broader audience and provide the community with exposure to a wide variety of musical genres. Headliner acts have included well-known artists such as Jonny Lang, The Dixie Chicks, and Herman's Hermits. Rochester's Down by the Riverside concerts have become a much anticipated community event where hundreds, sometimes thousands of people come together with friends, families, and neighbors to enjoy the simple pleasures of life—socializing, picnicking, and listening to music. So grab your lawn chair, picnic blanket, and cooler and join the community gathering where you'll more than likely run into a friend. Concessions are available at all concerts. All concerts begin at 7 p.m. and end at approximately 9:30 p.m. Opening acts typically perform for about 45 minutes. In the event of inclement weather, concerts are held inside the Civic Center.

Jake and Jenny Outdoor Day

NWTF Representative, (507) 282-7344, www.nwtf.org
The Minnesota Sportsman's Club is located at 6251 20th Street SE, Rochester, MN 55904, (507) 282-9808

Jake and Jenny Outdoor Day is an annual event sponsored by the Hiawatha Valley Chapter of the National Wild Turkey Federation that has won four National Awards from the NWTF. The event, held on the last Saturday in July, provides kids ages 4 to 12 with an introduction to shooting sports and fishing. Additional nature-related activities include turkey, duck, and goose calling and dog retrievals. All equipment is provided for the activities, which are held at the Southern Minnesota Sportsman's Club and Quarry Hill Park. Pre-registration is preferred because a limited number of entries are available. The nominal participation fee includes lunch and member-ship in the NWTF's Jake's Program. Please call for more information.

Valley Street Machines Annual Car and Truck Show & Swap Meet

Valley Street Machine Club, P.O. Box 6893, Rochester, MN 55903, (507) 282-1798, hjalmerdik.com/vsm
The Olmsted County Fairgrounds is located at 16th Street and 3rd Avenue SE, Rochester, MN 55904, (507) 285-8231

The Valley Street Machines Annual Car and Truck Show & Swap Meet has been sponsored by Rochester's Valley Street Machine Club for nearly 20 years. Cars, trucks, and motorcycles of all types and vintages may be viewed at the show. Newcomers are encouraged to shine up their street machines and enter them in the show. Prizes are awarded in about 26 classes. This show is held at the Olmsted County Fairgrounds in early July. Please call the fairgrounds or check the Rochester Post-Bulletin for the date of the show.

HAMMOND
Hammond Classic Car Show

Hammond Ball Park, (507) 753-2440, (507) 753-2086 (Hammond City Hall)
Take Hwy. 63 north to County Road 11, follow signs to Hammond.

The tiny town of Hammond, 18 miles north of Rochester, hosts an Annual Classic Car Show on the Fourth of July. The show features about 200 cars, and awards are given in approximately 28 classes. Car owners wanting to show their cars may register at the gate. Food concessions are available. Admission fee.

HARMONY
Minowa Carver's Annual Show & Sale
Slim's Woodshed & Museum, P.O. Box 594, 160 1st Street NW, Harmony, MN 55939, (507) 886-3114, www.slimswoodshed.com

Slim's Woodshed and Museum of Harmony hosts the Annual Minowa Wood Carver's Show and Sale. Woodcarvers from throughout the United States and the Midwest exhibit their work at this event, which is held during the first weekend of July. A woodcarving class or workshop is usually offered at the show. Small admission fee.

LANESBORO
Old-Fashioned Barn Dance
Sons of Norway Hall, Parkway Avenue South, Lanesboro, MN 55949, (507) 498-5452
Lanesboro Visitor's Center, (507) 467-2696, 800-944-2670, www.lanesboro.com

Kick up your heels and come for an evening of fun at Lanesboro's Old-Fashioned Barn Dances. The dances are a re-creation of old-style barn dances reminiscent of the early 20th century. They are held at the Sons of Norway Hall and feature square, circle, and couples dancing with live music and calling. All dances are taught, and partners are not needed. Dances are held once a month in March, April, May, June, July, August, and September on a Saturday evening, usually late in the month, from 8 p.m.–11 p.m. Contact the Lanesboro Visitor's Center or visit www.lanesboro.com to obtain exact dates of the dances. Admission fee.

OWATONNA
Festival of the Arts
Central Park, Main Street and East Park Square, Owatonna, MN
Arts Center: (507) 451-0533, Visitor's Bureau: (507) 451-7970, 800-423-6466, www.owatonna.org

Festival of the Arts is an annual event held in Owatonna's downtown Central Park, adjacent to Wells Fargo Bank, formerly National Farmers' Bank, designed by world-renowned architect, Louis Sullivan. The event features exhibits by over 50 regional artists, live entertainment, and ethnic foods. This event is usually held the last Saturday and Sunday in July. Please call the Owatonna Arts Center or Visitor's Bureau for more information.

Owatonna Extravanganza
Village of Yesteryear, 1448 Austin Road, Owatonna, MN 55060, (507) 451-1420
Located on the Steele County Fairgrounds, 1525 South Cedar Avenue, Owatonna, MN 55060, (507) 451-5305, www.scff.org

The Owatonna Extravaganza is held at the Village of Yesteryear on the Steele County Fairgrounds. The village features several buildings that date back to the 1800s including log cabins, a general store/post office, blacksmith shop, country school, railroad station, and the Dunnell mansion. The extravaganza commemorates the days of yesteryear with handcrafted demonstrations, blacksmithing, wagon rides, horse exhibitions, musical entertainment, an ice cream social and more. This one-day event is held on a weekend in mid-July. Please call the Village of Yesteryear for more information.

PRESTON
Evening of Leisure
Historic Forestville, Forestville State Park, Preston, MN 55965, (507) 765-2785, (507) 352-5111, www.mnhs.org
Located 4 miles south of State Hwy. 16 on Fillmore County Road 5, then 2 miles east on Fillmore County Road 118.

Historic Forestville, a turn of the century historic village located in Forestville State Park, hosts an old-fashioned "Evening of Leisure" on a Saturday evening in late July and late August. Guides in period costumes welcome visitors to participate in music, storytelling, and games reminiscent of the late 19th century such as horseshoes, croquet, checkers and euchre. Refreshments are served. Please call Historic Forestville for specific dates and times of this event. Admission fee.

RACINE
Buffalo Fest
Burr Oak Buffalo Ranch & Trading Post, RR 1, Box 30, 78291 280th Street, Racine, MN 55967, (507) 378-5413, e-mail: burroak@hmtel.com

The Burr Oak Buffalo Ranch and Trading Post coordinates their annual Buffalo Fest so that it is held on the same weekend as the Antique Engine and Tractor Show just down the road in Spring Valley. Approximately 125 head of buffalo are raised on the 200-acre ranch. A sample of Buffalo Fest activities includes blacksmith and wood-carving demonstrations, tomahawk throwing, black powder gun making, horse-drawn and tractor-driven hayrides, kids' games, crafts, sales of fur trade era goods, and food concessions. Buffalo meat as well as other buffalo related products and souvenirs are available for sale at the Trading Post. Shipping is available for buffalo meat purchases. This event is held in mid-July. Please contact the Ranch for specific dates.

SPRING VALLEY
Antique Engine and Tractor Show
P.O. Box 23, Spring Valley, MN 55975, (507) 437-4940
Show grounds are located 20 miles south of Rochester on Hwy. 63 next to Deer Creek Campground.

The Root River Antique Historical Power Association hosts the Annual Antique Engine and Tractor Show in Spring Valley. The event features a variety of engine and tractor exhibits, demonstrations of traditional crafts such as rosemaling, spinning, tatting, and chair caning, a parade of tractors, square dancing, tractor pulls, musical entertainment, pancake breakfasts and more. This show is held in mid-July on the same weekend as the Buffalo Fest mentioned below. Please call for a specific dates. Admission fee.

WABASHA
Delta Queen Steamboat Docking
Wabasha Area Chamber of Commerce, P.O. Box 105, Wabasha, MN 55981, (651) 565-4158, 800-565-4158, www.wabashamn.org
Winona Visitor's Center, Hwys. 14/16 and Huff Street, Winona, MN 55987, (507) 452-2278, (507) 452-2272, 800-657-4972, www.visitwinona.com
American Queen Steamboat Company: www.deltaqueen.com

Experience the majesty and grandeur of a steamboat docking as the Delta Queen makes its scheduled stops in Wabasha and Winona. The Delta Queen regularly stops at these Mississippi River towns during its excursions to and from St. Paul. Call the

Wabasha Visitor's Center, Winona Visitor's Center, or the American Queen Steamboat Company for a schedule of summer and fall dockings.

Riverboat Days

Wabasha Area Chamber of Commerce, P.O. Box 105, Wabasha, MN 55981, (651) 565-4158, 800-565-4158, www.wabashamn.org

Wabasha's Riverboat Days, an annual festival that has been celebrated for 25 years, takes place in this Mississippi riverfront community during late July. Events at the festival typically include a beverage tent and food vendor court, a Princess Pageant, Lumberjack Show, Classic Car Show, Golf Tournament, Grande Parade, dances, an Arts and Crafts Show, Canine Frisbee Championship, Fireman's Water Fight, a River Run, live music, kiddie games and more. Please contact the Wabasha Area Chamber of Commerce for more information.

WINONA

Delta Queen Steamboat Docking

Wabasha Area Chamber of Commerce, P.O. Box 105, Wabasha, MN 55981, (651) 565-4158, 800-565-4158, www.wabashamn.org
Winona Visitor's Center, Hwys. 14/16 and Huff Street, Winona, MN 55987, (507) 452-2278, (507) 452-2272, 800-657-4972, www.visitwinona.com
American Queen Steamboat Company: www.deltaqueen.com

Experience the majesty and grandeur of a steamboat docking as the Delta Queen makes its scheduled stops in Wabasha and Winona. The Delta Queen regularly stops at these Mississippi River towns during its excursions to and from St. Paul. Call the Wabasha Visitor's Center, Winona Visitor's Center, or the American Queen Steamboat Company for a schedule of summer and fall dockings.

August

Small Town Festivals and County Fairs in August

Small towns in southeastern Minnesota typically celebrate summer with a community festival. Events commonly held at these festivals include parades, street dances, food vendors, local sports tournaments, family fun nights, pancake breakfasts, city-wide rummage sales, carnival games and rides, fireworks, concerts and more. Please call for specific dates and a schedule of events.

Buffalo Bill Days

Lanesboro, MN 55949, 800-944-2670
First weekend in August

Corn on the Cob Festival

Plainview, MN 55964, (507) 534-2229
Third weekend in August

Festival in the Park

Kasson, MN 55944, (507) 634-7744
Second weekend in August

Gladiolus Days

St. Charles, MN 55972, (507) 932-3020
Third week and weekend in August, usually the weekend before Labor Day weekend

Goodhue County Fair
Goodhue County Fairgrounds, 44217 County 6 Boulevard, Zumbrota, MN 55992,
(507) 732-5001 (during fair), www.mfcf.com
Held the first full week in August

Houston County Fair
1310 East Main Street, Caledonia, MN 55921, (507) 724-3397, www.mfcf.com
Held the second or third week in August

Mower County Fair
Mower County Fairgrounds,12th Street SW between 4th and 6th Avenues, Austin, MN 55912
(507) 433-1868, www.mfcf.com
Begins the first Tuesday in August

Steele County Fair
Steele County Fairgrounds,1525 South Cedar Avenue, Owatonna, MN 55060,
(507) 451-5305, www.scff.org or www.mfcf.com
Held during the week of August 17th. Call to confirm dates

Uff-Da Days
Ostrander, MN 55961, (507) 657-2465
First full weekend in August

Wilder Fest
Spring Valley, MN 55975, (507) 346-1015
Third weekend in August

Southeastern Minnesota Prairie Day
Minnesota Department of Natural Resources, 500 Lafayette Road, St. Paul, MN 55155-4040,
(651) 296-6157, 888-MINNDNR (646-6367), www.dnr.state.mn.us

The Minnesota DNR sponsors a statewide Prairie Day in order to promote the
preservation of Minnesota's prairie lands. The event typically includes educational presentations and excursions onto a prairie within southeastern Minnesota. Prairie Day is
usually scheduled in mid-August, although the location varies from year to year. Please
call the DNR for the date, time, and location of this event.

ROCHESTER
Annual Butterfly Count
Quarry Hill Nature Center,701 Silver Creek Road, Rochester, MN 55906, (507) 281-6114,
www.rochester.k12.mn.us/quarryhill or www.monarchwatch.org
Accessible from County Road 22, also called East Circle Drive.

Quarry Hill Nature Center and the Zumbro Valley Audubon Society sponsor an
Annual Butterfly Count in July or August. The count is open to any school-aged children and adults who are interested in butterflies. Participants assist nature center staff
with catching, identifying, tagging, counting, and releasing butterflies at Quarry Hill
Park and other sites in the Rochester area. No experience is necessary and a practice
count is usually held for prospective participants. Bring binoculars and a butterfly guidebook if you have them. Please call Quarry Hill Nature Center for more information.

Blues Fest
Central Park, 1st Avenue & 2nd Street NW, Rochester, MN
Downtown Business Association, P.O. Box 416, Rochester, MN 55903, (507) 287-3577,
(507) 285-8233

Blues Fest, an annual event sponsored by the Downtown Business Association of Rochester, takes place in Central Park on the second Saturday in August. Live bands perform an afternoon and evening of blues music for the community. Free admission. Concessions are available. Please double-check the Rochester Post-Bulletin for the date and time of this event.

Days of Yesteryear
Olmsted County Historical Society, 1195 Circle Drive SW, Rochester, MN 55902, (507) 282-9447, www.olmstedhistory.com

Experience the Days of Yesteryear at the Olmsted County History Center. This annual event has been held for more than 25 years and provides visitors with an authentic depiction of life in the late 19th and early 20th centuries. Demonstrations include the operation of a steam-powered sawmill, shelling and grinding corn, blacksmithing, butter churning, tatting, quilting, rug hooking, woodcarving, chair caning, rope making, spinning, basketweaving and more. Visitors also have the opportunity to visit a one-room school house, view farming displays and an antique tractor pull, watch an old-time baseball game, enjoy musical entertainment, and attend a Sunday worship service. Food vendors are available on the grounds. Call the Olmsted County Historical Society for more information. Small admission fee.

Olmsted County Gold Rush Days
Olmsted County Fairgrounds, 16th Street and 3rd Avenue SE, Rochester, MN 55904, (507) 285-8231

Olmsted County Gold Rush Days, an annual antique show and flea market, draws thousands of people to the Rochester area in a search of special treasures and collectibles. Collectors flock to Gold Rush Days to peruse the wares of more than 1,000 vendors who sell everything from antique furniture, toys, vintage jewelry, books, paintings, china and whatever else you can imagine. This event is held at the Olmsted County Fairgrounds in mid-August. Free admission.

Greek Festival
Saints Anargyroi Greek Orthodox Church, 703 West Center Street, Rochester, MN 55901, (507) 282-1529, 800-634-8277

Experience the warmth of the Greek community at the Annual Greek Festival, a two-day event that has been sponsored by the Saints Anargyroi Greek Orthodox Church of Rochester for 40 years. The well-attended festival provides an authentic taste of Greek culture for the people of southeastern Minnesota with Greek music, dancing, and food. The festival is held in late August. Please call the church for more information or check the Rochester Post-Bulletin for dates, times, and location of the festival. Free admission.

National Night Out
Rochester Law Enforcement Center, Crime Prevention Unit, 101 4th Street SE, Rochester, MN 55904, (507) 281-6056
Rochester Neighborhood Resource Center, 700 4th Avenue SE, Hawthorne Education Center, Room 301, Rochester, MN 55904, (507) 529-4150, www.rneighbors.org

National Night Out, an annual crime prevention event held in nearly 9,000 communities nationwide for more than 18 years, takes place in Rochester on the first Tuesday in August. The event, sponsored by the Rochester Police Department's Crime Prevention Unit and the Rochester Neighborhood Association, is designed to strengthen neighborhoods and increase safety awareness by learning about drug and crime prevention. Neighborhood picnics and parties encourage residents to become better acquainted, and Rochester police, McGruff the crime dog and his nephew Scruff, firefighters, and city officials visit neighborhoods throughout the city. Please call the Crime Prevention Unit for more information or to register your neighborhood picnic.

Peace Lantern Ceremony

Rochester International Association, 300 11ᵗʰ Avenue NW, Rochester, MN 55901, (507) 289-5960, ext. 24
This event is held in Rochester's Silver Lake Park, Silver Lake Drive NE, Rochester, MN 55906, (507) 281-6160, www.ci.rochester.mn.us/park

The Rochester Peace Lantern Ceremony began in 1985 as a way to commemorate the atomic bombings on Hiroshima and Nagasaki, Japan in 1945 and offer prayers for future peace. Floating peace lanterns originated as a Buddhist tradition of remembrance for the deceased but continues to be used as a prayer ceremony in many countries. The annual Peace Lantern ceremony in Rochester, held in early August at Silver Lake Park, offers the community an opportunity to join together in unity and hope for a peaceful world. Please contact the Rochester International Association for more information.

Lifeguard Olympics

Southeastern Minnesota Chapter of the American Red Cross, 310 14ᵗʰ Street SE, Rochester, MN 55904, (507) 287-2200, semn.redcross.org

The Lifeguard Olympics is an annual event sponsored by the Southeastern Minnesota Chapter of the American Red Cross. Lifeguards from Olmsted, Dodge, and Fillmore Counties as well as other Red Cross Chapters compete in a series of fun events and simulated rescues. This event is usually held in July or August. Please contact the Red Cross to confirm the date, time, and location of this event. Free.

Rochester Roosters Old Time Baseball

Olmsted County History Center's Schmitt Field, 1195 West Circle Drive SW, Rochester, MN 55902, (507) 282-9447, www.olmstedhistory.com

The Rochester Roosters is a vintage baseball team that plays the game of American baseball as it originated in the mid-1800s. Players dress in period uniforms and compete with other vintage teams using replica balls and bats in a league that plays by 1860s rules. Games and tournaments are played periodically throughout the summer. Please contact the Olmsted County History Center or visit their website for a schedule. Admission fee: two bits (25 cents).

BERNE/WEST CONCORD

Berne Swiss Fest

West Concord (Berne), MN 55985, (507) 527-2622, 800-322-2478, (507) 356-4340, www.mantorville.com
Take Hwy. 14 west to the Mantorville exit, follow Hwy. 57 north about 7 miles to Berne/West Concord and follow signs to Swiss Fest.

Little Switzerland may be found just 30 miles from Rochester at the Berne Swiss Fest in rural West Concord. The Berne Swiss Fest, a celebration of the community's Swiss heritage, has been a tradition for more than 50 years. The festival grounds, located at Zwingli United Church of Christ, are transformed into a small Swiss village with an atmosphere reminiscent of the homeland. Authentic entertainment and activities include folk dancing, flag throwing, handbell choir concerts, Swiss Wrestling, a Swiss Costume Style Show, yodeling, Alphorn blowing, children's story-time, sack races, stone throwing and more. The festival also features guest artists from Switzerland, Swiss foods, demonstrations, and Swiss imports and products for sale. This event is held during the first weekend in August. Small admission fee.

CHATFIELD
Chatfield Western Days
Chatfield Tourist Information Center, Center of City Park, Chatfield, MN 55923, (507) 867-3966, (507) 867-3810, www.ci.chatfield.mn.us

Chatfield's Western Days, an annual festival in the "Chosen Valley," has been a community tradition for more than 35 years. The festival features a theatrical performance by local actors as well as concerts in the park, food vendors, a carnival, classic car show, sporting tournaments, a craft and flea market, grand parade, fireworks and more. More information may be obtained by calling the Chatfield Tourist Information Center.

HOUSTON
Money Creek Junction Bluegrass Festival
Cushon's Peak Campground, RR 1 Box 257A, 18696 State Hwy. 16, Houston, MN 55943, (507) 896-7325, e-mail: camppeak@acegroup.cc
Located 2 miles west of Houston off Hwy. 16.

Cushon's Peak Campground, situated on 180 acres of farmland and woods between the towns of Houston and Rushford, is the site of the Money Creek Junction Bluegrass Festival. Families are welcome at this weekend event, which is held in mid–May and mid–August. The festival includes performances by bluegrass bands, workshops for young musicians or others interested in learning about bluegrass instruments and music, and open mike sessions. Camping is available at the campground, and the Root River State Trail runs adjacent to the campground. Please see Chapter 12, Campgrounds, for detailed information about Cushon's Peak Campground. Day and weekend passes are available for the festival.

ORONOCO
Oronoco Gold Rush Days
P.O. Box 266, Oronoco, MN 55960, (507) 367-4405, www.mn-community.org/oronoco

Oronoco Gold Rush Days is another huge antique show and flea market held in mid–August, usually the same weekend as the Olmsted County Gold Rush Days. The small town of Oronoco, just 12 miles north of Rochester, hosts over 1,000 vendors at this event. Thousands of antique collectors and bargain hunters from around the region gather in Oronoco to look through the treasure trove of goods that are for sale. This event takes place throughout Oronoco. Please contact the city office for more information. Free admission.

PRESTON
Evening of Leisure
Historic Forestville, Forestville State Park, Preston, MN 55965, (507) 765-2785, (507) 352-5111, www.mnhs.org
Located 4 miles south of State Hwy. 16 on Fillmore County Road 5, then 2 miles east on Fillmore County Road 118.

Historic Forestville, a turn of the century historic village located in Forestville State Park, hosts an old-fashioned "Evening of Leisure" on a Saturday evening in late July and late August. Guides in period costumes welcome visitors to participate in music, storytelling, and games reminiscent of the late 19th century such as horse-shoes, croquet, checkers and euchre. Refreshments are served. Please call Historic Forestville for specific dates and times of this event. Admission fee.

Chapter 11: Seasonal Events: Fall

Autumn in Historic Bluff Country

Autumn in southeastern Minnesota's bluff country is a magical time of year. The rolling hills, valleys, and waterways are transformed into a majestic landscape with a medley of vibrant fall colors that rival New England's panorama during this time of year. Of course, Minnesota tradition is to celebrate this majestic beauty with lots of fall festivals. The abundance of small town festivals in southeastern Minnesota during the fall season offers something for just about everyone. In fact, the towns of Caledonia, Chatfield, Harmony, Houston, Lanesboro, Spring Grove, and Wykoff are just some of the locales that host festivals. A complete calendar of fall festivals and events in southeastern Minnesota as well as a brochure with several self-guided driving tours may be obtained by contacting Southeastern Minnesota Historic Bluff Country, P.O. Box 609, 15 2nd Street NW, Harmony, MN 55939, (507) 886-2230, 800-428-2030, www.bluffcountry.com

September

Small Town Festivals in September and October

Small towns in southeastern Minnesota typically celebrate fall with a community festival. Events commonly held at these festivals include parades, food vendors, local pageants, sports tournaments, family fun nights, dances, pancake breakfasts, arts and crafts shows, carnival games, local tours, concerts and more. Please call for specific dates and a schedule of events.

Apple Fest
La Crescent, MN 55947, (507) 895-2800, www.lacrescent.com
Held the third weekend in September

Johnny Appleseed Days
Lake City, MN 55041, (651) 345-4123, 800-369-4123, www.lakecity.org or www.lakecitymn.org
Held the first weekend in October

Marigold Days
Mantorville, MN 55955, (507) 635-5464, www.mantorville.com
Held the weekend after Labor Day

Watermelon Days
Kellogg, MN 55945, (507) 767-4953, www.mississippi-river.org
First weekend after Labor Day

ROCHESTER
All-Breed Dog Show
Rochester Kennel Club, P.O. Box 5803, Rochester, MN 55903, rmkc.8m.com
Olmsted County Fairgrounds, 16th Street and 3rd Avenue SE, Rochester, MN 55904, (507) 285-8231

The Rochester Kennel Club sponsors an Annual All-Breed Dog Show at the Olmsted County Fairgrounds in mid-September. A diverse variety of dog breeds are represented at the show, which typically expects the presentation of about 1,000 dogs. Small admission fee.

Golden Generation Show
Mayo Civic Center, 30 Civic Center Drive SE, Rochester, MN 55904, (507) 287-2222
Rochester Post-Bulletin, 18 1st Avenue SE, Rochester, MN 55904, (507) 285-7600

The Golden Generation Show, an award winning trade show for people over 50 and their families, is sponsored by the Rochester Post-Bulletin in conjunction with the Rochester Senior Center, Rochester Community Education, and Mayo Civic Center. The show offers seniors a variety of educational seminars, more than 100 exhibits, entertainment and prizes. This event is held in mid-September. Please call the Rochester Post-Bulletin for the date, time, and location or check the newspaper. Small admission fee.

Olmsted County Gold Rush Days
Olmsted County Fairgrounds,16th Street and 3rd Avenue SE, Rochester, MN 55904, (507) 285-8231

Olmsted County Gold Rush Days, an annual antique show and flea market, draws thousands of people to the Rochester area in a search of special treasures and collectibles. Collectors flock to Gold Rush Days to peruse the wares of more than 1,000 vendors who sell everything from antique furniture, toys, vintage jewelry, books, paintings, china and whatever else you can imagine. This event is held at the Olmsted County Fairgrounds in late September. Free admission.

Quarry Hill Nature Center Fall Harvest Festival
Quarry Hill Park and Nature Center, 701 Silver Creek Road, Rochester, MN 55906, (507) 281-6114, www.rochester.k12.mn.us/quarryhill or e-mail: grmunson@rochester.k12.mn.us
Accessible from County Road 22, also called East Circle Drive.

The Annual Fall Harvest Festival, a family event at Quarry Hill Nature Center, offers an incredible selection of nature-related activities for kids of all ages. Children and adults may explore the wonder of nature in a carnival-like atmosphere that features cave tours, rock climbing, and canoeing as well as nature-related arts and crafts such as pumpkin painting, candle rolling, sand painting, raptor bracelets, plaster animal tracks, cookie decorating and more. A fun and exciting day awaits those who attend the Fall Harvest Festival, which is held during a weekend in mid-September. Concessions are available at the festival. Activity and food tickets may be purchased on site. Please call Quarry Hill Nature Center for more information.

BYRON
Great Southern Grass Drag Nationals & Swap Meet
Byron Sno-Bears, P.O. Box 743, Byron, MN 55920, (507) 775-2497

The Great Southern Grass Drag Nationals and Swap Meet, an annual event hosted by the Byron Sno-Bears, provides snowmobile enthusiasts with the opportunity to race their sleds before the snow flies. The Swap Meet features antique displays as well as exhibits and information by snowmobile dealers, area snowmobile clubs, parts suppliers and more. The event is held on the fourth Sunday in September and the race grounds are located about one mile north of Douglas, just off County Road 3. Douglas is a small town located five miles northwest of Rochester. Food and beverages are available on the grounds. Please contact the Byron Sno-Bears for more information.

HARMONY
Root River Trail Wagon Ride
Southeastern Minnesota Historic Bluff Country, P.O. Box 609, 15 2nd Street NW, Harmony, MN 55939, (507) 886-2230, 800-428-2030, www.bluffcountry.com

The Root River Trail Ride is an annual event that provides seniors and handi-capped individuals with the opportunity to take a wagon ride along the Root River Trail. Morning and afternoon departures as well as long and short rides are available. This event is held in early September. Please contact Historic Bluff Country for the date, times, and location of the ride. Please note that reservations must be made with Historic Bluff Country to participate in this event. Free.

LAKE CITY
Wild Wings Fall Festival
Wild Wings Gallery, 2101 South U.S. Hwy. 61, Box 100, Lake City, MN 55041, (651) 345-5355, 800-248-7312, www.wildwings.com

The Wild Wings Gallery of Lake City, known among collectors for its display and sales of quality paintings, prints, sculptures, and wood carvings of nature and wildlife "themed" art by renowned artists, has been hosting a Fall Festival for more than 30 years. Thousands of people from throughout the United States come to the annual festival, which was awarded the "Best Outdoor Show" by U.S. Art magazine in 1999. Festival activities include an original art show and sale, well-known artists on location, kids' activities, wildlife and nature demonstrations, musical entertainment and more. This weekend event takes place in mid-September. Please call Wild Wings for more information. Free admission.

LANESBORO
Fall Weekend Getaway at Eagle Bluff
Environmental Learning Center
Route 2, Box 156A, 1991 Brightsdale Road, Lanesboro, MN 55949, (507) 467-2437, 888-800-9558, www.eagle-bluff.org or e-mail: hello@eagle-bluff.org

Eagle Bluff Environmental Learning Center's Fall Weekend Getaway is a great way for families and friends to enjoy an outdoor experience during the beautiful season of autumn. Singles, couples, and families are welcome to register for the entire weekend including an overnight stay or may choose to participate in one or more activities as a day guest. A typical weekend itinerary includes some type of outdoor recreation such as hiking, archery, the tree tops high ropes course in addition to a banquet and musical entertainment. Please contact Eagle Bluff for dates, cost, pro-gram information, and registration materials.

MABEL
Hesper-Mabel Steam Engine Days
Steam Engine Park, Mabel, MN 55954, (507) 493-5350

Hesper-Mabel Steam Engine Days is an annual event held in Mabel, "Rural America's Steam Engine Capital. The event, held the weekend following Labor Day, is located in Mabel's Steam Engine Park, which is adjacent to the Mabel Steam Engine Museum. The celebration features steam engine displays and demonstrations of their use in threshing and sawing wood, a steam engine parade, arts and crafts show, carnival, and stage shows. Please call the museum for more information. Admission fee.

October

ROCHESTER
Fall Festival at Sunrise Cottages
4220 55th Street NW, Rochester, MN 55901, (507) 286-8528

Sunrise Cottages, an assisted living center in northwest Rochester, holds an annual Fall Festival on the last Saturday in October. Families with young children are welcome to participate in free activities such as pumpkin painting, face painting, a costume parade and trick or treating with the residents. Please contact Activity Coordinator at Sunrise Cottages for more information.

Fire Prevention Week
Rochester Fire Station #1, 530 South Broadway; Rochester Fire Station #2, 702 Silver Lake Drive NE; Rochester Fire Station #3, 2755 2nd Street SW; Rochester Fire Station #4, 1875 41st Street NW

The Rochester Fire Department observes National Fire Prevention Week in early October with open houses at its four fire stations. Tours, equipment demonstrations, and fire safety information are provided for the public, and Sparky the fire dog is usually present at one of the stations. In addition to this, Sparky's Fire Safety House, a small trailer, is on site at one the stations and gives kids the opportunity to practice a simulated fire escape. Please check the Rochester Post-Bulletin for dates and times or call (507) 285-8963 for more information.

Halloween at Charter House
211 2nd Street NW, Rochester, MN 55901, (507) 266-8572

Charter House, a retirement living center in downtown Rochester, welcomes trick or treaters to visit on Halloween. Trick or treaters have their photo taken with the Charter House Queen of Pumpkins and receive a bag of treats. Please call Charter House to confirm the time of this event.

KROC Women's Fall Expo
Mayo Civic Center, 30 Civic Center Drive SE, Rochester, MN 55904, (507) 287-2222, www.mayociviccenter.com
KROC Radio, 122 4th Street SW, Rochester, MN 55902, (507) 286-1010, www.kroc.com

The KROC Women's Fall Expo has become an annual Rochester event. Held at the Mayo Civic Center, the day-long expo features musical entertainment, special guests, exhibitors, shopping and prize drawings of special interest for today's woman. Concessions are available. Free admission.

Mayo Clinic Community Safety Fair
Sponsored by Mayo Clinic Department of Emergency Medicine and Mayo Eugenio Litta Children's Hospital and the Department of Pediatrics, (507) 255-5066, (507) 284-2511
This event is usually held at Mayo Civic Center, 30 Civic Center Drive SE, Rochester, MN 55904, (507) 287-2222, www.mayociviccenter.com

This family event provides an interactive learning experience for children and their parents. Activities include practicing school bus safety on real school buses and fire escape plans in Sparky's Fire Safety House, role playing 911 calls with dispatchers, and learning about bike helmets, water safety, first aid, poisons, gun safety and more. Children may also explore an on-site ambulance, fire truck, and police car. Child car seat safety inspections and free safety information are available for parents. The date, time, and location of this event may be found in the Rochester Post-Bulletin or by calling the number listed above. Free admission.

Ski Swap

Olmsted County Fairgrounds, 4-H Building, 16th Street and 3rd Avenue SE, Rochester, MN 55904, (507) 285-8231
Coffee Mill Ski Area, Box 127, Hwys. 60 & 61, Wabasha, MN 55981, (651) 565-2777, www.coffeemillski.com
Mount Frontenac Ski Area, Box 180, Hwy. 61 North, Frontenac, MN 55026, (651) 388-5826, 800-488-5826, www.mountfrontenac.com

Avid skiers and snowboarders flock to the Annual Ski Swap sponsored by the Mt. Frontenac, Coffee Mill, and Hiawatha Nordic Ski Patrols. Ski and snowboard equipment and clothing may be checked-in on the morning of the swap. Patrons are welcome to browse and buy from noon to 8 p.m., and unsold items and/or checks may be picked up the following day.

BYRON

Halloween Festival and Party at Oxbow Park

Oxbow Park, Byron, MN 55920, (507) 775-2451

Oxbow Park offers alternative to trick-or-treating with an annual Halloween program for children ages 4 to 10. Children may wear their costumes at this nonthreatening event, which usually involves a short hike, Halloween treats, and learning about the animals associated with Halloween. Refreshments are provided. This event is held rain or shine, and preregistration is required. Free, but donations welcome.

Tweite's Pumpkin Patch

1821 Frontier Road SW, Byron, MN 55920, (507) 634-4848, www.tweite.com

The magic of Fall comes alive at Tweite's Pumpkinville and Gift Barn. Pumpkinville is an autumn wonderland that not only has short wagon rides to their U-pick pumpkin patch, but an assortment of wholesome outdoor activities for families. In addition to wagon rides, Pumpkinville has Storybook Land with scenes from popular Mother Goose rhymes, a Harvest Town play area with a huge sandbox and riding toys, a 16-foot tepee, a three tower castle, a small corn maze, and more. An entertainment schedule includes puppet and magic shows. Admission fee.

WELCH

Welch Village Fall Festival and Ski & Snowboard Swap

Welch Village Ski Area, P.O. Box 146,County Road 7, Welch, MN 55089, (651) 258-4567, (651) 222-7079, www.welchvillage.com

Welch Village Ski Area hosts an annual Fall Festival and Ski and Snowboard Swap in early to mid-October. Shop for new and used ski and snowboard equipment and drop your equipment off for a pre-season tune-up while your browse a craft fair with decorative and utility products, clothing, seasonal food items and more. Enjoy a savory lunch at the barbecue pit and a slice of old-fashioned pie before you head home. Season ski passes will be available for purchase at this event. Please call for more information.

WINONA
Winona Polish Apple Day—Smaczne Jabika
Polish Museum, 102 Liberty Street and 363 East 2ⁿᵈ Avenue, Winona, MN 55987, (507) 454-3431

The Polish Museum of Winona celebrates Apple Day with a variety of children's activities such as folk dancing, Polish paper cutting, and storytelling as well as musical entertainment, genealogies, and a country store with baked goods, jellies and jams, crafts, books, and fresh-picked apples. Food and apple pie are also available. This event is held on a Saturday or Sunday in mid-October. Free admission.

ZUMBRO FALLS
Bluff Valley Lights
Bluff Valley Campground, Bluff Valley Road, RR 1, Box 194, Zumbro Falls, MN 55991, (507) 753-2955, 800-226-7282, www.bluffvalley.com or e-mail: camp@bluffvalley.com

Bluff Valley Campground offers a spectacular autumn light show and family entertainment from mid-October through late November. The "Brilliant Nights of Autumn Lights" is the first autumn drive-through light show in North America. The drive-through tour includes eleven "themed" areas, more than 410 light displays and over 155 light displays with sequential animation. In addition to this, families have the opportunity to purchase a night light wristband to participate in glow-in-the-dark activities such as A"Maze"N'Lites, the Night Light driving range, mini-golf, disc golf, and wagon tour. A dinner buffet and free live entertainment by area high school students is also available. For more information, call Bluff Valley Campground or check out their website. Price varies by activity.

November

ROCHESTER
Fantasy of Wreaths
Rochester Repertory Theater, 314½ South Broadway, Rochester, MN 55904, (507) 289-7800, www.rochesterrep.org or e-mail: BoxOffice@RochesterRep.org

A truly unique display of holiday wreaths may be seen at the Fantasy of Wreaths, sponsored by the Rochester Repertory Theater in mid-November. A creative assortment of wreaths is contributed to this silent auction by community members of all ages. Patrons are welcome to view the wreaths and/or bid on them during the event. Please call the Rep for dates, time, and location of this event.

Festival of Trees: A Celebration of Giving
Hiawatha Homes, 1530 Greenview Drive SW, Rochester, MN 55902, (507) 289-4040
This event is usually held at the Mayo Civic Center, 400 5ᵗʰ Avenue SW, Rochester, MN 55902 (507) 287-2222, www.mayociviccenter.org

The Annual Festival of Trees is sponsored by Hiawatha Homes of Rochester, a non-profit organization that provides residential services to people with developmental disabilities. The annual event, held during Thanksgiving week and weekend, is a great kick-off for the holiday season. The gallery of trees offers a spectacular display of traditionally decorated trees as well as some novel creations. Special events are held at the festival throughout the week and include different activities on Senior Citizen's Day, Thanksgiving Day, Children's Day, Family Day, an evening Dinner

Dance, and Gourmet Gospel Brunch. Please check the Rochester Post-Bulletin for the festival's schedule of events and location or call Hiawatha Homes for more information. Admission fee.

Golf Equipment Swap Meet

Rochester Indoor Golf Center, 2700 W. Country Club Road, Rochester, MN 55903, (507) 288-4851
Located 1 mile west of Saint Mary's Hospital.

The Rochester Indoor Golf Center hosts an annual Golf Equipment Swap Meet. This event, held the weekend following Thanksgiving, is a place where golfers may buy and sell new and used equipment. They also have the opportunity to try the equipment at the domed, indoor driving range before they buy it. Please contact the Rochester Indoor Golf Center for more information.

Mayowood Mansion Holiday Tours

Olmsted County History Center, 1195 West Circle Drive SW, Rochester, MN 55902, (507) 282-9447,
www.olmstedhistory.com
The Mayowood Mansion is located at 3720 Mayowood Road SW, Rochester, MN 55902.

Mayowood Mansion is a 23,000-square-foot, 48-room estate that was built in 1910–1911 by the Mayo brothers and served as the residence for three generations of the Mayo family. The historic estate, located in southwest Rochester, is now owned by the Olmsted Historical Society. The mansion is adorned with festive decorations during the Christmas season, which are contributed by area clubs and businesses, private collectors and neighborhood associations. Walk-through and guided holiday tours are available from early to mid-November. Please call the Olmsted County History Center for tour dates, times, reservations and ticket purchases.

The Rescue of Santa

Rochester Peace Plaza, 100 1st Avenue, Rochester, MN
Sponsored by the Downtown Business Association, P.O. Box 416, Rochester, MN 55903,
(507) 287-3577, (507) 285-8233

Santa is rescued from atop the 100 1st Avenue Building at the Peace Plaza. This event is held the Friday after Thanksgiving early in the evening. Additional activities include visits with Santa, lighting of the Peace Plaza's Christmas tree, singing Christmas carols, music by Trombones Anonymous, and carriage rides.

WABASHA

Eagle Watch at Riverfront

Wabasha, MN 55981, (651) 565-4989, www.eaglewatch.org or e-mail: 4eagles@wabasha.net

The Eagle Watch Observation Deck offers breathtaking views from the banks of the Mississippi and is a prime spot for eagle watching. If you're unable to locate the 500-square-foot deck by the grand 17-foot wooden eagle statue carved by Jim Smit of Nelson, Wisconsin, just look for the deck at the intersection of Pembroke Avenue and Lawrence Boulevard. Volunteers from the National Eagle Center staff the deck on Saturdays and Sundays from 1 p.m. to 3 p.m. (early November through March) to answer questions and assist with eagle spotting. Visitors may use spotting scopes and binoculars provided by the National Eagle Center. Please note that volunteers are available when weather conditions are 10°F or above, and there is no rain.

Part IV:
Outdoor Activities

Chapter 12: Campgrounds provides detailed information on campgrounds in the southeastern Minnesota area ranging from primitive sites to facilities with a large selection of recreational amenities and full RV hook-ups

Chapter 13: Horseback Riding, Hay & Sleigh Rides presents a guide to horseback riding and hay & sleigh rides in the area.

Chapter 14: Nature Centers contains information about facilities that offer basic educational displays to those with naturalist-led programs and activities.

Chapter 15: Farmers' Markets, Gardening, Orchards, Berry Picking & Christmas Tree Farms provides information on where to rent a garden plot, find a farmer's market, pick your own berries, or cut your own Christmas tree.

Chapter 16: Parks guides the reader to small town parks and playgrounds as well as Minnesota State Parks in the region.

Chapter 17: Zoos & Wildlife provides information about places to experience farm animals and wildlife such as small public and private petting zoos, llama farms, fish hatcheries, buffalo ranches, and eagle centers.

Chapter 12: Campgrounds

State Park Campgrounds

Campground facilities at Minnesota State Parks vary from park to park. To obtain information about campgrounds within southeastern Minnesota State Parks, please contact the parks directly or the DNR at 800-246-CAMP (2267). Additional contact information may be found in Chapter 16.

ROCHESTER

Autumn Woods RV Park

1067 Autumn Woods Circle SE, Rochester, MN 55904, (507) 289-1123
From Hwy. 63 South, take the airport exit, turn right, drive 50 feet and turn right onto 11th Avenue SW. Autumn Woods is ½ mile down the road.

Autumn Woods RV Park is a year-round campground that is located just one mile from the Rochester International Airport, yet offers a country setting within the city. The new campground opened in August 2001 and has 30 open and shaded sites with full hook-ups, phone access, and picnic tables. On-site amenities include a secure, fenced-in location, handicapped-accessible bathrooms with showers and flush toilets, coin-operated laundry, a pay phone, central modem hook-up, and area transportation via local shuttles. A camp store will be available in the future. Pets allowed. No tent camping permitted or on-site recreational facilities. Reservations requested, but walk-ins welcome.

Cost: $$$
Season: open year-round

Rochester/Marion KOA Kampgrounds

5232 65th Avenue SE, Rochester, MN 55904, (507) 288-0785, 800-562-5232

This KOA is located on the outskirts of Rochester in Marion Township near the junction of I-90 and Hwy. 52 South. The campground is situated in an open, rural area with 79 grassy, level sites and two cabins for rent. Amenities include 58 shaded and open campsites with water and electric hook-ups, flush toilets, hot showers, coin-operated laundry, a dump station, access to a phone and modem, and camp store with wood, ice, and groceries. In addition to having a playground, pool, and recreation room on the premises, the campground is in close proximity to southeastern Minnesota's Historic Bluff Country, which has numerous opportunities for biking, canoeing, hiking, fishing, and scenic drives. Reservations requested.

Cost: $$–$$$
Season: mid-March–October

Silver Lake RV Park

1409 North Broadway, Rochester, MN 55906, (507) 289-6412

Silver Lake RV Park in northeast Rochester is a metro campground that is adjacent to Silver Lake Park with easy access to both the Zumbro River and Rochester's Bike Trail System. The 15-acre fenced-in facility is handicapped accessible and has 58 shaded sites with picnic tables and full hook-ups including cable TV. A limited number of sites have telephone hook-ups. On-site services include flush toilets, hot showers, coin-operated laundry, phone and modem access, cable TV hook-ups, and public transportation to Mayo Medical Center and local hospitals. A grocery store and gas station are within walking distance of the campground. Pets allowed. No tents. Reservations requested, but walk-ins are welcome.

Cost: $$–$$$
Season: April–November

Willow Creek Campground
5525 Hwy. 63 South, Rochester, MN 55904, (507) 282-1414, (507) 285-5955

Willow Creek Campground, formerly Van's Campground, is a no-frills facility that has 38 shaded sites with water and electric hook-ups, firepits, and picnic tables. The campground is just a few miles from the Rochester International Airport, and is susceptible to highway noise due to its location off Hwy. 63 South. Showers and flush toilets are available. No laundry facilities or phone on the premises. New owners plan to develop both basic services and recreational activities at the campground. Please call for updated information. Camping is by reservation or on a first come, first served basis.

Cost: $$–$$$
Season: April–December

ALTURA
Lazy D Campground & Trail Rides
RR 1, Box 252, Altura, MN 55910, (507) 932-3098, www.lazyd-camping-trailrides.com
8 miles north of Saint Charles at the junction of Hwy. 74 and County Road 39

Lazy D is a family campground just a few miles from southeastern Minnesota's popular Whitewater State Park. The Whitewater River, a premier trout stream in southeastern Minnesota, runs through the center of the campground; and many of the campsites are on the banks of the river. The large, grassy, and shaded campsites at Lazy D can accommodate tents, RVs, pop-ups and 5th wheel campers. Fifty-five of the 80 sites have electric and water. There is also a cabin (sleeps 5 people) available for rent, which is located in a secluded, wooded area of the campground. Other amenities at Lazy D include remodeled rest rooms with coin-operated showers, a camp store with limited groceries, ice, wood, and camping supplies, a pay phone, and dump station. A playground, heated pool, indoor game room, volleyball, tether ball, basketball, horseshoes, trail rides, hayrides, covered wagon rides, inner tubing, fishing, and an on-site antique carriage museum are the recreational activities available at Lazy D. Hiking trails and a swimming beach are nearby at Whitewater State Park. Pets on leashes are allowed. Reservations requested, but walk-ins welcome.

Cost: $$
Season: April–November

BYRON
Oxbow Park
Oxbow Park, 5731 County Road 105 NW (@ Olmsted 4 & 5 intersection), Byron, MN 55920, (507) 775-2451, www.olmstedpublicworks.com or e-mail: oxbow@venturecs.net

Oxbow Park is located in the scenic Zumbro River Valley. The 572-acre park has 29 semi-primitive campsites with running water, rest rooms, showers, and a playground, but no electric or water hookups. A group campsite with vault toilets and water is also available for overnight or day use by youth groups. In addition to camping, Oxbow has almost eight miles of maintained hiking trails, four picnic areas with covered shelters including one with a playground and ball field, a nature center, an outdoor zoo with 30 species of native Minnesota animals, and access to the banks of the Zumbro River that wind through the park. The Oxbow Nature Center has a small exhibit of regional snakes and animal artifacts and is the home base for the park's interpretive programs, which are usually held on Saturday mornings and afternoons. If you are planning a camping trip to Oxbow, you may want to call ahead to check the Nature Center's weekly program topic and schedule. Chapters 14 and 17 respectively provide more detailed information about Oxbow's Nature Center and Oxbow's Zollman Zoo. Please note that campsites, picnic areas, and shelters are available on a first come, first served basis; however, youth groups and organizations may reserve Oxbow's group campsite.

Cost: $
Season: May–October

CALEDONIA
Camp Winnebago
19708 Camp Winnebago Road, Caledonia, MN 55921, (507) 724-2351

Although Camp Winnebago primarily serves individuals with developmental disabilities, the lower section of the camp has been developed into a small public campground. The campground offers 20 open and shady sites, ten with water and electric, four with electric only, and six primitive sites. Facilities include picnic tables and fire rings at each campsite, a dump station, and enclosed portable toilets. No showers or modern rest rooms are available. Campers have access to three picnic shelters with electric (reservations required for shelters), firewood, and a pay phone at the main camp. On-site recreational opportunities include fishing, creek splashing, and several miles of hiking trails. Pets are permitted. Reservations requested, but walk-ins welcome on first come, first served basis.

Cost: $–$$
Season: May–October

Dunromin' Park Campground
Route 1, Box 146, Caledonia, MN 55921, (507) 724-2514, 800-822-2514, dunromin@means.net
Located 4½ miles south of Caledonia on Hwy. 76.

Wow! Look no further than Dunromin' Park Campground for a camping experience with all the amenities for family fun. The 148-acre campground is situated in a beautiful, rural area of southeastern Minnesota. Dunromin's 106 campsites are large, grassy, and partly shaded with some located on a terraced hillside or near a creek. All campsites have fire rings and picnic tables, and water and electric hook-ups are available at 86 of the sites. On-site rest rooms have hot showers with private dressing rooms and flush toilets. Recreational facilities and activities are plentiful at Dunromin' and include a large heated pool with lights, a wading pool, an 18-hole miniature golf course, a large shelter, youth center with video games, pool table and jukebox, a modern playground, basketball courts, tetherball, a sand volleyball court, horseshoe pits, ball fields, and shuffleboard. Nature lover's will enjoy on-site hiking trails, berry picking, bird watching, and fishing. Organized activities have included euchre tournaments, scavenger hunts, kids' tractor pulls, horseshoe and volleyball tournaments, hayrides, fireworks, bonfires, sing-alongs, skits, square dances, carnivals, "themed" weekend events, arts and crafts, and bingo. Additional services at the campground are gated security, pop-up camper and tipi rentals, funcycle rentals, dump station, propane gas exchange, coin-operated laundry, snack bar, and a complete store with groceries, firewood, ice, camping supplies, and gifts. Pets allowed. Reservations requested.

Cost: $$–$$$
Season: May–October

CANNON FALLS
Cannon Falls Campground
30365 Oak Lane, Cannon Falls, MN 55009, (507) 263-3145, 888-821-2267, www.cannonfallscampground.com
From Hwy. 52, take Hwy. 19 east for 2½ miles to Oak Lane.

Cannon Falls Campground is conveniently located midway between Rochester and the Twin Cities. The 150-site campground is set in a rural area with both open and shaded sites. All sites have electricity and water, and hook-ups with sewer are also available. Campground facilities include picnic tables, fire rings, flush toilets, hot showers with private dressing areas, a dump station, pay phone, coin-operated laundry, LP gas tank refills, and an air-conditioned store and lounge with RV supplies, ice, wood, and basic groceries. Recreational opportunities are abundant at the campground as well as in the regional area. The campground boasts a heated pool, playground, large recreation hall, volleyball, basketball, video arcade, horseshoe pits, softball field, hiking trails, and "themed" weekends with organized activities throughout the summer. Campers have easy access to the Cannon Valley Bike Trail, tubing and canoeing on the Cannon River, and the historic towns of Red Wing and Northfield. Treasure Island Casino and the Mall of America are just a short drive from the campground. Pets are permitted. Reservations requested.

Cost: $$–$$$
Season: May–mid-October

EYOTA
Chester Woods Park
8378 Hwy. 14 East, Eyota, MN 55934, (507) 285-7050, www.olmstedpublicworks.com, e-mail: chesterw@venturecs.net

Chester Woods is an Olmsted County Park located just 7 miles east of Rochester. The campground at Chester Woods has 52 sites that loop through a quiet, wooded area of the park. Campground amenities include 37 campsites with electric hook-ups, picnic tables, fire rings, centrally located rest rooms with flush toilets and hot showers, two handicapped-accessible campsites, several water spigots, a pay phone, dump station, and firewood for sale. Recreational facilities within the park and adjacent to the campground are two playgrounds (one handicapped accessible), several informal playing fields, a swimming beach at the 118-acre Chester Lake, seven separate picnic areas with covered shelters, 6 miles of hiking trails, equestrian trails, a boat launch (electric motors only), canoe and paddleboat rentals, and a fishing pier. Nature programs and hikes are occasionally presented by park naturalists during summer weekends. Pets are allowed. Group camping is not permitted. Reservations are required and must be received a minimum of five days prior to the reservation date. Reservations by mail guarantee a campsite, but specific sites may only be reserved in person. Advance payment in full is required to secure a campground reservation. In addition to campground reservations, a daily or annual entrance permit must be purchased for admittance to the park.

Cost: $–$$
Season: mid-May–mid-October

HARMONY
Amish Country Camping
RR 2, Box 41B, Harmony, MN 55939, (507) 886-6731, www.bluffcountry.com/austins.htm or e-mail: mohair@means.net

Amish Country Camping is located in rural southeastern Minnesota on Austin's Angora Goat Farm in the heart of Amish country. The farm has four primitive campsites with a fire rings, picnic tables, and a portable potty. RVs are welcome. At Amish Country Camping you will experience the sights, sounds, and scents of country living. An Amish neighbor will bring firewood for campers. Call for reservations. Please see Chapter 17 for more information on Austin's Angora Goat Farm.

Cost: $
Season: open year-round

Harmony Municipal Campground
Campground located at junction of 4th Street NE and 2nd Avenue NE near North Park
For camping information, contact the Harmony Visitor's Center, 45 Center Street East, P.O. Box 141, Harmony, MN 55939, (507) 886-2469,www.harmony.mn.us

The city of Harmony has a small, clean campground with shaded areas and picnic tables. The quiet campground is off the beaten path, but only a few miles from the Harmony-Preston Valley State Trail. There are six sites with water and electric, and numerous primitive sites. Rest rooms with toilets and sinks are available at North Park across the street. Public showers are available for rent at Slim's Woodshed and Bunkhouse (160 1st Street NW, Harmony, (507) 886-3114). North Park also has a golf course, tennis courts, a baseball field, basketball courts, a playground, and picnic shelter. Campsites may be used on a first come, first served basis.

Cost: $
Season: April–November

HOUSTON
Cushon's Peak Campground
RR 1, Box 257A, 18696 State Hwy. 16, Houston, MN (507) 896-7325, e-mail: camppeak@acegroup.cc
Located 2 miles west of Houston off Hwy. 16

Cushon's Peak is the backdrop for this campground that is a little piece of heaven on earth. Cushon's Peak Campground is situated on 180 acres of farmland and woods between the towns of Houston and Rushford. Judy and Tom Vix warmly welcome campers to their campground, which has 44 triple big campsites with electric and water hook-ups as well as primitive sites for single tent campers or large groups. Campground amenities include a bathhouse with heated showers and flush toilets, fire rings, picnic tables, a dump station, and portable toilets in the primitive

area. The Root River Bike Trail, which runs through the campground, is an especially attractive feature of Cushon's Peak in addition to the five miles of hiking and
walking trails, playground, two miles of riverfront on the Root River, canoe and
tube launch, fishing pond, Lloyd's Landing—a sandbar for swimming in the Root
River—frequent wildlife sightings, and a huge 104-by-48-foot recreation building
with a basketball hoop, pool table, Ping-Pong, arcade games, and on-site tube
rentals. Cushon's Peak also hosts the annual Money Creek Bluegrass Festival, which
is a weekend event held in May and August. The development of a children's play
area, miniature golf course, horseshoe pits, and a small store are also underway. Pets
are permitted. Reservations requested.

Cost: $–$$
Season: June–August; weekends in May, September, and October

Houston Municipal Campground at South Park
South Park, Houston, MN
From Hwy. 16 in Houston, follow South Grant Street until you see the South Park entrance. Contact
the Houston City Clerk, 105 West Maple Street, Houston, MN 55943, (507) 896-3234

Primitive camping is available at Houston's South Park. The park offers a rustic setting atop a high bluff overlooking the city. No water access. Pit toilets. Campers
have access to public rest rooms with flush toilets and showers at Trailhead Park
(215 West Plum Street) in Houston. Camping is available on a first come, first served
basis, but the city of Houston requests that campers check-in with the City Clerk.

Cost: $
Season: open year-round

Money Creek Haven
Route 1, Box 154, 18502 County Road 26, Houston, MN 55943, (507) 896-3544

Money Creek Haven is a huge, full-service campground for RVs and tents.
Approximately 195 open, shaded, and grassy campsites with picnic tables and fire
rings are available. There are 44 sites with full hook-ups, 140 sites with water and
electric, and 11 primitive sites. Campground services include a large picnic shelter,
coin-operated laundry, flush and nonflush toilets, hot showers, a pay phone, dump
station, and a convenience store with a limited supply of groceries, ice, and firewood
for sale. An on-site restaurant is open seven days per week and serves breakfast,
lunch, dinner, and a Friday fish fry. A unique feature of Money Creek Campground
is the huge spring-fed swimming pool with patio area. Horseshoe pits, volleyball
courts, basketball, hiking trails, a playground, fishing pond, and recreation room with
video games and pool tables round out the selection of on-site recreational activities. Money Creek is also a popular campground with hunting, fishing, and biking
enthusiasts. The Root River Bike Trail is only about 6 miles from the campground.
A large dining room in the restaurant and the outdoor picnic shelter may be
reserved by groups for special events. The Haven Inn, a lodge with 8 clean, quiet
rooms is also located on the premises. Pets are permitted. Reservations requested,
but walk-ins are welcome.

Cost: $$
Season: mid-April–October

LAKE CITY

Camp Lacupolis Campground

RR 4 CL 1, Lake City, MN 55041, (651) 565-4318, (507) 324-5216 (winter), www.camplacupolis.com
or e-mail: bea@camplacupolis.com or lacupolis@clear.lakes.com
Located 9 miles south of Lake City on Hwy. 61

Camp Lacupolis is a fishing village that has been located on the lower banks of the
Mississippi River's Lake Pepin since the 1860s. Accommodations at the camp vary
from rustic fishing cabins with mini-kitchens, bathrooms, air conditioning and grills
to modern, year-round cabins that have two or three bedrooms. Additional accommodations include four rooms at Camp Lacupolis's modern lodge or an on-site,
lakeside campground (with water and electric hook-ups) for those who prefer the
RV lifestyle. Regardless of what accommodations you choose, you will enjoy the
breathtaking views of Lake Pepin from the Camp's lakeside deck. The fishing village
provides the following services: boat launching, dockside gas and oil, bait and tackle
supplies, fish cleaning facilities and freezer space for your catch of the day, fishing
boat and motor rentals, a 60 slip protected harbor for docking boats, and a coffee
shop with snacks. Camp Lacupolis will also assist guests with obtaining fishing maps
or arranging appointments with private fishing guides. Small pets are allowed in the
fishing cabins. Please note that the lodge and modern cabins may be rented
throughout the year. Call for reservations.

Cost: $$–$$$$$
Season: mid-May–October

Hok-Si-La Park and Campground

Hwy. 61 North, Lake City, MN 55041, (651) 345-3855, www.lakecitygov.com
Located 2 miles north of Lake City on Hwy. 61/63

Welcome to southeastern Minnesota's Shangri-La. Hok-Si-La is a tents-only, primi-
tive campground situated on the banks of Lake Pepin. It is a quiet, peaceful retreat
for campers because vehicles are only permitted in the campground for unloading
and loading camping gear and then must remain in the parking lot. The 30-plus
campsites are located in shaded, wooded areas of the park and many have views of
Lake Pepin. Group camping is permitted in a designated area. A few water spigots
are scattered throughout the campground, and campers have access to a centrally
located bathhouse with flush toilets and modern showers. Additional campground
and park amenities include picnic tables, fire rings, outhouses, an adjacent boat
launch, a wide sandy swimming beach (no lifeguard), nature and hiking trails, vol-
leyball courts, playground equipment, and an on-site camp store connected to a
small interpretive center with animal displays. The store sells a limited number of
groceries, camping supplies, coffee, candy, ice, and firewood. Hok-Si-La also has
three screened-in shelters and a modern Dining Hall with a kitchen and cooler
available for rent. Pets are permitted. Reservations requested, but walk-ins welcome.

Cost: campsites: $–$$$; shelters and dining hall: $$–$$$$
Season: May–October

Lake Pepin Campground & Trailer Court

1818 North High Street, Lake City, MN 55041, summer (651) 345-2909, winter (651) 345-2749

This Lake City campground offers views of Lake Pepin from most of its 156 open,
level sites. All sites have picnic tables and fire rings, but electric hook-ups are only

available at 40 of the sites. Due its location on Highway 61, Lake Pepin Campground lacks a private atmosphere, but is in close proximity to area attractions. Lake Pepin and Waterman's Restaurant are across the street, downtown Lake City is just one mile away, and campers will find easy access to outdoor activities such as boating, fishing, swimming, and eagle watching. Rest rooms with flush toilets and hot showers, a public phone, dump station, on-site playground, and small store with snacks, ice, and firewood are on the premises. Tents are permitted. Reservations requested, but walk-ins welcome.

Cost: $–$$
Season: mid-April–mid-October

LANESBORO

Eagle Cliff Campground and Lodge

Hwy. 16, Route 1, Box 344, Lanesboro, MN 55949, (507) 467-2598

Eagle Cliff is a secluded, country campground situated on the Root River, just 3 miles from Lanesboro. In addition to the campground, Eagle Cliff also has a modern lodge and on-site bicycle, canoe, tube, and kayak rentals that are open to the public. The 100-plus site campground welcomes both tent and RV campers and has a group camping area. The 46 sites with full hook-ups are in an open area; however, most of the campground's primitive areas and sites with partial hook-ups are shaded. There are also a limited number of riverfront tent sites. Campground facilities include picnic tables, fire rings, centrally located laundry and hot showers, flush and nonflush toilets, a dump station, pay phone, and a small store with ice, firewood, and basic groceries. At Eagle Cliff, campers also have an on-site game room, playground, open field, the opportunity to swim and fish in the Root River as well as easy access to the Root River Bike Trail in Lanesboro and Whalan. Pets are permitted. Reservations requested.

Cost: $$–$$$
Season: April–November

Highway 250 Campground

Lanesboro, MN 55948, (507) 467-2527
Take Parkway Avenue North to Ashburn Street East (Hwy. 250), follow Hwy. 250 past the bridge, campground will be on your right.

Highway 250 Campground is situated on the northern edge of Lanesboro between the Root River Trail and the Root River. The campground offers 49 shaded and open sites with water and electric hookups, fire rings, picnic tables, and modern rest rooms with showers. On-site recreational facilities include canoe and tube rentals, horseshoes, and volleyball. Downtown Lanesboro is within walking distance of the campground.

Cost: $$
Season: April–October

Riverview Campground

West Pleasant Street, Lanesboro, MN 55949, (507) 467-3722, 800-944-2670
Follow Parkway Avenue South to West Pleasant Street, turn right. Campground is located off West Pleasant Street near the river and dam.

Riverview Campground is a Lanesboro City campground located a short distance from Sylvan Lake Campground. The open campground is situated between the

Lanesboro school's football field and the Root River dam. Sixteen sites with water and electric hook-ups and a tents-only area are available on a first come, first served basis. The campsites are equipped with picnic tables and fire rings. Campers have access to a picnic shelter, and firewood is available for a donation. No rest rooms are located on the premises, but campers may use the bathroom and shower facilities at Sylvan Park.

Cost: $–$$
Season: mid-April–mid-November

Sylvan Park Campground
202 Parkway Avenue, Lanesboro, MN 55949, (507) 467-3722, 800-944-2670

Although Sylvan Park is situated in the heart of Lanesboro, this municipal campground has a semi-rustic setting. Sylvan Park's quiet campground has a tents-only area with numerous sites and 27 sites in an RV/trailer-only section with electric and water hook-ups. Flush toilets, coin-operated showers, and a dump station are available. Firewood is available for a small donation. The beautiful park is heavily shaded and has a small pond, large gazebo, modern playground, a basketball court, sand volleyball court, horseshoe pits, a ball field, tennis courts, and six picnic shelters. In addition to this, the park is within walking distance to downtown restaurants, shopping, the Cornucopia Art Center, Commonweal Theater, Scenic Valley Winery, local museums, the Root River Bike Trail, and area outfitters that rent bicycles, canoes, and tubes. It's also a special treat to meet the Amish people who come to Sylvan Park on Saturdays to sell their baked goods, quilts, and baskets. Pets are allowed. Campsites available on a first come, first served basis.

Cost: $–$$
Season: mid-April–mid-November

MAZEPPA
Ponderosa Campground
RR 1, Box 209, Mazeppa, MN 55956, (507) 843-3611, 800-895-0328

Ponderosa Campground is an 80-site RV park located next to Lake Zumbro. The campground is attractive for boaters because it has an on-site boat launch, boat docking for seasonal campers, and boat tie-ups for weekend visitors. Some campsites are shaded, but all have water and electric hook-ups, fire rings, and picnic tables. Other campground features are a traffic control gate, pay phone, nonflush toilets, dump station, hot showers, horseshoe pits, playground equipment, on-site fishing and a camp store with ice, wood, snacks, and basic grocery items. A small swimming area located near the boat launch is accessible via a very small and very steep beach. Reservations requested.

Cost: $$
Season: mid-April–mid-October

ORONOCO
Oronoco Park Campground
310 3rd Avenue NW, Oronoco, MN 55960, (507) 367-4526

Nestled a short distance from Highway 52 on the shores of Lake Shady is Oronoco Park. This 35-acre park offers eight primitive sites for tent and RV camping in a beautiful shaded area. Campground facilities include picnic tables and fire rings at each campsite, access to potable water and electricity (via an extension cord to the bathroom), hot showers, and pit toilets. Recreational amenities at the park include a picnic shelter, gazebo, playground, volleyball courts, horseshoe pits, grill and fire rings. Campsites are available on a first come, first served basis. Reservations are suggested for groups wanting to use the picnic shelter on a specific date. Firewood is available at the campground, and a country store with a phone, ice, and basic groceries is located about ¼ mile from the campground.

Cost: $
Season: May–Labor Day

PETERSON
Peterson Municipal Campground
P.O. Box 11, Peterson, MN 55962, (507) 875-2587
Located on Fillmore Street.

A quiet 10-site campground, suitable for both RV and tent camping, is nestled in Peterson's City Park. Water and electric hook-ups are available as is firewood for a donation. Rest rooms have flush toilets and sinks with running water, but no showers. The Root River Bike Trail is easily accessible from the campground, and the park has a playground and ball field. Campsites may be reserved through the City of Peterson or used on a first come, first served basis. Long-term camping is permitted with reservations. Pets are allowed.

Cost: $
Season: April–November, weather permitting

PINE ISLAND
Wazionja Campground
6450 120th Street NW, Pine Island, MN 55963, (507) 356-8594

Wazionja Campground is a jewel! The peaceful campground is easily accessible from Hwy. 52, just north of Rochester. The well-landscaped, woodsy, and ultra-quiet area along the Zumbro River provides the setting for Wazionja's 100 shaded and open campsites. Amenities include full and partial hook-ups, meticulously clean bathrooms with flush toilets and hot showers, coin-operated laundry, a pay phone, and a small store with ice, firewood, candy and ice cream. What makes Wazionja special is its emphasis on building a community within the campground. Campers organize ice cream socials, gather together in the evenings at the community fire ring and help tend the community garden, where all are welcome to its harvest. The campground also has two beautiful lodges, both with fireplaces and one with a kitchen. The lodges are used by campers as well as area residents for special events and meetings. Additional facilities include a recreation room, game room, horseshoe pits, a playground, a centrally located modem, on-site fishing, and easy access to bicycling on the Douglas State Trail. Nearby communities provide opportunities for hiking and canoeing. Pets are permitted. Reservations requested, but walk-ins welcome.

Cost: $–$$
Season: mid-April–mid-October

PRESTON
Fillmore County Fairgrounds Campground
413 East Fillmore Street, Preston, MN 55965, (507) 765-4733

The Preston-Harmony Recreation Trailhead is just a few yards away from this no-frills campground in Preston. The campground has 40 open sites with picnic tables and fire rings as well as access to potable water, rest rooms, showers, a pay phone, firewood, a dump station, three picnic shelters, and some electric hook-ups. Campsites are available on a first come, first served basis. Please note that the campground is closed during the third week of July due to the Fillmore County Fair.

Cost: $–$$
Season: April–November

Hidden Valley Campground
Hwy. 16 & 52, Preston, MN 55965, (507) 765-2467, www.hiddenvalleycampground.com or e-mail: info@hiddenvalleycampground.com

Come to Hidden Valley Campground for relaxing, peaceful, old-fashioned family camping at its best. The 140-acre rural campground is shaded by 30-year-old willow, oak, and pine trees. In addition to this, the south branch of the Root River borders the campground, and there are 3½ miles of hiking trails that meander through woods and ravines leading you to "the bluff." Hidden Valley has 35 plus sites, some with water and electrical hook-ups. Picnic tables and fire rings are available at all sites. Other facilities include outdoor toilets, a dump station, and firewood for sale. Additional amenities at Hidden Valley are a recreation area that has sand volleyball, horseshoe pits, basketball, tetherball, softball fields, swings, slides and monkey bars as well as great trout fishing in the Root River, on-site tube rentals, and easy access to the Root River Bike Trail. Canoeing is available through local outfitters. Development of a central building with flush toilets, showers, sinks, a pay phone, and vending machines is underway.

Cost: $–$$
Season: mid-April–mid-October

Maple Springs Campground
Route 2, Box 129B, Preston, MN 55965, (507) 352-2056, www.exploreminnesota.com

Nestled in a valley and bordered by the spring-fed Forestville Creek, Maple Springs Campground has 49 shaded and open campsites as well as a separate area for keeping horses and horse trailers. Campground facilities include 14 sites with water and electric hook-ups, picnic tables, fire pits, cold running water, pit toilets, and a Trading Post with ice, firewood, groceries, ice cream, fishing bait and tackle, and gifts. Outdoor enthusiasts enjoy fishing, hiking, bird watching and creek splashing at Maple Springs. A special feature of the campground is its connection to Forestville State Park via hiking and equestrian trails. Pets are permitted. Reservations requested, but walk-ins are welcome.

Cost: $–$$
Season: April–November

The Old Barn Resort
Route 3, Box 57, Preston, MN 55965, (507) 467-2512, 800-552-2512, www.exploreminnesota.com or www.bluffcountry.com

The Old Barn Resort, located on the Root River State Recreational Trail, is one of southeastern Minnesota's most popular campgrounds. As you approach the resort, the "Old Barn" comes into view. Originally built in 1884, the 50-by-100-foot white barn is now a National Historic site. It was restored in 1988 and is now the heart of the resort with a restaurant and bar, banquet rooms, a 54 bed hostel and a clubhouse for the resort's on-site golf course. The 170-site, tiered campground has large, grassy sites with scenic views of the countryside. Open and shaded sites are available, 65 with full hook-ups, 65 with partial hook-ups, and about 40 tent sites. Three bathroom facilities with showers and flush toilets are conveniently located throughout the campground. A dump station, grocery store with ice, snacks, and supplies, coin-operated laundry, firewood, and a pay phone are available also on site. If camping isn't your style, plan to stay at the hostel, which has rooms that can accommodate one person or a group of sixteen. The hostel's rest rooms and showers are just down the hall, and guests have access to a kitchenette and TV/sitting room. Whether they stay at the campground or the hostel, families of all shapes and sizes love the recreational opportunities at The Old Barn. The resort's location on the south branch of the Root River provides easy access to trout fishing, canoeing, and tubing. In addition to this, the Root River State Recreation Trail is connected to the campground. Canoe, tube, bicycle and bicycle trailer rentals are conveniently located on site for those wanting to partake in these activities. Other recreational amenities include a 30-by-60-foot heated, indoor pool, a 9-hole golf course and driving range, playground, a hiking trail, river access via a boat ramp, regularly scheduled entertainment, organized children's programs, a recreation room with arcade games, horseshoe, volleyball, and basketball areas, and a couple of large grassy areas for activities such as playing Frisbee and kite-flying. The restaurant serves breakfast on weekends and holidays, and lunch and dinner are served seven days a week. Pets are permitted. Reservations are usually needed 2–4 months in advance, especially for holiday weekends.

Cost: $$–$$$
Season: April–November

RUSHFORD
North End Park Campground
Hwy. 43, Rushford, MN 55971, (507) 864-7720

This small city campground is located across the street from the Creekside Community Park. Seven small campsites are available, five with electric and water hook-ups and two with water only. All sites have picnic tables and fire pits. Flush toilets and a picnic shelter are located on the premises. Firewood is sometimes available on the premises or may be purchased locally. Register at Larry's Mobil located at the intersection of Highways 16 and 43. Campsites are available on a first come, first served basis.

Cost: $–$$
Season: May–November

SPRING GROVE
Supersaw Valley Campground
Route 2, Spring Grove, MN 55974, (507) 498-5880
Located 3.2 miles north of Spring Grove on County Road. 4, then 2.5 miles west on County Road 19.

Situated in the picturesque Supersaw Valley, this 200-acre campground is surrounded by bluffs that are 300–400 feet high. Riceford Creek, a trout-stocked stream, runs through the campground. The 106-site campground has open and shaded sites with full and partial hook-ups as well as a primitive camping area. Facilities at the campground include flush toilets, hot showers, a public phone, coin-operated laundry, a dump station, snack bar, and camp store with groceries, ice, firewood, camping supplies, and toys. The secluded campground has plenty of recreational amenities such as a 30-by-60-foot swimming pool, a large playground, an 18-hole miniature golf course, volleyball, basketball, horseshoe pits, picnic shelters, a recreation room with pool tables and arcade games, on-site biking and fishing, 4.5 miles of scenic hiking trails as well as hayrides and organized children's games during weekends. Pets are permitted. Reservations requested.

Cost: $$–$$$
Season: May–September

Trollskogen Park & Campground
3rd Avenue SW, Spring Grove, MN 55974, (507) 498-5221

This small campground is located in Spring Grove's beautiful Trollskogen Park. The shady, hillside park is equipped with three sites that have water and electric hook-ups and one primitive site. Picnic tables and fire pits are located on the premises. Campground amenities include picnic shelters, rest rooms with flush toilets and showers, drinking water, and a playground. Equestrian trails may also be accessed from the park. Campsites are available on a first come, first served basis.

Cost: $
Season: April–October

SPRING VALLEY
Deer Creek Campground and Speedway
25262 Hwy. 63 South, Spring Valley, MN 55975, (507) 346-2342 (track phone), (507) 754- 6107 (office), www.deercreekspeedway.com

Although this 50-site campground is in a rural location, it doesn't lack for excitement because it is next to the Deer Creek Speedway, a WISSOTA sanctioned stock car racing track. The grassy, shaded campground has water, electric, and sewer hook-ups at 25 sites, nonflush toilets, a dump station, firewood for sale, and playground equipment. Pets are allowed. Reservations requested.

Cost: $$
Season: April–mid-October

STEWARTVILLE
Ironwood Springs Christian Ranch
7291 County Road 6 SW, Stewartville, MN 55976, (507) 533-9933 (stables), 888-533-4316 or (507) 533-4315 (information and reservations), www.ironwoodsprings.com, e-mail: iscr2000@aol.com

Ironwood Springs, a nonprofit, nondenominational year-round camp, is located in rural Stewartville along the Root River on 200 rural, wooded acres. The camp's mission is "to provide an atmosphere and opportunity for adults and children to get to know themselves, others and God better. We strive to do this through our lives, words, and activities." The Ironwood Springs Ranch campground facilities are open to the public only during summer weekends due to the schedule of week-long summer camps for youths and families; however weekday camping is permitted when there are no camps scheduled. The campground is situated in a shady, wooded area west of the Main Lodge and has 26 electric and 7 nonelectric sites. In addition to this, Edgewood Park, another area the Ranch has 12 open, electrical sites. Campground facilities and recreational amenities include flush toilets, hot showers, public phones, firewood for sale, a dump station, recreation center, a pool, playgrounds, tennis courts, basketball courts, and an on-site horse stable with trail rides. Occasionally, there are concerts or other live entertainment at Ironwood Springs. Please note that Ironwood Springs does not provide trash receptacles, and campers are required to dispose of their own trash. Ironwood Springs welcomes inquiries about use and rental of their Main Lodge, cabins, dormitory, and Log Chapel. The facility has been used by community organizations, schools, scouts, clubs, day care groups, businesses, and organizations working with the disabled for retreats, as well as trail and wagon rides, birthday parties, sleigh rides, snow tubing, banquets, and other special events. Call the camp to request a brochure or newsletter, obtain a current schedule of camps or special events such as the Quilting Retreat and Annual National Wheelchair Sports and Recreation Camp, or to make campground reservations. Pets are permitted. Reservation required.

Cost: $$
Season: Memorial Day weekend–Labor Day weekend

THEILMAN
Whippoorwill Ranch Kampground
RR 1, Box 145, Theilman, MN 55945, (507) 534-3590
Located west of Theilman on Wabasha County Road 4.

Whippoorwill Ranch is a very large RV park with a small area for tent camping. The campground has approximately 200 open sites with full and partial hook-ups. West Indian Creek, which borders the campground, runs next to the tent camping area. On-site facilities include flush toilets, showers, coin-operated laundry, a public phone, and a clean, air-conditioned restaurant and lodge with a bar, video games, pool table, kids' movie room, an adults-only social hall, and general store. Although the recreational facilities are a bit outdated, there is a lot to choose from such as horseshoes, shuffleboard, miniature golf, bocce ball, croquet, volleyball, basketball, a ball field, and a sandy area with a swimming pond. Outdoor lovers will appreciate the on-site hiking trails, fishing pond, and native trout stream. Whippoorwill also has a large hall and two pavilions that may be rented for parties and special events. Pets are permitted. Reservations requested.

Cost: $–$$$
Season: mid-April–mid-October

WINONA
Pla-Mor Campground & Marina
Route 6, Box 18-1, Winona, MN 55987, (507) 454-2851, 877-454-2267
Located 6 miles south of Winona on Hwy. 14/61 between mile markers 19 and 20.

The Pla-Mor Campground & Marina and former Winona KOA, both owned by Gordie and Ann Rasmussen, have merged to form a new, larger Pla-Mor Campground & Marina. One side of the campground is situated on a riverbank of the Mississippi and the other is nestled in a bluff just across the highway. The Pla-Mor is set in a scenic area of the Mississippi River Valley that has been affectionately nicknamed the "Little Smokies of Minnesota" for its breathtaking views and resemblance to the Smoky Mountains. The bluff side of the campground has a spring-fed stream and 72 open, wooded, and hilltop sites with picnic tables and fire rings. Approximately 65 sites have water and electric hook-ups. Facilities on the bluff side include a large picnic shelter, flush and nonflush toilets, hot showers, a public phone, modem access, coin-operated laundry, a dump station, LP tank refills, a snack bar, and a small store with groceries, ice, and firewood. On-site recreational amenities include a swimming pool with sun deck, playground, game room, horseshoe pits, volleyball, basketball, canoe rentals, fishing, organized weekend activities, and a challenging hiking trail that winds up high atop a bluff. The river side of the Pla-Mor has about 35 large, grassy, open and wooded campsites with picnic tables, fire rings, and water and electric hook-ups. It also has a playground, boat launch, daily and seasonal boat slip rentals, volleyball, access to fishing, a picnic shelter, recreation field, and pontoon and canoe rentals. All campers have access to both sides of the campground. Arrivals via boat are welcome. Pets are allowed. Reservations requested.

Cost: $$–$$$
Season: mid-April–mid-October

Prairie Island Campground
1120 Prairie Island Road, Winona, MN 55987, (507) 452-4501

Prairie Island, located on the banks of the Mississippi River, is Winona's city campground. The 150-plus site campground has an open area for RVs with 86 electric hook-ups and a more rustic, wooded area for tent campers. Campground facilities include flush and pit toilets, hot showers, a dump station, pay phone, access to potable water, and a small convenience store with ice and firewood. Prairie Island's on-site recreational amenities include a picnic shelter, playgrounds, canoe rentals, a boat ramp, yard games, a long, but very narrow sandy beach, basketball, volleyball, miniature golf, organized weekend activities for kids (scavenger hunts, movies and Saturday morning cartoons shown in the parking lot), hiking, biking as well as swimming and fishing in the Mississippi. The campground is also in close proximity to many of Winona's historic sites and the Bob Welch Aquatic Center.

Cost: $–$$
Season: April–October

WABASHA
Pioneer Campsite Resort
130 Pioneer Drive, Wabasha, MN 55981, (651) 565-2242
From the junction of Hwy. 60 and U.S. Hwy. 61, go four miles south on U.S. 61, then ¾ mile north on County Road 30, then 2½ miles east on County Road 24, then ¼ mile east on Prairie Lane. Follow signs to campground.

Pioneer Campsite Resort is a family-oriented campground with a complete selection of recreational amenities. The campground is situated in the Hiawatha Valley near the mighty Mississippi River and has 220 grassy, shaded sites with water and electric hook-ups available at many of the sites. Campground facilities include flush and nonflush toilets, hot showers, a dump station, coin-operated laundry, a pay phone, weather shelter, and a camp store with groceries, ice, pizza, snacks, and firewood. On-site recreational amenities include a swimming pool, arcade, ball field, horseshoe pits, volleyball and basketball courts, a playground, hiking trails, wagon rides, miniature golf, canoe and paddleboat rentals, a self-guided fitness course, organized activities, and Sunday worship services. Campers also have easy access to the Mississippi River backwaters, a boat ramp, and fishing near dam number four. Reservations are strongly suggested.

Cost: $$
Season: mid-April–mid-October

WELCH
Hidden Valley Campground
27173 144th Avenue Way, Welch, MN 55089, (651) 258-4550

Welch is home to the Hidden Valley Campground, a grassy, rural facility situated near the Cannon River. The campground has approximately 200 sites, 100 with water and electric as well as flush toilets, hot showers, a dump station, public phone, recreation room, and pavilion. Ice and firewood are available on the premises. Recreational amenities include a playground, on-site hiking, canoeing, biking, fishing, and river swimming. Reservations suggested, but walk-ins welcome.

Cost: $$
Season: May–October

ZUMBRO FALLS
Bluff Valley Campground
Bluff Valley Road, RR 1, Box 194, Zumbro Falls, MN 55991, (507) 753-2955, 800-226-7282, www.bluffvalley.com or e-mail: camp@bluffvalley.com

Wow! Bluff Valley Campground (BVC), nestled into a scenic bluff and bordered by the Zumbro River, offers both a secluded, rustic location and a wealth of recreational amenities. The 275 campsites, all with water and electric hook-ups, are situated along the Zumbro River and beside the campground's wooded bluffs. Although the campsites are tucked within a hillside terrain, most of them are grassy, level, and shaded. Campground facilities include picnic tables, fire rings, public water faucets, flush and nonflush toilets, hot showers, a dump station, pay phone, traffic control gate, a well-stocked convenience store with groceries, ice and firewood, propane refills, and snack bar. In terms of recreation, there is something for everyone at BVC. Recreational amenities include two riverfront beaches, tube rentals and shuttles, a heated pool with "kids' beach," playgrounds, a driving range (golf), miniature golf course, horseshoe pits, badminton, croquet, sand volleyball courts, a softball field, large game room with pool tables, air hockey, and video games, Frisbee golf, on-site fishing and biking, more than five miles of hiking trails, a live music hall, amphitheater as well as organized entertainment and activities such as movies, wagon rides, karaoke, arts and crafts, rainy day activities, "themed" weekends, a Saturday morning pancake breakfast, and Sunday morning worship service. Recreation equipment may be checked out at the office, free of charge. Pets are permitted. Reservations are recommended, but not necessary except to reserve a specific site. Call BVC for reservations or to obtain a current activity schedule.

Cost: $$$–$$$$
Season: mid-April–October

Bluff Valley Lights

Bluff Valley Campground offers a spectacular autumn light show and family entertainment from mid-October through late November. The "Brilliant Nights of Autumn Lights" is the first autumn drive-through light show in North America. The drive-through tour includes eleven "themed" areas, more than 410 light displays and over 155 light displays with sequential animation. In addition to this, families have the opportunity to purchase a night light wristband to participate in glow-in-the-dark activities such as A"Maze"N'Lites, the Night light driving range, mini-golf, disc golf, and wagon tour. A dinner buffet and free live entertainment by area high school students is also available. For more information, contact Bluff Valley Campground at (507) 753-2955, 800-226-7282 or check out www.Lights@BluffValley.com Price varies by activity.

Zumbro Valley Sportsmen's Park

Sportmen's Park, Hwy. 63, Zumbro Falls, MN 55991, (507) 753-2568

Tents and RV campers are welcome at Sportsmen's Park in Zumbro Falls. The small primitive campground, located on the banks of the Zumbro River, has shaded and unshaded sites, electric hook-ups, pit toilets, access to a water spigot, picnic tables, fire rings, a covered picnic shelter, volleyball net, and on-site canoe rentals. Firewood is sold on the premises. Campsites are rented on a first come, first served basis, but the picnic shelter must be reserved for group functions.

Cost: $
Season: May–October

ZUMBROTA
Shades of Sherwood

RR 1, Box 142, 14334 Sherwood Trail, Zumbrota, MN 55992, (507) 732-5100

Shades of Sherwood is a rural campground on the Zumbro River with all the amenities families love. Some of its 200-plus sites are open, but most are in shaded areas with grassy pads. The 77-acre campground has water and electric hook-ups for 200 sites, flush and chemical toilets, hot showers, picnic tables, fire pits, coin-operated laundry, a dump station, propane exchange, and an on-site camp store with groceries, ice, and firewood. An abundance of recreational activities offered at Shades of Sherwood makes it a winner with families. The campground boasts five playgrounds, a recreation room, free wagon and mini-train rides, hiking trails, a large arcade, heated pool, and some organized activities. Canoeing, fishing, and bicycling is available within the area. Pets allowed. Reservations strongly suggested.

Cost: $$
Season: May–October

Chapter 13: Horseback Riding, Hay & Sleigh Rides

Horseback Riding

ALTURA
Lazy D Trail Rides & Carriage Company
RR 1, Box 252, Altura, MN 55910, (507) 932-3098
Located 8 miles north of St. Charles on County Road 74.

Lazy D offers a one-hour trail ride that crosses the Whitewater River and climbs the bluff overlooking the scenic Whitewater River Valley. Trail rides are available from May through October and can accommodate up to 15 people, but require a four-person minimum. Riders must be seven years old to ride alone, and children under age seven may ride double with an adult. Children under the age of two are not permitted on horseback. Regularly scheduled trail rides leave from the Lazy D Campground on Saturdays and Sundays during the summer months or by reservation at other times. Lazy D also has on-site pony rides for children. Helmets are not provided.

Cost: $$, ½ price for children
Hours: Saturday and Sunday, or by reservation

ROCK DELL
Riverside Trails
Rock Dell, MN 55920, (507) 285-5223
Call for directions.

Riverside Trails arranges off-site trail rides at Chester Woods Park in Eyota and Forestville State Park in Preston for beginning and experienced riders. Inexperienced riders are required to visit the Ranch, located a short distance from Rochester in the rural Rock Dell area, for an introductory lesson prior to the trail ride. Trail rides are approximately one hour long at Chester Woods Park and two hours long at Forestville State Park; however, this does not include travel time to and from the parks. Riders are responsible for their own transportation to the parks and may choose to meet the guide or follow them to the designated park. Trail rides are limited to a maximum of six participants. Riders must be age seven and older and are encouraged to bring their own helmets. No double riding is permitted. Riverside Trails also offers overnight camping trips, pony rides, pony wagon rides, and pony birthday parties as well as horseback riding lessons for children age four and older and adults. Call for more information or to make reservations.

Cost: pony rides: $; trail rides: $$$–$$$$
Hours: by reservation

STEWARTVILLE
Ironwood Springs Christian Ranch
7291 County Road 6 SW, Stewartville, MN 55976, (507) 533-9933 (stables), 888-533-4316 or (507) 533-4315 (information and reservations), www.ironwoodsprings.com, e-mail: iscr2000@aol.com

Ironwood Springs Christian Ranch offers half-hour or hour long trail rides for individuals, families, or groups throughout the year. The stable has the capacity to accommodate a maximum of 12 people for group trail rides. Riders must be 8 years old to ride alone; however children under age eight may saddle up with an adult. Children under age two are not permitted on trail rides. Ironwood Springs provides riding helmets for both children and adults. All children under 18 years of age are required to wear helmets, but this is optional for adult riders. Please call the stables to arrange trail rides, and call general information and reservations to schedule use of the lodge or other facilities.

Cost: $–$$
Hours: Monday–Friday, call for times and reservations; Saturday, 9 a.m.–4:30 p.m. (weather conditions permitting); Sundays, closed
    summer: Monday–Friday, call for times and reservations; Saturday, 9 a.m.–5:45 p.m.; Sunday, 2 p.m.–5:45 p.m.

Horseback Riding Lessons

Horse stables and farms in close proximity to Rochester that offer horseback riding lessons are:

Bear Creek Farm
2725 Marion Road SE, Rochester, MN 55904, (507) 536-0456

The Paddock School of Horsemanship
7500 Valleyhigh Road NW, Byron, MN 55920, (507) 775-6912, (507) 775-6818 (Arena)

Turn Crest Stable
Hwy. 14, Kasson, MN 55944, (507) 634-4474, e-mail: turncrest@ll.net

Horseback Riding Trails

Horseback riding trails in and around Rochester include:

Chester Woods Park
8378 Hwy. 14 East, Eyota, MN 55934, (507) 285-7050, (507) 287-2624, www.olmstedpublicworks.com, e-mail: chesterw@venturecs.net

Chester Woods Park has approximately 8–9 miles of equestrian trails that are open to the public from May 1st to November 1st. Some sections of the trails are hardened, but all form interconnected loops that meander through woods, prairies, hills, and fields. Please call the park for current trail conditions before your ride. Trails are occasionally closed due to poor conditions.

Cost: park entrance: $; bridle fee: $
Season: May 1st–November 1st

Douglas State Trail
Trailheads located in Rochester on County Road 4 (Valleyhigh Drive NW) behind IBM, in Douglas at County Road 14 off Hwy. 52, and in Pine Island at Pine Island Park, just off the Hwy. 52 exit. (507) 285-7176

The Douglas State Trail has a 12-mile equestrian trail that is located along side the paved blacktop trail that runs from Rochester to Pine Island. The trail is open to the pubic and no riding permits are required; however, the equestrian path is converted to a snowmobile trail during the winter season.

Cost: free
Season: spring–fall

Horseback Riding Trails and Campgrounds in Southeastern Minnesota State Parks

Southeastern Minnesota State Parks that have horse campsites and riding trails are Forestville/Mystery Cave State Park and Lake Louise State Park. For more information about the parks and their facilities, contact the Minnesota DNR at 888-MINNDNR, (651) 296-6157 or www.dnr.state.mn.us. Camping and lodging reservations at the state parks may be made by calling The Connection at 800-246-CAMP or (952) 922-9000.

Minnesota Horse Trails and Campgrounds

Minnesota Horse Council, 10355 Riverdale Drive NW, PMB 202, Suite 500, Coon Rapids, MN 55448, (612) 576-1757, www.horses-mn.org

To obtain a brochure with a map and detailed information about horse trails and campgrounds throughout the state of Minnesota, contact the Minnesota Horse Council.

Hay & Sleigh Rides

ALTURA
Lazy D Trail Rides & Carriage Company

RR 1, Box 252, Altura, MN 55910, (507) 932-3098
Located 8 miles north of St. Charles on County Road 74.

There's a lot to choose from at Lazy D Trail Rides and Carriage Company. Whether you're interested in hayrides, sleigh rides, covered wagon rides, or carriage rides—Lazy D has them all! All rides take place in the scenic Whitewater River Valley and are pulled by a team of draft horses. Hay, sleigh, and covered wagon rides have a seating capacity of 16–17 people and are approximately 45–60 minutes in length. Hour-long antique carriage rides can accommodate 2–4 people and are available with or without a picnic lunch. All rides depart from the Lazy D Campground.

Cost: $$$
Hours: by appointment

BYRON
Tweite's Pumpkin Patch

1821 Frontier Road SW, Byron, MN 55920, (507) 634-4848, www.tweite.com

The magic of fall comes alive at Tweite's Pumpkinville and Gift Barn. Pumpkinville is an autumn wonderland that not only has short wagon rides to their U-pick pumpkin patch, but an assortment of wholesome outdoor activities for families. In addition to wagon rides, Pumpkinville has Storybook Land with scenes from popular Mother Goose rhymes, a Harvest Town play area with a huge sandbox and riding toys, a 16-foot tepee, a three tower castle, a small corn maze, and more. An entertainment schedule includes puppet and magic shows.

Cost: $–$$
Hours: open seasonally from late September through October; Friday–Saturday, 10 a.m.–5:30 p.m.; Sunday, 1 p.m.–5:30 p.m.

HARMONY
Tom Jarland Carriage Service
Route1, Box 259, Harmony, MN 55939, (507) 886-6302

Tom Jarland offers horse-drawn hayrides and sleigh rides throughout the year. The wagons used for hayrides can accommodate 15–25 people with passengers sitting on seats or hay bales. Sleigh rides have hay bale seating with a passenger capacity of 10–15 people. Although blankets are provided for sleigh rides, you may want to bring extras on a very cold day. A horse-drawn carriage is available for special events.

Cost: $$$
Hours: by appointment

ROCK DELL
Riverside Trails
Rock Dell, MN 55920, (507) 285-5223
Call for directions.

Riverside Trails is located a short distance from Rochester in the rural Rock Dell area. Horse-drawn hayrides are offered during the summer and warmer months of spring and fall. Hay bales are nestled in the center of the wagons, which can accommodate about 20 people. Wagons also have wooden seats with backrests and side rails. Advanced reservations are required.

Cost: $$$
Hours: by appointment

STEWARTVILLE
Ironwood Springs Christian Ranch
7291 County Road 6 SW, Stewartville, MN 55976, (507) 533-9933 (stables); (507) 533-4315 or 888-533-4316 (information and reservations), www.ironwoodsprings.com, e-mail: iscr2000@aol.com

Horse or tractor pulled wagon and sleigh rides are available on the scenic grounds of Ironwood Springs Christian Ranch. Wagon and sleigh rides are approximately one hour long and have a seating capacity for about 25 adults or 35 children. Blankets are provided for sleigh rides. Reservations are needed for both wagon and sleigh rides, but no minimum number is required. Groups may also make arrangements to use the lodge or other facilities at Ironwood Springs when they make their reservation.

Cost: $$$
Hours: by appointment

Chapter 14: Nature Centers

ROCHESTER
Quarry Hill Park and Nature Center
701 Silver Creek Road, Rochester, MN 55906, (507) 281-6114, www.rochester.k12.mn.us/quarryhill
Accessible from County Road 22, also called East Circle Drive.

Quarry Hill Park and Nature Center is truly a Rochester treasure. This hands-on environmental education center is a place where children, youth, adults, and families are encouraged to explore the beauty and biology of nature. The Nature Center, located on the scenic grounds of Quarry Hill Park, supports a diverse variety of habitats on its nearly 300 acres. The meadow, forest, and prairie landscapes as well as the sandstone cave, stream, and two-acre fishing pond provide both a classroom for Nature Center programs and a recreational haven for visitors who are welcome to hike on the more than five miles of hiking trails that meander through the park.

The exhibit hall has a large collection of live and mounted animal displays, touch tables with animal bones and skins, a life-size T-Rex skull model, an indoor bird viewing area, a 1,700 gallon native fish aquarium, and smaller tanks with turtles, frogs, and snakes. Other resources at Quarry Hill Nature Center include a library with nature-related books and magazines, classrooms, an auditorium that seats up to 100 people, and cross-country ski and snowshoe rentals during the winter months. Recreational facilities at the park include tennis courts, a baseball diamond, playground, picnic area, and paved bike trail that connects to Rochester's Bike Trail System.

Quarry Hill and Rochester Community Education co-sponsor and support nature classes, programs, and workshops open to the general public. A wide variety of classes are available for children, youth, adults, and families throughout the year. Regularly scheduled programs include Parent-Child Classes, Full Moon Hikes, Cave Tours, Bird Sundays, Adventure Trips for Teens, and Family Nature Days and Nights. Program topics have included birding, fossils, rock climbing, canoeing, snowshoeing and snowshoe making, caving, animal tracks, and other seasonal or special topics. Quarry Hill also provides science and nature programs to more than 35,000 students annually through area public and private schools. Please call Quarry Hill for information about current events and programs or birthdays parties at the nature center. Information about the Quarry Hill Fall Festival may be found in Chapter 11.

Cost: free, donations welcome; small fee for ski and snowshoe rentals
Hours: Monday–Saturday, 9 a.m.–5 p.m.; Sundays, noon–5 p.m.

ALTURA
Whitewater State Park Geological Center
RR 1, Altura, MN 55910, (507) 932-3007, www.dnr.state.mn.us/parks_and_recreation/state_parks
or e-mail: info@dnr.state.mn.us

The Visitor Center at Whitewater State Park is home to an interpretive Discovery Center. The exhibit features information about area history and how land use in the Whitewater Valley has affected the watershed. Children and adults may explore specimens from animal remains such skins, skulls, birds, and turtle shells at the touch tables. Mounted birds of prey are also an interesting display in the interpretive center. An indoor trail center, equipped with large windows and a wood burning stove, is adjacent to the Discovery Center and provides visitors with the opportunity to view both a wooded area of the valley and a bird feeding station. Other facilities at the Visitor Center include the park office, an indoor classroom/auditorium, and an outdoor amphitheater. For more information about the Discovery Center, nature programs, or Whitewater State Park, call the park office or visit the park website. Please see Chapter 16 for more specific information about the park.

Cost: day pass: $; annual state park permit: $$
Hours: mid-April–mid-October: Sunday–Thursday, 8 a.m.–4 p.m.; Friday and
   Saturday, 8 a.m.–10 p.m.
   mid-October–mid-April: daily, 8 a.m.–4 p.m.

BYRON
Oxbow Nature Center and Zollman Zoo
Oxbow Park, 5731 County Road 105 NW (at Olmsted 4 & 5 intersection), Byron, MN 55920,
(507) 775-2451, www.olmstedpublicworks.com, e-mail: oxbow@venturecs.net

The Oxbow Nature Center offers a classroom area and small exhibit of regional snakes and animal artifacts. The facility provides a home base for the park's large variety of nature programs. Designed for families, the interpretive programs are usually held on Saturday mornings and afternoons. Program topics change seasonally and have included Children's Zoo Hour, Snake Feeding, Otter Feeding, Birds of Prey, Maple Syruping, Prairie Walk, Night Hikes, Tree Identification, Bats, and Feeding the Bison. The Oxbow Park staff also provides environmental and outdoor education to thousands of school children annually through field trips to the nature center and zoo.

The Dr. Paul E. Zollman Zoo is adjacent to the Oxbow Nature Center. This outdoor zoo opened in 1969 and is currently owned and operated by Olmsted County. The zoo is named in honor of Dr. Paul E. Zollman, a retired veterinarian, as a tribute to his dedication and service to both the treatment of injured animals and the Olmsted County Parks. The zoo houses 30 species of native Minnesota animals. Live animal exhibits include eagles, owls, hawks, otters, gray wolf, cougar, bear, red fox, porcupine, domesticated farm animals, and the playful prairie dogs. A majority of the animals can not be returned to the wild due to injuries that would jeopardize their survival. Oxbow's large animal collection of bison, elk, and white tailed deer is located in the Gordon Yeager Memorial Area across the street from the main zoo area. A restored prairie, pioneer home and antique farm implement display also gives visitors the opportunity to experience a touch of Minnesota's past.

Oxbow Nature Center and Zoo is located in Oxbow Park. The scenic 572-acre park, set in the Zumbro River Valley, has approximately eight miles of maintained hiking trails, four picnic areas with covered shelters including one with a playground and ball field, and a semi-primitive camping area with a playground, running water, rest rooms and showers. Fishing is permitted along the shores of the Zumbro River as it winds through the park.

Call Oxbow Nature Center for information about current nature programs. Campsites, picnic areas and shelters are available on a first come, first served basis.

Cost: free, donations welcome, minimal fee for camping
Hours: nature center and zoo: Labor Day–Memorial Day, daily, 12–4 p.m.
  Memorial Day–Labor Day, daily, 12–8 p.m.
  park: daily, 7 a.m.–10 p.m.

HOUSTON
Houston Nature Center
215 West Plum Street, Houston, MN 55943, (507) 896-HOOT (4668), www.houstonmn.com

The Houston Nature Center lies at the trailhead of the Root River Bike and
Recreation Trail in Houston. The local naturalist will greet you and introduce you
to Alice, the Great-Horned Owl. Visitors may view and touch exhibits of local fossils, animal skins, and bird talons and wings, or take a hike around the nearby marsh
that is home to nearly 100 species of native prairie and wetland plants. Children and
adults are welcome to attend naturalist-led educational programs throughout the
summer months. A schedule of weekly programs is available from Memorial Day
weekend to Labor Day weekend. Program topics vary, but have included Beginning
Bird Identification, Birds of Prey, Bird Hike, Frog Walk, and Prairie Walk. Please call
for a current schedule of program topics. Speakers from the Houston Nature Center
are also available to give programs at your school, organization or club from
September to May. A multi-purpose room in the nature center may be reserved for
community meetings or events. Please call for details. A small gift shop is located in
the nature center.

Cost: free, donations welcome
Hours: Memorial Day weekend–Labor Day: Thursday & Sunday, 12:30 p.m.–4:30
  p.m.; Friday, Saturday & Monday, 9:30 a.m.–4:30 p.m.

LANESBORO
Eagle Bluff Environmental Learning Center
Route 2, Box 156A, 1991 Brightsdale Road, Lanesboro, MN 55949, (507) 467-2437, 888-800-9558,
www.eagle-bluff.org or e-mail: hello@eagle-bluff.org

Eagle Bluff Environmental Learning Center is an accredited special function school
located in southeastern Minnesota's picturesque bluff country. The Eagle Bluff mission is "to develop and foster educational opportunities for individuals of all ages
that will create universal awareness, enhance respect, and promote personal responsibility of the natural world." The professional staff at Eagle Bluff accomplish this by
"awakening the student's curiosity about the natural world by involving them in
hands-on activities in an outdoor setting and by providing a learning experience
that is exciting and meaningful." Although the grounds of Eagle Bluff are open to
the public year-round, reservations are required for all programs and events.

The 80-acre residential environmental education center is situated on a bluff overlooking the Root River Valley near the historic town of Lanesboro. The Eagle Bluff
campus is surrounded by 1,000 acres of limestone bluffs, hardwood forest, and farmland, which is accessible to the school for its outdoor education programs. The
modern facilities at Eagle Bluff include a dormitory and dining facility with the
capacity to serve 248 people, two treetop high ropes courses, a group challenge
course, orienteering courses, interpretive nature trails, a limited mobility trail, cross-
country ski trails, a canoe launch, recycling center, demonstration prairie garden,

basketball and volleyball courts, archery and shooting sports ranges along with Native American and Pioneer Life interpretive sites, pond and river study sites, and an indoor rock climbing wall and archery range. The Discovery Center building has classroom space, an auditorium, library, and small gift shop.

There is truly something for everyone at Eagle Bluff. The extensive selection of one day and residential programs consist of environmental education for adults and students in kindergarten through twelfth grade. Choose from wildlife, forestry, karst, cultural, conservation lifestyle, adventure life skills and nature life skills themes. Additional classes routinely offered include Outdoor Skills Programs (OSP) for youth and adults, Family Get-Away Weekends, Sunday Brunch with a Naturalist, Team Building Activities (treetop high ropes courses, indoor rock climbing, and group challenge course), Firearms Safety and Advanced Hunter Education, Becoming an Outdoors Woman, Women in the Outdoors as well as a variety of Evening Programs (night hike, paper making, campfire, owl pellets, concerts) and summer youth camps. Visit the Eagle Bluff website or call for more information about their programs and facilities. Better yet, arrange a tour of this southeastern Minnesota treasure, hike the interpretive trails or challenge yourself on the Treetops High Ropes Course when it is open to the public, but be sure to call for dates, times and reservations.

Eagle Bluff is also a retreat and conference center that has been used for wedding receptions, retreats, reunions, professional conferences, and other special events. Organizations, clubs, churches, and families are encouraged obtain a copy of the Conference and Special Events Guide for more information about Eagle Bluff's conference and banquet facilities.

Cost: program fees vary
Hours: Monday–Friday, 8 a.m.–4:30 p.m.; Saturday–Sunday, 10 a.m.–4 p.m.

WABASHA
The National Eagle Center and EagleWatch Observation Deck
River Vista Park, 152 Main Street, Wabasha, MN 55981, (651) 565-4989, www.eaglewatch.org or e-mail: 4eagles@wabasha.net

As the "Gateway to the Upper Mississippi River National Wildlife and Fish Refuge," Wabasha is a great place to view the American Bald Eagle because the Mississippi River Valley is a migration corridor for the eagles. The National Eagle Center was organized as a grassroots citizen science response to the spontaneous presence of eagles in the area and the people who observe them.

The temporary home of The National Eagle Center (NEC) is located on West Main Street adjacent to the banks of the Mississippi River. The NEC has interpretive exhibits, an aviary, observation deck, a video library, information about environmental education programs, and a gift shop with eagle-related products and souvenirs. Plans are currently underway to construct a permanent home for the NEC—The National Eagle Interpretive Building is scheduled to open in approximately 2004.

While visiting the NEC, resident eagles Harriet and Angel invite you to have a "nose-to-beak" experience at the aviary. Your visit will be up close and personal since Harriet and Angel are not kept in cages or behind glass; however, they are tethered to their perches. Although both eagles underwent rehabilitation at the University of Minnesota Raptor Center, they are unable to be released into the wild due to the nature of their wing injuries. Volunteers and/or staff are available to answer questions about the eagles, and visitors are welcome to take photographs of Harriet and Angel.

The EagleWatch Observation Deck, just a short walk from the NEC, offers breath-taking views from the banks of the Mississippi and is a prime spot for eagle watching. If you're unable to locate the 500-square-foot deck by the grand 17-foot wooden eagle statue carved by Jim Smit of Nelson, Wisconsin, just look for the deck at the intersection of Pembroke Avenue and Lawrence Boulevard. The EagleWatch deck is open 24 hours a day, but is staffed by volunteers from early November through March on Saturdays and Sundays from 1 p.m. to 3 p.m. Volunteers will answer questions about the eagles and assist with eagle spotting. Spotting scopes and binoculars, provided by the NEC, may be used by visitors. Please note that volunteers are available when weather conditions are 10°F or above, and there is no rain.

Cost: free, donations welcome
Hours: Tuesday–Friday, 9 a.m.–4 p.m.; Saturday and Sunday, 10 a.m.–4 p.m.; Monday, closed

The Nature Conservancy
59 Main Street West, Wabasha, MN 55981, (651) 565-4011, www.tnc.org/minnesota

The Nature Conservancy is a worldwide organization with the mission "to preserve the plants, animals, and natural communities that represent the diversity of life on Earth by protecting the lands and waters they need to survive." The Minnesota chapter has offices in different regions of the state. The southeastern Minnesota office is located in Wabasha and manages the Weaver Dunes Scientific and Natural Area in Wabasha County. The landscape of this 697-acre preserve consists of dry sand prairie and an oak savanna, and supports the world's best population of the endangered Blanding's turtle. Call the Nature Conservancy to learn about volunteer opportunities available at Weaver Dunes, located just six miles southeast of Kellogg, Minnesota.

Chapter 15: Farmers' Markets, Gardening, Orchards, Berry Picking & Christmas Tree Farms

Farmers' Markets

Community Supported Agriculture

Community supported agriculture (CSA) establishes a relationship between local farmers and community members by providing locally grown produce that is both fresh and organic. Members of the community purchase season "subscriptions" from CSA farms and receive a variety of seasonal produce on a weekly basis for a designated period of time. The following CSA farms sell produce subscriptions:

Earthen Path Farm
RR 1, Box 52BB, Lake City, MN 55041, (507) 753-2080

Many Hands Farm
RR 1, Box 125, Theilman, MN 55945, (507) 534-3047

The Downtown Rochester Farmers' Market
P.O. Box 6554, Rochester, MN 55903
Farmers' Market Parking Lot, 400 block of 4th Street SE, Rochester, MN
Located one block east of Civic Center Drive.

Rochester's open air Farmers' Market is a popular place on Saturday mornings from spring to fall. Browse among 60-plus vendors for fresh fruits, vegetables, flowers, herbs, plants, fresh meats, cheeses, breads and other products. No resales or manufactured products are sold at the Farmers' Market.

Cost: free admission
Season: May–October: Saturday mornings: 7:30 a.m.–noon

The Greater Rochester Grower's Market, Inc.
West Parking Lot, Miracle Mile Shopping Center, 16th Avenue NW, Rochester, MN

This seasonal Farmers' Market is conveniently located in the west parking lot of the Miracle Mile Shopping Center. This small-sized market features five to six vendors who sell fresh produce, meats, and plants.

Cost: free admission
Season: June–October, Wednesdays, 2 p.m.–6 p.m.; Saturdays, 8 a.m.–2 p.m.

Gardening

Annual Garden Tours

Annual garden tours are listed below. Information about the garden tours may usually be found in the Rochester Post-Bulletin or by contacting the organization directly for specific dates, times, and cost.

Friends of the Chatfield Public Library Garden Tour
314 South Main Street, Chatfield, MN 55923, (507) 867-3480
Scheduled every other year in mid-July, usually the second weekend in July

Garden Path Tour

Women's Resource Center, 77 East 5th Street, Winona, MN 55987, (507) 452-4440

Mayowood Garden Tour and Private Garden Tour

1195 West Circle Drive, Rochester, MN 55902, (507) 282-9447
Held on the last Saturday in June

Rochester Garden & Flower Club's Tour

(507) 282-4265, www.dwebsite.com/gardenclub
Held on the third Thursday in July

Annual Spring Gardening Seminar

Rochester Community Education, 201 8th Street NW, Rochester, MN 55901, (507) 285-8350,
www.rochester.k12.mn.us/community-ed

This annual event is cosponsored by Rochester Community Education and the
Olmsted County Master Gardeners in mid-March. The seminar includes a keynote
speaker and two hour-long sessions, each with a few choices of different gardening
topics. Topics have included shade gardening, lawn care options, gardening with
children, wildlife in the urban garden, floral basics, and growing vegetables in a small
area. For more information or registration materials, call Rochester Community
Education or look for the Annual Spring Gardening Seminar in the Winter/Spring
Community Education catalog.

Garten Marketplatz Perennial Farm

5225 County Road 15 SW, Byron, MN 55920, (507) 281-1023, www.gartenmarketplatz.com
Located 6 miles SW of Rochester, take Salem Road (County 25) 3 miles to Olmsted County 15, drive
south on County Road 15 for 3 miles.

Spend a leisurely afternoon strolling through the garden displays at Garten
Marketplatz. Visitors to the 10-acre, Civil War era farm are invited to relax and
enjoy the country atmosphere at the Garten by bringing a picnic lunch, letting the
children romp around on the play fort, listening to songbirds, or conversing with a
friend. The farm features more than 750 varieties of perennials as well as a large
selection of annuals, herbs, trees, and shrubs. The friendly and knowledgeable staff is
eager to assist even the novice gardener with garden planning and plant selection.
The "Garten House," located in an 1860s brick home, provides customers with a
pleasurable shopping experience away from the hustle and bustle of the retail nursery. Distinctive garden decor and accessories such as sculptures, benches, gazing
balls, garden flags, and more are displayed throughout the grounds and in the Garten
House. In addition to garden-related gifts, the Garten House also has a variety of
decorative items for the home, including a unique selection of indoor fountains.

Special events at a Garten Marketplatz? That's right! Garten Marketplatz not only
offers gardening classes, but some good old-fashioned fun out in the country by
hosting a Spring Celebration Open House (first and second weekends in May)
complete with Kettle Korn and 1919 Keg Rootbeer, Pictures in the Garden by
Sonja's Studio, a Community Garage Sale (August), and special events for Memorial
Day, Father's Day, the fourth of July, Labor Day, and in November and December,
their nostalgic "Christmas in the Country" displays and gift show. Looking for a
place to hold your meeting or special event? Reserve the garden greenhouse. The
Garten will also provide space, free-of-charge, for nonprofit organizations sponsoring a community fundraiser. Remember, if you just want to get some dirt under

your fingernails, at Garten Marketplatz, "there's always room for one more at the potting bench."

Cost: varies by purchase
Hours: open daily, call for seasonal hours

Minnesota Master Gardener Program

Olmsted County Extension Service, 1421 3rd Avenue SE, Rochester, MN 55904, (507) 285-8253, www.mg.umn.edu/, www.olmstedcounty.com/extension

The Minnesota Master Gardener Program, currently administered by the University of Minnesota Extension Service, is an educational program that was created in 1977 to provide volunteers with professional training in horticulture. In order to become a Master Gardener, individuals must complete an application process followed by coursework including the Master Gardener Core Course, 48 hours of classroom instruction, and a 50 hour volunteer internship. Upon completion of these require-ments, Master Gardeners must follow county guidelines in their volunteer work and remain up-to-date with horticultural topics through educational conferences. The Master Gardener is also required to volunteer a minimum of 25 hours annually by assisting the County Extension Service and their community with horticultural programs. Typical activities performed by a Master Gardener include teaching classes and workshops, guiding and supervising school gardens and community plantings, fielding phone inquiries regarding home horticulture, judging 4-H exhibits, and writing newspaper columns. If you're interested in becoming a Master Gardener, contact your County Extension office.

Rochester Garden and Flower Club

(507) 282-4265,www.dwebsite.com/gardenclub

Anyone interested in gardening, beginner to expert, is welcome to join the Rochester Garden and Flower Club. The club holds monthly meetings on the third Thursday of every month, except in May and July, at 7:30 p.m. Meetings typically feature a speaker who presents a program on a specific topic or current gardening technique, and a hands-on workshop is usually held every other month. Additional club activities include an Annual Plant Sale and Annual Garden Tour, held the third Thursday in May and the third Thursday in July, respectively. Membership in the Rochester Garden and Flower Club also includes membership in the Minnesota State Horticultural Society, the Club's parent organization, and a subscription to *Northern Gardener Magazine*.

Rochester's Municipal Garden Plots

Rochester Park and Recreation Department, 201 4th Street SE, Room 150, Rochester, MN 55904, (507) 281-6160, www.ci.rochester.mn.us/park

Several 20-by-30-foot garden plots, owned by the City of Rochester, are available for rent in Essex Park and Zumbro Park South. The plots are tilled in the spring, weather permitting. Reservations for garden plots may be made in person or by mailing in the fee after January 1st of each year.

Cost: $
Hours: dawn–11 p.m.

Orchards

Berry Farms (U-Pick & Pre-Picked)

The strawberry picking season is typically from early June through the first week of July. You may pick your own or buy pre-picked berries at the farms listed below. Many of these farms also raise raspberries or other berries that are available from mid-summer to early fall. Call to confirm picking conditions, hours and cost.

Chester Berry Farm

9546 10th Street SE, Rochester, MN 55904, (507) 269-4748
Take U.S. Hwy. 14 East to Olmsted County Road 102, drive 1 mile north, turn right onto 10th Street.

Preston Apple and Berry Farm

645 Hwys.16 and 52 East, Preston, MN 55965, (507) 765-4486

Red's Berries

58619 280th Avenue, Byron, MN 55955, (507) 635-5299. www.redsberries.com
From U.S. Hwy. 14 West in Byron, turn north (right) on County Road 5, drive 7 miles on County Road 5 and look for signs. Red's Berries will be on the left side of the road.

Sekapp Farms

3415 College View Road SE, Rochester, MN 55904, (507) 282-4544
Located one mile east of Rochester on County Road 9

Sterling Berry Farm

5542 23rd Street NE, Rochester, MN 55906, (507) 252-1309
Located 3 miles east of Broadway on U.S. Hwy. 14, then 3 miles north on County Road 11

ROCHESTER
Sekapp Orchard

3415 Collegeview Road East, Rochester, MN 55904, (507) 282-4544, www.mnfarmtours.com
Located one mile east of Rochester on County Road 9.

Although Sekapp Orchard is located on the outskirts of Rochester, you'll feel like you're out on the farm. A flavorful experience awaits those eager to sample many of the apple varieties, which include Duchess, Beacon, Paula Red, Wealthy, Honeygold, McIntosh, Haralson, Regent, Fireside, Cortland, and more. Squashes, cucumbers, peppers, onions, and tomatoes are some of the fresh vegetables available in season. The orchard salesroom also has apple cider, honey, jams, jellies, and maple syrup for sale. It's especially fun for children to visit Sekapp's in October when there is an abundant supply of pre-picked pumpkins scattered throughout the yard. Seasonal decorations such as decorative gourds and Indian corn are also available.

Cost: varies by purchase
Season: mid-July–December

ELGIN
Wescott Orchard and Agriproducts

RR 1, Box 13, Elgin, MN 55932, (507) 876-2891, www.wescottagriproducts.com
Located one mile east of Elgin on County Road 25.

Wescott Orchard and Agriproducts, a fruit packager and distributor, opens as a fall retail outlet for the public during the apple season. The orchard offers eighteen varieties of apples, freshly pressed cider, locally made honey, jams and jellies, caramel apples, and other apple related products.

Cost: varies by purchase
Season: open year-round, 8 a.m.–4:30 p.m.

KASSON
King's Orchard
2763 County Hwy. 34, RR 1, Box 50, Kasson, MN 55944, (507) 634-7830
Located on Hwy. 14 near Kasson

King's Orchard is a family-owned business that has been in operation since 1980. The orchard raises approximately 20 apple varieties, and customers are welcome to sample many types of apples. The orchard store sells pre-picked apples, apple cider, apple-related accessories, seasonal decorative items, honey, produce, jams and jellies as well as fresh produce, flowers, pumpkins, squash, and gourds. You pick and pre-picked raspberries are available from early July to early August.

Cost: varies by purchase
Season: August–November: Monday–Saturday, 9 a.m.–7 p.m.; Sunday, noon–6 p.m.

LA CRESCENT
La Crescent: Apple Capital of Minnesota
La Crescent is also known as the "Apple Capital of Minnesota" and the "Gateway to Apple Blossom Scenic Drive." The Apple Blossom Scenic Drive runs north from La Crescent for approximately seven miles and takes you to some of the most spectacular views of the Upper Mississippi River Valley from southeastern Minnesota's blufflands. In addition to magnificent scenery, you will see charming homes and farms along the way as well as the opportunity to stop by an orchard or two. To access Apple Blossom Scenic Drive, go to Main Street in La Crescent and follow the apple-shaped signs for the scenic drive. As you head north on Apple Blossom Drive the road will be renamed Winona County Road 1 at the county line. After completing the seven mile scenic drive you may turn right on Winona County Road 12 for a steep descent into Dakota. Interstate 90 may be accessed from Dakota. Another option is to turn left on Winona County Road 12 to Nodine and drive north to Interstate 90 and Great River Bluffs State Park. Please contact the La Crescent Chamber of Commerce, P.O. Box 132, La Crescent, MN 55947, (507) 895-2800, 800-926-9480 or check out www.lacrescent.com for more information about Apple Blossom Scenic Drive or apple orchards in the La Crescent area.

LAKE CITY
Pepin Heights Orchard
Hwy. 61, Lake City, MN 55041, 800-652-3779, www.pepinheights.com
Located 1½ miles south of Lake City on Hwy. 61.

Stepping into the Pepin Heights Orchard store is like experiencing a celebration of autumn. The inviting atmosphere encourages visitors to browse among not only an assortment of apples, but a huge selection of gifts, seasonal decorations, and specialty food items. As Minnesota's largest orchard, Pepin Heights sells a wide variety of premium apples including Honeycrisp, Cortland, McIntosh, Paula Red, Sweet Sixteen,

Honeygold, Fireside, Regent, Gala, Delicious, Chestnut Crab, Haralson, Cortland and more. Apples are sold by the bushel or pound. For a refreshing treat, try Pepin Heights Sparkling Cider or one of the many other flavors of apple cider such as apple-cranberry, apple-blackcherry or apple-raspberry. A variety of specialty foods sold at the orchard includes confections, jellies and jams, fruit butters, syrups, baking mixes, crackers, and cheeses as well as fresh pies, cheesecakes, caramel apples, apple turnovers, fritters and muffins. Pumpkins, gourds, fall bouquets, wreaths, mums, and Indian corn round out the selection of the seasonal decorations for sale. Custom gift baskets may be ordered and shipping is available. No orchard tours or pick-your-own apples.

Cost: varies by purchase
Season: August–Christmas Eve: open daily, 9 a.m.–6 p.m.; call for late fall hours

MAZEPPA
Apple Ridge Orchard
County Road 1, Mazeppa, MN 55956, (507) 843-3033, www.appleridgeorchard.com

Family fun awaits visitors at Apple Ridge Orchard. Located in the rolling country-side of Mazeppa, Apple Ridge provides tractor-pulled wagon rides out to the orchard and pumpkin patch for a "u-pick" experience. Visitors enjoy an abundance of fresh air and a festive fall atmosphere on the wagon rides that are available on weekends during the harvest season. Children also like to feed and watch the fenced-in, barnyard animals at the orchard. If you're just out for a scenic drive, stop by the Apple Ridge store to purchase freshly pressed cider, apples, apple products, and pumpkins.

Cost: varies by purchase
Hours: call for current hours

PRESTON
Pine Tree Orchards, Inc.
County Road 17, Preston, MN 55965, (507) 765-2408
Located off Hwy. 52 South on County Road 17.

Pine Tree Orchard's on-farm store sells a large variety of apples, apple cider, apple-related gifts, jams, jellies, and gift baskets. There is also an on-site apple bakery with pies, breads, donuts, and caramel apples for sale. Orchard tours are available by reservation from September through October. During selected dates in October, the orchard offers wagon rides to the pumpkin patch where customers may pick their own pumpkins. Call for times regarding wagon rides.

Cost: varies by purchase
Season: August–December: open daily, 9 a.m.–6 p.m.

Preston Apple and Berry Farm
645 Hwy. 16 and 52 East (off Hwy. 52 on County Road 17), Preston, MN 55965, (507) 765-4486

The Preston Apple and Berry Farm, located on the south edge of Preston, has an inviting country store atmosphere. In addition to 28 apple varieties, the farm offers apple cider, an on-site bakery with fresh and frozen apple pies, turnovers, muffins, apple bars, apple donuts, and caramel apples as well as pumpkin, peach, pecan, and raspberry pies. Free coffee is available with a bakery purchase. Sample a variety of apples while you browse through the large selection of food and garden products including wild rice, honey, popcorn, nuts, Wisconsin cheese and cheese curds, squash, perennials, calico corn, mums, flower bulbs, gourds, and small pumpkins. A full line of Watkin's products as well as Amish-made candies, jams, and baskets are also available. Customers may pick their own strawberries (June–July) and raspberries (July–September), but should call before coming to pick. Garden seeds and bedding plants are available in April and May. Wagon rides to the pumpkin patch are offered on Sunday afternoons during September and October. The Preston Apple and Berry Farm also takes orders for Michigan blueberries, cherries, and peaches. Gift boxes and shipping are available.

Cost: varies by purchase
Season: May–December: daily, 9 a.m.–7 p.m. (open at 7 a.m. during strawberry season); mid-January–mid-March: closed

Christmas Tree Farms

ROCHESTER
Choose and Cut Fraser Firs
2230 48th Street NE, Rochester, MN 55906, (507) 289-8811, www.fraserfirs.net
Located one mile north of Shopko North on U.S. Hwy. 63 North, turn right at Stock Lumber (48th Street), drive one mile, tree farm will be on the right side of the road.

Choose and Cut Fraser Firs is a 13-acre tree farm that exclusively grows Fraser firs. Lighted fields provide customers with the opportunity to search for the perfect Christmas tree during the evening hours. Cut your own tree, select a pre-cut tree, or have one of the staff cut the tree of your choice. Enjoy a handful of free peanuts while you wait for your tree to be trimmed. Customers may also purchase Christmas tree stands and fresh wreaths fashioned from the farm's trees. Shake and bale service, and delivery is available. Saws and twine provided.

Chris Manahan Tree Farm
1820 55th Avenue NE, Rochester, MN 55906, (507) 289-1159

Cut your own tree from a selection of spruce and pines on this small 7-acre tree farm. Saws and twine provided.

Schulz Christmas Trees
85th Street SE, Rochester, MN 55904, (507) 288-3999
Located off Hwy. 63 South between 80th and 85th Streets just past the Rochester airport exit.

Family traditions have been made at Schulz Christmas Trees since 1965. Customers are brought out to the fields of the 160-acre farm by horse-drawn sleigh (weekends only) to search for just the right Christmas tree and receive a return ride with their tree in tow. Several varieties are available including Scotch pine, Norway pine, white pine, Colorado blue spruce, Black Hills spruce, balsam fir, and Fraser fir. Pre-cut trees and wreaths are also available. Saws and twine provided.

FOUNTAIN
Spruce Pine Tree Farm
RR 1, Fountain, MN 55935, (507) 285-1168
Located 35 miles south of Rochester on the west side of U.S. Hwy. 52.

A good old-fashioned romp in the woods awaits visitors of Spruce Pine Tree Farm. Customers are likely to spot wildlife as they roam throughout the 110-acre tree farm situated in rural southeastern Minnesota. The 110-acre rural tree farm has an abundant selection of trees including white, Scotch, and red pine; blue, Black Hills, white and Norway spruce; and balsam, Fraser, Douglas, and concolor firs. Although the trees are shaped and trimmed, the farm itself is not manicured. Pre-cut trees are available. Saws and twine provided.

KELLOGG
Mountainland Timber Tree Farms
Pine Tree Road, Kellogg, MN 55945, (507) 767-4555, (763) 753-4938

A family-oriented experience at this tree farm includes horse-drawn wagon rides the first three weekends of the season, a visit from Santa the first two weekends in December, and hot cider and cookies. Cut your own tree or select a pre-cut tree from this 70-acre farm, which grows balsam firs, Scotch pines, white pines, Norway pines and spruce trees. A gift shop is located on the premises. Wreaths, garland, and crosses are also available. Saws and twine provided.

Nielsen Tree Farm
RR 1, Box 27, Kellogg, MN 55945, (507) 767-2296, (507) 767-4476
Located just off Hwy. 61 on County Road 84 between Weaver and Kellogg.

Wander through this 160-acre tree farm to find just the right Christmas tree or select a pre-cut tree at Nielsen Tree Farm. Well-maintained roads provide the customer with the opportunity to drive throughout the farm to look for their tree. Tree varieties include white, Scotch, and Norway pines; blue, Black Hills, and white spruce; and balsam and Fraser firs. Meet Rudy the white-tailed buck and feed the fawns while you're out on the farm. Shake and bale service available. Saws and twine provided.

SPRING VALLEY
Hellrud's Christmas Trees
Route 1, Box 123, Spring Valley, MN 55975, (507) 346-2389
Located 1 mile south of Minnesota Hwy. 16 between Spring Valley and Wykoff.

Cut your own tree at this 18-acre farm, which was once the site of a stage coach stop. Varieties include Scotch pine, white pine, white spruce and Colorado blue spruce. Saws and twine provided.

ZUMBRO FALLS
Windmill Haven
Zumbro Falls, MN 55991, (507) 753-2415
Drive 1½ miles north of Zumbro Falls on U.S. Hwy. 63 to County Road 72. Farm is 1 mile east on County 72.

Cut your own tree on this four-acre tree farm that grows Fraser firs, balsam firs, white pine, and Austrian pine. No pre-cut trees are available. Saws and twine provided. Cookies and cider are served on weekends.

Chapter 16: Parks

Rochester City Parks

Rochester Park and Recreation Department

201 4th Street SE, 150 City Hall, Rochester, MN 55904, (507) 281-6160, www.ci.rochester.mn.us/park

The Rochester Park System is a community treasure! The city of Rochester boasts more than 2500 acres of parkland and 70-plus parks. Park amenities include a diverse array of facilities including playgrounds, neighborhood and community parks, sports complexes and playing fields, an archery range, indoor and outdoor swimming pools, a public beach with fishing pier, indoor and outdoor ice rinks, natural areas, garden plots, three golf courses and a golf learning center, a running track, an outdoor tennis center, 29-plus miles of paved recreation trails, a dog park, historic sites and more. A comprehensive list of the Rochester Parks with their locations and facilities is provided below. A map of the Rochester Park and Recreation System including the paved bike/recreation trails may be found in Appendix 2. Please note that athletic facilities and playing fields within the parks may not be reserved. They are available on a first come, first served basis; however, city and youth sponsored athletic teams have priority to use park facilities and fields for organized league games.

Hours: 6 a.m.–11 p.m.; except Essex, Foster-Arend, and Quarry Hill Parks, 6 a.m.–sundown

Information about specific park and recreation facilities and/or activities is located in the following chapters:

Chapter 6: Historic Sites
Chapter 14: Nature Centers
Chapter 15: Gardening
Chapter 18: Recreational Sports
Chapter 20: Winter Recreation

Picnic Shelters

The following parks have picnic shelters that may be reserved by calling the Rochester Park and Recreation Department (507) 281-6160. Reservations may be made beginning on January 15th for the current year only. Shelters may be reserved for use during the months of May through September.

Bear Creek Park
Central Park
Cooke Park
East Park
East Silver Lake Park
Eastwood Park
Essex Park

Foster-Arend Park
Kutzky Park
Quarry Hill Park
Slatterly Park
Soldiers Field Memorial Park
Three Links–Silver Lake Park
West Silver Lake Park

Rochester Park & Recreation Department • Park System

2564.38 Acres

NORTHWEST PARKS

Feature matrix — an "X" indicates the feature is present at that park.

Park	Acres	Undeveloped	Picnic Shelter	Restrooms	Play Equipment	Baseball Fields	Softball Fields	Basketball	Football Fields	Volleyball	Tennis Courts	Horseshoes	Soccer Fields	Swimming	Hockey	X-Country Ski	Sledding Hills	Special Features
Allendale, 3000 Block of 18th Ave NW	8				X	X					X							
Arborglen, 31st Ave & Arbor Dr NW	4.2				X													
Cascade Lake, 3rd St & W Circle Dr NW	60	X													X			Heritage House
Central, 1st Ave & 2nd St NW	1.6		X	X								X						
Cimarron, 48th St & 20th Ave NW	3.0																	
John R. Cooke, 7th St & 7th Ave NW	12.7		X	X	X	X			X	X	X	X	X					
Crescent, 28th St & 15th Ave NW	.6				X													
Diamond Ridge, 46th Ave & Valley Dr NW	4				X	X							X					
Elton Hills, 13th Ave & 22nd St NW	1.7				X													
Elton Hills Run, 9th Ave & 30th St NW	5	X			X													
Essex, 5455 West River Road NW	160.7		X	X	X					X		X				X	X	Archery Range/Trails
Foster-Arend, 37th St & East River Rd	40.7		X	X	X					X		X		X				Lake/Beach/Fishing
Goose Egg, 9th St & 2nd Ave NW	2.8				X						X							
Indian Heights, 600 Block Terracewood Dr NW	36.5	X															X	Trails
E. Starr Judd, 3rd St & 36th Ave NW	6.7				X						X							
Kings Run, 50th St & 18th Ave NW	11				X													
Kutzky, 2nd St & 13th Ave NW	24.1		X	X	X	X		X	X	X	X	X	X					Tennis Center
Lincolnshire, 48th St & West Circle Dr NW	25	X																
Lutheran School, 2619 9th Ave NW	8				X	X			X	X	X		X					Property Leased
Manor, 3rd St & 42nd Ave NW	11.3			X	X	X						X			X			
Nachreiner, 22nd St & 25th Ave NW	4.5				X	X									X			
North, Fairway Dr & 44 Ave NW	7				X								X					
Northern Hills, 4805 W Circle Dr NW	200		X															Golf Course
Northern Hills Prairie, West Circle Dr NW	7	X																
Northgate, 24th St & 21st Ave NW	2.4		X		X			X										Spray Pool
Northwest, 4400 Block of 56th St NW	9				X													
Recreation Center, 21 Elton Hills Dr NW	15													X	X			Gym/Ice Rinks/Pool
Riverview West, West River Parkway NW	11																	Open Play Field
Rolling Green, 38th St & 21st Ave NW	.3				X													
Schmidt, 63rd St & 24th Ave NW	20				X	X												
Thompson Mill Race, 13th St & 3rd Ave NW	4.1				X										X		X	Historical Site
Viking, 26th St & 2nd Ave NW	7.5				X								X					
Watson Sport Complex, 41st St & West River Rd	55				X													
Wedgewood Hills, 52nd Ave NW	5.1				X													
Zumbro North, 41st St & West River Road NW	106	X																

Silver Lake, John R. Cooke, and Slattery Parks are fully accessible and meet the intent of the Americans with Disabilities Act requirements.

		SOUTHEAST PARKS	Acres										Notes

SOUTHEAST PARKS

Park	Acres	Notes
Bear Creek, Hwy 14 & Marion Rd SE	124	Trails
Eastwood, Hwy 14 E	188.4	Golf Course
Carl & Jean Canine Park, Pinewood Rd SE	6	
Homestead, 8th St & 15th Ave SE	28.5	
Joyce, Melody St & Hilltop Ave SE	2	
Mayo Memorial, E Center St & Civic Center Dr	26.9	Mayo Civic Center
McQuillan, 1655 Marion Rd SE	10	Softball Complex
Meadow, 20th St & 5th Ave SE	5	
Meadow Park Estates, 16th St & 11th Ave SE	3.5	
Slatterly, 10th St & 11th Ave SE	34.6	Frisbee Golf
Smetka, 11th Ave & Pinewood Rd SE	60	

NORTHEAST PARKS

Park	Acres	Notes
Buckridge, 5500 Portland Ct NE	13	
Century Hills, North of Century High School	9	
East Park, East Center St & 15th Ave NE	35	Frisbee Golf
Hawthorn Hills, 1925 48th St NE	206	Golf Learning Cntr.
Mayo Field, 403 East Center Dr	11.4	Maintenance Cntr.
Northern Hgts, 22nd St & 10th Ave NE	49	Trails
Northern Hgts East, Viola Hgts Rd & Nor Valley Dr	6.14	
Northern Slopes, 30th St & 6th Ave NE	2	Property Leased
Parkwood Hills, 22dn Ave & Parkwood Hills Dr NE	6.1	
Quarry Hill, 9th St & 19th Ave NE	264	Trails/Nature Center
Silver Lake, 7th St & 2nd Ave NE	125.8	Lake/Pool
Viking Hills, Whiting Lane NE	1.33	

SOUTHWEST PARKS

Park	Acres	Notes
Balhy Heights Tot Lot, 21st & Folwell Dr SW	.3	
Balhy Meadows, Balhy Hills Dr & Fox Valley Dr	6.1	
Bamber Ridge, 36th St & Halling Place SW	2.4	
Dinah Olin Bird Sanctuary, Skyline Dr SW	.5	Wildlife Area
Eagle Ridge, 4th St & Aspen Lane SW	6.04	
Elmcroft, 25th St & Oakridge Ave SW	4	
Fox Valley, Co Rd 22 & Fox Valley Rd SW	7	
Pine Ridge Estates, 22nd St & 5th Ave SW	5.1	No Public Access
Plummer Gardens, 1091 Plummer Lane SW	11	Historic Home
St Mary's, 4th St & 9th Ave SW	5.9	
Second Street, 2nd St & 23rd Ave SW	35	Property Leased
Soldiers Memorial Field, 244 E Soldiers Field Dr	145.3	Golf Course/Pool
South Point, South Point Dr SW	9	
Southern Hills, 11th Ave & Southern Hills Dr SW	3.87	
Southern Woods, 11th Ave & 48th St SW	20	
Younge, Fox Valley Dr & 23rd Ave SW	4	Property Leased
Zumbro South, From 5th Ave to Bamber Valley Rd	177	
Zumbro West, 1st St & 19th Ave SW	1	Trails
Mini-Parks & Parkways	21.7	

Rochester's Favorite Parks

The following Rochester Parks are perennial favorites and worth a visit: Bear Creek Park, Cooke Park, Essex Park, Foster-Arend Park and Lake, Kutzky Park, Mayo Memorial Park, Silver Lake Park and the Silver Lake Adventure Playground, Slatterly Park, Soldiers Field Memorial Park, and Quarry Hill Park and Nature Center.

Carl and Jean Frank Canine Park

The Carl and Jean Frank Canine Park, located at 11th Avenue SE and Pinewood Road in Rochester, provides a safe place for dog lovers to unleash their pets. The six-acre, fenced-in park has an open grassy area with a "doggie obstacle course" and creekside trail that wanders through the woods. Water and "mutt mitts" for cleaning up after your dog are available at the park. Park hours are 5 a.m.–11 p.m.

Rochester Adopt-a-Park Program

The Adopt-A-Park program was started in 1991. Families, groups, and organizations may volunteer to pick up litter and check for vandalism at their adopted park about twice a month. A three-year commitment is required to participate in the program, and the city will place a sign at the park's entrance to either recognize the group or in memory or honor of a loved one. Call Park and Rec for more info at (507) 281-6160.

Olmsted County Parks

Chester Woods Park

8378 Hwy. 14 East, Eyota, MN 55934, (507) 285-7050, www.olmstedpublicworks.com, e-mail: chesterw@venturecs.net

Chester Woods Park, located just 7 miles east of Rochester, has become a local favorite since it opened in the spring of 1995. The parkland is situated on the head-waters of Bear Creek, and it features 1335 acres of woods, prairie, stream, and bluffs that surround the park's 118-acre Chester Lake. Park facilities open to the public include a 52-site campground, two playgrounds (one handicapped accessible), several informal playing fields, a swimming beach with bathhouse at Chester Lake, seven separate picnic areas with covered shelters, 6-plus miles of hiking trails, 8–9 miles of equestrian trails, cross-country ski trails, a boat launch (electric motors only), canoe and paddleboat rentals, and a fishing pier. Nature programs and hikes are presented by park naturalists throughout the year. Pets are allowed in the park.

Cost: $
Hours: daily, 7 a.m.–10 p.m.

Graham Park and Arena at the Olmsted County Fairgrounds

16th Street SW and 3rd Avenue SE, Rochester, MN 55904, (507) 281-6189, (507) 285-8231, www.ci.rochester.mn.us/park

Graham Park, otherwise known as the Graham Arena Complex, is located on the Olmsted County Fairgrounds. The complex is primarily used as an exhibition facility and hockey arena. Annual events typically hosted at Graham Arena from April through September include arts and crafts shows, sporting events, concerts, antique shows, home and recreation shows as well as dog, horse, and livestock exhibitions. The arenas are converted into ice rinks during the winter months in order to provide the playing space needed to support Rochester's youth, high school, and adult hockey programs.

Cost: varies by event
Hours: vary by event

Oronoco Park

310 3rd Avenue NW, Oronoco, MN 55960, (507) 367-4526 or (507) 285-8231, www.mn-community.org/oronoco
Located off County Road 12, ½ mile east of Hwy. 52 North.

Oronoco Park is situated on the shores of Lake Shady, just a short distance from Highway 52 as it passes through Oronoco. The park's facilities are located in both open and shady areas and include several picnic areas, one picnic shelter, a playground, volleyball courts, horseshoe pits, grills, and a small campground with pit toilets and showers. A small sandy beach provides a play area and launching site for canoes and paddleboats. The White Bridge Boat Launch is available for boaters needing a standard size launch. It is located off County Road 12 between Oronoco and Sandy Point, adjacent to the Sandy Point Supper Club.

Cost: free
Hours: 7 a.m.–10 p.m.

Oxbow Park and Zollman Zoo

Oxbow Park, 5731 County Road 105 NW (at Olmsted 4 & 5 intersection), Byron, MN 55920, (507) 775-2451, www.olmstedpublicworks.com or e-mail: oxbow@venturecs.net

Oxbow Park is located in the scenic Zumbro River Valley. The 572-acre park has almost eight miles of maintained hiking trails, four picnic areas with covered shelters including one with a playground and ball field, a nature center, an outdoor zoo with 30 species of native Minnesota animals, a semi-primitive campground, a group campground for youth organizations, and access to the banks of the Zumbro River that wind through the park. The Oxbow Nature Center has a small exhibit of regional snakes and animal artifacts and is the home base for the park's interpretive programs, which are usually held on Saturday mornings and afternoons. During the winter months, the park maintains groomed cross-country ski trails, and snowshoe rentals for children and adults are available on weekends for a nominal fee. Chapters 12, 14 and 17, respectively, provide more detailed information about Oxbow's Campgrounds, Nature Center and Zollman Zoo. Please note that picnic areas and shelters are available on a first come, first served basis.

Cost: free
Hours: park: 7 a.m.–10 p.m.
  nature center and zoo: noon–8 p.m. (summer); noon–4 p.m. (winter)

CHATFIELD
Chatfield City Park

Hwy. 52/Main Street, Chatfield, MN 55923, (507) 867-3810, www.ci.chatfield.mn.us

This beautiful, old-fashioned city park is near the Chosen Valley Elementary School and within walking distance to downtown shops and restaurants. The center of the park is adorned with a sculptured fountain surrounded by a flower garden. There are plenty of shaded areas with picnic tables and benches, a large playground, band shell, rest rooms, and a Tourist Information Center located in the park.

Cost: free
Hours: park: dawn–10:30 p.m.
  tourist information center: May–mid-October; daily, 10 a.m.–4 p.m.

LAKE CITY
Hok-Si-La Park and Campground
Hwy. 61 North, Lake City, MN 55041, (651) 345-3855,www.lakecity.org or
www.mississippi-river.org/lakecity.html
Located 2 miles north of Lake City on Hwy. 61/63.

Hok-Si-La is an absolutely beautiful 250-acre-plus park that is situated on the shores of Lake Pepin. Visitors will find a peaceful atmosphere at the wooded, shady park, which has a wide, sandy swimming beach (no lifeguards), picnic tables, nature and hiking trails, playground equipment, volleyball courts, a nearby boat launch, and an on-site camp store connected to a small interpretive center with animal displays. Three screened-in shelters and a modern Dining Hall with a kitchen and cooler available for rent. Pets are permitted in the park. Use of the campground, shelters, and Dining Hall requires reservations. The park may be used during the winter months for hiking and cross-country skiing.

Cost: free
Hours: 8 a.m.–10 p.m.

McCahill Park
Hwy. 61, Lake City, MN 55041, (651) 345-2213, www.lakecity.org or
www.mississippi-river.org/lakecity.html
Located 3 blocks south of Hwy. 63.

Located near the Lake City Yacht Club's boat harbor, McCahill Park sports a large, modern playground, a tier one skate park, shaded picnic tables, and access to fishing from the pier. This is a great place to take a break as you travel along the Great River Road. Rest rooms are available.

Cost: free
Hours: 6 a.m.–11 p.m.

Ohuta Park
Lyon Avenue, Lake City, MN 55041, (651) 345-2213, www.lakecity.org or
www.mississippi-river.org/lakecity.html
Located 3 blocks east of Hwy 61.

Ohuta Park, otherwise known as "wave park," is a scenic oasis overlooking Lake Pepin and the surrounding bluffs. The park is easily identified by the contemporary wave-like statue that adorns its grounds in honor of Ralph Samuelson, the Father of Waterskiing, who discovered the sport from the shores of Lake Pepin in 1922. The park boasts a picnic area, playground facilities, and a sandy beach with a swimming area and a bathhouse. Lifeguards are on duty at the swimming beach during the summer. Riverwalk, a 2.5 mile pedestrian walkway that provides picturesque views of Lake Pepin, is within walking distance of Ohuta Park. Rest rooms are only available seasonally in the bathhouse.

Cost: free; swimming beach, $
Hours: park: 6 a.m.–11 p.m.
  swimming beach: open June–Labor Day, call for hours

Patton Park

Lyon and Oak Streets, Lake City, MN 55041, (651) 345-2213, www.lakecity.org or
www.mississippi-river.org/lakecity.html
Located one block south of the Hwy. 61–63 junction.

The image of a quaint small town park comes to life at Patton Park. The attractively
landscaped park occupies one city block and has a beautiful gazebo and fountain.
Cement walkways intersect the park, and there are many shaded areas with picnic
tables and park benches. No rest rooms are available.

Cost: free
Hours: 6 a.m.–11 p.m.

Roshen Park

Hwy. 61, Lake City, MN 55041, (651) 345-2213, www.lakecity.org or
www.mississippi-river.org/lakecity.html
Located near the south end of Lake City on Hwy. 61.

Lake City's Roshen Park offers beautiful views of Lake Pepin and has a great picnic
area for both large and small groups. Park facilities include a playground, tennis
courts, picnic shelters, and rest rooms. Picnic shelters may be used free of charge on
a first come, first served basis.

Cost: free
Hours: 6 a.m.–11 p.m.

LANESBORO
Sylvan Park

202 Parkway Avenue, Lanesboro, MN 55949, (507) 467-3722, 800-944-2670, www.lanesboro.com

Sylvan Park is a quiet haven within walking distance to Lanesboro's Award Winning
Main Street, which is the home to a delightful variety of restaurants, shops, the
Cornucopia Art Center, Commonweal Theater, Scenic Valley Winery, local museums,
the Root River Trail, and area outfitters that rent bicycles, canoes, and tubes. The
beautiful park is heavily shaded and has a small pond, large gazebo, modern playground, picnic tables and shelters, rest rooms, and a municipal campground. Come
enjoy a picnic in the park, fish in the pond, or feed the ducks before strolling downtown or pedaling the Root River Trail. During summer weekends, stop by the park to
meet the Amish people who come to Sylvan Park to sell their baked goods, quilts, and
baskets. See Chapter 12 for more information about the Sylvan Park Campground.

Cost: free
Hours: dawn–10 p.m.

MABEL
Steam Engine Park

South Main Street, Mabel, MN 55954, (507) 493-5299

Steam Engine Park is a fun place to stop as you wander through rural southeastern
Minnesota. The open, spacious park is located next to Mabel's Steam Engine

Museum. The park offers visitors a playground with swings, horseshoe pits, volleyball courts, picnic tables and park benches, two picnic shelters and bathrooms with flush toilets. Please note that the Steam Engine Museum (see Chapter 7) is open by appointment only, except during Steam Engine Days in September. Picnic shelters may be reserved free of charge.

Cost: free
Hours: 6 a.m.–10 p.m.

PLAINVIEW
Eastwood Park
510 2ⁿᵈ Avenue NE, Plainview, MN 55964, (507) 534-3701, www.plainviewmn.com

This popular park has a lot of recreational facilities including a softball field, two tennis courts with a practice hitting board, modern playground equipment, a sand volleyball court, basketball court, an archery range, an open ice-skating rink and a hockey rink with a warming house, a large picnic area with grills, and two picnic shelters with electricity. Park shelters may be reserved on a first come, first served basis. Rest rooms are available at the park.

Cost: park: free; shelter rental: $$–$$$, no rental fee for nonprofit groups
Hours: park: 6 a.m.–10 p.m.
  warming house: Monday, Tuesday, Thursday, and Friday, 3:30p.m.–5 p.m. &
  7 p.m.–9 p.m.; Saturday and Sunday, 1 p.m.–5 p.m. & 7 p.m.–9 p.m.

Eckstein Athletic Field
390 North Wabasha, Plainview, MN 55964, (507) 534-3701, www.plainviewmn.com

Eckstein Field is the site of Plainview's Community Swimming Pool as well as numerous recreational facilities including a lighted combination softball/baseball/football field, two little league baseball fields, two lighted tennis courts, a lighted basketball court, a half basketball court, and a paved walking trail that is almost one mile long.

Cost: park: free; pool: $
Hours: park: 6 a.m.–10 p.m.
  pool: open June–August, call for hours

Wedgewood Park
210 3ʳᵈ Street SW, Plainview, MN 55964, (507) 534-3701, www.plainviewmn.com

Plainview's oldest park features a large, handicapped-accessible playground with an interesting variety of play structures that are fun for both younger and older children. Wedgewood Park also has shaded and unshaded picnic areas as well as a large picnic shelter with electricity and lights. Park shelters may be reserved on a first come, first served basis. Rest rooms are available near the park.

Cost: free; shelter rental: $$–$$$, no rental fee for nonprofit groups
Hours: 6 a.m.–10 p.m.

RUSHFORD
Magelssen Bluff Park
Rushford, MN 55971, (507) 864-2444

Located on Hwy. 30 West just outside the city of Rushford. Take Hwy. 43 to Hwy. 30 West, turn right at sign for scenic overlook. Park is up the hill.

Rushford—these bold white letters displayed on the side of Magelssen Bluff capture the attention of visitors who enter the town. The limestone bluff located on the west edge of Rushford is actually a city park with overlooks that offer breathtaking views of area farms, several city landmarks, the Root River Bike Trail, and Rush Creek. As you explore the park, you will see what is considered to be the fifth largest tree in Minnesota—a bur oak that is approximately 175–200 years old. Park facilities include many picnic areas with tables and shelters, a playground, hiking trail, and toilets.

Cost: free
Hours: dawn–dusk; open seasonally from late spring–early fall

Magic Kingdom Park
Creekside Park, Hwy. 43 and Mill Street, Rushford, MN 55971, (507) 864-2444

Wow! The Magic Kingdom Playground in Creekside Park is a child's dream come true. Imaginary play rules at this playground that was constructed from wood and tires in 1990 by local families and volunteers. The playground sports wooden castles, tunnels, challenging obstacles, a "tire" horse and tire swings, standard swings, and baby swings. Additional sporting facilities at the park include ball fields as well as tennis, volleyball and basketball courts. The beautifully maintained park also has four picnic shelters with water and electric, a gazebo, and rest rooms with flush toilets. Picnic shelters may be reserved free of charge, but donations are suggested.

Cost: free
Hours: dawn–dusk

STEWARTVILLE
Bear Cave Park
10th Street NW, Stewartville, MN 55976, (507) 533-4745, www.stewartvillemn.com

Bear Cave Park is Stewartville's outdoor sports complex. It has several fields for soccer, softball and baseball, tennis courts, volleyball courts, Frisbee golf, newer playground equipment, a sandbox, picnic tables with two shelters, grills, walking and hiking paths, a native prairie grass area with an observation deck, and access to Florence Park via a path and bridge that crosses the Root River.

Cost: free
Hours: 8 a.m.–10 p.m.

Florence Park
Lake Shore Drive, Stewartville, MN 55976, (507) 533-4745, www.stewartvillemn.com

Lake Florence Park was renamed Florence Park by the city of Stewartville after a 1993 flood destroyed the dam that formed Lake Florence. The lake bed has since been replaced with parkland and the natural area continues to provide recreational facilities for residents and visitors. The nicely landscaped park has lots of shaded areas with picnic tables and shelters, one fully enclosed picnic shelter (available from mid-May to mid-October), a huge playground, volleyball courts, paved walking and recreation trails, a small pond, and rest rooms. Visitors may also access Bear Cave Park from Florence Park via a paved trail with a bridge that crosses the Root River.

During the winter months, the pond is used for open skating, and an ice rink with a warming house is available for hockey players. Meadow Park South, located at 2ⁿᵈ Avenue NE in Stewartville, also has two outdoor hockey rinks and a warming house.

Cost: free; picnic shelter rental: $$$
Hours: park: 8 a.m.–10 p.m.
   warming house: Monday–Friday, 3 p.m.–9 p.m.; Saturdays and school holidays,
   10 a.m.–9 p.m.; Sundays, 1 p.m.–9 p.m.

WINONA
Garvin Heights Park and Lookout
Garvin Heights Road, Winona, MN 55987, (507) 457-8258, www.visitwinona.com
From Hwy. 14/61, drive south on Huff Street to the top of the bluff on County Road 44.

A great place to begin your tour of Winona is Garvin Heights Park, which is situated high atop a 575-foot bluff that overlooks Winona and the Mississippi River Valley. The drive to the park offers scenic views and the majestic vistas seen from the bluff top extend for 20–30 miles up and down the river. Picnic areas are available at the park, but there are no rest room facilities. Access may be limited during the winter months.

Cost: free
Hours: daily, 24 hours a day

Lake Park
Lake Park Drive, Winona, MN 55987, (507) 457-8258, www.visitwinona.com
Lake Park may be accessed from Lake Park Drive, Huff, Sarnia, and Gilmore Streets.

Lake Winona is the central landmark of this magnificent park. Parkland surrounds the 300-acre lake and provides residents and visitors with a wide variety of recreational opportunities. Park facilities include a 5.5 mile multi-use paved recreation trail that runs around the lake, a historic band shell, the Winona Veterans' Memorial, a rose garden with 1,000 plants, picnic areas, tennis courts, a disc golf course, and softball fields. Those who love aquatic activities will enjoy the three boat docks (limited to 10 horsepower engines), four fishing piers and swimming beach.

Cost: free
Hours: daily, 8 a.m.–10 p.m.

Levee Park
Between Walnut and Johnson Streets on the Mississippi River, Winona, MN 55987, (507) 457-8258, www.visitwinona.com

Levee Park stretches out alongside the mighty Mississippi and offers spectacular views of the riverfront. Visitors may relax by sitting on a park bench, strolling on the riverside walkway, or picnicking at one of the many tables scattered throughout the park. If you're having trouble finding Levee Park, just look for the actual size steamboat replica located on its premises. This replica houses the Julius C. Wilkie Steamboat Center (507) 454-1254, a major Winona attraction, which is open seasonally from Memorial Day to Labor Day.

Cost: free
Hours: daily, 5 a.m.–11 p.m.

ZUMBROTA
Covered Bridge Park
Zumbrota City Hall, 175 West Avenue, Zumbrota, MN 55992 (507) 732-7318, www.zumbrota.com
Located on Hwy. 58 just past downtown Zumbrota.

Zumbrota's Covered Bridge Park features both historic sites and modern recreational facilities. The park's namesake, the Zumbrota Covered Bridge, was built in 1869 and currently stands 116 feet from its original location. Not only is the bridge on the National Register of Historic Sites, but it is also the last standing covered bridge in Minnesota. Other historic sites at the park include a railway depot (circa 1878) and an old country school house. The Kids' Kingdom Playground, designed by local school children and constructed by over 1,000 community volunteers, is a highlight of the park. In addition to swings, slides, and a sandbox, the playground sports an obstacle course, mazes, a catwalk, covered bridge, pirate ship, and a shaded picnic area. Other park facilities include shaded picnic areas, a picnic shelter, ball fields, sand volleyball courts, horseshoe pits, a municipal swimming pool, a campground, 5 miles of scenic walking trails, snowmobile trails, and an ice rink. The picnic shelter may be reserved by calling City Hall.

Cost: park: free; shelter rental: $$$
Hours: sunrise–10 p.m.

Zumbrota Covered Bridge Music and Arts Festival
A great time to visit the Covered Bridge Park is during this annual festival, which is held on the third Saturday of June. The festival features arts and crafts, antiques, flea markets, food vendors, sports tournaments, a parade, and a street dance. Please call Zumbrota City Hall at (507) 732-7318 for more information about the festival and other community activities held at the park.

Southeastern Minnesota State Parks

Minnesota Department of Natural Resources (DNR) 500 Lafayette Road, St. Paul, MN 55155-4040, (651) 296-6157, 888-MINNDNR (646-6367), www.dnr.state.mn.us

Basic information about southeastern Minnesota's State Parks is provided below. Park visitors may obtain more detailed information about park facilities and amenities by calling the park's office or the DNR, visiting the DNR website or stopping by the park office during a visit. Request a copy of the Minnesota State Parks Traveler Newsletter for extensive information about the parks and their scheduled activities and special events. State parks require visitors to purchase a daily or annual entrance permit for admittance to the parks. An annual permit is valid at all Minnesota State Parks. The parks are listed alphabetically by town.

ALTURA
Whitewater State Park
RR 1, Box 256, Altura, MN 55910, (507) 932-3007
Located 3 miles south of Elba on State Hwy. 74.

As southeastern Minnesota's favorite state park, Whitewater offers outdoor enthusiasts and day trippers the opportunity to explore the blufflands and spring-fed streams of the Whitewater River Valley. The park remains a popular destination because it provides visitors with the facilities to participate in outdoor recreational activities throughout the year. An added bonus is that the park is virtually mosquito-free due to the lack of standing water in the area. Park amenities include interpretive exhibits, a visitor's center, camping, a group center with winterized cabins, extensive hiking trails with handicapped accessibility, picnic areas with shelters, a sandy swimming beach, excellent trout fishing, snowshoeing, cross-country ski trails, a warming house, year-round naturalist programs, and a nature store gift shop. No horses, ATVs or snowmobiles are permitted in the park, but bikes are allowed on established roads.

CALEDONIA
Beaver Creek Valley State Park
RR 2, Caledonia, MN 55921, (507) 724-2107
From I-90, drive south on State Hwy. 76 for 24 miles, then take Houston County Road 1 west for 4 miles.

Beaver Creek Valley State Park is located in the southeastern most corner of Minnesota near Caledonia. The park's valley walls are composed of sandstone and dolomite and rise up about 250 feet from the spring-fed Beaver Creek. Outdoor enthusiasts love the 706-acre park, which boasts an abundance of wildflowers, migratory songbirds, a variety of wildlife, and some of the best trout streams in the state. Additionally, the park's terrain and shady areas provides visitors with a naturally cool environment in the summer. Camping, hiking, picnicking, snowshoeing, interpretive exhibits, and a nature store gift shop are available at the park.

LAKE CITY
Frontenac State Park
29223 County Road 28 Boulevard, Lake City, MN 55041, (651) 345-3401
Located 10 miles southeast of Red Wing on U.S. Hwy. 61, turn left on County Road 2.

Frontenac not only offers visitors the opportunity to explore nearly 3000 acres of forests, prairies, wetlands, river flats and bluff tops, but is also bustling with shore-birds, songbirds, and raptors. In addition to this, the mighty Mississippi River and Lake Pepin are just a short distance from the park. Amenities at Frontenac State Park include several miles of hiking, snowmobile, and cross-country ski trails as well as facilities for snowshoeing, a sledding hill with warming house, camping, fishing, picnicking, seasonal naturalist programs, and a nature store gift shop.

LEROY
Lake Louise State Park
12385 766th Avenue, LeRoy, MN 55951, (507) 324-5249
Located 1.5 miles north of LeRoy on County Road 14.

Lake Louise State Park is considered an "oasis" amid the farmlands of southeastern Minnesota and nearby Iowa. The 1150-acre parkland is primarily level with open fields and hardwood forests. Additionally, Lake Louise and the Upper and Lower Iowa Rivers are situated within the park's boundaries. Recreational facilities at the park include camping and horse camping, a swimming beach, fishing, picnicking, surfaced bike trails, carry-in boat access (electric motors only), seasonal naturalist programs, a nature store gift shop as well as snowshoeing, hiking, cross-country ski-ing, and snowmobile trails.

OWATONNA
Rice Lake State Park
Route 3, Owatonna, MN 55060, (507) 455-5871
Located 7 miles east of Owatonna on Rose Street.

Rice Lake State Park has marshes, lakes, meadows, and woods among its 1,000 acres as well as the shallow wetlands of Rice Lake. Native Americans once harvested wildlife from this lake that currently attracts large numbers of waterfowl during the migratory seasons. Bird watching and wildflower identification are popular activities with park visitors who also have access to camping and canoe camping, hiking trails, picnic areas, lake fishing, drive-in boat access (inquire about current boat restrictions), snowshoeing, cross-country skiing and snowmobile trails with an on-site warming house, interpretive exhibits, year-round naturalist programs, and a nature store gift shop.

PLAINVIEW
Carley State Park
c/o Whitewater State Park, Route 1, Box 256, Altura, MN 55910, (507) 932-3007
Located 4 miles south of Plainview on Wabasha County Road 4.

Rustic and secluded, Carley State Park provides visitors with a true back-to-nature experience with its majestic white pine trees and blankets of bluebells in the spring. The park offers primitive camping, picnicking, bird watching, snowshoeing, hiking and cross-country ski trails, trout fishing on the north branch of the Whitewater River, and an abundance of spring wildflowers.

PRESTON
Forestville/Mystery Cave State Park
Route 2, Box 128, Preston, MN 55965, Main Park (507) 352-5111, Cave (507) 937-3251
Located 4 miles south of State Hwy. 16 on Fillmore County Road 5, then 2 miles east on Fillmore County Road 118.

This park provides visitors with a variety of natural wonders as well as a step into the past at Historic Forestville's restored 1800s village, once owned by Thomas Meighen. Forestville State Park supports a diverse array of habitats including prairies, savannas, oak woodlands, and maple and basswood forests. Moreover, Mystery Cave is located within the park's boundaries and is an excellent example of the region's karst topography. Park facilities include camping and horse camping, picnic areas with shelters, fishing, several miles of hiking, horseback riding, cross-country ski and snowmobile trails, a winter warming shelter, snowshoeing, interpretive exhibits, seasonal naturalist programs, a nature store gift shop, and guided tours of Historic Forestville and Mystery Cave. Please see Chapters 5 and 6 for more information about Mystery Cave and Historic Forestville, respectively.

WINONA
Great River Bluffs State Park
Route 4, Winona, MN 55987, (507) 643-6849
From the north, take U.S. Hwy. 61 about 12 miles southeast of Winona to County Road 3. Park entrance will be 4 miles down the road. From I-90, take exit 266 (County Roads 12 and 3) and follow the signs to the park.

Great River Bluffs State Park is situated along Minnesota's Apple Blossom Scenic Drive and offers visitors absolutely breathtaking views of the Mississippi River Valley. The variety of natural habitats in the park is expansive and includes hardwood forests of oak, hickory, basswood, sugar maple, green ash and black walnut trees as well as remnant plantations of white pine. An especially unique plant in the park is "goat prairie," so named because it grows on 40–50° slopes, upon which only a goat could graze. Park facilities include a campground, bicycle campground (located off Hwys. 14/61), hiking trails, picnic areas, a nature store gift shop, snowshoeing, a sledding hill, and cross-country ski trails for both diagonal and skate skiing.

John A. Latsch State Park

c/o Whitewater State Park, Route 1, Box 256, Altura, MN 55910, (507) 932-3007
Travel north from Winona on U.S. Hwy. 61 for approximately 12 miles.

John A. Latsch, a Winona businessman and founder of the Izaak Walton League, is the namesake of this state park because he was instrumental in establishing this land as a state park. The park's 1500 acres consists of blufland, prairie, flood plain and oak forests. Visitors willing to hike up the ½ mile ravine will enjoy stunning vistas of the Mississippi River and eagle watching from the three bluffs—Faith, Hope, and Charity. A small campground, picnic area, and ½ mile hiking trail is available in the park. There is no on-site naturalist, but information about the park may be obtained by contacting the naturalists at Whitewater State Park. Please note that there is no public phone at this park.

Chapter 17: Zoos & Wildlife

ROCHESTER
Canada Geese at Silver Lake Park
Silver Lake Park, North Broadway Avenue and 13th Street NE, Rochester, MN
For more information contact the Rochester Park and Recreation Office, 201 4th Street SE, Room 150, Rochester, MN 55904, (507) 281-6160, www.ci.rochester.mn.us/park

A prime attraction in Rochester for both residents and visitors is the abundant population of Giant Canada Geese at Rochester's Silver Lake. Small numbers of the Giant Canada Geese first flocked to Rochester in 1947 after 12 large geese from Nebraska, donated by a former Mayo Clinic patient, were released at Silver Lake. Shortly thereafter, a new Rochester power plant located near Silver Lake began to use the lake as a source of cooling water, thus creating an ice-free lake throughout the winter. It is believed that the almost extinct subspecies of Giant Canada Geese was initially attracted to the combination of an ice-free lake and the small flock of resident geese at Silver Lake during their annual fall migration in 1948. It is estimated that 500 of the Canada Geese that migrated to Rochester that year settled in for the entire winter season. Today, Silver Lake is home to the world's largest concentration of Giant Canadian Geese, which number from 30,000–35,000 during the fall migration. Visitors to Silver Lake Park, especially children, like to feed and mingle among the large numbers of geese. Goose food is available for purchase from vending machines located near the parking lot on the west side of Silver Lake Park.

Cost: free, small fee for vending machines
Hours: 5 a.m.–11 p.m.

Goose Poop Art
Goose Poop Art? It's true. Gary Blum originally created Goose Poop Art in 1983 as a special gift for a couple that was relocating from Rochester. Apparently, the wife was not crazy about Rochester's geese and what they left behind, so Gary decided to have a little fun and make the couple a commemorative picture of Rochester out of goose poop. In 1994, Gary decided to test the demand for his Goose Poop Art since he had received a lot of requests for his unique artwork. After displaying his Goose Poop Art at just one craft show, Gary received national and international publicity on radio, television, and in newspapers. So if you're interested in a unique souvenir or gift from Rochester, consider Gary's Goose Poop Art, which may be viewed or purchased locally at Natalie's Hallmark Shop, 101 1st Avenue SW, Subway Level of the Marriott Hotel, (507) 288-4715; Soldiers Field Best Western, 401 6th Street SW, (507) 288-2677; by calling Gary directly at (507) 289-5537, or visiting his website at http://pages.prodigy.net/gooseguy. E-mail: gooseguy@prodigy.net.

Kennellamas
702 23rd Street SW, Rochester, MN 55902, (507) 288-0984

Arthur and Lois Kennel established Kennellamas in 1981 on a 10-acre parcel of land in southwest Rochester. Formerly in a rural area, the llama farm is now surrounded by a residential neighborhood known as Apple Ridge. Dr. and Mrs. Kennel began raising llamas as a family endeavor when their children were young. Now retired, the couple continues to breed and raise llamas and welcomes group visits by schools, scouts, vacation bible schools, seniors, individuals with special needs, veterinary students and other organizations and clubs. Tours generally include a 10–15 minute educational talk about the llamas and an opportunity to touch and lead the llamas. Visitors are also shown llama wool and some of the woven goods made from the wool. Picnic areas on the farm are available for use by tour groups and guests. If you can not make it out to the farm, you may arrange to have Kennellamas bring a llama to you for your special event.

Cost: free
Hours: by appointment

Mayo Clinic Peregrine Falcon Program

Mayo Clinic, 200 1st Street SW, Rochester, MN 55905, (507) 284-2511, www.mayoclinic.org
Located on subway level of Mayo Clinic Building adjacent to Patient and Visitor Coffee Shop.

Young peregrine falcons were nearly extinct due to pesticide use in the Upper Midwest. In the mid-1970s, Mayo Clinic was invited to participate as a release site for captive-raised peregrine falcons because the Medical Center's buildings were a similar height to their natural nesting habitats, an abundant pigeon population in downtown Rochester would provide a steady diet for the birds, and the lack of natural enemies in the area would encourage their survival. The program has successfully bred several young falcons atop Mayo Clinic buildings. Visitors may view photographs of the falcons and watch a video of their nesting box via closed-circuit TV at the exhibit located on the subway level of the Mayo Clinic building.

Woodruff's Llamas

804 Mayowood Road, Rochester, MN 55902, (507) 282-3854

A familiar Rochester sight is the llama farm located at the crossroads of 16th Street SW and Mayowood Road. Tours may be arranged to visit the 7½-acre farm where Sandy and Jim Woodruff have raised and bred llamas for over 17 years. These gentle, curious animals provide an interesting experience to visitors as they learn first hand about the llamas while petting, feeding and leading them. The Woodruffs have hosted visits to their farm for a variety of community groups and schools and also participate in the sponsorship of 4-H kids who do not live on a farm, but want to pursue llama breeding and care as a 4-H project. Occasionally, they will bring their llamas to special events at schools, nursing homes, or other facilities.

Cost: free
Hours: by appointment

BYRON

Zollman Zoo at Oxbow Park and Nature Center

Oxbow Park, 5731 County Road 105 NW (at Olmsted 4 & 5 intersection), Byron, MN 55920, (507) 775-2451, www.olmstedpublicworks, e-mail: oxbow@venturecs.net

The Dr. Paul E. Zollman Zoo is adjacent to the Oxbow Nature Center. This outdoor zoo opened in 1969 and is currently owned and operated by Olmsted County. The zoo is named in honor of Dr. Paul E. Zollman, a retired veterinarian, as a tribute to his dedication and service to both the treatment of injured animals and the Olmsted County Parks. The zoo houses 30 species of native Minnesota animals.

Live animal exhibits include eagles, owls, hawks, otters, gray wolf, cougar, bear, red fox, porcupine, domesticated farm animals, and the playful prairie dogs. A majority of the animals can not be returned to the wild due to injuries that would jeopardize their survival. Oxbow's large animal collection of bison, elk, and white-tailed deer is located in the Gordon Yeager Memorial Area across the street from the main zoo area. A restored prairie, pioneer home and antique farm implement display also gives visitors the opportunity to experience a touch of Minnesota's past.

Oxbow Nature Center and Zoo is located in Oxbow Park. The scenic 572-acre park, set in the Zumbro River Valley, has approximately eight miles of maintained hiking trails, four picnic areas with covered shelters including one with a playground and ball field, and a semi-primitive camping area with a playground, running water, rest rooms and showers. Fishing is permitted along the shores of the Zumbro River as it winds through the park.

Please see Chapter 14 for more information about the Oxbow's Nature Center and/or call for a current schedule of nature programs. Campsites, picnic areas and shelters are available on a first come, first served basis.

Cost: free, donations welcome, minimal fee for camping
Hours: zoo and nature center: Labor Day–Memorial Day, daily, noon–4 p.m.;
  Memorial Day–Labor Day, daily, noon–8 p.m.
  park: daily, 7 a.m.–10 p.m.

Farm Tours

Country Heritage Adventures
5209 County Road 21 NE, Elgin, MN 55932, (507) 282-6604, ww.mnfarmtours.com

Offers guided farm and orchard tours. Please see Chapter 5 for more information.

CHATFIELD
Pease Wildlife Museum
Thurber Building, 21 2nd Street SE, Chatfield, MN 55923, (507) 867-3810

The William Pease Wildlife Museum opened in 1989 as a tribute to the late William Pease who was an avid Chatfield outdoorsman. The museum displays Pease's collection of animal mounts and skins. Full animal mounts on display include a great blue heron, bald eagle, badger, leopard, snowy, screech and great horned owls, a wild turkey, snapping and bog turtles, a hawk, as well as other waterfowl and native Minnesota fish. Visitors may also view a variety of animal skins such as black bear, raccoon, red fox, mink, otter, muskrat, rattlesnake, otter, mink, lynx, and mountain lion. An interesting exhibit is the two-headed baby pig that was born on the Pease Farm. Other memorabilia in the museum includes Pease's Model T, antique fishing and hunting gear, and soap box derby race cars.

Cost: free
Hours: open by appointment only

Chatfield and William Pease Wildlife Management Areas
Both in rural Chatfield, these wildlife management areas are open to the public for hunting, trapping, and hiking.

The Chatfield Wildlife Management Area is located 6–7 miles west of Chatfield on Fillmore County Road 2. This area was the first piece of land purchased with state conservation wildlife funds collected from license plate donations. Look for a red-wood sign and small parking lot designating this area.

The William Pease Wildlife Management Area is two miles southwest of Chatfield. To access this area, take Hwy. 52 to Fillmore County Road 5, turn right on County 5, drive three miles, turn right onto County Road 102, follow this road until there is a fork in the road, take the left fork. This will bring you to the William Pease Wildlife Management Area, which is also the site of the Chatfield Fish & Game Club. For more information about the wildlife areas or Fish & Game Club, contact Dave's Barbershop, 225 South Main Street, Chatfield, MN 55923, (507) 867-3856 or write to The Chatfield Fish & Game Club at Box 392, Chatfield, MN 55923.

ELBA
Crystal Springs State Fish Hatchery
County Road 112, Elba, MN, (507) 796-6691
Take Hwy. 74 through Elba to Winona County Road 26, take a right and follow 26 to Winona County Road 37, follow 37 and take a left on Winona County Road 112. Hatchery will be about 1 mile down 112.

Visitors may view a newly renovated Rainbow Trout Observation Runway before entering the small, but interesting, Visitor's Center. A tank display of brown, rainbow, and brook trout, and an observation area of the hatchery's production raceway are the two main exhibits. Other exhibits include educational posters with information on the Minnesota Watershed and photographs of different fish species such as bass, perch, sunfish, crappies, catfish, and pike. Organized tours may be arranged for schools, scouts, clubs or family groups. Tours are not available for casual visitors.

Cost: free
Hours: Monday–Friday, 8 a.m.–4 p.m.; Saturday & Sunday, closed

HARMONY
Austin's Angora Goats and Mohair Gifts
RR 2, Box 41B, Harmony, MN 55939, (507) 886-6731, www.bluffcountry.com/austins.htm or e-mail: mohair@means.net

Ada and Jim Austin welcome you to visit their angora goat farm and gift shop. Ada is eager to introduce you to her babies in the "Kids Krib" and answer questions about their herd of 200 angora goats. Touch one of the baby angora goats at the "Kids Krib," and feel the luxurious hair that is the source of mohair wool. After learning about the goats, step into the gift shop where you may sample and/or pur-chase goat meat, cheese, milk, and fudge.

The gift shop also displays and sells handmade mohair-blend woolen products including sweaters, socks, blankets, coats, slippers, hats, capes, scarves, baby sweaters, and mittens. Eighty percent of the gift shop merchandise is handcrafted by approxi-mately fifteen professional mothers who spin, card, and knit the wool. Some of the truly unique gifts that you will find at Austin's are the handcrafted Santas and Woodsmen with mohair beards. Other items for sale include angora hides, goat skulls, raw mohair, dyed mohair and mohair-blend yarns.

Picnic tables are available for use by visitors. Primitive camping facilities are also located on the property. Please see Amish Country Camping in Chapter 12 for more information on the campground.

Cost: free
Hours: call for hours

HOUSTON
Money Creek Buffalo Ranch
Route 1, Box 72, Houston, MN 55943, (507) 896-2345, www.buffalogal.com, e-mail: sales@buffalogal.com

The Money Creek Buffalo Ranch is home to Cody, the movie star buffalo who had a major role in *Dances With Wolves* and has also appeared in the movie *Radio Flyer* as well as commercials for Energizer® batteries and Subway®. Visit the Money Creek Buffalo Ranch to meet Cody and take a Buffalo Gal Ranch Tour. Buffalo Gal Tours provide visitors with a first hand experience of a working buffalo ranch situated among the rolling pastures and bluffs of southeastern Minnesota. In addition to a herd of over 200 buffalo, the Ranch also has other animals including white-tailed deer, peacocks, Russian wild boar, Mouflon sheep, and a Shetland pony. Guided tours are available for groups as small as families or as large as an entire bus load. A lunch featuring buffalo meat is provided to large groups as part of the tour but must be requested for small group tours. Sunrise Breakfast Tours and Sunset Dinner Tours are also available. After your tour, stop by the Ranch's unique gift shop. The gift shop sells a complete line of buffalo meat and jerky products as well as one of a kind gift items and collectibles. Contact the Money Creek Buffalo Ranch via telephone or online to make arrangements for your group tour. The Buffalo Gal website has information about tours, holiday specials, the nutritional content of buffalo, buffalo recipes and cooking tips, rustic lodging available at the ranch, and a place to order meat and meat gift packages. By the way, Cody is available to make appearances at private parties, parades, fairs, and other special events.

Cost: small family groups: free (lunch available upon request for fee); large groups: $ fee per person (includes lunch)
Hours: by appointment

VanGundy's Elk Farm & Antler Shed Gift Shop
3383 State Hwy. 76, Houston, MN 55943, (507) 896-2380

At VanGundy's, "if we're home, we're open." Visitors may stop by the farm by chance or call ahead for a tour. Larry and Patty VanGundy began raising Rocky Mountain Elk, once native to Minnesota, in 1993. Their private elk farm started with six cows and one bull and currently has a total of 68 elk. The Antler Shed Gift Shop is a stunning gallery with an impressive variety of unique elk-related products from antlers to art work to medicinal supplements. VanGundy's sells "Vital-Ex" and other Velvet Antler products and supplements. Many scientific studies have indicated that these supplements increase energy, relieve arthritis symptoms, enhance mood and promote general wellness. While browsing through the gallery, take a few minutes to view the video of the "bugling bulls," which is both interesting and entertaining.

Cost: free
Hours: by chance or reservation

LANESBORO
Avian Acres Native Bird Supply & Petting Zoo
Route 2, Box 5, Lanesboro, MN 55949, (507) 467-2996, 800-967-BIRD (2473), www.aawildbirdsupply.com

Avian Acres Petting Zoo is situated on the rolling countryside of rural Lanesboro. The privately-owned zoo has a wide variety of animals including a miniature horse, donkey, llama, deer, ferrets, bunnies, raccoons, ducklings, emu, fox, peacocks, pheasants, chinchillas, goats, and exotic birds. Avian Acres provides a wonderful opportunity for families to enjoy the outdoors while they pet, feed, and observe the animals. Children love to frolic on the farm and find it irresistible to stop feeding the animals from ice cream cones full of corn feed. The zoo grounds are meticulous and prior to your self-guided tour, owner Bob will verbally guide you through the zoo.

After touring the zoo, stop by the barn to shop for birding and butterfly supplies. Novice and experienced bird watchers alike will find what they are looking for among the incredible selection of over 800 bird and butterfly feeders and houses, bird baths, heaters, fountains, and hangars. Try the best selling "Bob's Mix" or take home custom bird seed mixes that will attract your favorite birds. Avian Acres also carries birding optics, nature-related books, CDs and videos. Nationwide shipping via UPS and personal delivery within the region is available.

Cost: $ (zoo admission)
Hours: open daily, year-round, 9 a.m.–7 p.m.

Lanesboro State Fish Hatchery
State Hwy. 16, Lanesboro, MN 55949, (507) 467-3771

The Lanesboro State Fish Hatchery is the largest fish hatchery in southeastern Minnesota. It produces over one million brown trout and approximately 300,000 rainbow trout per year for northern Minnesota lakes and streams. The hatchery has a small classroom area with educational posters and video tapes. Guided tours are available for groups but must be arranged in advance. The hatchery is in the process of developing a self-guided tour of its facility for use by casual visitors. Tours are not currently available for drop-in visitors.

Cost: free
Hours: Monday–Friday, 7 a.m.–4:30 p.m.

MABEL
Brumm's Petting Zoo & Gifts
State Hwy. 43, 7 miles north of Mabel (look for sign), (507) 493-5507, e-mail: tcbrumm@means.net

As you travel off the beaten path on southeastern Minnesota's country roads, make arrangements to visit Brumm's Petting Zoo in the rural Mabel area. The zoo has a variety of animals and birds including chinchillas, prairie dogs, a pot-bellied pig, miniature horses and donkeys, pygmy goats, angora goats, llamas, Suffolk, Barbado and Mouflon sheep, emu, geese, ferrets, chickens, ducks, rabbits, and more. Brumm's Petting Zoo has become a popular attraction at local fairs and festivals and welcomes requests to set up their petting zoo at your special event. Snacks are sold at the zoo and picnic areas are located on the grounds. An on-site gift shop sells animal and Indian figurines as well as other craft items. The Brumm's are also in the business of buying, selling, and trading animals.

Cost: $ (on-site visits)
Hours: by appointment

PETERSON
Peterson State Fish Hatchery
Route 1, Box 85A, Peterson, MN 55962, (507) 875-2625
As you drive east on State Hwy. 16 (from the Lanesboro area), turn south (right) on County Road 25. The hatchery will be approximately one mile down County Road 25. Look for the hatchery domes.

The Peterson State Fish Hatchery primarily raises Lake Trout for inland lakes. The hatchery is available for scheduled tours that involve learning about the daily routines of feeding and cleaning the fish as well as monitoring water quality. The Visitor's Center features self-guided tours and a hiking trail that highlights local habitats. Reservations are needed for guided tours.

Cost: free
Hours: Monday–Friday, 7 a.m.–3:30 p.m.
 visitor's center: Monday–Friday, 8 a.m.–3 p.m.; Saturday and Sunday, call for morning hours

RACINE
B.E.A.R.C.A.T. Hollow
P.O. Box 1117, Racine, MN 55967, (507) 378-2221
Located 13 miles south of Rochester on Hwy. 63 South, turn left on 785th Avenue and follow the road to B.E.A.R.C.A.T. Hollow.

B.E.A.R.C.A.T. Hollow celebrated its Grand Opening in the spring of 2001. The nonprofit zoo and educational facility is privately owned and operated by Nancy and Ken Kraft. B.E.A.R.C.A.T. is an acronym for Beautiful Endangered and Rare Conservation and Therapy, which defines the zoo's mission as a sanctuary for rare and endangered animals, rescue animals or those that have been injured. The animals are typically rehabilitated and kept at the zoo or are traded to similar private zoo operations throughout the United States.

B.E.A.R.C.A.T. Hollow is home to a black bear, liger (a lion tiger hybrid), Bengal tiger, grizzly bears, camels, lynx, African lions and more. The friendly and knowledgeable zoo staff gives guided, train-drawn tours of the big animal areas. Guided tours generally last one hour. Self-guided tours are permitted in the petting zoo area, which houses fawns, donkeys, goats, and chickens. Fun and educational programs may be arranged for schools, nursing homes, day care centers, animal therapy, holiday parties or other special events. The zoo has a small gift area with animal related artwork and clothing for sale as well as a concession booth with snacks and a picnic area. Future plans at B.E.A.R.C.A.T. Hollow include the development and construction of an educational center and bunkhouse.

Cost: $$, all admission fees go toward the care and feeding of the animals
Hours: summer: May–October, open daily, call for times
 winter: call for days and times

Burr Oak Buffalo Ranch & Trading Post

RR 1, Box 30,78291 280ᵗʰ Street, Racine, MN 55967, (507) 378-5413, e-mail: burroak@hmtel.com

The Burr Oak Buffalo Ranch has 200 acres of land upon which a rotational grazing system with native grasses is used to raise approximately 125 head of buffalo. Tours of the ranch are available to visitors via hayride, but must be arranged in advance. A fun time to visit the Ranch is during the Annual Buffalo Fest in mid-July. It is usually scheduled on the same weekend as the Annual Antique Engine and Tractor Show just down the road in Spring Valley. The Trading Post is generally open on Saturday and Sunday afternoons and sells buffalo meat as well as other buffalo related products and souvenirs. Buffalo, also known as bison, is considered the new healthy red meat because it is raised without hormones and antibiotics and has 30% more protein, 50% less cholesterol, and 70% less fat than beef without the gamey taste. Shipping is available if you want to purchase buffalo meat but can't make it out to The Trading Post. Burr Oak also sells its buffalo meat at the Rochester Downtown Farmers' Market from May to October.

Cost: free
Hours: tours: by appointment
   trading post: Saturday and Sunday afternoons, call to confirm hours

WABASHA
The National Eagle Center and EagleWatch Observation Deck

River Vista Park, 152 Main Street, Wabasha, MN 55981, (651) 565-4989, www.eaglewatch.org or e-mail: 4eagles@wabasha.net

As the "Gateway to the Upper Mississippi River National Wildlife and Fish Refuge," Wabasha is a great place to view the American Bald Eagle because the Mississippi River Valley is a migration corridor for the eagles. The National Eagle Center was organized as a grassroots citizen science response to the spontaneous presence of eagles in the area and the people who observe them.

The temporary home of The National Eagle Center (NEC) is located on West Main Street adjacent to the banks of the Mississippi River. The NEC has interpretive exhibits, an aviary, observation deck, a video library, information about environmental education programs, and a gift shop with eagle-related products and souvenirs. Plans are currently underway to construct a permanent home for the NEC—The National Eagle Interpretive Building is scheduled to open in approximately 2004.

While visiting the NEC, resident eagles Harriet and Angel invite you to have a "nose-to-beak" experience at the aviary. Your visit will be up close and personal since Harriet and Angel are not kept in cages or behind glass; however, they are tethered to their perches. Although both eagles underwent rehabilitation at the University of Minnesota Raptor Center, they are unable to be released into the wild due to the nature of their wing injuries. Volunteers and/or staff are available to answer questions about the eagles, and visitors are welcome to take photographs of Harriet and Angel.

The EagleWatch Observation Deck, just a short walk from the NEC, offers breathtaking views from the banks of the Mississippi and is a prime spot for eagle watching. If you're unable to locate the 500-square-foot deck by the grand 17-foot wooden eagle statue carved by Jim Smit of Nelson, Wisconsin, just look for the deck at the intersection of Pembroke Avenue and Lawrence Boulevard. The EagleWatch deck is open 24 hours a day, but is staffed by volunteers from early November through March on Saturdays and Sundays from 1 p.m. to 3 p.m. Volunteers will answer questions about the eagles and assist with eagle spotting. Spotting scopes and binoculars provided by the NEC may be used by visitors. Please note that volunteers are available when weather conditions are 10°F or above, and there is no rain.

Cost: free, donations welcome
Hours: Tuesday–Friday, 9 a.m.–4 p.m.; Saturday and Sunday, 10 a.m.–4 p.m.; Monday, closed

WINONA
Prairie Island Nature Area
1120 Prairie Island Road, Winona, MN 55987, (507) 452-4501, www.visitwinona.com

Prairie Island Nature Area is within the boundaries of Prairie Island Park on the banks of the Mississippi River. In addition to picnic areas and playgrounds, the Nature Area has an enclosed Deer Park and a one-mile interpretive nature and wildlife trail. The level, looped trail can be hiked in approximately 30 to 45 minutes.

Upper Mississippi National Wildlife and Fish Refuge
Headquarters: Winona District, 51 East 4th Street, Winona, MN 55987, (507) 452-4232, www.umesc.usgs.gov/umr_refuge.html

The Upper Mississippi National Wildlife and Fish Refuge was established in 1924 in order to preserve the bottom lands of the upper Mississippi River for fish, migratory birds, wildlife, and people. The refuge spans over 261 river miles with more than 200,000 acres of water marsh, wooded islands, forest, and prairie from Wabasha, Minnesota, to Rock Island, Illinois. The sanctuary is home to 292 bird species, 57 mammal species, 45 species of amphibians and reptiles, and 118 species of fish. Approximately three million people annually visit the refuge to participate in fishing, hunting, boating, camping, picnicking, bird watching, nature study, and sight seeing activities. Despite its popularity, the area remains virtually unspoiled by visitors and modern technology. Please contact the Refuge headquarters for Public Use Regulations and permit information prior to your visit.

Cost: free
Hours: open 24 hours a day, year-round

Part V:
Sports & Recreation

Chapter 18: Recreational Sports provides extensive information about classes, clubs, leagues, and facilities available in the region including archery, ballroom dancing, baseball, bike trails, billiards, bowling, boxing, canoeing, dancing, fitness clubs, football, indoor and outdoor golf, martial arts, rowing, rugby, skateboard parks, adult sports leagues, soccer, swimming, tennis, track, volleyball and walking as well as youth sports organizations and adaptive recreation programs

Chapter 19: Spectator Sports is a guide to spectator sports available in the area including automobile and motocross racing, figure skating, water skiing, collegiate baseball, professional volleyball, and an 1860s baseball league.

Chapter 20: Winter Recreation informs the reader about cross-country ski trails, downhill ski areas, ice skating, sledding and toboggan hills as well as places to go snowshoeing and snowmobiling.

Chapter 18: Recreational Sports

Adaptive Recreation Programs

Ironwood Springs Christian Ranch—
National Wheelchair Sports & Recreation Camp

7291 County Road 6 SW, Stewartville, MN 55976, (507) 533-9933 (stables), 888-533-4316 or (507) 533-4315 (information and reservations), www.ironwoodsprings.com, e-mail: iscr2000@aol.com

Ironwood Springs Christian Ranch, a nonprofit, nondenominational year-round camp, is located in rural Stewartville along the Root River on 200 rural, wooded acres. The camp's mission is "to provide an atmosphere and opportunity for adults and children to get to know themselves, others and God better." The Ranch offers a National Wheelchair Sports and Recreation Camp and Camp Jornada for kids with cancer and their families during the summer months. Ironwood Springs also organizes the Annual Slumberland Wheelchair Race, which is scheduled for mid to late June. The event is held in Rochester and includes a variety of divisions from junior to elite races. Facilities and recreational amenities at Ironwood Springs include the Main Lodge with recreation center, cabins, a dormitory, Log Chapel, campground, an outdoor swimming pool, playgrounds, tennis courts, basketball courts, a miniature farm with animals, horse stables, and walking and hiking trails. Call the Ranch for a current camp schedule and race information.

PossAbilities Youth Recreation Program

PossAbilities: 1808 3ʳᵈ Avenue SE, Rochester, MN 55904, (507) 281-6116, www.possAbilities.org
YMCA: 709 1ˢᵗ Avenue SW, Rochester, MN 55902, (507) 287-2260, www.rochfamy.org

PossAbilities of Southern Minnesota, in conjunction with the Rochester Area Family Y, offers an after school recreation program and summer recreation program for middle school and high school students with disabilities. Peer companions support and assist the students as they participate in a variety of aquatic, gym, and arts and crafts activities. Please contact PossAbilities or the Y for more information.

RideAbility

Pine Island, MN 55963, (507) 356-8154, (507) 824-2854
Call for directions.

RideAbility is a recreational and therapeutic horseback riding program for children with disabilities and their families. The equestrian program is designed to boost self-confidence and provide a shared activity for families whose children have different abilities. Please call RideAbility for more information and a class schedule.

Rochester Adaptive Recreation Program

Rochester Park and Recreation Department, 201 4ᵗʰ Street SE–Room 150, Rochester, MN 55904, (507) 281-6160, (507) 287-7980, www.ci.rochester.mn.us/park

The Rochester Park and Recreation Department offers an Adaptive Recreation program for youth and adults. All individuals ages five and older with a physical and/or mental disability are eligible to participate in the sports and recreation programs; however, a physician's authorization is required. Year-round programs and activities are typically held after school, during the evening hours, and on weekends.

Basketball, bowling, floor hockey, kickball, swimming, volleyball, hiking, cycling, inline skating, softball, and horseshoes are a sample of the sports offered through the program. Special Olympics Sports Training is also available in conjunction with the Rochester Area Special Olympics for the sports of basketball, volleyball, swimming, cross-country skiing, horseback riding, bowling, track and field, softball, and cycling. Social and recreational activities offered include arts and crafts, music, dances, playground programs, teen activities, movies and more. Registration for adaptive recreation programs is held on a quarterly basis. Please contact the Park and Recreation Department for more information. Transportation is available through ZIPS [(507) 288-8404] for a nominal fee.

Rochester Area Disabled Athletics and Recreation, Inc.—RADAR

539 North Broadway, Rochester, MN 55906, (507) 280-6995, http://radarsports.tripod.com or e-mail: radarsports@aol.com

RADAR, a nonprofit organization established in 1985, promotes athletics and recreation for individuals with disabilities in the Rochester and southeastern Minnesota area. The group's mission is to enhance the quality of life for individuals with disabilities and their families. Athletic activities offered by RADAR include basketball, hunting, fishing, archery, bowling, billiards, golf, water skiing and track. Recreational programs available include movie nights, games nights, crafts, and other social activities. Children, youth, and adults are welcome to participate in RADAR programs and events. Please contact RADAR or visit their website for more information.

Rochester Area Special Olympics

Adaptive Recreation, Rochester Park and Recreation Department, 201 4th Street SE–Room 150, Rochester, MN 55904, (507) 287-7980, www.ci.rochester.mn.us/park

Rochester Area Special Olympics is a community-based athletic training program for individuals with mental and/or physical disabilities. Individuals, ages five through adulthood, with mental and developmental disabilities are eligible to participate in Special Olympics programs. Sports training is available for children between the ages of five and eight, but competition is not permitted until an athlete is eight years old. Special Olympians have the opportunity to meet new friends, develop healthy leisure skills, and learn good sportsmanship in addition to competing at local, regional, and state events. Please call the Adaptive Recreation Department for more information.

Rochester Youth Soccer Association—RYSA

P.O. Box 6402, Rochester, MN 55903, (507) 280-7584, www.rysa.org

TopSoccer is an adaptive program run in conjunction with Rochester Park and Recreation Department for boys or girls, ages 6–19, who have a mental or physical disability. TopSoccer participants register through Rochester Park and Recreation Department for sessions in March and June. Please call RYSA or visit www. rysa.org for more information.

Arcades

Chateau Theatres

971 East Circle Drive, Rochester, MN 55906, (507) 536-7469, www.chateautheatres.com

Chateau Theatres celebrated its "Magical Grande Opening" in December 2001. The 14 screen movie theater is reminiscent of the Historic Chateau Theatre in downtown Rochester, which is now the site of Barnes & Noble Booksellers. Patrons are greeted by Chester the dragon upon entering the theater and will find the lobby an attraction in itself. The medieval castle setting, complete with balconies, towers, and flags, is set under a night sky with twinkling "star" lights. An arcade, party room, and food court with seating for more than 100 people are available at the theater. The arcade features video games, pinball, photo booths, and more. The public is welcome to use the arcade and eat at the food court without going to a movie. The Chateau also offers a free children's movie on Saturday mornings as well as a monthly movie day for senior citizens with free showings of classic movies, and midnight movie showings for reduced prices. Please call for a current schedule of these special showings. Birthday party packages are available at the Chateau.

Cost: $
Hours: Monday–Friday, 11 a.m.–midnight; Sunday–Saturday, 11:30 a.m.–midnight

Colonial Lanes

1828 14th St. NW, Rochester, MN 55901, (507) 289-2341

After bowling a game or two, children and adults alike will have fun playing pinball and video games in the arcade room at Colonial Lanes. The arcade is equipped with about 10 video games. Birthday party packages are available at Colonial Lanes.

Cost: $
Hours: Monday & Wednesday, 11 a.m.–10:30 p.m.; Tuesday; 9 a.m.–10:30 p.m.;
     Thursday, 9 a.m.–11:30 p.m.; Friday, 11 a.m.–12:30 a.m.; Saturday & Sunday,
     9 a.m.–12:30 a.m.; daily closing times may vary depending upon number
     of customers

Machine Shed Arcade

Galleria Mall–Centerplace, Rochester, MN 55904, (507) 529-8438

The Machine Shed Arcade, located in Rochester's Galleria Mall, is a full-sized arcade with redemption games suitable for all ages. Children, youth, and adults will enjoy testing their skill and luck as they play a wide variety of games. Birthday party packages are available at the Machine Shed.

Cost: $
Hours: Monday–Friday, 9:30 a.m.–8:30 p.m.; Saturday, 9:30 a.m.–5:30 p.m.; Sunday,
     noon–5 p.m.

Mr. Pizza

1729 South Broadway, Rochester, MN 55902, (507) 288-1488

A small arcade area with a limited number of games is located in Mr. Pizza's rear dining room. This family restaurant offers great pizza and a relaxed atmosphere where parents may allow kids to move around and play arcade games while they wait for their pizza or relax after their meal. Mr. Pizza welcomes patrons to use their restaurant for birthday parties with advance notice.

Cost: $
Hours: Sunday–Saturday, 11 a.m.–11 p.m.

Archery Ranges

Archery Headquarters

5510 North Hwy. 63, Rochester, MN 55901, (507) 282-3507

Archery Headquarters of Rochester provides bowhunters and archery enthusiasts with AAA service in addition to a well-stocked shop with a full line of archery and bowhunting equipment, supplies, and clothing. An indoor shooting range, video rentals, archery lessons, and leagues are also available on site. The indoor range is set up for target shooting from a distance of 20 yards and is also equipped with the DART Interactive Archery System. The DART System provides the video projection of hunting scenarios with North American, Alaskan, African, or small game animals. Individual bowhunter, 2-person bowhunter, 300 spot target, DART, couples, and youth leagues run from January through March. Open shooting is available during store hours when leagues are not scheduled. Archery equipment may be rented for a nominal fee.

Cost: $
Hours: Monday–Friday, 10 a.m.–8 p.m.; Saturday, 10 a.m.–5 p.m.; Sunday, noon–4 p.m.

Rochester Archery Club

P.O. Box 6701, Rochester, MN 55903, www.rochesterarcheryclub.com

The Rochester Archery Club, an affiliate of the Minnesota Bowhunters Association, is open to youth and adults interested in target archery, bowhunting, bowfishing, and conservation issues. Membership includes access to a 40-acre archery range, monthly meetings and social hours, a newsletter, membership to the Minnesota Bowhunters Association, an annual awards banquet, and a variety of special events such as wild game potlucks, guest speakers, 3D shoots, hog roasts, and small game hunts. The practice range, located in northwest Rochester along 75th Street NW, has targets at marked distances from 10 to 60 yards as well as a field course with life-sized animal targets at unmarked distances on a variety of terrains. New members, both novice and experienced, are welcome to join the club. Nonmembers are welcome to attend some events. Contact the club for more information about youth and adult memberships, upcoming meetings, and a current schedule of events.

Essex Park

5455 West River Road NW, Rochester, MN 55901, (507) 281-6160, www.ci.rochester.mn.us/park

An archery range, located at Essex Park in northwest Rochester, is open to the public during park hours. The range has thirteen hay bales set up in an open field that is flanked by two wooded areas and an open field. Archers may shoot from the ground or a raised platform resembling a mock tree stand. Archers must bring their own target to mount on the hay bales.

Cost: free
Hours: 6 a.m.–dusk

Ballroom Dancing (see also Dance and Square and Round Dancing)

Fred Astaire Dance Studio

11 4ᵗʰ Street SE, Rochester, MN 55904, (507) 282-9811, www.fredastaire.com

Fred Astaire Dance Studio of Rochester provides instruction for singles, couples, or youth in Ballroom, Latin, Salsa, Night Club, Country, and Swing Dancing. Practice dances are held at the studio on the second and fourth Thursdays of the month from 9 p.m.–10 p.m. Dancers interested in competition have the opportunity to participate in competitive events twice a year. Introductory lessons are reasonably priced and those interested in continuing may choose to continue their instruction through Fred Astaire's Bronze, Silver, and Gold level programs.

Cost: $$–$$$$$
Hours: Monday–Friday, 3 p.m.–10 p.m.

Pla-Mor Ballroom

2045 Hwy. 14 East, Rochester, MN 55904, (507) 282-5244

Step back in time to the 1930s and 1940s at the Pla-Mor Ballroom in southeast Rochester. The Pla-Mor boasts a beautiful 3,000-square-foot maple dance floor and can accommodate up to 900 people. Saturday evening dances feature live bands from Minnesota and Wisconsin that play a medley of polkas, waltzes, country tunes, and more. The Pla-Mor serves popcorn, beer, and nonalcoholic beverages. Guests are permitted to BYOB, snacks, and food. Singles, couples, and families with young children are all welcome at the Pla-Mor.

Cost: $; children under 12 free
Hours: Saturday, 8 p.m.–midnight

Southern Minnesota Chapter of the United States Amateur Ballroom Dancers Association—USABDA

P.O. Box 7354, Rochester, MN 55903, (507) 281-1034, www.usabda.org The Eagles Club is located at 409 1ˢᵗ Avenue SW, Rochester, MN 55902, (507) 289-5931.

The USABDA Chapter of Southern Minnesota, a nonprofit organization that promotes and sponsors amateur ballroom dancing in the region, welcomes people of all ages and dancing abilities to join them at their monthly dances. Dances are held on the first Friday of the month at the Eagle's Club Ballroom in Rochester and the third Friday of the month at the Rochester Senior Center. All dancers are invited to begin their night with a complimentary, one-hour lesson followed by an evening of ballroom dancing. Dance styles taught include the Cha-Cha, Fox-trot, Mambo, Merengue, Polka, Rumba, Samba, Swing, Tango, Two-Step, Waltz, and more. Rhythm, Latin, and swing dances are held at the Senior Center. Please contact the club or visit their website for more information and a current dance schedule.

Cost: $
Hours: first Friday of the month, dance lesson: 7:30 p.m.; open dancing:
    8:30 p.m.–11:30 p.m.
    third Friday of the month, dance lesson: 7:15 p.m., open dancing: 8 p.m.–
    10:30 p.m.

Baseball

Rochester Roadrunners

Rochester, MN, www.geocities.com/Colosseum/Bleachers/3432/Baseball/Roadrunners2002.html,
e-mail: rochroadrunners@yahoo.com

The Rochester Roadrunners, a Class C amateur baseball team, is part of the Twin Rivers League. The team is open to players aged 16 and older. The Roadrunners' season runs from mid-May to mid-July with playoffs at the end of July. Organizational meetings for the upcoming season are usually held in December or January. Interested players should e-mail the club for more information.

Rochester Royals Baseball

P.O. Box 7316, Rochester, MN 55903, (507) 281-0612, www.rochesterusa.com/rochesterroyals
For ticket information, call (507) 281-0612 or (507) 280-0253.

The Rochester Royals is an adult amateur baseball team that plays in the Southern Minny League. Sanctioned by the Minnesota Baseball Association, any player aged 17 and older is eligible to try out for the Class B team. The Royals play approximately 40 games during their season, which runs from June 1st to September 4th. Players interested in trying out for the team should contact the organization by May 1st. The Rochester Blues, a Class C team affiliated with the Rochester Royals, is part of the Twin Rivers League. The Blues serve as a farm team to the Rochester Royals. Players interested in playing for the Blues should also contact the Rochester Royals organization.

Hiawatha Senior Baseball League

(507) 775-6693, www.scorebook.com/hiawathaseniorbaseball

The Hiawatha Senior Baseball League, an amateur baseball club for players age 28 and older, is comprised of seven teams from the southeastern Minnesota area. No tryouts are required to join a league team, but interested players should contact the league by early March. Teams play a 12-game regular season within the league, and double-elimination playoffs are held at the end of the season, which runs from April until August. New teams are welcome to join the league. Please call for more information.

Batting Cages

Recreation Lanes

2810 North Broadway, Rochester, MN 55906, (507) 288-2601

Five outdoor batting cages are available for use at Recreation Lanes during the spring and summer months. One batting cage is set at a slower speed so that children may safely practice hitting balls. Players may choose to hit either baseballs or softballs. An 18-hole mini-golf course is located adjacent to the batting cages.

Cost: $
Hours: April–Labor Day: Monday–Thursday, 10 a.m.–10 p.m.; Friday–Saturday, 10 a.m.–midnight; Sunday, noon–10 p.m.; hours may vary in early spring

Rochester Athletic Club
3100 19ᵗʰ Street NW, Rochester, MN 55901, (507) 282-6000, www.rochesterathleticclub.com

The Rochester Athletic Club is a members-only facility that has two batting cages. Daily guest passes are available; however, local residents are only permitted to use the club as a guest once every 60 days. Batting cages are set up so that players may choose to hit softballs or baseballs on either a fast-pitch or slow-pitch machine.

Cost: guest fee: $–$$; batting cage fee: $
Hours: Monday–Friday, 5 a.m.–10:30 p.m.; Saturday–Sunday, 7 a.m.–9 p.m.

Biking

Rochester Bike Trails
Residents and visitors of all ages enjoy exploring the 29 miles of paved trails that run throughout all quadrants of the city including the downtown area. Many of the trails are interconnected, and each one has its own character. Some of the trails have a distinctly urban feel while others pass through wooded areas. The trail system is also open to walkers, runners, and inline skaters. Please see Appendix 2 for a map of Rochester's bike trails or contact the Rochester Park and Recreation Department, 201 4th Street SE, Room 150, Rochester, MN 55904, (507) 281-6160, www.ci.rochester.mn.us/park for more information.

Bike Trails in Southeastern Minnesota
Cannon Valley Trail
Red Wing–Cannon Falls

Cannon Valley Trail, City Hall, 306 West Mill Street, Cannon Falls, MN 55009, (507) 263-0508, (507) 258-4141, www.cannonvalleytrail.com
The Red Wing trailhead is located on Old West Main Street and Bench Street, one block from Hwy. 61 with parking nearby.
The Cannon Falls trailhead originates near 3ʳᵈ Street in Cannon Falls. Parking at this trailhead is limited but may be accessed across from the ballpark on East Stoughton Street.
The Welch Station Access is located along County Road 7 between the Village of Welch and Welch Village Ski Area.

The Cannon Valley Trail, formerly a section of the Chicago Great Western Railroad, is a 19.7-mile paved trail that runs between Red Wing and Cannon Falls with a midpoint at Welch Station. The multiple-use trail winds along side the Cannon River and passes through a variety of natural habitats including marshlands, pastures, and wooded areas. Bicyclists, inline skaters, skateboarders, hikers, and cross-country skiers will enjoy spectacular views of the area as they travel along the trail. A Wheel Pass is required for all adults, aged 18 and up, who are riding on wheeled vehicles from April 1st through November 1st. Wheel passes are available at self-purchase stations along the trail, local businesses, and from trail attendants on weekends during the summer months. Voices of the Valley, an interpretive program held at the Welch Station Access, is scheduled for the first Saturday of every month from May through September from 11 a.m.–3 p.m. These entertaining programs are designed to educate trail users about the Cannon River Valley. Rest rooms and water are located at Cannon Falls, Welch Station Access, and Red Wing's Anderson Park. There are also rest rooms but no water at the Anderson

Memorial Rest Area, Cannon Bottom Road, and the Old West Main Parking Area in Red Wing. Maps, directions, and additional information may be obtained by contacting the Cannon Valley Trail Office.

Douglas State Trail
Rochester–Pine Island

Rochester Area Trails & Waterways, 2300 Silver Creek Road NE, Rochester, MN 55906, (507) 285-7176, www.dnr.state.mn.us.
Trailheads are located in Rochester on County Road 4 (Valleyhigh Drive NW) behind IBM, in Douglas at County Road 14 off Hwy. 52, and in Pine Island at Pine Island Park, just off the Hwy. 52 exit.

Trailheads for the Douglas State Trail originate in northwest Rochester and Pine Island with a midpoint in Douglas, the town for which the trail is named. This multiple-use trail is 12.5 miles in length with a paved treadway for inline skaters, bicyclists, hikers, and cross-country skiers. The trail was developed from an abandoned railroad track and passes over iron bridges and through some of southeastern Minnesota's richest farmland. A parking lot with rest rooms is located at each trailhead, and water is available at the Douglas and Pine Island trailheads.

Great River Ridge Trail
Elgin–Plainview

Plainview City Hall, (507) 534-2229

The Great River Ridge Trail is currently a 5-mile paved trail that runs between Elgin and Plainview. The trail passes through open country and has gently sloping terrain. The multiple-use trail and its trailheads are still under development with plans to extend it from Plainview to Eyota. Bikers may access the trail in Plainview at the intersection of 3rd Street SW and State Highway 42.

Harmony–Preston Valley State Trail
Harmony–Preston

Rochester Area Trails & Waterways, 2300 Silver Creek Road NE, Rochester, MN 55906, (507) 285-7176, www.dnr.state.mn.us
Harmony Visitor's Center, (507) 886-2469, 800-247-MINN(6466), www.harmony.mn.us
Preston Area Toursim, (507) 765-2100, 888-845-2100, www.bluffcountry.com
The Preston trailhead is located off Hwy. 52 on Fillmore Street (County Road 12), and the Harmony trailhead is located off Hwy. 52 on 4th Street SW.

The Harmony–Preston Valley State Trail is an 18-mile paved trail between the towns of Harmony and Preston that connects to the popular Root River State Trail at Isinours Junction, approximately 5.5 miles east of the Root River trailhead in Fountain. Although the northern section of the Harmony–Preston Valley trail is relatively flat, a series of hills and inclines provides challenging terrain along the southern portion of the trail between County Road 16 and Harmony. Inline skaters, bicyclists, hikers, and cross-country skiers are welcome to use the trail, which crosses Watson and Camp Creeks and passes through farmland and wooded areas. Camp Creek, located adjacent to Preston, is accessible via three fishing piers. Rest rooms and water are available in Preston and Harmony and at the Isinours Forestry Unit, one mile west of Isinours Junction.

Root River State Trail

Fountain–Houston

DNR Trail Center, Lanesboro Depot, Lanesboro, MN 55949, (507) 467-2552,
www.dnr.state.mn.us
Lanesboro Visitor's Center, (507) 467-2696, www.lanesboro.com, www.bluffcountry.com
Trailheads in Fountain, the Isinours Forestry Unit, Lanesboro, Whalan, Peterson, Rushford, and
Houston may be easily located by following signs to the Root River State Trail as you approach
these towns.

Southeastern Minnesota's Root River State Trail is the region's premier multi-use recreational trail and annually attracts thousands of outdoor enthusiasts who come to skate, bike, hike or ski in the Root River Valley. The 42-mile paved trail was developed from an abandoned railroad bed and meanders through an idyllic setting of picturesque farmlands, rolling pastures, limestone bluffs, and forested areas from Fountain to Houston. The trail is especially attractive to visitors because it passes through the small towns of Lanesboro, Whalan, Peterson, and Rushford before terminating in Houston. These charming towns capture the essence of rural Americana and each community offers a unique variety of recreational, historic, and cultural activities for visitors. Rest rooms and water are available at the small towns along the trail.

Minnesota Bike Trails & Rides

108 Main Street, P.O. Box 28, Nevis, MN 56467, (218) 652-3475, www.mnbiketrails.com

Minnesota Bike Trails & Rides is an annual publication that provides current information about paved biking trails throughout Minnesota as well as a calendar of more than 40 weekend rides and tours. Please write, call, or visit their website to get a copy of this valuable resource.

Bike Rentals in Southeastern Minnesota

HOUSTON
Classcycle Bikes of Houston
113 West Cedar Street (Hwy. 16), Houston, MN 55943, (507) 896-9433

LANESBORO
Capron Hardware
119 Parkway Avenue North, Lanesboro, MN 55949, (507) 467-3714

Historic Scanlan House Bed & Breakfast
708 Parkway South, Lanesboro, MN 55949, (507) 467-2158

Little River General Store
104 Parkway Avenue North, Lanesboro, MN 55949, (507) 467-2943, 800-994-2943

Root River Outfitters
102 South Parkway Avenue, Lanesboro, MN 55949, (507) 467-3400

PRESTON
Brick House on Main Coffeehouse and Gift Shop
104 East Main Street, Preston, MN 55965, (507) 765-9820

Root River Outfitters at the Old Barn Resort
RR 3, Box 57, Preston, MN 55965, (507) 467-2512, 800-552-2512, www.bluffcountry.com
Located 3 miles northeast of Preston.

Trailhead Inn
112 Center Street, Preston, MN 55965, (507) 765-2460
Located at Preston Trailhead of Root River State Trail.

PETERSON
Geneva's
318 Mill Street, Peterson, MN 55962, (507) 875-7733

RED WING
Four Seasons Bike Rental & Sales
2311 West Main Street, Red Wing, MN 55066, (651) 385-8614

Outdoor Store
1811 Old West Main Street, Red Wing, MN 55066, (651) 388-5358

Billiards

37th Street Billiards
275 37th St. NE, Rochester, MN 55906, (507) 282-0033, www.mnbilliards.com

37th Street Billiards offers pool players a place to play their favorite game 24 hours a day, seven days a week. The pool hall sports eight 7-foot tables and ten 9-foot tables, a small selection of video games, and a snack bar that serves pizza, burgers, hot dogs, appetizers, beer, pop, and juice. Rental cues are available for one dollar, and a limited number of cues and billiards accessories are sold on-site. Please call to inquire about leagues available for high school-aged youth and adults.

Cost: $
Hours: Sunday–Saturday, 24 hours a day

D & R Star
2207 7th Street NW, Rochester, MN 55901, (507) 282-6080, 800-788-9692, www.dnrstar.com

D & R Star, a Rochester company that provides vending services and concessions to area businesses in addition to owning the Family Fun Center and Machine Shed Arcade, is a major sponsor of local billiards leagues and regional tournaments. Dart leagues and tournaments are also available. Please contact D & R Star or visit their website for league information or a tournament schedule.

Jerry's Billiards
1207 7th Avenue NW, Rochester, MN 55901, (507) 292-8790, www.mnbilliards.com

Jerry's Billiards is a clean pool hall that serves youth and adults who love to shoot pool. Jerry's has 12 coin tables including four Diamond Smart tables and seven 9-foot tables. The facility also has two separate rooms that are used for league play and private parties. Jerry's sells new and used cues, repairs cues, and rents house cues. Bar cues may be used free of charge. A few video games, an air hockey table, four dart boards and a big screen TV are also available. The pool hall also has a snack bar, and alcoholic beverages are served on the premises. Please inquire for information about youth (ages 8 and up) and adult billiard leagues.

Cost: $; monthly memberships are available
Hours: Sunday–Saturday, 11 a.m.–1 a.m.

Bingo

Circus World Bingo

2828 Frontage Road East, Rochester, MN 55901, (507) 282-0988
Located off Hwy. 52 North. Take the 19th Street exit near Hillcrest Shopping Center and follow the Frontage Road to Circus World Bingo.

Come to Circus World Bingo, Rochester's largest bingo hall, to play a wide variety of progressive bingo games such as Crazy T, Four Corners, Big Diamond, Double Postage Stamp, Letter H, Black Out and more. The bingo hall offers both early bird and regular sessions as well as a section for smokers and an enclosed room for non-smokers. Circus World also sells bingo supplies and has an on-site snack bar with hot and cold beverages, sandwiches, pizza, popcorn, candy, and other treats.

Cost: $–$$
Hours: Tuesday–Sunday, early bird session: 6:30 p.m.–7:30 p.m.; regular session, 7:30 p.m.–9:30 p.m. Saturday & Sunday matinees: 1:30 p.m.–3:30 p.m.

Elks Lodge 1091

917 15th Avenue SE, Rochester, MN 55904, (507) 282-6702

The public is welcome to play bingo at the Elks Lodge on Tuesday and Friday evenings. The Elks Lodge offers progressive games with increased prizes and payouts. Snacks and beverages are available for purchase.

Cost: $–$$
Hours: Tuesday and Friday, 7:15 p.m.

Knights of Columbus Bingo

Knights of Columbus Hall, 2030 Hwy. 14 East, Rochester, MN 55904, (507) 288-1492

The Knights of Columbus invites the public to play bingo on Monday nights. A variety of popular bingo games are played, and a small nonsmoking section is available at the hall. Food and beverages are available for purchase.

Cost: $–$$
Hours: Monday, early bird session: 7:30 p.m.; regular session: 8 p.m.

Boat Rentals in Southeastern Minnesota

ROCHESTER
King's Marina

Lake Zumbro, 40 Shorewood Lane NE, Rochester, MN 55906, (507) 367-4585

Rents fishing boats and pontoons.

LAKE CITY

Sail Away of Lake City
P. O. Box, 196, Lake City, MN 55041, (651) 345-5225

Rents power boats to experienced boaters.

Sailboats, Inc.
Hansen's Marina, 35699 Hwy. 61 Boulevard, Lake City, MN 55041, (651) 345-6282

WABASHA

Great River Houseboats
P.O. Box 247, 1009 East Main Street, Wabasha, MN 55981, (651) 565-3376,
www.greatriverhouseboats.com

Rents houseboats, pontoons, and fishing boats.

Bowling

Colonial Lanes
1828 14ᵗʰ Street NW, Rochester, MN 55901, (507) 289-2341

Colonial Lanes is a family-friendly bowling alley with 20 lanes. All the lanes have retractable bumpers that may be used during open bowling sessions. Extreme Bowling is a regularly scheduled weekend event at Colonial Lanes, which features black lights, glow in the dark pins, a light show, music, and music videos. There is also an arcade room and bar and grill located on the premises. Adult, youth, and adult/child leagues are available. Please call for more information about specials, open bowling sessions, leagues, the Extreme Bowling schedule, and current hours.

Cost: $
Hours: call for current hours

Recreation Lanes
2810 North Broadway, Rochester, MN (507) 288-2601

Recreation Lanes is a smoke-free, family-friendly bowling alley with 16 lanes that are all equipped with bumpers. Bumper may be used during open bowling sessions. Thunder Alley is held on Fridays and Saturdays and features bowling with black lights, fog, a light show, and music. A small selection of video games as well as a bar and grill are also located at Recreation Lanes. Adult, youth, and adult/child leagues are available. In addition to this, Recreation Lanes has five outdoor batting cages and an 18-hole, handicapped-accessible miniature golf course available for patrons during the spring and summer months. Please call for more information about specials, open bowling sessions, leagues, the Thunder Alley schedule, batting cages, and mini-golf.

Cost: $
Hours: winter: Monday–Thursday, 10 a.m.–11 p.m.; Friday, 10 a.m.–1 a.m.;
    Saturday, 8:30 a.m.–midnight; Sunday, 9 a.m.–10 p.m.
    summer: Monday–Thursday, 10 a.m.–10 p.m.; Friday–Saturday, 10 a.m.–11 p.m.;
    Sunday, noon–10 p.m.

Bowling Alleys in Southeastern Minnesota

BYRON
Byron Lanes
501 Frontage Road NE, Byron, MN 55920, (507) 775-6000

CALEDONIA
Starlite Bowling Center
114 West Bissen Street, Caledonia, MN 55921, (507) 725-3825

CHATFIELD
Chosen Valley Lanes
118 Main Street, Chatfield, MN 55923, (507) 867-3080

HAYFIELD
Spare Time Lanes
18 2nd Street NE, Hayfield, MN 55940, (507) 477-3492

PINE ISLAND
Pine Island Lanes
416 3rd Avenue NE, Pine Island, MN 55963, (507) 356-4893

PLAINVIEW
Gopher Lanes
211 West Broadway Street, Plainview, MN 55964, (507) 534-3286

PRESTON
B & B Olympic Bowl
401 Kansas Street, Preston, MN 55965, (507) 765-2522

RUSHFORD
Nordic Lanes
403 South Mill Street, Rushford, MN 55971, (507) 864-7799

ST. CHARLES
Legion Unity Lanes
1148 Whitewater Avenue, St. Charles, MN 55972, (507) 932-3490

SPRING VALLEY
Valley Lanes
208 South Broadway Avenue, Spring Valley, MN 55975, (507) 346-7661

STEWARTVILLE
Stewartville Bowl
101 10th Street NW, Stewartville, MN 55976, (507) 533-8330

WABASHA
Pioneer Lanes
218 West 2nd Street, Wabasha, MN 55981, (651) 565-3911

WINONA

Westgate Bowl
Westgate Shopping Center, 1429 West Service Drive, Winona, MN 55987, (507) 454-3133

Winona Bowl
526 Cottonwood Drive, Winona, MN 55987, (507) 452-6441

ZUMBROTA

Evergreen Lanes
110 Mill Street, Zumbrota, MN 55992, (507) 732-7013

Boxing

Fourth Street Youth Boxing Gym
615 1st Avenue SW, Rochester, MN 55902, (507) 288-7458
Located adjacent to the Rochester Area Family YMCA.

The Fourth Street Gym in downtown Rochester provides a safe haven for youth interested in the sport of boxing. Membership at this Christian-affiliated gym is open to male and female amateur boxers, ages 8–36, of all skill levels. The facility has a practice ring, several types of punching bags, a weight room, and small locker room in an atmosphere reminiscent of a traditional boxing gym. Young boxers are trained in Olympic-style boxing by certified coaches who volunteer their time to run the gym. Local bouts provide an opportunity for boxers to compete against others of the same age, weight, and skill level. The gym also offers a Saturday morning bible study. Please call or drop in during open gym time for more information.

Cost: yearly insurance fee only
Hours: Monday–Thursday, 5:30 p.m.–8 p.m.; Saturday, 11:30 a.m.–2 p.m.
  bible study, 11:30 a.m.–12:30 p.m.

Silver Lake Gym
702 Silver Lake Drive NE, Rochester, MN 55906, (507) 285-0843, (507) 271-6405
Located in the lower level of the Silver Lake Firehouse. Please use the side entrance.

The Silver Lake Boxing Gym was established 55 years ago and continues to serve amateur boxers, ages 8–35, of all skill levels. The old-style boxing gym has a practice ring, several types of punching bags, a weight bench, and small locker room. Jim Tonjum and Penny Marshall, licensed and certified coaches, volunteer their time to run all aspects of the gym. Young boxers are taught Olympic-style boxing in an atmosphere that promotes safety, respect, and discipline. Local bouts provide an opportunity for boxers to compete against others of the same age, weight, and skill level. Gym membership is open to male and female boxers. Please call or drop in during open gym time for more information.

Cost: yearly insurance fee only
Hours: Tuesday, Thursday & Sunday, 5:30 p.m.–7:30 p.m.

Canoeing & Tubing

ROCHESTER
Silver Lake Canoe & Paddle Boats
West Silver Lake Drive, Rochester, MN 55906, (507) 282-3248, (507) 281-6160

Canoes and paddleboats are available for rent from Memorial Day through Labor Day at the lakeside pavilion on the west side of Silver Lake. Lifejackets and paddles are included with the rental.

Cost: $
Hours: Monday–Friday, 11 a.m.–8 p.m.; Saturday–Sunday, 10 a.m.–8 p.m.

CANNON FALLS
Cannon Falls Canoeing
615 North 5th Street, Cannon Falls, MN 55009, (507) 263-4657

Cannon Falls Canoeing offers canoe and kayak rentals for day or overnight trips along the Cannon River. Choose from a two-hour or five- to seven-hour day trip. Shuttle service, lifejackets, and paddles are included in the cost of the rental. Camping is available at Hidden Valley Campground in Welch for overnight trips. Please see Chapter 12, Campgrounds, for information about the campground.

Cost: $$–$$$$
Hours: Monday–Friday, 10 a.m.–5 p.m.; Saturday–Sunday, 9 a.m.–5 p.m.

LANESBORO
Eagle Cliff Canoe & Tube Rental
Eagle Cliff Campground, Route 1, Box 344, Lanesboro, MN 55949, (507) 467-2598

Eagle Cliff Campground, located just three miles east of Lanesboro on Highway 16, offers canoe, kayak, and tube rentals for day trips along the scenic Root River. Choose from an 8- or 16-mile day trip. Rental includes a shuttle service upriver, paddles, and lifejackets. Noncampers are welcome to rent canoes, kayaks, and tubes at Eagle Cliff. Please see Chapter 12, Campgrounds, for more information about Eagle Cliff Campground.

Cost: $–$$$
Hours: Monday–Friday, 9 a.m.–5 p.m.; Saturday–Sunday, shuttles leave at scheduled times throughout the day, please call for a schedule

Lanesboro Canoe Rental
301 Fillmore Avenue North, Lanesboro, MN 55949, (507) 467-2948

Canoe rentals are available for day or overnight trips. Rental includes shuttle service, lifejackets, and paddles. Please call for more information.

Cost: $$
Hours: daily, 8 a.m.–2 p.m. (last shuttle)

Little River General Store
104 Parkway Avenue North, Lanesboro, MN 55949, (507) 467-2943, 800-994-2943, www.LRGeneralstore.com

The Little River General Store offers canoe, kayak, and tube rentals for day and overnight trips along the scenic Root River. Little River provides newly updated equipment for all their rentals. Trips range in length from 3 to 5½ hours, and all rentals include shuttle service, lifejackets and paddles.

Cost: $–$$$
Hours: daily, 9 a.m.–5:30 p.m.; earlier by appointment; closing times tend to be later during the summer months, weather permitting

Root River Outfitters
P.O. Box 162, 102 South Parkway, Lanesboro, MN 55949, (507) 467-3400
Old Barn Resort, RR 3, Box 57, Preston, MN 55965, (507) 467-2512, 800-552-2512

Root River Outfitters rents canoes and tubes from their locations in downtown Lanesboro and the Old Barn Resort in Preston. Choose from a 2½ hour or 5- to 6-hour canoe trip along the Root River. Tube rentals are available for floats that range from 30 minutes to 3 hours. Rentals include shuttle service, lifejackets, and paddles. Overnight canoe rentals and a limited number of kayaks are also available. Please call for more information.

Cost: $–$$$
Hours: daily, 9 a.m.–7 p.m.

PETERSON
Geneva's
318 Mill Street, Peterson, MN 55962, (507) 875-7733

Geneva's offers canoe and tube rentals for day and overnight trips along the historic Root River. Day trips vary in length from two to ten hours. Rentals include shuttle service, lifejackets, and paddles.

Cost: $–$$$$
Hours: Monday–Friday, 10 a.m.–7 p.m.; Saturday–Sunday; 8 a.m.–8 p.m.

PRESTON
Root River Outfitters
P.O. Box 162, 102 South Parkway, Lanesboro, MN 55949, (507) 467-3400
Old Barn Resort, RR 3, Box 57, Preston, MN 55965, (507) 467-2512, 800-552-2512

Root River Outfitters rents canoes and tubes from their locations in downtown Lanesboro and the Old Barn Resort in Preston. Choose from a 2½ hour or 5- to 6-hour canoe trip along the Root River. Tube rentals are available for floats that range from 30 minutes to 3 hours. Rentals include shuttle service, lifejackets, and paddles. Overnight canoe rentals and a limited number of kayaks are also available. Please call for more information.

Cost: $–$$$
Hours: daily, 9 a.m.–7 p.m.

WELCH
Welch Mill Canoeing & Tubing
Route 1, Box 153, Welch, MN 55089, (651) 388-9857, 800-657-6760
Located between Hastings and Red Wing, off Hwy. 61 on Welch Village Road.

Travel along the Cannon River with canoe, kayak, or tube rentals from Welch Mill. Choose a 5-mile or 12-mile canoe or kayak trip. Small and large tube rentals are also available for day trips, which last from one to three hours. Rentals include shuttle service, lifejackets, and paddles. Tube rentals include an unlimited number of shuttles upriver for the day.

Cost: $–$$$
Hours: Monday–Friday, 10 a.m.–8 p.m.; Saturday–Sunday, 8 a.m.–8 p.m.

ZUMBRO FALLS
Zumbro Valley Canoe & Tube Rental
P.O. Box 145, Hwy. 63 North, Sportsman Park, Zumbro Falls, MN 55991, (507) 753-2568

Canoe or tube the Zumbro River with rentals and shuttle service from Zumbro Valley Canoe and Tube Rental located at Sportsmen's Park in Zumbro Falls. Choose from day trips ranging from three to eight hours via canoe or a four to five hour tubing trip. Rental prices include shuttle service, life jackets, and paddles. Overnight canoeing and camping trips are available upon request. Camping is available on-site at Sportsmen's Park and Bluff Valley Campground, adjacent to Zumbro Falls. Please see Chapter 12 for campground information.

Cost: $–$$$$$
Hours: daily, 9 a.m.–5 p.m.

Dance (see also Ballroom Dancing and Square and Round Dancing)

ROCHESTER
Allegro School of Dance
14½ 4th Street SW, Rochester, MN 55902, (507) 288-0125

Allegro School of Dance offers instruction in ballet, Pointe, tap, jazz, hip-hop as well as creative and lyrical dance. Classes are available for preschoolers through adults. A Move With Me class is also offered for parents and preschoolers. Please contact the studio for price information and a current class schedule.

Dance Dana & Company
2001 2nd Street SW, Rochester, MN 55902, (507) 288-0598

Dance Dana & Company provides instruction in classical ballet, Pointe, tap, jazz and lyrical styles. Classes are available for preschoolers through adults of all abilities. Please contact the studio for price information and a current class schedule.

Janet Lang Dance Studio
2625 Hwy. 14 West, Rochester, MN 55901, (507) 288-9653

Janet Lang provides dance instruction for preschoolers through adults. Dance styles taught at Janet Lang include classical ballet, Pointe, jazz, lyrical, tap, dance line, modern, hip-hop, swing, and clogging. Mom and Me classes are also available. Please call the studio for price information and a current class schedule.

Dance classes and programs are also available at the Rochester Athletic Club, (507) 282-6000, and through Rochester's Community Education program, (507) 285-8350. Please inquire for more information about their class offerings, schedules and prices.

Just for Kix

Rochester, MN, (507) 536-4952
Just for Kix National Office: P.O. Box 724, Brainerd, MN 56401, (218) 829-7107, www.justforkix.com

The Just For Kix program offers precision dance team instruction for boys and girls, ages 3 through 9th grade. The Rochester program is run by local Director, Jennifer Alleckson. Along with dance skills and styles, dancers are taught how to cooperate and work as a team. No auditions are necessary, and beginners as well as experienced dancers are welcome. Classes are held once a week from September through April. Please contact Just For Kix for price information and a current class schedule. Classes are also available in the Byron and Kasson areas.

KASSON
Kasson Ballet School

Manorwood Court, Kasson, MN 55944, (507) 288-9653

The Kasson Ballet School is run by Janet Lang Dance Studio of Rochester. The Kasson studio primarily offers classes in ballet, tap, jazz, hip-hop, and lyrical dancing. A more extensive class selection is available at the Janet Lang Studio. Please call the studio for price information and a current class schedule.

Fishing Guides

Lake Pepin Guide Service

211 Lyon Avenue East, Lake City, MN 55041, (651) 345-5801

Loren's Mississippi River Guide Service

1010 Lyon Avenue West, Lake City, MN 55041, 651-345-7550, www.walleyefirst.com/waalkens

Moving Waters Guide Service

1133 7th Avenue SW, Rochester, MN 55902, (507) 271-0362, www.movingwaters.net

Fitness Clubs

Northgate Health Club

1112 7th Street NW, Rochester, MN 55901, (507) 282-4445, www.northgatehc.com

Northgate Health Club is a private fitness club for adults and youth ages 15 and up. The facility has a large fitness area with a wide variety of cardiovascular and strengthening/toning equipment, an indoor walking track, a separate free weight room, an indoor swimming pool, a huge selection of aerobic and fitness classes, locker rooms with whirlpools and saunas, tanning beds, and an on-site nursery. Certified fitness trainers are available to design workout programs for members. Please call Northgate or visit their website for more information.

Cost: monthly membership fee
Hours: Monday–Thursday, 5 a.m.–11 p.m.; Friday, 5 a.m.–10 p.m.; Saturday, 6 a.m.–6 p.m.; Sunday, 10 a.m.–6 p.m.

Rochester Area Family YMCA

709 1st Avenue SW, Rochester, MN 55902, (507) 287-2260, www.rochfamy.org

The mission of the Rochester Area Family YMCA "is to practice Christian values by providing opportunities for everyone to build strong kids, strong families, and strong communities." Facilities at the Y include a Safe Start Fitness Center, a complete fitness center with cardiovascular equipment, Cybex and Nautilus machines, and a free weight area, rooms for group fitness classes, basketball and volleyball gyms, racquetball courts, a 25-yard, five-lane swimming pool, a community whirlpool, an indoor track, Kids' Gym, Junior Gym, a nursery, member lounge with game room, and a service center with rental equipment and limited merchandise for sale. In addition to the Men's/Boy's and Women's/Girl's Locker Rooms, the Y has a Family Locker Room, Special Needs Locker Room, and adults-only locker rooms for men and women. The Y offers a full selection of sports and recreational programs for preschoolers, youth, teens, and families as well as an on-site nursery school and resource center, which offers counseling, support groups, and life skills classes. A sample of available activities includes Toddlers in Motion, swimming lessons, karate training, Saturday flag football, summer sports camps and teams, family pool nights, home school gym classes, Teen Leader's Club, Father/Daughter Dances and much, much more. Membership is open to all persons in the community. Financial assistance and scholarships are available.

Cost: monthly membership fee; guest fee: $
Hours: winter: Monday–Thursday, 5 a.m.–10 p.m.; Friday, 5 a.m.–9 p.m.; Saturday, 7:30 a.m.–8 p.m.; Sunday, 11 a.m.–5 p.m.
summer: Monday–Thursday, 5 a.m.–9 p.m.; Friday, 5 a.m.–7:30 p.m.; Saturday, 7:30 a.m.–5:30 p.m.; Sunday, 11 a.m.–2 p.m.

Rochester Athletic Club

3100 19ᵗʰ Street NW, Rochester, MN 55901, (507) 282-6000, www.rochesterathleticclub.com

The Rochester Athletic Club (RAC) is an upscale, family-friendly fitness club with extensive indoor and outdoor facilities. Indoor facilities include aerobic studios, batting cages, two full-sized gymnasiums with basketball and volleyball courts, a large children's play area, junior gym for kids ages 7–12, a nursery, golfing cages and a 9-hole putting green, racquetball and squash courts, an indoor running/walking track, a 25-meter lap pool, family swimming pool and whirlpool, and ten championship tennis courts. Men's and Women's locker rooms have full amenities with towel service, saunas, whirlpools, and steam rooms. A family locker room that has private showers and changing areas is also available. Outdoor facilities include two regulation baseball/softball fields, a zero-depth entry swimming pool with 180-foot water slide, geyser forest, and mushroom waterfall as well as five 25-meter lap lanes, a large fenced-in sandy play area with playground equipment, mini-golf area, a regulation soccer field, six clay and two plexicushion tennis courts, two sand volleyball courts, a poolside snack bar, and locker rooms with changing areas and rinse showers. The RAC also offers a full schedule of fitness and sports classes and camps for children, youth, and adults as well as on-site massage therapy service, tanning beds, meeting rooms, a complete pro shop, and the Club Café and Deli. Please note that the Rochester Athletic Club is a members-only facility. Daily guest passes are available; however, local residents are only permitted to use the club as a guest once every 60 days. Special rates are available for relatives of members who live outside of southeastern Minnesota.

Cost: monthly membership fee; guest fee: $–$$
Hours: Monday–Friday, 5 a.m.–10:30 p.m.; Saturday–Sunday, 7 a.m.–9 p.m.

Rochester–Olmsted Recreation Center

21 Elton Hills Drive, Rochester, MN 55901, (507) 281-6167, www.ci.rochester.mn.us/park

The Rochester-Olmsted Recreation Center is not considered a fitness club, but has sporting and recreational facilities for water, ice, and gymnasium sports in addition to an exercise room and community meeting rooms. The Recreation Center boasts an Olympic caliber, 50-meter swimming pool with eight lanes, a handicapped-accessible ramp at the shallow end, and a removable bulkhead that may be used to divide the pool into two, 25-yard sections. The pool depth varies from 3.6 to 16 feet, and there are two, 1-meter, and two 3-meter diving boards at the pool. Poolside bleachers can accommodate more than 1,000 spectators. The Recreation Center offers Parent-Tot Swim, Open Swim, Lap Swim, Adult Lap Swim, and Family Swim sessions. Two full-sized, 85-by-200-foot indoor ice rinks for figure skating, hockey, and curling with spectator seating for more than 2500 people. Ice skating activities available for the general public include Open Skating, Adult Ice Skating, Adult Noon Ice Skating, Adult Open Hockey, Family Ice Skating, Parent-Tot Skating, and Open Freestyle Skating.

The gymnasium is designed for either competitive or recreational use. It has six basketball backstops, space for two practice volleyball or badminton courts, or may be set up to accommodate one official high school basketball court or one full size competition volleyball court. Adult Open Gym, Elementary & Middle School Open Gym, High School & Adult Open Gym, and Family Open Gym are regularly scheduled at the Rec Center. An exercise room with universal-style exercise equipment is also available for youth in 7th–12th grades and adults. Please call for current swimming, ice skating, gym and exercise room schedules.

Cost: $, memberships are available
Hours: public hours may vary depending on the event and practice schedules; call for current hours

Football

Rochester Giants

(507) 202-2119, www.eteams.com/rochestergiants

The Rochester Giants, a member of the Great Plains Football League, is a semi-professional football team that provides adults with the opportunity to play full contact football. Players in the league generally have experience playing high school, college, or professional football. The Giants compete against other teams in the Great Plains League, which has or has had teams from Minnesota, Iowa, Wisconsin, Nebraska, North Dakota, South Dakota, and Missouri. Please contact the Rochester Giants for more information about joining the team or to obtain a game schedule.

Go-Karts

Skyline Raceway

2250 40th Street SW, Rochester, MN 55902, (507) 287-6289

Rochester's only Go-Kart track may be found at Skyline Raceway. Single and double passenger Go-Karts are available at the quarter-mile track. A minimum height of 54 inches is required for drivers, and passengers in the double cars must be at least 36 inches tall. A 410-foot waterslide and mini-golf course as well as a picnic area with barbecue pits, horseshoe pits, a volleyball court, and concessions are also located at this amusement park.

Cost: $–$$
Hours: Memorial Day–Labor Day: open daily, noon–8 p.m. (weather permitting)
off-season: noon–6 p.m. (weather permitting)

Golf: Miniature Courses

ROCHESTER
Putter's Paradise at Recreation Lanes
2810 North Broadway, Rochester, MN 55906, (507) 288-2602

Putter's Paradise is a handicapped-accessible, 18-hole mini-golf course that provides players with an interesting landscape as well as challenging obstacles. After playing a round, try hitting baseballs or softballs at the batting cages located on the premises.

Cost: $
Hours: April–Labor Day: Monday–Thursday, 10 a.m.–10 p.m.; Friday–Saturday, 10 a.m.–midnight; Sunday, noon–10 p.m.; hours may vary in early spring

Skyline Raceway
2250 40th Street SW, Rochester, MN 55902, (507) 287-6289

Skyline Raceway has a nicely landscaped 9-hole miniature golf course that provides wholesome entertainment for both kids and adults. Other recreational facilities at Skyline Raceway include a quarter-mile Go-Kart track and 410-foot waterslide as well as a picnic area with barbecue pits, a volleyball court, horseshoe pits, and concessions.

Cost: $–$$
Hours: Memorial Day–Labor Day: open daily, noon–8 p.m. (weather permitting)
off-season: noon–6 p.m. (weather permitting)

BYRON
Links of Byron
222 2nd Avenue, Byron, MN 55920, (507) 775-2004

An 18-hole, championship miniature golf course is located just a short drive from Rochester at the Links of Byron. The mini-golf course is beautifully landscaped and has challenging features for players of all ages. Additional facilities at the Links of Byron include a 9-hole executive golf course, driving range, and clubhouse with screened-in porch and snack bar.

Cost: $
Hours: call for hours

KELLOGG
Miniature Golf at the L.A.R.K.
P.O. Box 39, Lark Lane, Kellogg, MN 55945, (507) 767-3387, www.larktoys.com

The L.A.R.K. Toy Company, which stands for Lost Arts Revival by Kreofsky, is a 31,000-square-foot complex that not only has an 18-hole miniature golf course, but features an enchanting handcarved and handpainted carousel, and is one of the largest children's specialty toy stores in the United States. Visitors to the L.A.R.K. can easily spend the day playing a round of mini-golf, browsing through the toy museum and specialty toy stores, riding the carousel, and eating lunch at The Rocking Café. So after putting your way through a mountain on the meticulously landscaped mini-golf course, plan to stay awhile and explore all that the L.A.R.K. has to offer. Birthday party packages are available at the L.A.R.K.

Cost: $
Hours: Monday–Friday, 9 a.m.–5 p.m.; Saturday–Sunday, 10 a.m.–5 p.m.
  winter: open Friday–Sunday in January & February
  mini-golf season: May–mid-October during store hours; evening mini-golf is available from June–Labor Day (call for evening hours)

STEWARTVILLE
Dairy Queen of Stewartville
920 North Main Street, Stewartville, MN 55976, (507) 533-8540

Enjoy the simple pleasures at DQ of Stewartville–an ice cream treat and a round of mini-golf. A no-frills, 18-hole miniature golf course with a few challenging obstacles is located on the premises.

Cost: $
Hours: spring & summer: Sunday–Saturday, 10:30 a.m.–10 p.m.

WABASHA
Foxes Mini Golf
1030 Bailey Avenue, Wabasha, MN 55981, (651) 565-4330

This 18-hole miniature golf course is located in Historic Wabasha. The course provides family fun for all ages by having a variety of easy and challenging holes. Please call to inquire about birthday party packages available at Foxes Mini Golf.

Cost: $
Hours: spring & fall: call for hours
  summer: Monday–Friday, 1 p.m.–9 p.m.; Saturday–Sunday, 11 a.m.–9 p.m.

WHALAN
Gator Greens Mini Golf
Whalan, MN 55949, (507) 467-3000, www.gatorgreens.net

Gator Greens Mini Golf, located in the tiny community of Whalan, offers a meticulously landscaped 9-hole miniature golf course adjacent to the Root River Recreation Trail. After a long trek on the bike trail, take a break and stretch your legs by playing a round at Gator Greens.

Cost: $

Hours: May–October: Friday–Sunday, call for hours; Monday–Thursday, by appointment

A visit to Whalan wouldn't be complete without stopping by the Aroma Pie Shop. Choose from a tasty selection of sandwiches, soups, pies, ice cream treats and other refreshing goodies. Located at 618 Main Street in Whalan. (507) 467-2623.

Golf: Indoor

Golf Etiquette Classes for Juniors

Hawthorn Hills Golf Learning Center, 1925 48th Street NE, Rochester, MN 55906, (507) 529-4119, www.ci.rochester.mn.us/park

Hawthorn Hills offers golf etiquette classes for junior golfers, ages 9–15. The 45-minute class is required to obtain a junior season ticket at the discounted rate. Please call Hawthorn Hills for class information.

Golf Headquarters

1920 South Broadway, Rochester, MN 55902, (507) 282-3424, 800-335-3424

The golf simulation rooms at Golf Headquarters offer golfers the opportunity to play at 32 different courses via video projection. Two golf simulators are available for rent by the hour during the winter months. Please call ahead for reservations. No rental clubs are available.

Cost: $$

Hours: Monday–Thursday, 10 a.m.–8 p.m.; Friday, 10 a.m.–6 p.m.; Saturday, 9 a.m.–5 p.m.; Sunday, 11 a.m.–4 p.m.

Rochester Indoor Golf Center

2700 West Country Club Road, Rochester, MN 55903, (507) 288-4851
Located 1 mile west of Saint Mary's Hospital.

The Rochester Indoor Golf Center (RIGC) is a 120-by-180-foot domed facility that is primarily used as an indoor driving range but may also be used for other activities that require a large space such as soccer, baseball, and football. The driving range can accommodate 12 hitters at a time and is also equipped with targets and a putting green. Golf instruction by a PGA professional, a complete pro shop with a selection of new and used clubs, club repairs and rentals are available on site. RIGC also hosts an annual Golf Equipment Swap Meet. This event, held the weekend following Thanksgiving, is a place where golfers may buy and sell new and used equipment.

Cost: $, discount punch cards and passes are available

Hours: open daily, 9 a.m.–7 p.m.

The Sandtrap

Hillcrest Shopping Center, Rochester, MN 55901, (507) 536-7768

Play the world's most famous courses at the Sandtrap, Rochester's indoor golf facility. The Sandtrap boasts real golf, played with regulation clubs and balls. State-of-the-Art Full Swing Golf Simulators record the speed, trajectory, bounce, and backspin of each shot. The shots are then duplicated on a screen in real time. You'll hear the splash in the pond or the ping if you hit the pin. Leagues are available and tournaments are occasionally scheduled. Call to reserve tee times. Food and beverages are available on site.

Cost: $–$$$, cost is per hour and per half hour on the driving range
Hours: 9 a.m.–10 p.m., earlier or later hours by tee time

Golf: Outdoor Courses

ROCHESTER

Eastwood Golf Course

3505 Eastwood Road SE, Rochester, MN 55904, (507) 281-6173, www.ci.rochester.mn.us/park

Eastwood, an 18-hole, par-70 municipal golf course, is located in southeast Rochester. The course has tree-lined fairways and hilly terrain with smaller greens and no water hazards. Tee times may be reserved up to two days in advance. Cart and club rentals, a driving range, practice putting green, pro shop, golf instruction, Men's and Women's leagues, and a clubhouse with restaurant are available at the course.

Cost: $$–$$$
Hours: Monday–Friday, 6:30 a.m.–dusk; Saturday–Sunday, 6 a.m.–dusk

Hawthorn Hills Golf Learning Center

1925 48th Street NE, Rochester, MN 55906, (507) 529-4119, www.ci.rochester.mn.us/park

Hawthorn Hills Golf Learning Center is an outstanding practice facility in northeast Rochester. In addition to golf instruction by a PGA professional, Hawthorn has a driving range with 40 hitting stations, a three-tiered putting green, pitching green with bunker, and a three-hole practice golf course. First Tee, an international program designed by the World Golf Federation to create affordable and accessible golf facilities for kids who would otherwise not have access to the game, is also offered at Hawthorn. Please contact the Learning Center for more information about the First Tee program or group and individual instruction. Club rentals are available.

Cost: $, call for cost of classes
Hours: open daily, 9 a.m.–8 p.m.

Maple Valley Golf and Country Club

8600 Maple Valley Road SE, Rochester, MN 55904, (507) 285-9100, www.maplevalleygolf.com

Maple Valley Golf and Country Club is one of southeastern Minnesota's most scenic golf courses. The Root River meanders through the 18-hole, par 71 golf course, which is surrounded by picturesque bluffs and mature trees. Tee times may be reserved up to five days in advance. Cart and club rentals, practice chipping and putting greens, a pro shop, Men's and Women's leagues, golf instruction and limited food and beverage service are available.

Cost: $$–$$$
Hours: open daily, dawn–dusk

Meadow Lakes Golf Club

70 45th Avenue SW, Rochester, MN 55902, (507) 285-1190, www.rochestersquare.com
Located 5 miles west of Mayo Clinic on 2nd Street SW.

Meadow Lakes Golf Club is an 18-hole, par-71 links-style golf course that challenges golfers with water hazards on 15 holes and two island greens. Tee times may be made up to five days in advance. Additional amenities include cart and club rental, a "state-of-the-art" practice facility with a driving range, five target greens, practice putting green, a pro shop, golf instruction, Men's and Ladies' leagues, and a clubhouse with restaurant and lounge. Please call for current specials and Couple's events.

Cost: $$–$$$
Hours: open daily, dawn–dusk

Northern Hills Golf Course
4805 West Circle Drive, Rochester, MN 55901, (507) 281-6170, www.ci.rochester.mn.us/park

Northern Hills, an 18-hole, par-72 course, is located in northwest Rochester. The challenging course has hilly terrain and a small creek that comes into play on several holes. Tee times may be made up to two days in advance. Cart and club rentals, a driving range, practice putting green, pro shop, limited golf instruction, Men's and Ladies' Days, and a club house with food and beverage service are available.

Cost: $$–$$$
Hours: Monday–Friday, 6:30 a.m.–dusk; Saturday–Sunday, 6 a.m.–dusk

Oak Summit Golf Course
2751 Airport Hwy. 16 SW, Rochester, MN 55902, (507) 252-1808, www.oaksummitgolf.com

Oak Summit, an 18-hole, par-71 golf course, is located on the outskirts of southwest Rochester near the Rochester International Airport. The course is situated on hilly terrain and challenges golfers with its sandtraps, five ponds, and small creek. Tee times may be reserved up to seven days in advance. Cart and club rentals, a driving range, practice putting green, pro shop, golf instruction, Men's, Women's, and Couple's leagues, and a clubhouse with limited food and beverage service are available.

Cost: $–$$
Hours: open daily, dawn–dusk

Rochester Golf and Country Club
3100 Country Club Road, Rochester, MN 55902, (507) 282-3170, www.rgcc.com

The Rochester Golf and Country Club is a private club open to members, members of participating clubs, and their guests. The 18-hole, par-71 championship course was designed by A.W. Tillinghast in 1926 and has received accolades from Golf Digest and the Golf Course Architects of America. RGCC has been ranked Minnesota's number three championship golf course and has hosted many regional, state, and national golf tournaments and events. The country club is situated in southwestern Rochester and offers beautiful landscapes and elegant facilities amid a secluded atmosphere. Additional golf amenities include a practice facility with a driving range, target greens, chipping and bunker areas, a 7,000-square-foot putting green, golf instruction, a full-service pro shop, golf leagues for men, women, and juniors, and club tournaments. Members may reserve tee times up to one week in advance. There is also an Olympic-sized swimming pool with diving well, a wading pool, deck, bath house, on-site swimming lessons, a snack bar, pool side patio with dining services, and fine and casual dining with banquet facilities. A variety of different memberships are available including social and house memberships, which entitles a member to clubhouse and pool privileges only.

Cost: $$$$$$
Hours: open daily, dawn–dusk

Soldiers Field Golf Course

244 Soldiers Field Drive SW, Rochester, MN 55902, (507) 281-6176, www.ci.rochester.mn.us/park

Soldiers Field Golf Course, Rochester's oldest city golf course, is just a few blocks from the downtown area. The Zumbro River flows through the 18-hole, par-70 course that has many mature trees and a relatively flat, easy to walk terrain. Tee times may be reserved up to two days in advance. Cart and club rentals, a pro shop, practice putting and chipping greens, Men's and Women's leagues, and a clubhouse with restaurant are available on site.

Cost: $$–$$$
Hours: Monday–Friday, 6:30 a.m.–dusk; Saturday–Sunday, 6 a.m.–dusk

Willow Creek Golf Course & Little Willow Executive 9-Hole Course

1700 48th Street SW, Rochester, MN 55902, (507) 285-0305, www.wpgolf.com/willowcreek

Willow Creek, an 18-hole, par-70 course, offers golfers the combination of a front nine that is relatively flat and open, and a challenging back nine that is tight with wooded areas and a creek that comes into play on several holes. Little Willow is a 9-hole, par-20 executive course that is great for beginning golfers, families, youth, or seniors unable to walk a regular course. Amenities at Willow Creek include cart and club rentals, a pro shop, driving range, practice putting green, golf instruction, and clubhouse with full bar and grill as well as banquet facilities. Men's and Women's leagues are available at Willow Creek and the Little Willow offers a Junior League program. Green fees are only $5 per person for families on Saturday and Sunday afternoons, after 3 p.m.

ADAMS

Cedar River Country Club

P.O. Box 311, Adams, MN 55909, (507) 582-3595
Located about one mile east of Adams on Hwy. 56.

The Cedar River runs through this scenic 18-hole, par-72 golf course. Tee times are readily available, but large groups are encouraged to make reservations. This small town country club offers cart and club rentals, a newly remodeled clubhouse with bar and grill, pro shop, a driving range and putting green, golf lessons, cart shed rentals, and Men's leagues. Men's Day is Wednesday from noon until dusk and includes supper. Ladies' Day is Thursday morning until noon and includes a lunch-eon. Memberships are available but not necessary to play at the course.

Cost: $$–$$$
Hours: open daily, dawn–dusk

BYRON

Links of Byron

Hwy. 14 West and County Road 5, Byron, MN 55920, (507) 775-2004

The Links of Byron sports a 9-hole, par-31 executive golf course, a driving range, and an 18-hole, championship miniature golf course. Tee times are not necessary. The Links offers cart and club rentals, a clubhouse with a screened-in porch that serves snacks and beverages, pro shop, golf instruction, and a couple's league. The driving range and mini-golf course are lighted for nighttime play.

Cost: $
Hours: Monday–Friday, 8 a.m.–dusk; Saturday–Sunday, 7 a.m.–dusk

CALEDONIA
Ma-Cal-Grove Country Club
15939 Hwys. 76/44, Caledonia, MN 55921, (507) 725-2733, www.bluffcountry.com

The Ma-Cal-Grove Country Club, named after the communities of Mabel, Caledonia and Spring Grove, is situated among the rolling hills of southeastern Minnesota. Nonmembers may reserve tee times for the 9-hole, par-36 golf course up to three days in advance. This small town country club offers cart and club rentals, a pro shop, a driving range and putting green, golf instruction, a clubhouse with bar and grill, and Ladies' and Men's Leagues. Ladies' Day is Wednesday until 3 p.m., and Men's Day is all day Thursday beginning at 10 a.m.

Cost: $$
Hours: open daily, 7 a.m.–dusk

CHATFIELD
Chosen Valley Golf Club
1801 South Main Street, Chatfield, MN 55923, (507) 867-4305

The 9-hole, par-35 golf course at Chosen Valley Golf Club is fairly flat with small rolling hills and some challenging raised greens. Tee times are not accepted at this course. Cart and club rentals, a pro shop, and clubhouse with bar and grill are available. Private golf instruction may be arranged.

Cost: $–$$
Hours: open daily, 8 a.m.–8 p.m.

DODGE CENTER
Dodge Country Club
Box 429, Hwy. 14 West, Dodge Center, MN 55927, (507) 374-2374

The Dodge Country Club, a 9-hole, par-36 golf course, is currently being expanded to an 18-hole course with a driving range. Tee times are not necessary. Cart and club rentals, a clubhouse with a full-service bar and restaurant, pro shop, a practice putting green, and Men's league are available at the country club.

Cost: $$
Hours: Monday–Friday, 8 a.m.–dusk; Saturday–Sunday, 6:30 a.m.–dusk

FRONTENAC
Mount Frontenac Golf Course
Box 180, Hwy. 61, Frontenac, MN 55026, (651) 388-5826, www.mountfrontenac.com

Mount Frontenac is a challenging 18-hole, par-71 golf course located atop the picturesque Mississippi River Bluffs. The course was rated second best in value for the 1998 season and the fourth most scenic course in 1999 by the Minneapolis Star Tribune. Tee times may be reserved up to ten days in advance. Cart and club rentals, a new clubhouse with a full-service bar and restaurant that seats 180 people, a pro shop, driving nets, a practice putting green, and Men's, Couple's, and Senior leagues are available.

Cost: $$–$$$
Hours: open daily, dawn–dusk

HARMONY
Harmony Golf Club
535 4ᵗʰ Street NE, Harmony, MN 55939, (507) 886-5622, www.harmonygolfclub.com

The Harmony Golf Club offers an easily walkable 9-hole, par-36 course with small, sloping greens. Tee times are not needed; however, reservations must be made for cart rentals. Cart and club rentals, a small pro shop, practice putting green, a clubhouse with a bar and grill as well as Men's, Ladies' and Couple's leagues are available. The club is closed on Tuesday afternoons for Ladies' Day and Thursday afternoons for Men's Day.

Cost: $$
Hours: open daily, 8 a.m.–dusk

HAYFIELD
The Oaks Golf Club
73671 170ᵗʰ Avenue, Hayfield, MN 55940, (507) 477-3233

The Oaks Golf Club, a 9-hole, par-72 course, is a relatively flat course with great greens, and a rolling brook that runs throughout the entire course. Nonmembers may reserve tee times up to five days in advance. Cart and club rentals, a driving range, practice putting green, pro shop, golf instruction including a youth golf program, a clubhouse with a bar and grill as well as Men's, Ladies', and Mixed leagues are available.

Cost: $$
Hours: Monday–Friday, 7:30 a.m.–dusk; Saturday–Sunday, 7 a.m.–dusk

HOUSTON
Valley High Country Club
9203 Mound Prairie Drive, Houston, MN 55943, (507) 894-4444, www.bluffcountry.com

Valley High Country Club, an 18-hole, par-71 course, is nestled among the bluffs of southeastern Minnesota in Houston. The challenging course has tree-lined fairways and undulating greens. Tee times are necessary for weekend and holiday play and may be made up to seven days in advance. Cart and club rentals, driving range, practice putting green, a clubhouse with a bar and grill, private golf lessons, a pro shop as well as Men's, Ladies', and Couple's leagues are available.

Cost: $$
Hours: open daily, dawn–dusk

KENYON
Kenyon Country Club
Hwy. 56 North Kenyon, MN 55946, (507) 789-6307

The 9-hole, par-34 golf course of the Kenyon Country Club, originally built in 1926 and 1927, has large oak trees, a couple of ponds, and small greens with a few sand traps. Nonmembers must make tee times three days in advance. Cart rentals, a pro shop, a clubhouse with a bar and grill, and Men's, Women's, and Couple's leagues are available. Golfers have access to a driving range across the street from the golf course. The course is closed on Wednesdays until 4 p.m. for women members and their guests and on Thursdays from noon until closing for men members and their guests.

Cost: $$
Hours: open daily, 8 a.m.–dusk

LA CRESCENT
Pine Creek Golf Course
3815 North Pine Creek Road, La Crescent, MN 55947, (507) 895-2410

Pine Creek is a 9-hole, par-35 golf course located in La Crescent adjacent to the Mississippi River Valley of La Crosse, Wisconsin. The course is hilly from holes four to nine, and two streams come into play toward the end of the course. Tee times may be reserved up to seven days in advance. Cart and club rentals, a pro shop, practice putting green, clubhouse with a bar and grill as well as a Men's Senior league and Ladies' league are available.

Cost: $
Hours: Monday–Friday, 6:30 a.m.–dusk, Saturday–Sunday; 6 a.m.–dusk

LAKE CITY
Lake City Golf Club
33587 Lakeview Drive, Lake City, MN 55041, (651) 345-3221, www.lakecitygolf.com

The Lake City Country Club boasts a recently expanded 18-hole, par-71 course designed by Gil Miller, Inc. The course challenges even experienced golfers with nine water hazards and a meandering stream that comes into play during the last three holes. Tee times may be reserved up to seven days in advance. Cart rentals, a pro shop, driving range, practice putting green, clubhouse with a bar and grill, and a Men's league are available. Ladies' Night is Wednesday evening, and Men's Night is Thursday evening.

Cost: $$–$$$
Hours: open daily, 8:30 a.m.–dusk

Lake Pepin Golf Course
RR 4, Box 761, Lake City, MN 55041, (651) 345-5768, www.lakepepingolf.com
Take Hwy. 61 South to County Road 4, turn right and follow road to top of hill, turn left on County Road 10 at the Y-intersection and another quick left onto the gravel road. Follow the gravel road for 2½ miles.

The Lake Pepin Golf Course, opened in 1997 and expanded in 2001, features stunning views of Lake Pepin from 12 of its 18 holes. Lake City's par-36 golf course also has rolling hills and a pond that comes into play at five holes. Tee times may be reserved up to seven days in advance. Cart and club rentals, a driving range with target greens, a practice putting green, golf instruction, a clubhouse with two full-service bars (no grill), and Men's, Ladies', and Mixed leagues are available.

Cost: $$
Hours: open daily, dawn–dusk

LANESBORO
Lanesboro Golf Club

Box 10, 900 Parkway South, Lanesboro, MN 55949, (507) 467-3742, www.lanesboro.com

The Lanesboro Golf Club is situated in southeastern Minnesota's historic bluff country. The 9-hole, par-35 course is long, narrow, and hilly. There are few, if any, even lies. No tee times are accepted. Cart and club rentals, a pro shop, practice putting green, golf instruction, a clubhouse with a bar and grill, and Men's and Ladies' leagues are available.

Cost: $–$$
Hours: dawn–dusk

LEWISTON
Lewiston Country Club

Route 2, Box 39, Lewiston, MN 55952, (507) 523-2060

The golf course at the Lewiston Country Club, a 9-hole, par-36 course is excellent for beginner and intermediate golfers. The course features wide-open fairways on gently rolling hills and several sand traps but no water hazards. A 9-hole, par-3 course is also located at the country club. This course is excellent for beginning golfers and children because all the holes are between 75 to 85 yards. Tee times for both courses may be reserved up to seven days in advance. Cart and club rentals, a small pro shop, a driving range, practice putting green, clubhouse with a bar and grill, and Men's Leagues are available.

Cost: $$
Hours: open daily, 7 a.m.–dusk

MABEL
Meadowbrook Country Club

RR 2, Box 210A, Mabel, MN 55954, (507) 493-5708
Located 1 mile east of Mabel on Hwy. 44.

Meadowbrook's 9-hole, par-36 golf course is situated on a relatively flat terrain. No tee times are accepted at this small town country club, which also offers cart and club rentals, a practice putting green, a Men's league, a clubhouse that serves beer and snacks (BYOB permitted). Ladies' Day is on Tuesdays from 2 p.m. until closing, and Men's Day is on Thursdays from 2 p.m. until closing.

Cost: $–$$
Hours: open daily, 8 a.m.–dusk

MANTORVILLE
Zumbro Valley Recreation Club
25202 615th Street, Mantorville, MN 55955, (507) 635-2821

The 9-hole, par-36 course at the Zumbro Valley Recreation Club challenges players with tree-lined fairways, rolling hills, and streams that come into play at four holes. Due to high demand, players are encouraged to call ahead for tee times. Weekend tee times may be reserved beginning on Wednesday of the same week. Cart and club rentals, a small pro shop, practice putting green, golf instruction, a clubhouse with a bar and grill, and a Men's league are available. Women's Day is held on Tuesday mornings until 11:30 a.m. and Wednesday afternoons from 4 p.m. until closing. Men's Day is held on Thursdays from 1 p.m. until closing.

Cost: $$
Hours: Monday–Friday, 7 a.m.–dusk; Saturday–Sunday, 6 a.m.–dusk

OWATONNA
Brooktree Golf Course
1369 Cherry Street, Owatonna, MN 55060, (507) 444-2467

Brooktree is a challenging 18-hole, par-71 golf course with a long front nine that has undulating greens and a back nine that demands accuracy. Nonmembers may reserve tee times up to three days in advance. Amenities include cart and club rentals, a pro shop, two practice putting greens, Men's, Women's, and Couple's leagues, and a clubhouse with restaurant.

Cost: $$–$$$
Hours: Monday–Friday, 7 a.m.–dusk; Saturday–Sunday, 6:30 a.m.–dusk

Havanna Hills
2213 34th Street NE, Owatonna, MN 55060, (507) 451-2577, www.hiddencreekmn.com

This is a par-27, 9-hole course, run by Hidden Creek Golf Club, that is great for golfers who want to work on their short game. A driving range and practice putting green are located on the premises. Tee times are on a first come, first served basis. Cart and club rentals, a pro shop, golf instructions, and Senior and Ladies' leagues are available.

Cost: $
Hours: open daily, dawn–dusk

Hidden Creek Golf Club
4989 East Rose Street, Owatonna, MN 55060, (507) 444-9229, 888-MOR-GOLF, www.hiddencreekmn.com

Hidden Creek sports an 18-hole, par-72 Scottish links-style course with rolling terrain, a creek, and five ponds. The golf club offers cart and club rentals, a pro shop, a driving range, practice putting green, golf instruction, and Men's and Women's leagues. Players must call ahead for tee times, which will be taken up to seven days in advance. A clubhouse with a bar and full service restaurant is available.

Cost: $$$–$$$$
Hours: open daily, dawn–dusk

Owatonna Country Club
1991 LeMond Road, Owatonna, MN 55060, (507) 451-1363

The Owatonna Country Club is a well-maintained 18-hole, par-71 championship course. The course terrain features many rolling hills and is generally played in four hours. Nonmembers may reserve tee times on a limited basis. The golf club offers cart and club rentals, a pro shop, driving range, practice putting green, golf instruction, and leagues for Men, Women, Couples, and Juniors. The country club also boasts a new 23,000-square-foot clubhouse with a full service restaurant and bar.

Cost: $$$$–$$$$$
Hours: open daily, dawn–dusk

PINE ISLAND
Pine Island Golf Course
Box 341, Pine Island, MN 55963, (507) 356-8252
Go south on Main Street, left on 7th Street.

This 18-hole, par-71 golf course is located on 80 acres in Pine Island, just 15 miles north of Rochester. The course has wide fairways, and several water hazards make it challenging for both novice and experienced golfers. Tee times may be reserved up to seven days in advance. Cart and club rentals, a driving range, practice putting green, small pro shop, golf instruction, and Men's, Women's, and Couple's Leagues as well as a clubhouse with a limited selection of sandwiches, snacks, and beverages are available.

Cost: $$
Hours: Monday–Friday, 6 a.m.–dusk; Saturday–Sunday, 5:30 a.m.–dusk

PLAINVIEW
Piper Hills Golf Club
Hwy. 42, Plainview, MN 55964, (507) 534-2613
Located just south of Plainview on Hwy. 42, adjacent to the Feed Mill.

Piper Hills offers a challenging 9-hole, par-36 course situated among the rolling hills of rural Plainview. Golf club facilities include cart and club rentals, a pro shop, driving range, practice putting green, golf lessons, Men's leagues, and a clubhouse with full service restaurant and bar. No advance tee times are necessary to play at Piper Hills.

Cost: $–$$
Hours: open daily, 8 a.m.–dusk

PRESTON
The Old Barn Resort
Route 3, Box 57, Preston, MN 55965, (507) 467-2512, 800-552-2512, www.bluffcountry.com, www.exploreminnesota.com

The Old Barn Resort offers a challenging 9-hole, par-35 course that plays over the Root River and through the Root River Valley, as well as a driving range and practice putting green. Cart and club rentals and golf lessons are also available. Tee times may be made one day in advance or upon check-in for resort guests. Additional facilities at the Old Barn, a favorite resort among area residents and visitors, include a campground, full-service bar and restaurant, a hostel, swimming pool, canoe and tube rental, and easy access to the Root River State Trail. Please see Chapter 12, Campgrounds, for detailed information about the resort.

Cost: $$
Hours: Monday–Friday, 9 a.m.–8 p.m.; Saturday–Sunday, 8 a.m.–8 p.m.

Preston Golf and Country Club
Hwy. 16 West, Preston, MN 55965, (507) 765-4485

This is a 9-hole, par-35 course on hilly terrain with tree-lined fairways and a limited number of sand bunkers. The facility offers cart and club rentals, a practice putting green, small pro shop, Senior league, and clubhouse with sandwiches, snacks, and beverages. Tee times are not accepted. Ladies' Day is on Tuesday from 2 p.m. until closing, and Men's Day is on Thursday from noon until closing.

Cost: $–$$
Hours: open daily, 7 a.m.–dusk

RUSHFORD
Ferndale Country Club
23239 Hwy. 16, Rushford, MN 55971, (507) 864-7626, www.ferndalecountryclub.com

This 9-hole, par-36 golf course is set in the scenic bluff country of southeastern Minnesota. Ferndale originally opened in 1931 but recently remodeled its clubhouse and added a driving range to its facility. Tee times may be made up to one week in advance. The facility has cart and club rentals, a practice putting green, pro shop, golf instruction as well as Men's, Women's, and Senior's leagues. A bar and grill is available in the clubhouse.

Cost: $$–$$$
Hours: Monday–Friday, 8 a.m.–dusk; Saturday–Sunday, 7 a.m.–dusk

ST. CHARLES
St. Charles Golf Club
1920 Park Road, St. Charles, MN 55972, (507) 932-5444, www.stcharlesgolfclub.com

St. Charles, the gateway to Whitewater State Park, offers an 18-hole, par-71 golf course with a number of ponds that come into play on the course. Players are encouraged to reserve tee times, which may be made up to seven days in advance. The facility has cart and club rentals, a driving range, practice putting green, pro shop, golf instruction, and Men's, Ladies' and Junior leagues. A clubhouse with bar and grill is available.

Cost: $$–$$$
Hours: open daily, dawn–dusk

SPRING VALLEY
Root River Country Club
Hwy. 63 South, Spring Valley, MN 55975, (507) 346-2501
Located 5 miles south of Spring Valley on Hwy. 63.

The Root River Country Club, a 9-hole, par-36 golf course, has an easy-to-walk terrain and an abundance of trees. The south branch of the Root River comes into play on four of the holes. Tee times are only required for weekend play and may be made one day in advance. The facility has cart and club rentals, a pro shop, practice putting green, Men's leagues, and a clubhouse with bar and grill.

Cost: $$
Hours: open daily, 7 a.m.–dusk

STEWARTVILLE
Riverview Greens Golf Course
1801 1ˢᵗ Avenue NE, Stewartville, MN 55976, (507) 533-9393, www.dhimmer.com

Riverview Greens, an 18-hole, par-67 golf course, challenges players with several water hazards created by the Root River as it runs through the course. The facility offers cart and club rentals, a practice putting green, golf instruction for juniors, and Women's, Men's, and Couple's leagues. Tee times may be reserved up to one week in advance. Development of a clubhouse with a pro shop and full-service restaurant and bar is currently underway.

Cost: $$
Hours: Monday–Friday, 8 a.m.–dusk; Saturday–Sunday, 7 a.m.–dusk

WABASHA
Coffee Mill Golf & Country Club
215 Skyline Drive, Wabasha, MN 55981, (651) 565-4332, www.coffeemillgolf.com

Coffee Mill Golf and Country Club, a 9-hole, par-36 course, is situated on gently rolling hills with tree-lined fairways and offers grand views of the bluffs along the Mississippi and Chippewa River Valleys. The country club offers cart and club rentals, a pro shop, practice putting green, and Men's and Ladies' leagues. The club-house has a bar that serves a selection of sandwiches, snacks and beverages. Tee times are not accepted. Coffee Mill is currently under expansion and will open as an 18-hole golf course with a driving range in June 2003.

Cost: $$–$$$
Hours: open daily, 7 a.m.–10 p.m.

WINONA
Cedar Valley
Winona, MN 55987, (507) 457-3129
Located off Hwy. 61 between Winona and La Crosse on County Road 9.

Cedar Valley offers golfers the opportunity to play up to 27 holes on three, separate 9-hole, par-36 golf courses. The courses are situated in a narrow, scenic valley and challenge players at several holes with a creek and trout stream that come into play. Tee times may be reserved up to seven days in advance. Cart and club rentals, a driving range, practice putting green, pro shop, golf instruction, and a clubhouse with bar and grill as well as a full-service restaurant are available. Men's Day is held on Wednesdays from 1:30 p.m.–4:30 p.m., and Ladies' Day is held on Thursdays from 4 p.m.–6:30 p.m.

Cost: $$–$$$
Hours: open daily, dawn–dusk

Westfield Golf Course

1460 West 5th Street, Winona, MN 55987, (507) 452-6901, www.visitwinona.com

This scenic, 9-hole par-36 course challenges golfers with its narrow fairways and water hazards at the 7th, 8th, and 9th holes. Tee times may be reserved up to two days in advance. Westfield Golf Course offers cart and club rentals, a driving range, practice putting green, pro shop, golf instruction, and a clubhouse with full bar and lunch service. Men's, Women's, and Couple's leagues are available.

Cost: $–$$
Hours: open daily, dawn–dusk

Winona Country Club

RR 3, Box 55, Winona, MN 55987, (507) 452-3535
Located off Hwy. 43 on County Road 17.

The Winona Country Club is a challenging 18-hole, par-71 course situated in a scenic valley surrounded by bluffs. The club is open to nonresident guests or guests accompanied by a member. Tee times may be reserved up to one month in advance. Services provided include cart and club rentals, a pro shop, driving range, two practice putting greens, a short game practice area, and golf instruction. Fine dining and a full-service bar are available at the clubhouse.

Cost: $$$$$
Hours: open daily, dawn–dusk

ZUMBRO FALLS
Zumbro Falls Golf Club

RR 1, Box 23, Zumbro Falls, MN 55991, (507) 753-3131, www.rochestersquare.com
Located 2 miles north of Zumbro Falls on Hwy. 63.

Zumbro Falls Golf Club is a 9-hole, par-36 course situated on very hilly terrain. Tee times may be reserved up to seven days in advance. The club offers cart and club rentals, a driving range, practice putting green, Men's and Women's leagues, and a clubhouse with a bar and grill.

Cost: $$
Hours: open daily, dawn–dusk

ZUMBROTA
Zumbrota Golf Club

17811 Sugarloaf Parkway, Zumbrota, MN 55992, (507) 732-5817
From Hwy. 52 North, take County Road 58 through Zumbrota, turn left onto Sugarloaf Parkway.

The Zumbrota Golf Club offers golfers a 9-hole, par-34 course with several sand traps and a creek that comes into play at two holes. Cart and club rentals, a small pro shop, driving range, practice putting green, golf lessons, Men's and Women's leagues, and a clubhouse with bar and grill are available at the club.

Cost: $$
Hours: open daily, dawn–dusk

Hiking

Rochester Park and Recreation Department

201 4th Street SE, 150 City Hall, Rochester, MN 55904, (507) 281-6160, www.ci.rochester.mn.us/park

The Rochester Park System has 9.8 miles of hiking trails located in the wooded, hilly areas of Essex, Eastwood, Northern Heights, Indian Heights, and Quarry Hill Parks. The trails are composed of turf, wood chips, or road rock. Please call Rochester Park and Recreation or visit their website for more information. Park locations may be found in Chapter 16.

Hiking in Southeastern Minnesota

If you're looking for hiking trails off the beaten path, *Hiking Minnesota* (John Pukite, Falcon Publishing Company, 1998) is an excellent guide of hard-to-find trails throughout the state with general descriptions, length, difficulty, and elevation gain along with DNR information and how to locate trails on USGS maps.

Hot Air Balloon Rides

Rochester Balloon Company

(507) 282-2932, www.rochesterballoon.com

Screwball Balloons

(507) 765-4913, www.geocities.com/samwho2

Windrider Ballooning

(715) 875-4966, 800-821-9484

Ice Skating

Please see Chapter 20 for information about indoor and outdoor hockey and ice skating facilities in the area. See Roller Skating sections earlier in this chapter.

Martial Arts

Martial Arts Fitness Center

2849 South Broadway, Rochester, MN 55904, (507) 281-4335, www.mafci.com

National Karate and Kickboxing

Northwest Plaza, 3526 55th Street NW, Rochester, MN 55901, (507) 280-6546, www.nationalkarate.com

Park Institute

3004 East Frontage Road, Hwy. 52 North, Rochester, MN 55901, (507) 288-9000.

Rochester Area Family YMCA

709 1st Avenue SW, Rochester, MN 55902, (507) 287-2260, www.rochfamy.org

Rochester Athletic Club

3100 19th Street NW, Rochester, MN 55901, (507) 282-6000, www.rochesterathleticclub.com

Paintball

Visit www.paintball.org or check out:

Back 80 Paintball Sports

Winona, MN 55987, (507) 523-2220, www.back80.com

Run-n-Gun Paint Ball Sports

RR 1, Box 248AB, Mazeppa, MN 55956, (507) 990-0913, www.run-n-gun.net

Play Centers: Indoor

Kids' Gym at Rochester Family YMCA

709 1st Avenue SW, Rochester, MN 55902, (507) 287-2260, www.rochfamy.org

YMCA members and guests are welcome to bring their children, ages 2–7, to the Kids' Gym for open play. The large indoor play area is equipped with tumbling mats, climbing towers, slides, and other toys that encourage active play and movement. Children must be accompanied by an adult at all times when playing in the Kids' Gym.

Cost: free for members; guest fee: $
Hours: Monday–Thursday, 5 a.m.–10 p.m.; Friday, 5 a.m.–9 p.m.; Saturday,
   7:30 a.m.–8 p.m.; Sunday, 11 a.m.–5 p.m.; building hours may be subject to
   change seasonally

Kids' Gym at the Rochester Athletic Club

3100 19th Street NW, Rochester, MN 55901, (507) 282-6000, www.rochesterathleticclub.com

The Rochester Athletic Club has a 2,200-square-foot play area designated exclusively for young children ages 0–6 years. This area provides plenty of room to romp and play. Play equipment includes balls, climbing towers, playhouses, slides, tumbling mats, a basketball hoop, and a variety of other large toys that encourage active play. Children must be accompanied by a parent or guardian (age 13 and older) at all times when in the Kids' Gym. Please note that the Rochester Athletic Club is a members-only facility. Daily guest passes are available; however, local residents are only permitted to use the club as a guest once every 60 days.

Cost: free for members; guest: $–$$
Hours: Monday–Friday, 5 a.m.–10:30 p.m.; Saturday–Sunday, 7 a.m.–9 p.m.

McDonald's Playplace

1306 Apache Drive SW, Rochester, MN 55902, (507) 288-2264

McDonald's offers tunnels and tube slides as well as ball pits in a play area designed for children ages 0–12. A small ball pit is designated for children three and younger. Other attractions include a table with child-activated music and lights, a fun house mirror, Lego table, and two computer games. The play area is exclusively for McDonald's customers and table time is limited to 30 minutes during busy times.

Children must wear socks in the playplace, but if you forgot yours, they are available on-site for one dollar a pair. Knee pads are also available for adult use. Birthday party packages are available at McDonald's Playplace.

Cost: free for McDonald's patrons
Hours: Monday–Friday, 9 a.m.–9 p.m.; Saturday–Sunday, 8 a.m.–9 p.m.

Pipsqueaks Indoor Play Zone

United Way of Olmsted County Gymnasium, 903 West Center Street, Rochester, MN 55902, (507) 281-6160, www.ci.rochester.mn.us/park or e-mail: pipsqueaks@charter.net

Pipsqueaks, an indoor playground designed for kindergarten-aged children and younger, opened its doors in Rochester in January 2003, thanks to the collaborative efforts of parent volunteers, the Rochester Park and Recreation Department and the United Way of Olmsted County. Pipsqueaks offers four play areas including an Infant/Crawler Zone, Climb and Slide Zone, Riding and Running Zone, and an Imagination Zone. Pipsqueaks offers Rochester residents and visitors a clean, safe place for the kids to romp around during the long winter months, a gathering spot for play groups, and the opportunity to meet new friends. Pipsqueaks hopes to expand by obtaining additional play equipment, extending its hours, and opening the facility to older children. Please contact the Parks and Recreation Department or the website listed above for up-to-date information. It is important to note that children may not be dropped off at the facility and must be under the direct supervision of a parent or guardian aged 16 and up.

Cost: $
Hours: fall–winter, call or visit website for hours of operation

Radio Controlled NASCAR Racing

Southside Speedway and Hobby Shop

2241 Marion Road SE, Rochester, MN 55904, (507) 281-3233, www.southsideracing.com

Southside Speedway has been tucked away in southeast Rochester for more than 10 years. Youth and adults interested in radio controlled NASCAR racing will find three, ⅒th scale race tracks and a complete hobby shop at Southside. State-of-the-art electronic timing devices are used for races at the indoor track, a high-banked, dirt oval that remains open year-round for races and leagues. The outdoor tracks, an off-road and asphalt course, are put into action during the warm weather months. Concessions are available on site. Please contact Kevin Guy at Southside for more information about races and leagues.

Cost: $
Hours: Monday–Tuesday, closed; Wednesday–Friday, 5 p.m.–9 p.m.; Saturday, 1 p.m.–midnight (winter), 1 p.m.–6 p.m. (summer), Sunday, 1 p.m.–6 p.m. Sunday races begin at 3 p.m.

ROCHESTER
Boys and Girls Club of America
1026 East Center Street, Rochester, MN 55904, (507) 287-2300, www.bgca.org

The Boys and Girls Club of Rochester has been a hit with kids aged 6–18 since it opened in February 2000. The youth club provides a safe place for children to participate in supervised activities and programs under the guidance of adult youth leaders. The facility is designed so that children in kindergarten through sixth grade are in a separate area from the kids in junior and senior high school. After school programs always begin with the "Power Hour." This is a quiet time for kids of all ages to complete homework assignments and receive tutoring. Children who do not have homework may spend the Power Hour participating in activities that support academic enrichment such as playing board or computer games. Kids earn points during the Power Hour that may be exchanged for prizes. Following the Power Hour, kids may choose to participate in open play or a variety of in-house clubs. There are a wide variety of clubs to choose from including, but not limited to A Passport to Manhood, World of Difference (diversity issues), TORCH (leadership), Fitness Authority (lifetime fitness), Juntos (Hispanic youth), and Keystone (life skills for teens). Recreational facilities include a gymnasium and outdoor playground, computer technology center, kids' game room, teen game room, lounge, a music room and recording studio, and an art room. Free snacks are also provided by the club. Membership is open to all boys and girls (kindergarten–12th grade) who are enrolled in school. Kids must pay an annual membership fee ($10), which includes full use of the club and its club-sponsored activities such as field trips.

Cost: membership fee only: $
Hours: Monday–Friday, 3 p.m.–8 p.m.; Saturday, 10 a.m.–5 p.m.

Junior Gym at the Rochester Area Family YMCA
709 1st Avenue SW, Rochester, MN 55902, (507) 287-2260, www.rochfamy.org

The YMCA Junior Gym is open to children ages 7 through 13 after school and during the early evening hours. Supervised recreational activities offered include standard gym games (basketball/volleyball), air hockey, foosball as well as computer and board games. A room next to the gym is designated as a homework area. Parents must remain in the building while their child is at the Junior Gym.

Cost: free for members; guests: $
Hours: Monday–Thursday, 4 p.m.–8 p.m.

Junior Gym at the Rochester Athletic Club
3100 19th Street NW, Rochester, MN 55901, (507) 282-6000, www.rochesterathleticclub.com

The Rochester Athletic Club Junior Gym is designed for children ages 7 through 12. The gym and play area is equipped with a tumbling area as well as a scaled down basketball court that functions as a playing field for other sports such as soccer, floor hockey, and kickball. Air hockey, table tennis, and foosball are some other recreational games available at the gym. Children must be supervised by an adult while in the Junior Gym when a staff person is not on duty. However, youth members may be checked into the Junior Gym by parents during designated times when a supervising staff person is present. The staff members encourage all youth to participate in free play or organized activities while maintaining a safe play environment. Please note that the Rochester Athletic Club is a members-only facility. Daily guest passes are available; however, local residents are only permitted to use the club as a guest once every 60 days.

Cost: free for members; guest: $–$$
Hours: club hours: Monday–Friday, 5 a.m.–10:30 p.m.; Saturday–Sunday, 7 a.m.–9 p.m.
 supervised Junior Gym hours (school year): Monday–Friday, 4 p.m.–8:30 p.m.;
 Saturday, 9 a.m.–5:30 p.m.; Sunday, 1 p.m.–5:30 p.m.
 supervised Junior Gym hours (summer): Monday–Thursday, 9 a.m.–noon &
 4:30 p.m.–8 p.m.; Friday, 9 a.m.–noon; Saturday, 9 a.m.–11:30 p.m.

Prairie Walls Climbing Gym
4420 19th Street NW, Rochester, MN 55901, (507) 292-0511, www.prairiewalls.com

Prairie Walls is a recreational rock climbing gym for both novice and seasoned rock climbers. The facility is a full-service, indoor rock climbing gym that features 7,000 feet of climbing surface with more than 100 marked and rated climbing routes. Additional features of the climbing gym include a bouldering area, a dedicated instruction wall and rappelling ledge, a padded landing surface under all climbing walls, and changing areas with showers and lockers. Classes available at the gym range from introductory lessons to advanced climbing techniques and everything in between. Prairie Walls also offers a Kid's Club for children ages 7 through 14; however, children under 7 may participate in the Kid's Club if a parent is on site. The Kid's Club is an open gym environment where kids climb under the supervision of staff members who perform safety checks and belaying while the kids climb. Reservations are requested so that a staff to climber ratio of 1 to 6 may be maintained. The fee for Kid's Club includes the use of a climbing harness. A Youth Rock Climbing Team is open to both new and experienced climbers interested in competitive climbing. Birthday party packages are available at Prairie Walls.

Cost: $$–$$$
Hours: Monday–Friday, 4 p.m.–10 p.m.; Saturday, noon–10 p.m.; Sunday, noon–
 6 p.m.; Wednesday hours in the summer are extended from noon–10 p.m.
 Kid's Club: Mondays and Fridays, 5 p.m.–7 p.m.

PLAINVIEW
The Union—Plainview Youth Center
346 West Broadway, Plainview, MN 55964, (507) 534-3802

The Union, Plainview's Youth Center, provides pre-teens and teens (5th–12th graders) a safe place to hang out and socialize with peers as well as opportunities that encourage responsibility and develop leadership skills through mentorships and job shadowing. Staffed by adult and youth volunteers, the Union offers both organized activities and "open" times when kids may use the recreational facilities, which include a lounge area, air hockey, foosball, a pool table, video and board games, Ping-Pong, a snack bar, and resource center with information on chemical use, teen mental health, smoking, and other issues. Dances, tutoring sessions, craft night, movie night, community projects, and game tournaments are some of the after school activities held at the youth center. Please call for a current activity schedule.

Cost: free
Hours: Monday, 3 p.m.–6 p.m.; Tuesday, 3 p.m.–9 p.m.; Wednesday, 3 p.m.–7 p.m.;
   Thursday, 3 p.m.–6 p.m.; Friday–Saturday, 3 p.m.–11 p.m.; Sunday, closed

WINONA
Rock Solid Youth Center
75 West 3rd Street, Winona, MN 55987, (507) 452-2125, www.dwebsite.com/rocksolidyouthcenter

The Rock Solid Youth Center of Winona is a great gathering place for junior and
senior high school youth. In addition to pinball and video games, Rock Solid offers
a unique variety of recreational activities such as the Bungee Run, Pedestal Joust,
and Climbing Wall and Cave. Additional recreational facilities available to youth
include pool tables, Ping-Pong, dart boards, N64, Super Nintendo, Sega Genesis,
and Internet access. Concerts, a climbing club, homework assistance, and make-over
nights are just some of the activities sponsored by the Rock Solid Youth Center.
Please call or check the website for a current activity schedule.

Cost: free
Hours: Tuesday & Thursday afternoons (6th–12th grades): 3:30 p.m.–6 p.m.;
   Wednesday evening, R.I.O.T. Youth Group (9th–12th grades): 7 p.m.–9 p.m.;
   Monday & Thursday evenings (6th–8th grades): 7 p.m.–9 p.m.; Friday & Saturday
   evenings (9th–12th grades): 7 p.m.–11 p.m.

Rock Climbing

Prairie Walls Climbing Gym
4420 19th Street NW, Rochester, MN 55901, (507) 292-0511, www.prairiewalls.com

Prairie Walls is a recreational rock climbing gym for both novice and seasoned rock
climbers. The facility is a full-service, indoor rock climbing gym that features 7,000
feet of climbing surface with more than 100 marked and rated climbing routes.
Additional features of the climbing gym include a bouldering area, a dedicated
instruction wall and rappelling ledge, a padded landing surface under all climbing
walls, and changing areas with showers and lockers. Prairie Walls offers youth and
adult classes from introductory lessons to advanced climbing techniques and everything in between. The Kid's Club, an open gym environment where kids climb
under the supervision of staff members who perform safety checks and belaying, is
available for youth ages 7 through 14. There is also a Youth Rock Climbing Team
for new and experienced climbers interested in competitive climbing. Competitive
events for all ages, such as the American Bouldering Series Indoor Climbing
Challenge, are held at Prairie Walls throughout the year. Please contact Prairie Walls
or visit their website for more information about classes, clinics, competitive events,
and birthday parties at the gym.

Cost: $$–$$$
Hours: Monday–Friday, 4 p.m.–10 p.m.; Saturday, noon–10 p.m.; Sunday, noon–
   6 p.m.; Wednesday hours in the summer are extended from noon–10 p.m.
   Kid's Club: Mondays and Fridays, 5 p.m.–7 p.m.

Roller Skating and Inline Skating

Indoor Rinks

BROWNSDALE
United Skates Roller Skating Center
Corner of SE Market and SE Railway Streets, Brownsdale, MN 55918, (507) 567-2539

United Skates is tucked away in the tiny town of Brownsdale but offers a huge 196-by-60-foot urethane floor for both inline and roller skaters in an atmosphere that takes you back to a simpler time. The center has a spacious carpeted area for donning and doffing skates and a limited number of coin-operated lockers. Public skating sessions are open to all ages and sometimes include skating games such as the limbo, train, backwards skate, the pole game, couples' skate, and the hokey pokey. Free passes are awarded to game winners. The concession area has seating for more than 100 people and sells a variety of snacks such as pizza, corn dogs, pretzels, ice cream, popcorn, cotton candy, pickles, and more. A selection of video games, pinball, foosball, and pool tables is also located in the concession area. Both roller skate (kids size 12 to adult size 12) and inline skate (kids size 8 to adult size 14) rentals are available. You may bring your own skates, but No plastic wheels are allowed on the rink. Please call United Skates for information about birthday party specials or to arrange a private skating party.

Cost: $
Hours: Friday, 7:30 p.m.–10 p.m.; Saturday, 2 p.m.–4:30 p.m. & 7:30 p.m.–
10 p.m.; Sunday, 2 p.m.–4:30 p.m.

HARMONY
Harmony Roller Rink
Hwy. 52 North, Harmony, MN 55939, (507) 886-4444

The Harmony Roller Rink provides area residents and visitors with a clean, modern facility to enjoy roller and inline skating. The roller rink sports a huge wooden floor that is surrounded by booth seating, a rink-side area with lockers for changing into skates, and a variety of arcade-style games such as pinball, foosball, and billiards. In addition to on-site concessions, skaters have access to Wheelers, a full-service restaurant connected to the rink. Skating sessions typically include a few group games such as the limbo, the dice game, and toilet seat races. Roller skate rentals (kids size 9 to adult size 14) are available, but the rink does not rent inline skates. The rink has seating accommodations for up to 500 people and may be rented for dances, banquets, wedding receptions, reunions, and other events. Birthday party packages are also available.

Cost: $
Hours: summer: open skate: Friday 7 p.m.–9:30 p.m.; Saturday and Sunday:
closed
winter: open skate: Friday 7 p.m.–9:30 p.m.; teen skate: Friday 9:30 p.m.-
11:30 p.m.; beginners skate: Saturday 9:30 a.m.–11:30 a.m.; open skate:
Sunday 1:30 p.m.–4 p.m.

OWATONNA
Owatonna Roller Rink
120 18ᵗʰ Street SW, Owatonna, MN 55060, (507) 451-9871, Office: (507) 455-9731, www.owatonnarollerrink.com

Folks have been rolling into the Owatonna Roller Rink since 1946 for some good old fashioned fun. The rink has a 110-by-52-foot masonite floor, but what really wows skaters is the schedule of monthly events that has something for everyone. In addition to Public Skating Sessions, the rink hosts a variety of "themed" skating events such as All-Night Skate, Adult Night, President's Day Skate, and Irish Luck Skate as well as Pizza Parties and Taco Days. Although rink-side seating is limited, there are a handful of video games on the premises. Skaters may purchase candy, chips, and soda at the concession area. Birthday party and group party packages are available. Roller skate (kids' size 9 to adult size 14) and inline skate (kids' size 10 to adult size 14) rentals are available. Please call the rink or visit their website for more information.

Cost: $
Hours: Friday, 7 p.m.–10 p.m.; Saturday, 1 p.m.–4 p.m. & 7 p.m.–10 p.m.; Sunday, 1 p.m.–4 p.m.

Zephyr Skate Tours and Vacations
If you've always wanted to learn how to inline skate or consider yourself an expert skater, check out the skate tours and travel packages offered by the Zephyr Tours Skate Camp. The camp offers a full schedule of Learn-To-Skate Tours, Standard Skate Tours, City Tours, Advanced Skate Tours, and Multi-sport Tours in the United States and Europe. In fact, the southeastern Minnesota community of Lanesboro is the site of Zephyr's Learn-To-Skate Tour for Women during the summer. For more information about Zephyr Skate Tours and to obtain a schedule, call Zephyr Tours at 888-758-8687, (406) 446-0275 or visit www.skatetour.com

Outdoor Roller Skating & Inline Skating Trails
Rochester Skating Trails
Rochester Park and Recreation Department, 201 4ᵗʰ Street SE, Room150 Rochester, MN 55904, (507) 281-6160, www.ci.rochester.mn.us/park

Inline skaters are welcome to use the extensive bike trail system throughout the city of Rochester. Please see Chapter 16 for more information about Rochester's bike trails and Appendix 2 for a map of these trails.

Douglas State Trail
Rochester–Pine Island

Rochester Area Trails & Waterways, 2300 Silver Creek Road NE, Rochester, MN 55906, (507) 285-7176, www.dnr.state.mn.us
Trailheads are located in Rochester on County Road 4 (Valleyhigh Drive NW) behind IBM, in Douglas at County Road 14 off Hwy. 52, and in Pine Island at Pine Island Park, just off the Hwy. 52 exit.

Trailheads for the Douglas State Trail originate in northwest Rochester and Pine Island with a midpoint in Douglas, the town for which the trail is named. This multiple-use trail is 12.5 miles in length with a paved treadway for inline skaters, bicyclists, hikers, and cross-country skiers. The trail was developed from an abandoned railroad track and passes over iron bridges and through some of southeastern Minnesota's richest farmland. A parking lot with rest rooms is located at each trailhead, and water is available at the Douglas and Pine Island trailheads.

Cannon Valley Trail
Red Wing–Cannon Falls

Cannon Valley Trail, City Hall, 306 West Mill Street, Cannon Falls, MN 55009, (507) 263-0508, (651) 258-4141, www.cannonvalleytrail.com
The Red Wing trailhead is located on Old West Main Street and Bench Street, one block from Hwy. 61 with parking nearby.
The Cannon Falls trailhead originates near 3rd Street in Cannon Falls. Parking at this trailhead is limited but may be accessed across from the ballpark on East Stoughton Street.
The Welch Station Access is located along County Road 7 between the Village of Welch and Welch Village Ski Area.

The Cannon Valley Trail, formerly a section of the Chicago Great Western Railroad, is a 19.7-mile paved trail that runs between Red Wing and Cannon Falls with a midpoint at Welch Station. The multiple-use trail winds along side the Cannon River and passes through a variety of natural habitats including marshlands, pastures, and wooded areas. Inline skaters, bicyclists, skateboarders, hikers, and cross-country skiers will enjoy spectacular views of the area as they travel along the trail. A Wheel Pass is required for all adults, aged 18 and up, who are riding on wheeled vehicles from April 1st through November 1st. Wheel passes are available at self-purchase stations along the trail, local businesses, and from trail attendants on weekends during the summer months. Voices of the Valley, an interpretive program held at the Welch Station Access, is scheduled for the first Saturday of every month from May through September from 11 a.m.–3 p.m. These entertaining programs are designed to educate trail users about the Cannon River Valley. Rest rooms and water are located at Cannon Falls, Welch Station Access, and Red Wing's Anderson Park. There are also rest rooms but no water at the Anderson Memorial Rest Area, Cannon Bottom Road, and the Old West Main Parking Area in Red Wing. Maps, directions, and additional information may be obtained by contacting the Cannon Valley Trail Office.

Great River Ridge Trail
Elgin–Plainview

Plainview City Hall, (507) 534-2229

The Great River Ridge Trail is currently a 5-mile paved trail that runs between Elgin and Plainview. The trail passes through open country and has gently sloping terrain. The multiple-use trail and its trailheads are still under development with plans to extend it from Plainview to Eyota. Bikers may access the trail in Plainview at the intersection of 3rd Street SW and State Highway 42.

Harmony–Preston Valley State Trail
Harmony–Preston

Rochester Area Trails & Waterways, 2300 Silver Creek Road NE, Rochester, MN 55906, (507) 285-7176, www.dnr.state.mn.us
Harmony Visitor's Center, (507) 886-2469, 800-247-MINN (6466), www.harmony.mn.us

Preston Area Tourism, (507) 765-2100, 888-845-2100, www.bluffcountry.com
The Preston trailhead is located off Hwy. 52 on Fillmore Street (County Road 12),and the
Harmony trailhead is located off Hwy. 52 on 4ᵗʰ Street SW.

The Harmony–Preston Valley State Trail is an 18-mile paved trail between the towns of Harmony and Preston that connects to the popular Root River State Trail at Isinours Junction, approximately 5.5 miles east of the Root River trailhead in Fountain. Although the northern section of the Harmony–Preston Valley trail is relatively flat, a series of hills and inclines provides challenging terrain along the southern portion of the trail between County Road 16 and Harmony. Inline skaters, bicyclists, hikers, and cross-country skiers are welcome to use the trail, which crosses Watson and Camp Creeks and passes through farmland and wooded areas. Camp Creek, located adjacent to Preston, is accessible via three fishing piers. Rest rooms and water are available in Preston and Harmony and at the Isinours Forestry Unit, one mile west of Isinours Junction.

Root River State Trail
Fountain–Houston

DNR Trail Center, Lanesboro Depot, Lanesboro, MN 55949, (507) 467-2552, www.dnr.state.mn.us
Lanesboro Visitor's Center, (507) 467-2696, www.lanesboro.com, www.bluffcountry.com
Trailheads in Fountain, the Isinours Forestry Unit, Lanesboro, Whalan, Peterson, Rushford, and Houston may be easily located by following signs to the Root River State Trail as you approach these towns.

Southeastern Minnesota's Root River State Trail is the region's premier ulti-use recreational trail and annually attracts thousands of outdoor enthusiasts who come to skate, bike, hike or ski in the Root River Valley. The 42-mile paved trail was developed from an abandoned railroad bed and meanders through an idyllic setting of picturesque farmlands, rolling pastures, limestone bluffs, and forested areas from Fountain to Houston. The trail is especially attractive to visitors because it passes through the small towns of Lanesboro, Whalan, Peterson, and Rushford before terminating in Houston. These charming towns capture the essence of rural Americana and each community offers a unique variety of recreational, historic, and cultural activities for visitors. Rest rooms and water are available at the small towns along the trail.

Rowing

Rochester Rowing Club
Box 1072, Rochester, MN 55905, (507) 289-0989, www.rrcmn.com or e-mail: info@rrcmn.com

The Rochester Rowing Club (RRC), established in 1990, is open to anyone who is interested in the sport of recreational rowing. The club is currently located on the west side of Silver Lake, adjacent to the Rochester Fire Station at 7th Street NE and West Silver Lake Drive. RRC owns eleven rowing shells of various sizes and its lakeside facility includes a boat shelter, equipment shack, and docks. Adult Learn to Row I and II, Master's Racing, High School and Junior Rowing, a College program, and Learn to Row Clinics are available through RRC. Novice and experienced rowers also have the opportunity to compete in regattas throughout the region. Membership is not required for participation in the Learn to Row programs. Please contact the club or visit their website for more detailed information.

Rugby

Rochester Rogues Rugby Football Club
(507) 536-0321, www.rochesterrogues.com e-mail: info@rochesterrogues.com

The Rochester Rogues was established in 1999 as a division III amateur rugby football club. The team plays competitive rugby during the spring and fall seasons. New players are welcome to join the club. Please call or visit the Rogues website for more information.

Shooting Sports

Eagle Bluff Environmental Learning Center
Route 2, Box 156A, 1991 Brightsdale Road, Lanesboro, MN 55949, (507) 467-2437, 888-800-9558, www.eagle-bluff.org or e-mail: hello@eagle-bluff.org

Eagle Bluff offers Firearms Safety, Advanced Hunter Education, and Bowhunter Education through the Minnesota Department of Natural Resources as well as Hunting Skills Clinics at their Environmental Learning Center in rural Lanesboro. Shooting facilities at Eagle bluff include a .22 and handgun range, a large bore/center fire range, a five-stand, sporting clays/shotgun range, and an indoor archery range. All participants must be accompanied by a certified Eagle Bluff shooting instructor at the ranges. Please contact Eagle Bluff for more information about these classes or their Outdoor Skills Program.

Youth Firearms Safety and Adult Hunter Education
Minnesota DNR, 500 Lafayette Road, St. Paul, MN 55155-4040, (651) 296-6157, 800-366-8917, www.dnr.state.mn.us.

The Minnesota Department of Natural Resources (DNR) offers Firearms Safety Training, Advanced Hunter Education, and Bowhunter Education Programs. Class schedules vary seasonally. Please contact the DNR for classes in the southeastern Minnesota area.

Sportsmen's Clubs
Please see Chapter 23 for a list of Conservation and Sportsmen's Clubs in the area.

There are several area Conservation and Sportsmen's Clubs that offer trapshooting and skeet shooting as well as rifle and archery ranges to their members. The clubs occasionally schedule events for nonmembers so that they may become acquainted with these sports. Contact information for these clubs may be found in Chapter 23.

Skateboard Parks

ROCHESTER

Board to Death Sports—Madrone Family Indoor Skate Park

8 4ᵗʰ Street SW, Rochester, MN 55902, (507) 292-5710, www.boardtodeathsports.com

Board to Death Sports opened its new indoor family skate park in November, 2002. The 2,500-square-foot, tier 2 park offers a wide variety of obstacles including ramps, ledges, and more for boarders, skaters and BMX bikers of different skill levels. All skaters, bladers, and bikers are required to wear safety gear. A skate shop, equipment rental, lessons, and concessions are available on-site. Check out the Board to Death website for an excellent listing of skate parks in the region.

Cost: membership fee; additional user fee ($) from Thursday–Saturday during school year
Hours: Monday–Saturday, 10 a.m.–10 p.m.; Sunday, 10 a.m.–8 p.m.

Silver Lake Skate Park

7ᵗʰ Street and East Silver Lake Drive NE, Rochester, MN 55906, (507) 281-6160, www.ci.rochester.mn.us/park
Located adjacent to Silver Lake Pool.

Rochester opened its first outdoor skate park in September, 2002. Located within Silver Lake Park, the popular tier 1 park offers open space and a few ramps for skateboarders, inline skaters, and BMX bikers to sport their tricks. There is no supervision at this park.

Cost: free
Hours: dawn–dusk

OWATONNA

Owatonna Skate Park

Morehouse Park, Owatonna, MN 55060, (507) 446-2330, www.ci.owatonna.mn.us
Take Hwy.14 East to I-35 South and exit on Bridge Street (#41). Go right onto Bridge Street, follow to Walnut Avenue and turn right at the power plant. Go to a "T" in the road and turn right. The park entrance will be straight ahead.

The Owatonna Skate Park offers boarders, bladers, and BMX bikers a tier 2 park with a wide variety of obstacles including ramps, jumps, and ledges of different heights and angles. All boarders, bladers and BMX bikers aged 17 and under must have a waiver and registration form signed by a parent in order to use the park. The use of protective equipment is required and may be rented for a nominal fee.

Cost: daily fee $; season passes and punch cards available
Hours: summer: Monday–Saturday, 11 a.m.–10:30 p.m.; Sunday, noon–9:30 p.m.
  fall: Monday–Friday, 4 p.m.–9 p.m.; Saturday, 1 p.m.–9 p.m.; Sunday, noon–9 p.m.

WINONA

Winona's 4.8 Skate Park

210 Zumbro Street, Winona, MN 55987, (507) 457-8258, www.cityofwinona-mn.com
Located at the East End Recreation Center.

Winona's 4.8 outdoor skate park features a low and high ledge, large spine ramp, ¼ pipe, transition bank, and a bump/bump with rail. The park is open to skateboarders, inline skaters, and BMX bikers. All skaters, bladers, and bikers are required to wear protective equipment. Separate shifts for bikers and skaters/boarders are scheduled at the park. Please call for a current shift schedule. Resident and nonresident memberships are available.

Cost: $

Hours: April, May, September, October (weather permitting): Monday–Friday, 4 p.m.–9 p.m.; Saturday–Sunday, 1 p.m.–9 p.m.
June–August, nonschool days and holidays: Sunday–Saturday, 1 p.m.–9 p.m.

Sports Leagues for Adults

Rochester Park and Recreation Department

201 4ᵗʰ Street SE, 150 City Hall, Rochester, MN 55904, (507) 281-6160, www.ci.rochester.mn.us/park

The Rochester Park and Recreation Department organizes competitive play among recreational sports teams for adults throughout the year. If you are interested in creating a new team or joining a pre-existing team, please contact the Parks and Recreation Department for registration information and cost. Available teams include:

Winter
Basketball: Men's
Broomball: Co-ed, Men's, and Women's
Curling: Co-ed, Men's, and Women's
Volleyball: Co-ed, Men's, and Women's

Spring
Volleyball: Co-ed, Men's, and Women's
Softball: Co-ed, Men's, and Women's

Summer
Softball: Co-ed, Men's, and Women's
Sandlot Volleyball: Co-ed, Men's, and Women's

Fall
Basketball: Men's and Women's
Touch Football: Men's
Softball: Co-ed, Men's, and Women's
Volleyball: Co-ed, Men's and Women's

Rochester Soccer Club

Rochester, MN, (507) 287-6316, www.rochestersoccerclub.org

The Rochester Soccer Club offers adult Co-ed and Women's leagues in the summer and fall and Co-ed and Open leagues during the winter. Men and women aged 16 and older are eligible to play. Please contact the club or visit their website for more information.

Southern Minnesota Adult Soccer Association—SMASA

P.O. Box 6504, Rochester, MN 55903, www.smasa.com

The SMASA, a member of the Minnesota Soccer Association, the United States Amateur Soccer Association, and the United States Soccer Federation, has an Open

Amateur League for men and women during the spring and summer months. The highly competitive league has teams representing many different ethnic groups from the Rochester community. Please contact the organization for more information.

Square and Round Dancing (see also Ballroom Dancing and Dance)

Square Dance Federation of Minnesota

www.squaredanceminnesota.com

There are several square and round dancing clubs in the southeastern Minnesota area. It is difficult to obtain direct contact information for these clubs because they do not have established meeting locations and club officers change yearly. An up-to-date listing of clubs, officers, and contact information may be found by visiting www.squaredanceminnesota.com.

Swimming: Indoor Pools & Waterparks

ROCHESTER

AmericInn Hotel & Suites of Rochester

5708 Hwy. 52 North, Rochester, MN 55901, (507) 289-3344

The AmericInn of Rochester welcomes the public to enjoy its swimming area. The modern facility has a warm spacious atmosphere with a pool ranging in depth from three feet to five feet, a hot tub, a handicapped-accessible rest room/changing area, poolside seating with tables and lounge chairs, and a few arcade games. It is recommended that visitors who are not registered hotel guests call ahead to check pool availability. No food is permitted in the pool area, but snacks may be eaten in the lobby area.

Cost: $
Hours: daily, 7 a.m.–midnight (adults only after 10 p.m.)

Holiday Inn South

1630 South Broadway, Rochester, MN 55902, (507) 288-1844

The Holiday Inn South opens its pool facilities to the public from Sunday through Thursday. An indoor pool, kiddie pool, and hot tub are located within a fenced-in area next to a recreation area with pinball, video games, air hockey, and a pool table. The pool depth varies from three to nine feet. A unisex sauna and separate changing areas for men and women are available for pool patrons. The changing areas have a toilet, sink, and shower, but no lockers. Weekend use of the facilities is dependent upon the hotel's occupancy. Please call ahead to check weekend availability.

Cost: $
Hours: Sunday–Thursday, 10 a.m.–10 p.m.; Friday–Saturday, 10 a.m.–11 p.m.

Rochester Area Family YMCA

709 1st Avenue SW, Rochester, MN 55902, (507) 287-2260, www.rochfamy.org

The YMCA has a 25 yard pool with a water temperature of 83° and a depth that ranges from three to ten feet. Swimmers are permitted to bring their own or use the water toys supplied by the Y during open swimming sessions. A waterslide and pool side basketball hoops are also available. Although a lifeguard is present during swimming sessions, children under age ten must be supervised by an adult.

Cost: free for members; guest: $
Hours: hours for open, family, and lap swimming vary; call the Y for a
  current schedule

Rochester Athletic Club

3100 19th Street NW, Rochester, MN 55901, (507) 282-6000, www.rochesterathleticclub.com

This members-only facility has an indoor family/aerobic pool with depths of three feet to four feet, two inches. There is no deep end or diving board, but water toys are allowed in the pool. A separate 25-meter, five lane lap swimming pool is located adjacent to the family pool as is a family hot tub. Lifeguards are on duty Monday, Wednesday, and Friday from 6:30–8:30 p.m. and Saturday and Sunday from 1:30 p.m.–4:30 p.m. during the school year. Water toys, flotation devices, and kickboards may be checked out at the Activities Desk. Daily guest passes are available; however, local residents are only permitted to use the club as a guest once every 60 days. Pool space may be limited during swimming lessons and water aerobics classes.

Cost: free for members; guest fee: $–$$
Hours: Monday–Friday, 5 a.m.–10:30 p.m.; Saturday–Sunday, 7 a.m.–9 p.m.

Rochester-Olmsted Recreation Center

21 Elton Hills Drive, Rochester, MN 55901, (507) 281-6167, www.ci.rochester.mn.us/park

The Rochester-Olmsted Recreation Center boasts an Olympic-caliber, 50-meter swimming pool with eight lanes, a handicapped-accessible ramp at the shallow end, and removable bulkhead that may be used to divide the pool into two, 25-yard sections. The pool depth varies from 3.6 to 16 feet, and there are two 1-meter, and two 3-meter diving boards at the pool. Pool side bleachers can accommodate more than 1,000 spectators. The Recreation Center offers Parent-Tot Swim, Open Swim, Lap Swim, Adult Lap Swim, Family Swim, and Adult Water Aerobics sessions. Please call the Recreation Center for a current schedule.

Cost: $
Hours: call for a current schedule

The Kahler Grand Hotel

20 2nd Avenue SW, Rochester, MN 55902, (507) 282-2581, 800-533-1655, www.kahler.com

The Kahler Grand Hotel offers Rochester residents the opportunity to use the hotel's pool and spa facilities by purchasing an annual pool membership. Surrounded by "Windows to the World" and a domed rooftop skylight, the pool provides outstanding views of the city from the Kahler's eleventh floor. A small changing area with a rest room, lockers, shower, and a sauna is available near the pool. An exercise room and small recreation area with foosball, a pool table, and video games are also located in the pool area.

Cost: call for current rates of annual pool membership
Hours: daily, 6 a.m.–10 p.m.

Waterpark at the Hawthorn Suites

2829 43rd Street NW, Rochester, MN 55901, (507) 281-1200, 800-527-1133, www.hawthorn.com

The indoor waterpark at the Hawthorn Suites of Rochester is for the exclusive use of hotel guests. The waterpark has a hot tub and two side by side pools, one with zero-depth entry that is only two feet deep. This pool, designed for very young children, has a slide, a "tipping bucket" rainmaker, and a mushroom waterfall. The adjacent pool ranges in depth from three to five feet and has two slides and two poolside basketball hoops. Hotel guests also have access to an exercise room and sport court with a basketball court and tennis net.

Cost: hotel room rates apply
Hours: daily, 7 a.m.–11 p.m.

OWATONNA
The Great Serengeti Indoor Waterpark at the Holiday Inn & Suites

2365 43rd Street NW, Owatonna, MN 55060, (507) 446-8900, 800-HOLIDAY, www.greatserengeti.com

Escape to the Great Serengeti Indoor Water Park at the Holiday Inn and Suites in Owatonna. The 14,000-square-foot, safari-themed water park is a sure cure for cabin fever with its python body slide, the lazy Zambizi River, an activity pool with basketball hoops, and the thrilling Kilimanjaro tube slide. Young children especially love to frolic among the water geysers and safari animals in the zero-depth entry wading pool. Adults enjoy the soothing sounds of the waterfall while relaxing in the whirlpool spa. The Café Zanzibar, located within the waterpark, serves beverages, snacks and the Green Mill's famous pizza. When you start to feel a bit waterlogged, take a break in the Lion's Den Arcade, which has a wide variety of games for people of all ages. Please note that the waterpark is for hotel guests only and is not open to the public. Continue your safari adventure by visiting Cabela's, the "World's Foremost Outfitter" of fishing, hunting, and outdoor gear, located within walking distance of the hotel.

Cost: hotel room rates apply
Hours: Monday–Thursday, 9 a.m.–9 p.m.; Friday, 9 a.m.–10 p.m.; Saturday,
   8 a.m.–10 p.m.; Sunday, 8 a.m.–9 p.m.

Swimming: Outdoor Pools & Swimming Areas

ROCHESTER
Foster-Arend Lake and Beach

4000 East River Road, Rochester, MN 55901, (507) 285-8316, www.ci.rochester.mn.us/park

Foster-Arend Lake and Beach is a popular place to play and cool off during the summer months. The spacious beach has soft sand, which is great for building sand castles or just running around. The 15-acre lake, once the site of an old gravel pit, has a designated swimming area. Please note that there are no lifeguards on duty at this facility. Stay within the roped-off swimming areas. The Parks and Recreation encourages both parental supervision and use of the "buddy system" at the lake, especially since there have been a number of drownings at the lake when swimmers have ventured outside the swimming area. Additional park facilities include a fishing pier, playground, volleyball net, and bathrooms. A beach umbrella is a must for all day or mid-day excursions at Foster-Arend since there are no shaded areas.

Cost: free
Hours: open daily, noon–8 p.m.

Rochester Athletic Club
3100 19th Street NW, Rochester, MN 55901, (507) 282-6000, www.rochesterathleticclub.com

Outdoor swimming facilities at the Rochester Athletic feature a zero-depth entry swimming pool that has a maximum depth of four feet, six inches. The child-friendly pool has a geyser forest, mushroom waterfall, and a 180-foot water slide as well as five, 25-meter lap lanes. Additional poolside recreational amenities include a huge, fenced-in sandy play area with playground equipment, a mini-golf area, tennis courts, a snack bar, and locker rooms with changing areas and rinse showers. The club provides plenty of lounge chairs, but the amount of shaded space at the pool is limited. Please note that the Rochester Athletic Club is a members-only facility. Daily guest passes are available; however, local residents are only permitted to use the club as a guest once every 60 days.

Cost: free for members; guests: $–$$
Hours: Monday Friday, 10:30 a.m.–dusk; Saturday–Sunday, 10 a.m.–dusk (weather permitting)

Silver Lake Municipal Pool
7th Street and East Silver Lake Drive NE, Rochester, MN 55906, (507) 281-6179, (507) 281-6160, www.ci.rochester.mn.us/park

A day's worth of fun awaits patrons of Silver Lake Pool, located adjacent to the popular Silver Lake Adventure Playground and Silver Lake Park. The eight lane, 50-meter pool ranges in depth from three feet, six inches to ten feet, six inches and has a diving board and drop slide. A fenced-in wading pool with a maximum depth of eighteen inches is available for young children. Shaded areas at the pool are limited, but the facility does have locker rooms with showers and a changing area. Other recreational facilities within walking distance of the pool include tennis courts, the Silver Lake Adventure Playground, soccer fields, biking and walking trails, sand volleyball courts, sheltered picnic areas, and Silver Lake with its famous Canada Geese.

Cost: $
Hours: June–late-August: open daily, noon–8 p.m. (weather permitting)

Skyline Raceway (Waterslide Only)
2250 40th Street SW, Rochester, MN 55902, (507) 287-6289

Skyline Raceway's 410-foot, seamless waterslide offers kids and adults a fun way to cool down on those hot summer days. Go-Karts and mini-golf are also available on the premises. Visitors have access to a large picnic area with barbecue pits, on-site concessions, and free use of volleyball courts and horseshoe pits. Reservations are suggested for large group events such as company picnics, family reunions, or parties

Cost: $–$$
Hours: Memorial Day–Labor Day: open daily, noon–8 p.m. (weather permitting)
   off-season: noon–6 p.m. (weather permitting)

Soldiers Field Municipal Pool

244 Soldiers Field Drive, Rochester, MN 55902, (507) 281-6180, (507) 281-6160,
www.ci.rochester.mn.us/park

This public pool is located in the Soldiers Field Park Complex, adjacent to downtown Rochester. The six lane, 50-meter pool ranges in depth from three feet, six inches to ten feet, six inches and has a modern bathhouse with showers and changing facilities. Pool amenities include a diving board, drop slide, and fenced-in wading pool that has a maximum depth of eighteen inches and two play features. Although the pool is not shaded, patrons can find many shaded areas within Soldiers Field Memorial Park, which also has bike trail access, tennis courts, an 18-hole golf course, two playgrounds, soccer and baseball fields, a running track, and sheltered and unsheltered picnic areas within walking distance of the pool. The park is also home to the Soldiers Field Veterans' Memorial, which was dedicated on June 25, 2000 as an honor and remembrance of veterans from Southeastern Minnesota (within a 50-mile radius of Rochester) who gave their lives in service to our country.

Cost: $
Hours: June–late-August: open daily, noon–8 p.m. (weather permitting)

ALTURA

The Swimming Beach at Whitewater State Park

RR 1, Box 256, Altura, MN 55910, (507) 932-3007, www.dnr.state.mn.us
Located 3 miles south of Elba on State Hwy. 74.

Whitewater State Park is a popular destination for families seeking summer fun at a sandy beach and swimming pond in a relatively mosquito-free environment. A large, grassy area with lots of shade trees borders the beach and provides a great place for a game of Frisbee or respite from the sun. Beach facilities include rinse showers and rest rooms with a changing area. No lifeguards are present at the beach. Additional park facilities that are available for use during the summer include a visitor's center with interpretive exhibits, picnic areas with shelters, extensive hiking trails (some with handicapped accessibility), a campground, group center, trout fishing streams, naturalist programs, and a nature store gift shop. No horses or ATVs are permitted in the park, but bikes are allowed on established roads.

Cost: daily ($) or annual ($$) state park permit required
Hours: open daily, 8 a.m.–dusk

EYOTA

Chester Woods Park and Beach

8378 Hwy. 14 East, Eyota, MN 55934, (507) 285-7050, www.olmstedpublicworks.com,
e-mail: chesterw@venturecs.net

Chester Woods Park, located just seven miles east of Rochester, has become a local favorite since it opened in the spring of 1995. A highlight of the park for many families is the swimming beach at Chester Lake. The 118-acre lake is situated on the headwaters of Bear Creek and is bordered by a huge sandy beach.

Beachgoers will encounter some steep and rocky sections on the beach as they walk down to the lake. Although there is a designated swimming area at the lake, there are no lifeguards on duty.

Visitors have access to a bathhouse with showers and a dressing area, and trees along the perimeter of the beach provide some shade cover. Additional park facilities include two playgrounds (one handicapped accessible), several informal playing fields, seven separate picnic areas with covered shelters, six-plus miles of hiking trails, eight to nine miles of equestrian trails, a boat launch (electric motors only), canoe and paddleboat rentals, a fishing pier, and a 52-site campground. Nature programs and hikes are presented by park naturalists during the summer months. Pets are allowed in the park.

Cost: $
Hours: daily, 7 a.m.–10 p.m.

LAKE CITY
Hok-Si-La Municipal Park
Hwy. 61 North, Lake City, MN 55041, (651) 345-3855, www.lakecity.org or
www.mississippi-river.org/lakecity.html
Located 2 miles north of Lake City on Hwy. 61/63.

Hok-Si-La is an absolutely beautiful 250-acre-plus park that is situated on the shores of Lake Pepin in Lake City, Minnesota. The park provides a peaceful atmosphere for those wishing to venture off the beaten path. A wide, sandy swimming beach (no lifeguards) awaits visitors who choose to play and swim or just relax at the lakeside beach. Park amenities also include a bathhouse with modern showers and toilets, picnic tables, nature and hiking trails, playground equipment, volleyball courts, a nearby boat launch, a primitive campground, an on-site camp store, and a small interpretive center with animal displays. Three screened-in shelters and a modern Dining Hall with a kitchen and cooler are available for rent. Pets are permitted in the park. Use of the campground, shelters, and Dining Hall requires reservations.

Cost: free
Hours: open daily, 8 a.m.–10 p.m.

Lake City Swimming Beach at Ohuta Park
Lyon Avenue, Lake City, MN 55041, (651) 345-2213, www.lakecity.org or
www.mississippi-river.org/lakecity.html
Located 3 blocks East of Hwy. 61 on Lyon Avenue.

Picturesque views of Lake Pepin and the surrounding bluffland may be seen when visiting Lake City's swimming beach at Ohuta Park. The wide, sandy swimming beach offers swimmers a lifeguard-protected area for water play and swimming with roped off areas and docks. Water shoes are recommended when swimming in the lake, which tends to have a somewhat rocky bottom. Additionally, visitors have access to a shaded picnic area and bathhouse with toilets, showers, and a changing area. If you're having trouble finding the swimming beach, just look for the "wave statue" in Ohuta Park. The contemporary statue honors Ralph Samuelson, the Father of Water-skiing, who discovered the sport from the shores of Lake Pepin in 1922. When you're ready to take a beach break, take a stroll on Riverwalk, a 2.5-mile pedestrian walkway, located within walking distance of the swimming beach.

Cost: $
Hours: June–Labor Day: open daily, 11 a.m.–7 p.m.; call to confirm hours

RUSHFORD
Rushford Aquatic Center
Hwy. 74, Rushford, MN 55971, (507) 864-2983, (507) 864-2444

The Rushford Aquatic Center offers residents and visitors of southeastern Minnesota a modern swimming facility. The zero-depth entry pool is handicapped accessible and has a drop slide, mushroom waterfall, and diving board that provides hours of entertainment for kids on a hot summer day. Locker rooms with showers and a picnic area are located on the premises.

Cost: $
Hours: open swim: Monday–Friday, 1:30 p.m.–5 p.m. & 6 p.m.–8 p.m.;
  Saturday–Sunday, 1 p.m.–7 p.m.
  lap swim: daily, 7 a.m.–8 a.m.

ST. CHARLES
Mel Brownell Family Aquatic Center
830 Whitewater Avenue, St. Charles, MN 55972, (507) 932-5386
Located just off Hwy. 14 next to the St. Charles High School.

A day trip to this spectacular aquatic center is a must for families. A 180-foot water slide and diving board wows the big kids while the little ones frolic in the zero-depth entry area, which has an alligator slide, water curtain, and tipping buckets of water. Six lap swimming lanes are also available at the pool. Patrons have access to a large sundeck surrounding the pool, a concession stand, picnic tables, and locker rooms with changing areas and showers. Please call to inquire about renting the aquatic center for parties or other group events.

Cost: $
Hours: open swim: daily, 1 p.m.–5 p.m. & 7 p.m.–9 p.m.
  lap swim: Monday–Friday, 7 a.m.–8 a.m. & 6 p.m.–7 p.m.; call to confirm hours

WINONA
Bob Welch Aquatic Center
780 West 4th Street, Winona, MN 55987, (507) 457-8210, (507) 457-8258,
www.cityofwinona-mn.com
Take Hwy. 61 to Huff Street, follow Huff Street to 5th Street, turn left on 5th Street, go to High Street, turn right and follow to the aquatic center.

Wow! Winona offers its residents and visitors a state-of-the-art aquatic playground. The Bob Welch Aquatic Center features an Olympic-sized swimming pool with a 208-foot waterslide, two diving boards, and a drop slide as well as a large zero-depth entry area that delights younger children with its mushroom waterfall and spray fountain. Additional recreational facilities at the aquatic center include a spacious deck, concession stand, shaded picnic area, large grassy area, two playgrounds, and a sand volleyball court.

Cost: $
Hours: daily, noon–7 p.m.

Small Towns in Southeastern Minnesota with Outdoor Pools

Byron Swimming Pool
500 Byron Avenue, Byron, MN 55920, (507) 775-6916

Caledonia Swimming Pool
521 North Winnebago Street, Caledonia, MN 55921, (507) 725-3450

Chatfield Swimming Pool
229 NE Union Street, Chatfield, MN 55923, (507) 867-3509

Dodge Center Swimming Pool
North Central Avenue, Dodge Center, MN 55927, (507) 374-6300

Hayfield Community Pool
324 2nd Street SE, Hayfield, MN 55940, (507) 477-2500

Kasson Swimming Pool
101 7th Street NW, Kasson, MN 55944, (507) 634-7755

La Crescent Swimming Pool
608 South 7th Street, La Crescent, MN 55947, (507) 895-8712

Lake City Swimming Pool
1125 West Marion Street, Lake City, MN 55041, (651) 345-3624

Pine Island Swimming Pool
411 3rd Avenue SE, Pine Island, MN 55963, (507) 356-4731

Plainview Community Swimming Pool
390 North Wabasha Street, Plainview, MN 55964, (507) 534-2701

Preston Swimming Pool
200 Park Street, Preston, MN 55965, (507) 765-2153

Spring Grove Swimming Pool
231 NE 5th Avenue, Spring Grove, MN 55974, (507) 498-5775

Spring Valley Swimming Pool
112 West Courtland Street, Spring Valley, MN 55975, (507) 346-7368

Stewartville Community Pool
500 4th Street SE, Stewartville, MN 55976, (507) 533-4745

Wabasha Swimming Pool
Hiawatha Drive East, Wabasha, MN 55981, (651) 565-2375

Wanamingo Swimming Pool
298 3rd Avenue, Wanamingo, MN 55983, (507) 824-2477

West Concord Pool
405 Eugene Street, West Concord, MN 55985, (507) 527-2935

Zumbrota Swimming Pool
385 Aqua Drive, Zumbrota, MN 55992, (507) 732-7318

Swimming Lessons

Adult swimming lessons are available through the Rochester Area Family YMCA [(507) 287-2260, www.rochfamyorg] and Rochester Park and Recreation Department [(507) 281-6160, www.ci.rochester.mn.us/park].

Children's swimming lessons are available through the Rochester Orcas Olympic Swim School [(507) 252-8569, www.swimorcas.com], Med-City Aquatics Champion Swim School [(507) 529-0653, www.medcityaquatics.org], the YMCA [(507) 287-2260, www.rochfamy.org], Rochester Park and Recreation Department [(507) 281-6160, www.ci.rochester.mn.us/park], and Community Education [(507) 285-8350, www. www.rochester.k12.mn.us/community-ed]. More information about the Rochester Orcas, Med-City Aquatics, and the YMCA Dolphins Swim Team may be found under youth sports organization toward the end of this chapter.

Tennis

Indoor Courts

Rochester Athletic Club
3100 19th Street NW, Rochester, MN 55901, (507) 282-6000, www.rochesterathleticclub.com

The Rochester Athletic Club (RAC) is an upscale, family-friendly fitness club with extensive indoor and outdoor facilities. Indoor tennis facilities at the RAC include ten championship courts. RAC tennis pros provide top-quality instruction and coaching for children, youth, and adults. Competitive leagues and tournaments are also available for novice and experienced players of all ages. Please note that the Rochester Athletic Club is a members-only facility. Daily guest passes are available; however, local residents are only permitted to use the club as a guest once every 60 days. Special rates are available for relatives of members who live outside of southeastern Minnesota. Please call to reserve court times.

Cost: monthly membership fee; guest fee: $–$$
Hours: Monday–Friday, 5 a.m.–10:30 p.m.; Saturday–Sunday, 7 a.m.–9 p.m.

Rochester Indoor Tennis Club
2700 West Country Club Road, Rochester, MN 55902, (507) 288-4851

The Rochester Indoor Tennis Club is a privately owned club open to both members and the general public.

Facilities at the tennis club include six plexicushion courts, a full-service pro shop, nursery care, and locker rooms. Membership includes reduced court fees, free use of ball machines with court time, membership at the Rochester Outdoor Tennis Center, advanced reservations, permanent court time privileges, and discounted fees for programs, activities and leagues. The club also offers professional private and group lessons for individuals ages four and up,

USA Junior and Adult programs and leagues, Round Robin Tournaments, Family Days and more. The club is also available for children's birthday parties or other social gatherings. Please call the club for more information.

Cost: monthly membership fee; public: $$
Hours: open daily, 8 a.m.–10 p.m.

Outdoor Courts
Rochester Athletic Club

3100 19th Street NW, Rochester, MN 55901, (507) 282-6000, www.rochesterathleticclub.com

The Rochester Athletic Club (RAC) is an upscale, family-friendly fitness club with extensive indoor and outdoor facilities. Outdoor tennis facilities at the RAC include six clay and two plexicushion tennis courts. RAC tennis pros provide top-quality instruction and coaching for children, youth, and adults. Competitive leagues and tournaments are also available for novice and experienced players of all ages. Please note that the Rochester Athletic Club is a members-only facility. Daily guest passes are available; however, local residents are only permitted to use the club as a guest once every 60 days. Special rates are available for relatives of members who live outside of southeastern Minnesota. Please call to reserve court times.

Cost: monthly membership fee; guest fee: $–$$
Hours: Monday–Friday, 5 a.m.–10:30 p.m.; Saturday–Sunday, 7 a.m.–9 p.m.

Rochester Outdoor Tennis Center

Kutzky Park, 2nd Street and 13th Avenue NW, Rochester, MN 55901, (507) 288-4851, (507) 281-6186, www.ci.rochester.mn.us/park

The Rochester Outdoor Tennis Center, a city-owned facility, is located in Kutzky Park. The facility has a clubhouse and 15 hard courts, four of which are lighted. The center is staffed by tennis pros who provide group and private instruction for youth and adults, coaching for tournament groups, and adult clinics in addition to organizing adult leagues and special tennis events. Season memberships are required to use the tennis center; however, non-members may pay a small fee to play as the guest of a member.

Cost: membership fee; call for current prices
Hours: open daily, 8 a.m.–10 p.m. (mid-May–mid-September)

Rochester Park and Recreation Department

201 4th Street SE, 150 City Hall, Rochester, MN 55904, (507) 281-6160, www.ci.rochester.mn.us/park

Outdoor tennis courts open to all tennis players are located at the Rochester parks listed below. Park addresses and locations may be found in Chapter 16. The tennis courts at Century [2525 Viola Road NE, (507) 287-7150], John Marshall [1510 114th Street NW, (507) 285-8693], and Mayo [1420 11th Avenue SE, (507) 285-8819] High Schools are also open to the public when there are no scheduled practices or events.

Allendale Park
Cooke Park
Elmcroft Park

Northern Heights Park
Quarry Hill Park
Silver Lake Park

Fox Valley Park	Slatterly Park
Goose Egg Park	Soldiers Field Memorial Park
Judd Park	Younge Park

Track

Conoco Kids' Classic

1417 14th Avenue NE, Rochester, MN 55906, (507) 282-1411, www.medcitymarathon.com

The Conoco Kids' Classic, open to children in grades one through eight, is a sister event to the Med-City Marathon. Children train for the 1.2 mile course by running a total of 25 miles between January 1st and the Med-City Marathon race date. On race day, the kids complete their marathon by running from Mayo Field to the actual Med-City Marathon finish line. Commemorative medals are awarded to all finishers. Registration must be completed prior to race day. Visit the Med-City Marathon website or call for more information and registration materials.

Med-City Marathon and Relays

1417 14th Avenue NE, Rochester, MN 55906, (507) 282-1411, www.medcitymarathon.com

Rochester's Med-City Marathon and Relays is a USATF-certified course sanctioned by the Road Runners Club of America. The 26.2-mile race starts and finishes at Soldiers Field Memorial Park. Individuals, two person and four person relay teams, and wheelchair racers may enter the marathon, which winds through Rochester on a combination of city streets and bike paths. Relay entries are limited and include Male, Female, Co-ed, and Corporate divisions. The popular race is held annually on the last Sunday in May. Visit the Med-City Marathon website or call for more information and registration materials.

Rochester Track Club

P.O. Box 6711, Rochester, MN 55903, (507) 285-9878, www.rochestertrackclub.com

The Rochester Track Club is open to people of all ages and abilities who are interested in track and field or distance running. The club provides programs for fitness, skill development, and competition in addition to sponsoring and supporting local road races. All-Comers Track Meets, sponsored by the Track Club, are held from June to mid-July on Tuesday evenings at 6 p.m. at Soldiers Field Memorial Park Track. Participants of all ages, preschoolers through adults, are welcome to compete in these informal meets. A complete race calendar with a list of area and regional races of all distances as well as contact information may be found on the club website.

Volleyball

National Volleyball Center

Century High School, 2601 Viola Road NE, Rochester, MN 55906, (507) 529-4199, (507) 281-6160, www.ci.rochester.mn.us/park

Rochester is fortunate to be the home of the National Volleyball Center (NVC). This world-class, multi-use facility has attracted national attention with its eight, 18-by-9-meter volleyball courts, which have Bio-Cushion II flooring, Olympic quality lighting, and 30-foot ceilings. There is on-court seating for 60 people at each court with additional spectator seating on the mezzanine level. Century High School is connected to the volleyball center and offers three additional volleyball courts with spectator seating for up to 2,000 people at the center court. In addition to this, the court space converts to six basketball courts or two indoor soccer fields. Although the NVC has been a training and tournament site for collegiate, Olympic and national level volleyball, it serves the local and regional areas by hosting high school tournaments, adult and youth leagues as well as volleyball clinics and summer camps. The NVC also regularly schedules open volleyball and court rentals are available at the facility. Call the NVC or visit the Rochester Park and Recreation website for more information about leagues, upcoming events, and an open volleyball schedule.

Rochester Park and Recreation Department

201 4ᵗʰ Street SE, Room 150, Rochester, MN 55904, (507) 281-6160, www.ci.rochester.mn.us/park

Outdoor volleyball courts are available at the Rochester parks listed below. Park addresses and locations may be found in Chapter 16.

Bear Creek Park
Cooke Park
East Park
Eastwood Park
Essex Park
Foster-Arend Park

Homestead Park
Kutzky Park
McQuillan Park
Meadow Park Estates
Slatterly Park
Soldiers Field Memorial Park

Walking

Walksport America

P.O. Box 16325, St. Paul, MN 55116, 800-757-WALK (9255), www.walksport.com
The Walksport program is held locally at Rochester's Apache Mall, (507) 288-8056.

Walksport America, a national mall walking program, provides walkers with the support and incentives they need to maintain their walking programs. Participants receive a swipe-card to track their progress, access to the Walksport website, free seminars, a newsletter, camaraderie with other walkers, and the opportunity to win prizes. Locally, Apache Mall of Rochester hosts Walksport by providing mall walkers with early access to the building from 7:30 a.m.–10 a.m., seven days a week. The mall is closed to walkers during special sale days throughout the year. Please contact Walksport or call Apache Mall for more information.

Youth Sports Camps

A diverse selection of Youth Sports Camps for all ages and skill levels are offered through the Rochester Area Family YMCA, Rochester Athletic Club (RAC), Rochester Community Education, Rochester Community and Technical College, Rochester Park and Recreation Department, and many of the Youth Sports Organizations mentioned below. Camps at both the RAC and YMCA are open to nonmembers. Information about summer camps may usually be obtained from these organizations in early spring.

Rochester Area Family YMCA
709 1ˢᵗ Avenue SW, Rochester, MN 55902, (507) 287-2260, www.rochfamy.org

Rochester Athletic Club
3100 19ᵗʰ Street NW, Rochester, MN 55901, (507) 282-6000, www.rochesterathleticclub.com

Rochester Community Education
Northrop Building, 201 8ᵗʰ Street NW, Rochester, MN 55901, (507) 285-8350,
www.rochester.k12.mn.us/community-ed

Rochester Community and Technical College
Continuing Education Office, Box 51, 851 30ᵗʰ Avenue SE, Rochester, MN 55904, (507) 280-3113

Rochester Park and Recreation Department
201 4ᵗʰ Street SE–Room 150, Rochester, MN 55904, (507) 281-6160, www.ci.rochester.mn.us/park

Youth Sports Organizations

Cheer America—Schools of Cheerleading, Pom Pom & Baton
Cheer America, 14870 Granada Avenue, #318, Apple Valley, MN 55124, (952) 997-7732,
www.cheeramericamn.com

Cheer America, a Minnesota nonprofit corporation, offers cheerleading programs in
Rochester for children and youth, ages 4–14. The program focuses on the development of cheerleading skills as well as physical fitness, coordination, flexibility,
working with others, making friends, and just having fun. Kids learn and practice
jumps, splits, choreographed Pom pom, dance, and cheer routines, and skills required
for high school tryouts, cheer competitions, and performances. Please call for more
information and a class schedule.

Ironwood Springs Christian Ranch—National Wheelchair Sports & Recreation Camp
7291 County Road 6 SW, Stewartville, MN 55976, (507) 533-9933 (stables), 888-533-4316 or
(507) 533-4315 (information and reservations), www.ironwoodsprings.com, e-mail: iscr2000@aol.com

Ironwood Springs Christian Ranch, a nonprofit, nondenominational year-round
camp, is located in rural Stewartville along the Root River on 200 rural, wooded
acres. The camp's mission is "to provide an atmosphere and opportunity for adults
and children to get to know themselves, others and God better." The Ranch offers a
National Wheelchair Sports and Recreation Camp and Camp Jornada for kids with
cancer and their families during the summer months. Ironwood Springs also organizes the Annual Slumberland Wheelchair Race, which is scheduled for mid to late
June. The event is held in Rochester and includes a variety of divisions from junior
to elite races. Facilities and recreational amenities at Ironwood Springs include the
Main Lodge with recreation center, cabins, a dormitory, Log Chapel, campground,
an outdoor swimming pool, playgrounds, tennis courts, basketball courts, a miniature farm with animals, horse stables, and walking and hiking trails. Call the Ranch
for a current camp schedule and race information.

Med-City Aquatics Champion Swim School & Club
Rochester, MN, (507) 529-0653, www.medcityaquatics.org

Med-City Aquatics Champion Swim School and Club, a member of USA Swimming, offers instruction from water acclimation to advanced stroke skills for children and youth, ages 3½ through 10. Young swimmers are placed in small groups according to their skill level and progress through the program as they master the elements of swimming. The Med-City Swim Club also offers training and competitive swimming opportunities for swimmers of all levels. Experienced coaches develop programs for the swimmers that encourage them to reach their potential according to their interest and abilities.

A Master's program is also available for adults who want to swim for fitness or train for competition. Please contact Med-City Aquatics or visit their website for more information.

Middle School Sports Program

Rochester Community Education, Northrop Building, 201 8th Street NW, Rochester, MN 55901, (507) 285-8350, www.rochester.k12.mn.us/community-ed

The Middle School Sports Program offered by Rochester Community Education is designed for boys and girls in sixth through eighth grades. The recreational sports program is open to students of all skill levels at each of the four middle schools. Program offerings vary by season and have included Boy's and Girl's Soccer, Girl's Volleyball, Boy's and Girl's Basketball, Boy's and Girl's Swimming, Girl's Softball, and Boy's and Girl's Track. Please contact Community Education or refer to a current brochure for more information.

PossAbilities Youth Recreation Program

PossAbilities: 1808 3rd Avenue SE, Rochester, MN 55904, (507) 281-6116, www.possAbilities.org
YMCA: 709 1st Avenue SW, Rochester, MN 55902, (507) 287-2260, www.rochfamy.org

PossAbilities of Southern Minnesota, in conjunction with the Rochester Area Family Y, offers an after school recreation program and summer recreation program for middle school and high school students with disabilities. Peer companions support and assist the students as they participate in a variety of aquatic, gym, and arts and crafts activities. Please contact PossAbilities or the Y for more information.

RideAbility

Pine Island, MN 55963, (507) 356-8154, (507) 824-2854
Call for directions.

RideAbility is a recreational and therapeutic horseback riding program for children with disabilities and their families. The equestrian program is designed to boost self-confidence and provide a shared activity for families whose children have different abilities. Please call RideAbility for more information and a class schedule.

Rochester Adaptive Recreation Program

Rochester Park and Recreation Department, 201 4th Street SE, Room 150, Rochester, MN 55904, (507) 281-6160, (507) 287-7980, www.ci.rochester.mn.us/park

The Rochester Park and Recreation Department offers an Adaptive Recreation program for youth and adults. All individuals ages 5 and older with a physical and/or mental disability are eligible to participate in the sports and recreation programs; however, a physician's authorization is required. Year-round programs and activities are typically held after school, during the evening hours, and on weekends. Basketball, bowling, floor hockey, kickball, swimming, volleyball, hiking, cycling, inline skating, softball, and horseshoes are a sample of the sports offered through the program. Special Olympics Sports Training is also available in conjunction with the Rochester Area Special Olympics for the sports of basketball, volleyball, swimming, cross-country skiing, horseback riding, bowling, track and field, softball, and cycling. Social and recreational activities offered include arts and crafts, music, dances, playground programs, teen activities, movies and more. Registration for adaptive recreation programs is held on a quarterly basis. Please contact the Parks and Recreation Department for more information. Transportation is available through ZIPS [(507) 288-8404] for a nominal fee.

Rochester All-Stars Youth Cheerleading

P.O. Box 7565, Rochester, MN 55903, (507) 280-8042, www.rochesterallstars.org

The Rochester All-Stars is a competitive cheerleading, dance, and tumbling group for girls in kindergarten through high school. Tryouts are held for the All-Star Youth, Junior, and Senior Squads during the month of April. The squads practice year-round in preparation for local, regional, and national competitions. Please call or visit the website for more information.

Rochester American Legion Baseball

Rochester, MN, (507) 281-1578, www.baseball.legion.org

The Rochester American Legion Post participates in the Legion's nationwide youth baseball program for teens, ages 18 and under, by supporting two local teams, the Rochester A's and the Rochester Patriots. Players have the opportunity to learn teamwork, discipline, leadership, and good sportsmanship while developing their baseball skills and having fun. Team rosters are generally made up of high school players, and the teams are divided and organized by the high school boundaries. Although the Rochester Redhawks are not a legion sponsored team, they also play in the Legion league. Sign-ups are held in early May, and the season runs from June first through August. Please call for more information.

Rochester Area Club Lacrosse—RACLX

Rochester, MN, (507) 536-0489, www.mn-lacrosse.com or www.raclax.homestead.com

The Rochester Area Club Lacrosse (a.k.a. the Rochester Rattlers), a member of the Minnesota Lacrosse Association, was formed in the spring of 2002 with one junior varsity team for local high school students. The Rochester program is expected to grow in the upcoming years and hopes to have both a varsity and junior varsity team. RACLX competes against other teams in the Minnesota Lacrosse Association. Male athletes in 8th through 12th grades interested in the sport are encouraged to contact the club for more information.

Rochester Area Disabled Athletics and Recreation, Inc.—RADAR

539 North Broadway, Rochester, MN 55906, (507) 280-6995, http://radarsports.tripod.com, e-mail: radarsports@aol.com

RADAR, a nonprofit organization established in 1985, promotes athletics and recreation for individuals with disabilities in the Rochester and southeastern Minnesota area. The group's mission is to enhance the quality of life for individuals with disabilities and their families. Athletic activities offered by RADAR include basketball, hunting, fishing, archery, bowling, billiards, golf, water skiing and track. Recreational programs available include movie nights, games nights, crafts, and other social activities. Children, youth, and adults are welcome to participate in RADAR programs and events. Please contact RADAR or visit their website for more information.

Rochester Area Family YMCA—Dolphins Swim Team

709 1st Avenue SW, Rochester, MN 55902, (507) 287-2260, www.rochfamy.org

The Rochester Area YMCA offers a competitive swimming program, the Dolphins Swim Team, for youth ages five through eighteen. The swimming season runs from October to March, and the Dolphins compete against other Y teams throughout the state. Please contact the Y for more information.

Rochester Area Gymnastics Academy—RAGA

4430 19th Street NW, Rochester, MN 55901, (507) 285-9262, www.ragagym.org

As the largest gymnastics facility in southeastern Minnesota, RAGA offers instructional programs for children and youth from 18 months to 18 years old. The 16,000-square-foot gym provides a safe environment with quality equipment for boys and girls gymnastics. Participation in gymnastics also promotes self-confidence, discipline, teamwork, and commitment. Gymnastics instruction for preschoolers through high school aged youth, special needs programs, and summer camps as well as professional coaching for competitive athletes are available. RAGA also organizes special events such as Kid's Night Out where parents can drop off their kids, ages 5 and older, for a fun-filled evening of gymnastics, obstacle courses, movies, arts and crafts, and more. Please contact RAGA or visit their website for more information.

Gymnastics Instruction and Coaching

Kathy's All-American Training Center

Pine Island, MN 55963, (507) 356-8933, (507) 635-5446

Ricochets Gymnastics Club

1802 2nd Street SW, Rochester, MN 55902, (507) 288-6963, www.flip4fun.com

Rochester Area Special Olympics

Adaptive Recreation, Rochester Park and Recreation Department, 201 4th Street SE, Room 150, Rochester, MN 55904, (507) 287-7980, www.ci.rochester.mn.us/park

Rochester Area Special Olympics is a community-based athletic training program for individuals with mental and/or physical disabilities. Individuals, ages 5 through adulthood, with mental and developmental disabilities are eligible to participate in Special Olympics programs. Sports training is available for children between the ages of five and eight, but competition is not permitted until an athlete is eight years old. Special Olympians have the opportunity to meet new friends, develop healthy leisure skills, and learn good sportsmanship in addition to competing at local, regional, and state events. Please call the Adaptive Recreation Department for more information.

Rochester Community Youth Basketball Association—RCYBA

P.O. Box 8443, Rochester, MN 55903, (507) 287-3264, www.rcyba.org

The RCYBA provides an organized basketball league for boys and girls in 5th through 8th grades. The program is designed to teach players the fundamentals of basketball including teamwork, strategy, and rules. Players are organized into "A" or

"B" Teams within the league based upon skill and experience or may try out for the Traveling Teams. Registration is usually held in early to mid-September with tryouts at a later date. Please contact RCYBA or visit their website for more information.

Rochester Diving Club

Rochester-Olmsted Recreation Center, 21 Elton Hills Drive, Rochester, MN 55901, (507) 281-6167, www.usadiving.org or e-mail: schmidtdeb@yahoo.com

The Rochester Diving Club, a member of U.S.A. Diving, provides lessons and coaching for youth interested in competitive diving. The club is open to youth, ages 5–18, of all abilities from novice to national age group competitors. An Introduction to Competitive Diving class is offered by the Diving Club through Rochester Community Education for beginners interested in the sport. All coaches are safety-certified through U.S.A. Diving. Please call the Rochester-Olmsted Recreation Center for contact information or e-mail Deborah Schmidt at the above address.

Rochester Figure Skating Club

21 Elton Hills Drive NW, Rochester, MN 55901, (507) 288-7536, www.web-site.com/rfsc

The Rochester Figure Skating Club (RFSC), an affiliate of the United Skates Figure Skating Association, offers instructional classes for all ages and skill levels. Youth programs include Preschool Classes, Junior Club, Advanced Junior Club as well as private and semi-private lessons. Professional coaching is available for competitive skaters interested in singles, dance, precision, and synchronized skating. Call the RFSC or check out their website for more information about their classes and competitive skating programs. Please see Chapter 19 for more information about RFSC Annual Ice Show.

Rochester Matmen—Youth Wrestling Club

Rochester, MN, (507) 280-6183, (507) 285-5053, www.matmen.org

The Rochester Matmen is a private, nonprofit youth wrestling club for boys and girls in kindergarten through 8th grades. The Matmen provide young wrestlers with a fun atmosphere where good sportsmanship and wrestling fundamentals are learned and practiced. Wrestlers have the opportunity to participate in matches with area clubs, inter-squad matches, and an overnight tournament. Qualifying wrestlers may compete in the NYWA Regional Tournament held in Rochester. Please contact the club or visit their website for more information.

Rochester Swim Club Orcas and Olympic Swim School

Rochester, MN, (507) 252-8569, www.swimorcas.com

The Rochester Orcas Olympic Swim School was established in 1949 and continues to provide outstanding swimming instruction and training for children and youth, ages 3 through college age. The Orcas operate as "a branch of the United States Olympic Committee through the United States of America Swimming, Inc." Unique to the Olympic Swim School are the instructional methods used to teach young swimmers. Swimmers are placed in small classes based upon their age and ability and are taught the fundamentals of the four competitive strokes in small increments. As swimmers progress through the program they learn to synthesize these skills into proper swimming techniques. In addition to this, the Orcas provide a solid training ground for developing and competitive swimmers. The Orcas training philosophy is to provide a challenging program in an enjoyable atmosphere.

Swimmers are placed in and advance through a series of training groups based upon their age, ability, attendance, attitude, and desire. The organization is staffed by caring, professional coaches who have had experience training swimmers who have been to Olympic trials. A Master's program is also available for adults wanting to swim for fitness or competition. Please contact the Orcas or visit their website for more information.

Rochester Youth Baseball Association—RYBA
P.O. Box 6631, Rochester, MN 55903, (507) 281-9672, www.rybamn.org

Boys and girls in Rochester School District #535, currently enrolled in 1st through 9th grades, are eligible to participate in organized baseball with the RYBA. T-ball, coach-pitched baseball, major and minor league teams for 4th through 8th grades, a 9th grade league, and a traveling program is available. Tryouts are only held for major league teams. Annual registration is usually in early March.

Rochester Youth Bowling
Colonial Lanes
1828 14th Street NW, Rochester, MN 55901, (507) 289-2341

Recreation Lanes
2810 North Broadway, Rochester, MN (507) 288-2601

Youth bowling leagues are available at Colonial Lanes and Recreation Lanes in Rochester. Fall, winter, and spring leagues are open to youth, ages six and older. The focus of the youth bowling leagues is learning to bowl, spending time with friends, and having fun. A limited number of summer leagues is also available. Please contact Colonial or Recreation Lanes for more information.

Rochester Youth Cheerleading Association—RYCA
Rochester, MN, (507) 280-8042, www.ryca.org

RYCA, a volunteer run and parent-coached organization, is open to all girls in 4th through 8th grades. No tryouts are necessary to join one of the cheerleading squads. The squads learn and practice cheering routines, which they perform at Rochester Youth Football games for teams of the same grade level. The cheering season runs from August to October. Please call or visit the website for more information.

Rochester Youth Fastpitch Softball Association
Rochester, MN, (507) 285-0810, www.ryfsa.com

The Rochester Youth Fastpitch Softball Association is open to boys and girls from age 7 to 18. Teams are organized according to age and the location of the player's home within Rochester. Association teams compete in the Southern Minny League from June through July. Sign-ups are generally held in early February. Please call for more information.

Rochester Youth Football Association—RYFA
P.O. Box 5764, Rochester, MN 55903, (507) 288-3438, www.ryfa.org

The RYFA provides boys and girls in 4th through 8th grades with the opportunity to play full contact football. Players learn fundamental football skills in an environment that promotes good sportsmanship. Annual registration is usually held in early July. Please call RYFA or visit their website for more information.

Rochester Youth Hockey Association—RYHA

P.O. Box 237, Rochester, MN 55903, (507) 280-6086, www.ryha.net

The RYHA provides girls and boys with the opportunity to play organized hockey in an environment that emphasizes fun, safety, and skill development. Teams are available for boys, ages 4–17, and girls, ages 4–15. Annual registration is usually held in September. An RYHA sponsored consignment sale is also held during registration. Please call RYHA or visit their website for more information.

Rochester Youth Soccer Association—RYSA

P.O. Box 6402, Rochester, MN 55903, (507) 280-7584, www.rysa.org

RYSA has provided youth in grades 1–12 with the opportunity to play organized soccer for more than 25 years. Available programs include Recreational Soccer, Traveling Soccer, Indoor Soccer, and TopSoccer.

The focus of Recreational Soccer is on participation and fun. Traveling Soccer is for boys and girls interested in more competitive play. The Indoor Soccer program is designed to keep soccer skills sharp throughout the winter months, and TopSoccer is an adaptive program run in conjunction with Rochester Park and Recreation Department for boys or girls, ages 6–19, who have a mental or physical disability.

Registration for Recreational Soccer, spring Traveling Soccer, and Indoor Soccer is held in the fall. Registration for Fall Traveling Soccer is held in June. TopSoccer participants register through Rochester Park and Recreation Department for sessions in March and June. Please call RYSA or visit www. rysa.org for more information.

Rochester Youth Softball—Girl's Slow Pitch

Rochester Park and Recreation Department, 201 4th Street SE, Room 150, Rochester, MN 55904, (507) 281-6160, www.ci.rochester.mn.us/park

A Slow Pitch Softball League, organized by the Rochester Park and Recreation Department, is available for girls entering 4th through 10th grade in the fall. Teams are organized by grade levels. Registration is usually held in early April. Please contact the Rochester Park and Recreation Department for more information.

Rochester Youth Volleyball Association—RYVA

826 10th Street SW, Rochester, MN 55902, (507) 529-4199, www.eteams.com/ryva, e-mail: smvjuniors@aol.com

The RYVA organizes and promotes volleyball programs for youth in the city of Rochester. The Association offers instructional programs and coaching, summer camps, and competitive play for boys and girls ages eight to eighteen. Please contact RYVA or visit their website for more information.

Rochester Youth Wrestling Association—RYWA

Rochester, MN, (507) 285-5086, www.rywa.com

The Rochester Youth Wrestling Association (RYWA) offers boys and girls in kindergarten through 6th grade the opportunity to learn about teamwork, self-discipline, sportsmanship, self-confidence and physical fitness through the sport of wrestling. Youths receive wrestling instruction by volunteer coaches and have the opportunity to compete in local and/or regional tournaments. Please contact the club or visit their website for more information.

Socrates Youth Futbol Club

Rochester, MN, (507) 280-8180, www.socratesfutbolclub.org

The Socrates Youth Futbol Club (SCFY), a Rochester youth soccer club sanctioned by the Minnesota Youth Soccer Association, provides European-style training for boys and girls of all ages and abilities. Professional coaches provide young players with a soccer program that focuses on technical, physical, and tactical training. The club's tournament-only teams emphasize player development through a high ratio of practice time to game time and offers specialized field training and goalie training. Registration for the summer season takes place in early fall. Please contact the Socrates Youth Futbol Club for more information.

Chapter 19: Spectator Sports

Automobile Racing

Deer Creek Speedway and Campground
25262 U.S. Hwy. 63, Spring Valley, MN 55975, (507) 754-6107, (507) 346-2342,
www.deercreekspeedway.com, www.wissota.org
Located on Hwy. 63 South, just north of Spring Valley.

Under new ownership of the Queensland family, Deer Creek Speedway sports
a 3/8 mile, banked clay track with seating for 3,000 people in the stands and
500 in the pit area. The speedway provides family entertainment in the form of
WISSOTA automobile racing. Racing divisions include Super Stock, Midwest
Modified, Street Stock, Dwarf Cars, and Late Model Racing. Races are held
on Saturday evenings from April through September. Concessions are available.
Please call Deer Creek Speedway or visit their website to obtain more information
about upcoming races. Information about the campground may be found in
Chapter 12, Campgrounds.

Cost: $–$$
Hours: Saturday, gates open at 3:30 p.m.; race time, 6:30 p.m.

Dodge County Speedway
mailing address: 825 3rd Avenue NE, Byron, MN 55920
physical address: North Mantorville Avenue, Kasson, MN 55944, (507) 634-4281, (507) 775-7091,
www.dodgecountyspeedway.com, www.wissota.org
Located 14 miles west of Rochester on Hwy. 14 in Kasson.

Fitzpatrick Promotions operates the Dodge County Speedway (DCS), a ⅓-mile,
semi-banked clay track with seating for 3500 people. Individuals of all ages come to
DCS to watch the WISSOTA sanctioned events, which include Super Stock, Street
Stock, Midwest Modified, and Late Model in addition to Dodge County Speedway
Modified races. Special races hosted at DCS also include the USMTS Modified
Touring Series and the Late Model Challenge Touring Series. Races are held on
Sunday evenings from April through September. Concessions are available. Please
call DCS or visit their website to obtain more information about upcoming races.

Cost: $–$$
Hours: Sunday, gates open 4 p.m.; race time, 6 p.m.

Steele County Speedway
Steele County Fairgrounds,1525 South Cedar Avenue, Owatonna, MN 55060, (507) 451-5305,
www.scff.org, www.wissota.org
Take Hwy. 14 West to the first Owatonna exit onto Cedar Avenue (County Road 45), drive to the first
stoplight, follow signs to fairgrounds.

The Steele County Speedway periodically runs races on its ½-mile, clay-based track
from Memorial Day to Labor Day. Races are scheduled throughout the season, on
major holidays (Memorial Day, July 4th, and Labor Day), and during the Steele
County Fair at the end of August. The Gopher 50, an annual event in early July,
attracts racers from throughout the nation. Racing fans may visit a museum at the
fairgrounds that displays archives of the Steele County Speedway. The museum is

open to the public during fair week. Seating capacity at the speedway is 4,400, and concessions are available. Please contact the fairgrounds for a current racing schedule.

Cost: $–$$
Hours: schedule varies, please call; gates open one hour before race time

Motocross Racing

Hurricane Hills

43560 232nd Avenue, Mazeppa, MN 55956, (507) 843-5154, www.hurricanehills.com
Take Hwy. 52 South to Hwy. 60 (Mazeppa/Zumbro Falls exit), follow Hwy. 60 into Mazeppa, turn left on County Road 1 at the Greenway Station. Drive through town and take the first tar road to the left (Wabasha County 12). Follow County Road 12, continue 1½ to 2 miles, turn right on 232nd Avenue (gravel road) and follow to the Hurricane Hills sign.

Hurricane Hills (HH) is an MX park located in rural Mazeppa. Races are held periodically during the racing season, which runs from April to October. Open riding is regularly available at the track on Tuesdays through Sundays from 10 a.m. until dark, weather permitting. Open riding on a Saturday before race day is from 10 a.m.–4 p.m. Riders must be HH club members to participate in open riding sessions and are encouraged to call ahead to check current track conditions. Camping is available on site. Please contact HH or visit their website to obtain a current race schedule.

Cost: $
Hours: Sunday, gates open, 6:30 a.m.; race time, 9:30 a.m.

Midway Recreation Park

RR 1, Box 85A, Kellogg, MN 55945, (507) 534-3276, (507) 534-3737 (race days only), www.geocities.com/midwaymx
Located on Hwy. 42 between Kellogg and Plainview.
From Hwy. 52: Turn onto Hwy. 12 East in Oronoco, follow Hwy. 12 to the Hwy. 63 intersection. Cross Hwy. 63 and follow Hwy. 247 for 12 miles into Plainview. Turn left at the only 4-way stop in Plainview onto Hwy. 42. The track is about 6 miles north of Plainview on Hwy. 42.
From Hwy. 61 South: Turn right at the Hwy. 61/Hwy. 42 junction just beyond the town of Kellogg. Follow Hwy. 42 about 7 miles to the track.

Midway Recreation Park, a motocross park owned and operated by Jack and Cindy Stamschror, is located in rural Kellogg. Midway hosts amateur and professional motocross and quad races including a Survivor Series and AMA District 23 Races. The Survivor Series is held on designated Sundays during the racing season, which runs from April through Labor Day. The track is used for practice on the Saturdays prior to race day. Please call Midway or visit their website for more information about upcoming races.

Cost: $
Hours: Sunday, gates open 6:30 a.m.; race time, 9:30 a.m.; race times may vary during special events

Spring Creek Motocross (MX) Park

RR 1, Box 32A Millville, MN 55957, (507) 753-2779, www.springcreekmx.com
From Rochester: Take Hwy. 63 North to Zumbro Falls, turn right onto Hwy. 60, drive east 9 miles on Hwy. 60 to Wabasha County Road 11, turn right at County Road 11, the park entrance is the first driveway on the right side.

From Hwy. 52: Take the Zumbrota exit and follow Hwy. 60 east 21 miles through Zumbro Falls to Wabasha County Road 11, turn right at County Road 11, the park entrance is the first driveway on the right side.

Spring Creek Motocross Park, a motor sports center located in rural Millville for nearly 40 years, is currently owned and operated by John and Greta Martin. During the past 15 years, the Martins have developed the facility into one of the best track layouts in the nation while also creating hillside seating that provides excellent viewing for spectators. Spring Creek hosts a variety of professional and amateur events during the racing season including one round of the renowned American Motorcycle Association (AMA) National Motocross Series. Big name riders are featured at this Pro National Race, which also has a full schedule of events such as open practice times, amateur races, awards ceremonies, an auction, fireworks, live bands, and a kids' play area. This weekend event draws crowds of 20,000 to 30,000 people. Spring Creek also hosts Super Series Races, held on designated Sunday mornings throughout the racing season, AMA District 23 Races for 125A and 250A riders, Harescrambles, Cross-Country, and open practices. Open practices are available at the Spring Creek track on designated dates from May through October. Spring Creek provides a groomed track with flaggers on the course and an ambulance on site for open practices. A primitive campground is also located on the premises. Please call Spring Creek for more information about upcoming races.

Cost: $; seniors 55 and older, free
Hours: Sunday, gates open 6:45 a.m.; race time, 9:30 a.m.; race times may vary during special events

Figure Skating

Rochester Figure Skating Club Annual Ice Show

Rochester-Olmsted Recreation Center, 21 Elton Hills Drive, Rochester, MN 55901, (507) 288-7536, www.web-site.com/rfsc

The Rochester Figure Skating Club (RFSC) presents its Annual Ice Show during the third weekend in April. This spectacular production showcases artistic and athletic performances by local youth of all ages and skating abilities. The combination of delightful performances by RFSC's younger skaters and the outstanding talent of its junior and senior skaters provides an entertaining show that will take your breath away. Admission fee.

Water Ski Shows

Rochester Water Ski Club

Box 193, Oronoco, MN 55960, (507) 367-4485

Shows are held at Fisherman's Inn, 8 Fisherman Drive NW, Oronoco, MN 55960.

The Rochester Water Ski Club was established more than 40 years ago and is currently an award winning team that performs public shows on Wednesday evenings at 7 p.m. throughout the summer. Club members and performers are primarily area teens, but range in age from four to fifty. The 1½-hour long water ski shows are performed on Lake Zumbro at the Fisherman's Inn Restaurant in Oronoco. The weekly shows include a variety of stunts and tricks including a ballet water dance line, pyramids, doubles, barefoot skiing, jumps, and more. Special shows are usually performed for the RochesterFest, Fourth of July, and Labor Day celebrations. These shows are held at Silver Lake Park in Rochester. Please check the Rochester Post-Bulletin for dates and times of these special shows. Free.

Cost: free, donations welcome
Hours: Wednesdays, 7 p.m. (June–September)

Rochester Amateur Sports Commission

150 South Broadway, Suite A, Rochester, MN 55904, (507) 252-9914, www.rochesterusa.com/sports

The Rochester Amateur Sports Commission (RASC), a nonprofit organization that was incorporated in 1991, was established to promote Rochester as a venue for major national and international amateur sporting events. Since its inception, the RASC has assisted Rochester in becoming known throughout Minnesota, the United States, and the world as a hospitable community with the capability and facilities to host major sporting events. Amateur events that have been held in Rochester include the NCAA Division II Women's Basketball Championship, the International Tug of War Championship, NCAA National Volleyball and Wrestling Championships, AAU Junior Olympic Games, and Star of the North games. Please call RASC or visit their website for more information about the organization, upcoming sporting events, or volunteer opportunities.

Sports Teams

Minnesota Chill—Women's Professional Volleyball
National Office: United States Professional Volleyball, 1 Lincoln Centre, 4th Floor, Oakbrook Terrace, Illinois, 60181, (630) 575-USPV (8778), 888-THE-USPV (843-8778), www.uspv.com
Mayo Civic Center is located at 30 Civic Center Drive SE, Rochester, MN 55904, (507) 287-2222, www.mayociviccenter.com Ticketmaster: (507) 252-1010 or www.ticketmaster.com

The Minnesota Chill, a Rochester-based women's professional volleyball team, tri-umphed during the United States Professional Volleyball League's (USPV) inaugural season in 2001–2002 by winning the league championship. The USPV is unique because it is the first women's professional sports league to precede the development of a men's league. The organization had four teams in its first season and plans to expand the league to eight teams in its second season. It will then add four teams per season until the league reaches about 20 teams. The Chill and other USPV fran-chised teams recruits players from top collegiate programs, the U.S. National Team, USPV National Athlete Tryout Camp, and free agent signings. These elite female athletes not only play world-class volleyball, but provide exciting and entertaining matches for the fans. The Chill quickly developed a loyal fan base as young children to seniors flocked to the matches to support the team who has won the hearts of Rochester by playing great volleyball as well as becoming involved in the commu-nity. Youth and adult volleyball enthusiasts will be interested to note that summer volleyball skill and team camps for youth and adults are offered by the Minnesota Chill. Please call the local office for more information about these camps. The USPV season runs from about January to May. The Minnesota Chill plays home games at the Mayo Civic Center in downtown Rochester. Tickets may be purchased at the Mayo Civic Center or through Ticketmaster.

Rochester Honkers Baseball Club

Northwoods League, P.O. Box 482, Rochester, MN 55903, (507) 536-4579, (507) 289-1170, www.northwoodsleague.com or www.rochesterhonkers.com
Home games are played at Mayo Field, 403 Center Street East, Rochester, MN.

The Rochester Honkers, a local baseball club, is a member of the Northwoods League. The Northwoods League is a summer baseball league that was founded in 1994 and is comprised of teams from the upper Midwest. Top collegiate players from throughout the United States are recruited to play in the amateur league, which is operated like a professional minor league team; however, the players are not paid so that they maintain their NCAA eligibility. The Honker's season runs from early June through mid-August with home games played at Mayo Field in downtown Rochester. Home games often feature special promotions such as Scout Night, Kid's Buck Day, Fan Appreciation Night, Team Trading Card Night and more. Please call the Honkers, visit their website, or check the Rochester Post-Bulletin for a current schedule. In addition to grandstand seating, Mayo Field has a limited number of luxury boxes and seating on raised deck near left field. Season tickets and group rates are available.

Cost: $–$$$$$
Hours: gates open one hour before game time; weekday & Saturday games:
   7:05 p.m.; Sunday games: 5:05 p.m.; call to confirm game times

Rochester Roosters Old Time Baseball

Olmsted County History Center's Schmitt Field, 1195 West Circle Drive SW, Rochester, MN 55902, (507) 282-9447, www.olmstedhistory.com

The Rochester Roosters is a vintage baseball team that plays the game of American baseball as it originated in the mid-1800s. Players dress in period uniforms and compete with other vintage teams using replica balls and bats in a league that plays by 1860s rules. Games are played periodically throughout the summer, during RochesterFest in June, and a Vintage Baseball Tournament is held at the Days of Yesteryear Festival in August. Please contact the Olmsted County History Center or visit their website for a schedule. Admission fee is two bits, in other words, 25 cents.

Chapter 20: Winter Recreation

Cross-Country Ski Trails In and Around Rochester

Chester Woods Park

8378 Hwy. 14 East, Eyota, MN 55934, (507) 285-7050, www.olmstedpublicworks.com, e-mail: chesterw@venturecs.net

Chester Woods Park is an Olmsted County Park located just seven miles east of Rochester. The park, a favorite among local residents, maintains approximately five to six miles of groomed cross-country ski trails during the winter months. A daily or annual park permit is required for entrance into the park.

Cost: $
Hours: daily, 7 a.m.–10 p.m.

Douglas State Trail

Rochester–Pine Island

Rochester Area Trails & Waterways, 2300 Silver Creek Road NE, Rochester, MN 55906, (507) 285-7176, www.dnr.state.mn.us
Trailheads are located in Rochester on County Road 4 (Valleyhigh Drive NW) behind IBM, in Douglas at County Road 14 off Hwy. 52, and in Pine Island at Pine Island Park, just off the Hwy. 52 exit.

The Douglas State Trail, a 12.5-mile multiple-use trail, is groomed for cross-country skiers during the winter months. Trailheads for the Douglas State Trail originate in northwest Rochester and Pine Island with a midpoint in Douglas, the town for which the trail is named. Users must purchase the Great Minnesota Ski Pass. Information about the pass may be found in the next section, Cross-Country Ski Trails in Southeastern Minnesota.

Oxbow Park and Zollman Zoo

Oxbow Park, 5731 County Road 105 NW (@ Olmsted 4 & 5 intersection), Byron, MN 55920, (507) 775-2451, www.olmstedpublicworks.com, e-mail: oxbow@venturecs.net

Oxbow Park is an Olmsted County Park located in the scenic Zumbro River Valley. The 572-acre park maintains about two miles of groomed cross-country ski trails when snow conditions are adequate. Skiers may warm up in the small nature center located in the park.

Cost: free
Hours: park: 7 a.m.–10 p.m.
  nature center and zoo: noon–8 p.m. (summer); noon–4 p.m. (winter)

Rochester Park and Recreation Department

201 4ᵗʰ Street SE, 150 City Hall, Rochester, MN 55904, (507) 281-6160, www.ci.rochester.mn.us/park

When snow conditions permit, the city of Rochester maintains groomed cross-country ski trails at the parks and golf courses listed below. Please contact Rochester's Parks and Recreation Department for information about current conditions. Telephone numbers for golf course clubhouses are provided below; however, these may not be open during the winter season. Cross-country ski equipment may only be rented at Quarry Hill Park and Nature Center.

Eastwood Golf Course
3505 Eastwood Road SE, Rochester, MN 55904, (507) 281-6173

Essex Park
5455 West River Road NW, Rochester, MN 55901, (507) 281-6160

Hawthorn Hills Golf Learning Center
1925 48th Street NE, Rochester, MN 55906, (507) 529-4119

Northern Hills Golf Course
4800 West Circle Drive, Rochester, MN 55901, (507) 281-6170

Quarry Hill Park and Nature Center
701 Silver Creek Road NE, Rochester, MN 55906, (507) 281-6114

Soldiers Field Golf Course
244 East Soldiers Field Drive, Rochester, MN, (507) 281-6176

Cross-Country Ski Trails in Southeastern Minnesota

Minnesota Department of Natural Resources—DNR
500 Lafayette Road, St. Paul, MN 55155-4040, (651) 296-6157, 888-MINNDNR (646-6367), www.dnr.state.mn.us

Basic information about southeastern Minnesota's State Parks is provided in Chapter 16. Park visitors may obtain more detailed information about park facilities and amenities by calling the park's office or the DNR, visiting the DNR website or stopping by the park office during a visit. Request a copy of the Minnesota State Parks Traveler Newsletter for extensive information about the parks and their scheduled activities and special events. State parks require visitors to purchase a daily or annual entrance permit for admittance to the parks. An annual permit is valid at all Minnesota State Parks. Cross-country skiers aged 16 and over must also purchase a Great Minnesota Ski Pass for use of public ski trails. Daily ski passes are available at the state parks. One-season and three-season ski passes are available through Minnesota's Electronic Licensing System (ELS). These may be purchased at more than 1700 locations around the state, typically where hunting and fishing licenses are sold. Please call the DNR Information Center or visit the DNR website for a list of ELS locations. State parks with cross-country ski trails are listed alphabetically by town.

ALTURA
Whitewater State Park
RR 1, Box 256, Altura, MN 55910, (507) 932-3007
Located 3 miles south of Elba on State Hwy. 74.

Whitewater State Park, southeastern Minnesota's favorite state park, offers cross-country skiers approximately seven miles of groomed trails with access to a visitor's center. The park remains a popular destination because it provides visitors with the facilities to participate in outdoor recreational activities throughout the year including a group center with winterized cabins.

CANNON VALLEY
Cannon Valley Trail
Red Wing–Cannon Falls

Cannon Valley Trail, City Hall, 306 West Mill Street, Cannon Falls, MN 55009, (507) 263-0508, (651) 258-4141, www.cannonvalleytrail.com
The Red Wing trailhead is located on Old West Main Street and Bench Street, one block from Hwy. 61 with parking nearby.
The Cannon Falls trailhead originates near 3rd Street in Cannon Falls. Parking at this trailhead is limited, but may be accessed across from the ballpark on East Stoughton Street.
The Welch Station Access is located along County Road 7 between the Village of Welch and Welch Village Ski Area.

The 19.7-mile Cannon Valley Trail, formerly a section of the Chicago Great Western Railroad, is groomed for both classical and skate skiing during the winter months. The trail runs between Red Wing and Cannon Falls with a midpoint at Welch Station. Cross-country skiers will enjoy spectacular views of the area as they travel along the trail, which winds alongside the Cannon River and passes through a variety of natural habitats including marshlands, pastures, and wooded areas. There are no warming facilities along the trail.

HARMONY
Harmony–Preston Valley State Trail
Harmony–Preston

Rochester Area Trails & Waterways, 2300 Silver Creek Road NE, Rochester, MN 55906, (507) 285-7176, www.dnr.state.mn.us
Harmony Visitor's Center, (507) 886-2469, 800-247-MINN(6466), www.harmony.mn.us
Preston Area Tourism, (507) 765-2100, 888-845-2100, www.bluffcountry.com
The Preston trailhead is located off Hwy. 52 on Fillmore Street (County Road 12), and the Harmony trailhead is located off Hwy. 52 on 4th Street SW.

The Harmony–Preston Valley State Trail is an 18-mile trail between the towns of Harmony and Preston that connects to the popular Root River State Trail at Isinours Junction, approximately 5.5 miles east of the Root River trailhead in Fountain. Although the northern section of the Harmony–Preston Valley trail is relatively flat, a series of hills and inclines provides challenging terrain along the southern portion of the trail between County Road 16 and Harmony. The trail is groomed for cross-country skiers during the winter months.

LAKE CITY
Frontenac State Park
29223 County Road 28 Boulevard, Lake City, MN 55041, (651) 345-3401
Located 10 miles southeast of Red Wing on U.S. Hwy. 61, turn left on County Road 2.

Frontenac State Park, located adjacent to the mighty Mississippi River and Lake Pepin, maintains 6.5 miles of groomed cross-country trails and a warming house for skiers. Eagle spotting is common during the winter months at this park since it is located in the migration corridor for these birds of prey. Skate skiing is available nearby at the Mississippi National Golf Links [409 Golf Links Drive, Red Wing, MN 55066; (651) 388-1874].

Hok-Si-La Municipal Park
Hwy. 61 North, Lake City, MN 55041, (651) 345-3855, www.lakecitygov.com
Located 2 miles north of Lake City on Hwy. 61/63.

Welcome to southeastern Minnesota's Shangri-La. Hok-Si-La is situated along the banks of Lake Pepin and provides cross-country skiers a mile or two of groomed trails. Skiers will enjoy the quiet beauty of winter as they ski through the park's peaceful setting. Outhouses are available in the parking lot.

LANESBORO
Root River State Trail
Fountain–Houston

DNR Trail Center, Lanesboro Depot, Lanesboro, MN 55949, (507) 467-2552, www.dnr.state.mn.us
Lanesboro Visitor's Center, (507) 467-2696, www.lanesboro.com, www.bluffcountry.com
Trailheads in Fountain, the Isinours Forestry Unit, Lanesboro, Whalan, Peterson, Rushford, and Houston may be easily located by following signs to the Root River State Trail as you approach these towns.

Southeastern Minnesota's Root River State Trail is the region's premier multi-use recreational trail and annually attracts thousands of outdoor enthusiasts. The 42-mile trail is groomed during the winter months and provides cross-country skiers with an idyllic setting as it meanders through picturesque farmlands, rolling pastures, limestone bluffs, and forested areas. A Candlelight Ski is held at the trail during February. Please see Chapter 8 for more information.

LEROY
Lake Louise State Park
12385 766 Avenue, LeRoy, MN 55951, (507) 324-5249
Located 1.5 miles north of LeRoy on County Road 14.

Lake Louise State Park, considered an "oasis" amid the farmlands of southeastern Minnesota, provides skiers with approximately three miles of cross-country ski trails within the 1,150-acre park. Parkland is primarily level with open fields and hard-wood forests. No warming house is available.

OWATONNA
Rice Lake State Park
Route 3, Owatonna, MN 55060, (507) 455-5871
Located 7 miles east of Owatonna on Rose Street.

Approximately 2.5 miles of cross-country ski trails are situated among the 1,000 acres of marshland, lakes, meadows, and woods at Rice Lake State Park. A warming house, interpretive exhibits, and year-round naturalist programs are also available.

PLAINVIEW
Carley State Park
c/o Whitewater State Park, Route 1, Box 256, Altura, MN 55910, (507) 932-3007
Located 4 miles south of Plainview on Wabasha County Road 4.

Carley State Park provides cross-country skiers with five miles of trails in a rustic and secluded atmosphere. A peaceful experience awaits skiers who come and ski amid the majestic white pines of this region. No warming facilities are available at this park.

Great River Ridge Trail
Elgin–Plainview

Plainview City Hall, (507) 534-2229

The Great River Ridge Trail is currently a 5-mile paved trail that runs between Elgin and Plainview. This section of the trail passes through open country and has gently sloping terrain. The multiple-use trail and its trailheads are still under development with plans to extend it from Plainview to Eyota. Skiers may access the trail in Plainview at the intersection of 3rd Street SW and State Highway 42.

PRESTON
Forestville/Mystery Cave State Park
Route 2, Box 128, Preston, MN 55965, main park: (507) 352-5111, cave: (507) 937-3251
Located 4 miles south of State Hwy. 16 on Fillmore County Road 5, then 2 miles east on Fillmore County Road 118.

Explore the diverse array of habitats including prairies, savannas, oak woodlands as well as maple and basswood forests as you ski through Forestville/Mystery Cave State Park. The park offers approximately 11 miles of cross-country ski trails and a warming house.

WINONA
Great River Bluffs State Park
Route 4, Winona, MN 55987, (507) 643-6849
From the north, take U.S. Hwy. 61 about 12 miles southeast of Winona to County Road 3. Park entrance will be 4 miles down the road. From I-90, take exit 266 (County Roads 12 and 3) and follow the signs to the park.

Cross-country skiers will find the views of the Mississippi River Valley at Great River Bluffs State Park absolutely breathtaking. The park offers nine miles of cross-country ski trails and a one-mile skate-ski trail. No warming facilities are available at the park.

Downhill Skiing

Coffee Mill Ski Area
Box 127, Hwys.60 & 61, Wabasha, MN 55981, (651) 565-2777, www.coffeemillski.com

Coffee Mill Ski Area, located along Great River Road in Wabasha, offers area residents and visitors magnificent views of the Mississippi River Valley and the opportunity to ski in a coulee. The bowl-shaped ski area provides easy lift accessibility and protection from the winter elements. Although there are only eleven slopes at the ski area, Coffee Mill boasts the longest vertical drop south of Duluth. Skiers will find a balanced selection of easy, intermediate, and difficult runs, and snowboarders like the 240-foot-long half-pipe with 12-foot sidewalls. The 8,000 foot, octagon-shaped chalet welcomes skiers to warm up with infra-radiant heat and houses a cafeteria as well as the rental shop and ski school. The ski school offers group and private lessons for skiers of all abilities, and free lessons are provided for first time skiers aged six and older. A ski racing program is also available. Please contact Coffee Mill for detailed information about the ski school, ski rentals, racing program, and special rates for college students, seniors, and families. Season passes are available.

Cost: $–$$$
Hours: Monday (holidays), 10 a.m.–8 p.m.; Tuesday, closed; Wednesday & Thursday, 3 p.m.–9:30 p.m., Friday, 1 p.m.–10 p.m.; Saturday, 10 a.m.–10 p.m.; Sunday, 10 a.m.–8 p.m.

Mount Frontenac Ski Area

Box 180, Hwy. 61 North, Frontenac, MN 55026, (651) 388-5826, 800-488-5826, www.mountfrontenac.com

Mount Frontenac Ski Area, nestled in the bluffs of the Mississippi and Hiawatha River Valleys, is located on Great River Road between Lake City and Red Wing. Frontenac has been a popular destination for ski enthusiasts in southeastern Minnesota since 1969. Frontenac attracts ski and snowboard enthusiasts of all levels due to its short lift lines, a well balanced selection of easy and challenging slopes, its family atmosphere, and reasonable prices. Facilities include a total of 13 runs, the Main Chalet, which is suitable for families, and the T-Bar Adult Chalet for those aged 21 and older. The Frontenac Ski School maintains a regular schedule of group lesson times during weekday evenings, weekends, and holidays as well as private lessons for skiers of all abilities and ages. The Ski School Kid's Club has a Snow Cubs program for four to five year olds and a Snow Bears program for six to eleven year olds. Snowboarding lessons are also available. The Frontenac Adult Ski Team (FAST) is open to adults interested in recreational racing, and the Junior Race Team provides youth with an opportunity to practice skiing skills and experience ski racing. Please contact Mount Frontenac for detailed information about the ski school, ski rentals, racing program, monthly specials, and special rates on Deep Discount Nights, College Nights, and Family Days. Season passes are available.

Cost: $$–$$$
Hours: Monday & Tuesday, closed; Wednesday, Thursday, Friday, 4:30 p.m.–10 p.m.; Saturday, 9:30 a.m.–10 p.m.; Sunday, 10 a.m.–8 p.m.; call for holiday hours

SKILINK™ Ski Club for Kids

Welch Village SKILINK™ Learning Center, Welch, MN 55089, (651) 258-4567, (651) 222-7079, www.welchvillage.com

The Welch Village SKILINK™ Ski Club is designed for young skiers and snowboarders, ages 8–17, of all skill levels. The Ski Club schedules six Saturday meetings during December and January. Ski Club enrollment includes bus transportation from Tyrol Ski Shop in Rochester to Welch Village, two hours of ski instruction, and free time to ski or snowboard on each Saturday. Skiers are grouped by ability and have the same instructor throughout the six-week program. Ski and snowboard rental packages are available. Please contact the Welch Village SKLINK Learning Center for more information.

Steeplechase Ski & Snowboard Area

Route 1, Box 168B, Mazeppa, MN 55956, (507) 843-3000, www.skisteeplechase.com
From Rochester, take Hwy. 52 North to Olmsted County Road 18 in Oronoco. Turn right on County Road 18, drive north on County 18 for about 5 miles, and follow the signs to Steeplechase.

Steeplechase Ski and Snowboard Area, southeastern Minnesota's newest ski facility, opened in January 2001. The Steeplechase Chalet, located above the slopes, greets skiers as they approach the ski area, which is set in a wooded valley between Oronoco and Mazeppa, just thirteen miles from Rochester. The newly renovated chalet, an old church relocated from Oronoco, is a beautiful building with cathedral ceilings and an authentic clock tower that provides a warm, comfortable atmosphere for families. The chalet is home to the Steeplechase Ski and Snowboard School, a full-service rental shop, game room on the lower level, and a cafeteria with a delicious selection of hot foods and snacks. Steeplechase offers a variety of runs from gentle cruisers for beginners to challenging black diamonds for the expert skier and the Holtork Airfield Terrain Park for snowboarders and freestyle skiers. However, a majority of the slopes are geared toward beginner and intermediate skiers. Ski and snowboard lessons are available for skiers and boarders of all abilities. Adults and youth may also participate in recreational ski and snowboard racing at Steeplechase. Opportunities include Slalom Ski Races for men, women, and youth during week-day evenings and weekends, and a traveling ski and snowboard team for youth. Please contact Steeplechase for more detailed information about lessons, ski racing, and equipment rentals. Season passes are available.

Cost: $$–$$$

Hours: Tuesday–Friday, 1 p.m.–10 p.m.; Saturday, 10 a.m.–10 p.m.; Sunday, 10 a.m.–8 p.m.; holidays, 10 a.m.–10 p.m.

Welch Village Ski and Snowboard Area

P.O. Box 146, County Road 7, Welch, MN 55089, (651) 258-4567, (651) 222-7079, (651) 222-7079, www.welchvillage.com

Welch Village Ski and Snowboard Area, southeastern Minnesota's premier ski resort, was rated "A Choice Family Resort" by *Ski Magazine* readers in 2001. As the # 4 ski area in the Midwest for families, Welch offers a total of 50 slopes with a variety of green, blue, and black runs as well as a SKILINK™ Learning Center, a Main Chalet, adults-only East Chalet, overnight accommodations for groups of 25 or more at six slope-side mountain cabins, a full-service rental shop, ski accessory shop, tune-up and repair center, and a ski and bag check. Approximately half of the runs are suitable for beginner and intermediate skiers. The remaining black diamond runs are geared for expert skiers. Snowboarders are attracted to Welch's three terrain parks with a half-pipe, rail slides, table tops, and more. The lift lines at Welch are minimal due to a total of eight chair lifts including three quad chair lifts, four double chair lifts, and one triple chair lift.

The Welch Village Learning Center provides lessons and workshops for skiers and snowboarders of all ages and abilities. The Learning Center features SKILINK™, a trademarked learn-to-ski program, used by ski instructors to teach individuals of all ages to ski and snowboard. Other programs available at the Learning Center include Discovery Workshops (private or semi-private lessons), Adult Twos & Fours Packages, Women's Ski Clinics with Jeanne Thoren, the SKILINK™ Kids' Club (ages 4–10), and Ski and Ride Lessons for groups. Youth and adults interested in recreational ski racing may participate in SKILINK™ Junior Development Race League (Jr. DevoTeam) and Welch Adult Race Program (WARP), respectively. Please contact Welch for detailed information about the ski school, ski rentals, the racing program, group rates, monthly specials, and special rates on Saturday Night Alive, Overnight Lock-Ins, 4-H & Scout Nights, Home School Outdoor Fun Days, and Family Days. Season passes are available.

Ice Skating: Indoor Rinks

ROCHESTER

Rochester-Olmsted Recreation Center

21 Elton Hills Drive, Rochester, MN 55901, (507) 281-6167, www.ci.rochester.mn.us/park

The Rochester-Olmsted Recreation Center is equipped with two full-sized, 85-by-200-foot indoor ice rinks for figure skating, hockey, and curling and has seating for more than 2500 spectators. The rinks are used by the Minnesota Ice Hawks Hockey Team, the Rochester Figure Skating Club, Rochester's Youth Hockey Association, and local high school hockey teams. Ice skating activities available for the general public include Open Skating, Adult Ice Skating, Adult Noon Ice Skating, Adult Open Hockey, Family Ice Skating, Parent-Tot Skating, and Open Freestyle Skating. Skate rentals are available.

Cost: $
Hours: call for a current schedule

KASSON
Four Seasons Arena
100 11ᵗʰ Street NE, Kasson, MN 55944, (507) 634-2222, www.dcyh.org
Located at Dodge County Fairgrounds.

The Four Seasons Arena, home of the Dodge County Youth Hockey Association, is located on the premises of the Dodge County Fairgrounds and offers a full-sized ice rink with bleachers that can accommodate about 500 people. The rink is open year-round and regularly schedules Open Skate, Open Hockey, and Open Freestyle Skate. Skate rentals are available.

Cost: $
Hours: call for a current schedule

LA CRESCENT
La Crescent Community Arena
531 South 14ᵗʰ Street at Abnet Field, La Crescent, MN 55947, www.lacrescent.com

The La Crescent Community Arena has a full-sized ice rink with spectator seating for about 350 people. The rink offers an Open Skate on designated days from October through March. Skate rentals are available. Please call the arena for more information about the open skating schedule or the learn to skate, figure skating, and hockey programs.

Cost: $
Hours: call for a current schedule

WINONA
Bud King Ice Arena
670 East Front Street, Winona, MN 55987, (507) 454-7775
Located at the end of St. Charles Street along the Mississippi River.

The Bud King Arena is a full-sized hockey arena with spectator seating for approximately 150 people. The arena is open from June through mid-March and serves Winona's youth and adult hockey leagues, a figure skating club, and a co-ed broomball league. The rink also offers open skating to the public. Please call for additional information about these activities. Skate rentals are available.

Cost: $
Hours: call for a current schedule

Figure Skating Organizations

Professional Skater's Association
3006 Allegro Park SW, Rochester, MN 55902, (507) 281-5122,www.skatepsa.com

Rochester is fortunate to be the headquarters for the Professional Skater's Association (PSA). PSA is an international organization responsible for the education and credentialing of skating coaches. Membership is open to figure skating coaches, judges, performing professionals, eligible skaters, and friends or patrons of the sport. The "Blades to Bronze" exhibit, a permanent collection of bronze sculptures at the PSA headquarters, depicts the accomplishments of well-known skaters. Visitors are welcome to view the sculptures during office hours (Monday–Friday, 8 a.m.–5 p.m.).

Rochester Figure Skating Club
21 Elton Hills Drive NW, Rochester, MN 55901, (507) 288-7536, www.web-site.com/rfsc

The Rochester Figure Skating Club (RFSC), an affiliate of the United Skates Figure Skating Association, offers instructional classes for all ages and skill levels as well as professional coaching for competitive skaters interested in singles, dance, precision, and synchronized skating. Call the RFSC or check out their website for more information about their classes and competitive skating programs. Please see Chapter 19 for more information about RFSC Annual Ice Show.

Outdoor Hockey Rinks

Rochester Park and Recreation Department
201 4th Street SE, Room 150, Rochester, MN 55904, (507) 281-6160, www.ci.rochester.mn.us/park

The Rochester Park and Recreation Department maintains several outdoor hockey rinks from late December through February. The rinks are lighted for night skating and all have warming houses. The public is welcome to use these rinks for open skating when there is not a hockey game. Please contact Rochester Park and Recreation for more information about the hockey rinks. Use of the rinks is free.

Allendale Park
3000 block of 18th Avenue NW, Rochester, MN 55901

Cooke Park
7th Street and 7th Avenue NW, Rochester, MN 55901

Manor Park
3rd Street and 42nd Avenue NW, Rochester, MN 55901

Mayo High School
1420 11th Avenue SE, Rochester, MN 55904

Nachreiner Park
22nd Street and 25th Avenue NW, Rochester, MN 55901

Northern Heights Park
22nd Street and 10th Avenue NW, Rochester, MN 55906

Viking Park
26th Street and 2nd Avenue NW, Rochester, MN 55901

Zumbro Park South
5th Avenue and Mayowood Road SW, Rochester, MN 55902

Outdoor Ice Skating Rinks

Rochester Park and Recreation Department
201 4th Street SE, Room 150, Rochester, MN 55904, (507) 281-6160, www.ci.rochester.mn.us/park

The Rochester Park and Recreation Department maintains a couple of public skating rinks from late December through February. These outdoor rinks are designated for skating only. No hockey is permitted. The rinks are lighted for night skating and have warming houses. Please contact Rochester Park and Recreation for more information about the skating rinks. Use of the rinks is free.

Mayo High School
1420 11th Avenue SE, Rochester, MN 55904

Northern Heights Park
22nd Street and 10th Avenue NW, Rochester, MN 55906

Warming House Hours: Mondays–Thursdays, 4:30 p.m.–8 p.m.; Saturdays, 10 a.m.–5 p.m.; Sunday, noon–5 p.m.
Holiday Hours: December 24, 10 a.m.–3 p.m.; December 25, closed; December 26–30, 10 a.m.–3 p.m.; December 31, 10 a.m.–3 p.m.; January 1, closed

Sledding and Toboggan Hills

Hills designated for sledding and tobogganing in and around Rochester are available at the city and state parks listed below. Warming facilities are only available at Frontenac State Park.

Rochester Parks
Eastwood Golf Course
305 Eastwood Road SE, Rochester, MN 55904, (507) 281-6160, www.ci.rochester.mn.us/park

Essex Park
5455 West River Road NW, Rochester, MN 55901, (507) 281-6160, www.ci.rochester.mn.us/park

Judd Park
3rd Street and 36th Avenue NW, Rochester, MN 55901, (507) 281-6160, www.ci.rochester.mn.us/park

State Parks

Carley State Park
c/o Whitewater State Park, Route 1, Box 256, Altura, MN 55910, (507) 932-3007
Located 4 miles south of Plainview on Wabasha County Road 4.

Frontenac State Park
29223 County Road 28 Boulevard, Lake City, MN 55041, (651) 345-3401
Located 10 miles southeast of Red Wing on U.S. Hwy. 61, turn left on County Road 2.

Great River Bluffs State Park
Route 4, Winona, MN 55987, (507) 643-6849
From the north, take U.S. Hwy. 61 about 12 miles southeast of Winona to County Road 3.
Park entrance will be 4 miles down the road. From I-90, take exit 266 (County Roads 12 and
3) and follow the signs to the park.

Snow Tubing at Ironwood Springs Christian Ranch
RR 1, Stewartville, MN 55967, Information & Reservations, (507) 533-4315, 888-533-4316,
www.ironwoodsprings.com

Snow tubing on the steep hill at Ironwood Springs Christian Ranch is a thrilling
experience for children, youth, and adults. Two hours of snow tubing at Ironwood
Springs includes the use of a tube, tow rope, and warming house. Hot water is provided in the warming house, but visitors must bring their own snacks, hot chocolate
mix, and cups. Reservations are required.

Snowshoeing

Rochester Park and Recreation Department
201 4th Street SE, 150 City Hall, Rochester, MN 55904, (507) 281-6160, www.ci.rochester.mn.us/park

Snowshoeing is permitted throughout the Rochester park system, except on
groomed cross-country ski trails. Snowshoes may be rented at Quarry Hill Park &
Nature Center [701 Silver Creek Road NE, Rochester, MN 55906,
(507) 281-6114, www.rochester.k12.mn.us/quarryhill] or Tyrol Ski & Sports [1923
2nd Street SW, Rochester, MN 55902, (507) 288-1683, www.tyrolskishop.com].

Please see Chapter 16, Parks, for a complete listing of Rochester parks and their
locations.

Olmsted County Parks
Snowshoeing is permitted on the grounds of Chester Woods Park and Oxbow Park.
These Olmsted County Parks are in close proximity to Rochester and provide a
backcountry setting for those wanting to snowshoe amid the peaceful surroundings of
nature. Chester Woods Park requires the purchase of a daily or annual park permit and
does not have snowshoe rentals or warming facilities. Oxbow Park does not require
an entrance fee and rents snowshoes on weekends from noon to 3 p.m. or by appointment. Snowshoers may warm up in the small nature center located in the park.

Chester Woods Park
8378 Hwy. 14 East, Eyota, MN 55934, (507) 285-7050,
www.olmstedpublicworks.com, e-mail: chesterw@venturecs.net

Cost: $
Hours: daily, 7 a.m.–10 p.m.

Oxbow Park

5731 County Road 105 NW (@ Olmsted 4 & 5 intersection), Byron, MN 55920,
(507) 775-2451, www.olmstedpublicworks.com, e-mail: oxbow@venurecs.net

Cost: free, $ for snowshoe rental
Hours: park: 7 a.m.–10 p.m.
  nature center: noon–4 p.m.

Snowhoeing at Southeastern Minnesota State Parks

Snowshoeing is permitted in all southeastern Minnesota State Parks. Snowshoe
rentals are only available at Great River Bluffs State Park and Whitewater State Park.
State Parks with warming facilities include Beaver Creek Valley, Forestville/Mystery
Cave, Frontenac, Rice Lake, and Whitewater.

Beaver Creek Valley State Park

RR 2, Caledonia, MN 55921, (507) 724-2107
From I-90, drive south on State Hwy. 76 for 24 miles, then take Houston County Road 1 west
for 4 miles.

Carley State Park

c/o Whitewater State Park, Route 1, Box 256, Altura, MN 55910, (507) 932-3007
Located 4 miles south of Plainview on Wabasha County Road 4.

Forestville/Mystery Cave State Park

Route 2, Box 128, Preston, MN 55965, main park: (507) 352-5111, cave: (507) 937-3251
Located 4 miles south of State Hwy. 16 on Fillmore County Road 5, then 2 miles east on
Fillmore County Road 118.

Frontenac State Park

29223 County Road 28 Boulevard, Lake City, MN 55041, (651) 345-3401
Located 10 miles southeast of Red Wing on U.S. Hwy. 61, turn left on County Road 2.

Great River Bluffs State Park

Route 4, Winona, MN 55987, (507) 643-6849
From the north, take U.S. Hwy. 61 about 12 miles southeast of Winona to County Road 3.
Park entrance will be 4 miles down the road. From I-90, take exit 266 (County Roads 12 and
3) and follow the signs to the park.

Lake Louise State Park

12385 766 Avenue, LeRoy, MN 55951, (507) 324-5249
Located 1½ miles north of LeRoy on County Road 14.

John A. Latsch State Park

c/o Whitewater State Park, Route 1, Box 256, Altura, MN 55910, (507) 932-3007
Travel north from Winona on U.S. Hwy. 61 for approximately 12 miles.

Rice Lake State Park

Route 3, Owatonna, MN 55060, (507) 455-5871
Located 7 miles east of Owatonna on Rose Street.

Whitewater State Park

RR 1, Box 256, Altura, MN 55910, (507) 932-3007
Located 3 miles south of Elba on State Hwy. 74.

Snowmobiling

There are hundreds—if not thousands—of miles of snowmobile trails throughout southeastern Minnesota. Snowmobile enthusiasts may obtain trail maps and information about snowmobile laws, licenses, and safety training from the Minnesota Department of Natural Resources. Contact the DNR at DNR Information Center, 500 Lafayette Road, St. Paul, MN 55155-4040, (651) 296-6157, 888-MINNDNR (646-6367), www.dnr.state.mn.us

The Minnesota United Snowmobilers Association (MnUSA), a state-wide organization, is also an excellent resource for snowmobilers seeking information about the sport. MnUSA provides snowmobilers with up-to-date news, trip planners, trail maps, locations and conditions, safety training, a calendar of events, a list of snowmobile clubs throughout the state, classified ads and more. Contact the MnUSA at Minnesota United Snowmobilers Association, 7040 Lakeland Avenue North, Suite 212, Brooklyn Park, MN 55428 or visit their website at www.mnsnowmobiler.org

Southeastern Minnesota State Parks that maintain snowmobile trails include Forestville/Mystery Cave, Frontenac, Lake Louise, and Rice Lake. Additional information about these parks may be found throughout this chapter or in Chapter 16, Parks. A list of snowmobile clubs in southeastern Minnesota may be found in Chapter 23, Special Interest Groups and Clubs.

Snowmobile Challenge Cup

Coffee Mill Ski Area, Hwys. 60 & 61, Wabasha, MN 55981, (651) 565-2777, www.coffeemillski.com

The Snowmobile Challenge Cup, held at Coffee Mill Ski Area in mid-December, features amateur and semi-professional snowmobile races in 22 different age and specialty divisions. Top racers from throughout the Midwest as well as beginners compete for cash and prizes. Please call (651) 388-5513 for more information or to register for the races. Food and beverages are available at this event.

Part VI:
Bits & Pieces

Chapter 21: Birthday Party Places provides a guide of interesting venues that have special activities for children's birthday parties and/or birthday party packages.

Chapter 22: Health, Wellness, & Spiritual Resources includes health education resources and alternative healing providers as well as retreat centers and camps.

Chapter 23: Special Interest Groups & Clubs is an extensive list of groups and clubs in the area.

Chapter 24: Unique Shopping highlights a handful of unique shopping opportunities in the southeastern Minnesota area.

Rochester Community Education and PAIIR (Parents Are Important In Rochester)

Rochester's Community Education and PAIIR programs are second to none. PAIIR offers parenting classes and workshops as well as parent/child classes for those with a child or children between birth and kindergarten age. Community Education serves the community with adult, youth and preschool enrichment classes and programs. There are hundreds of classes to choose from in a variety of areas including art, music, theater, business, communications, foreign language, computers, food & entertaining, gardening & plants, health & safety, leisure, hobbies & crafts, nature, parenting & family, self-improvement, community awareness, sports, trips & tours and much more. Adult and family literacy, English as a Second Language, G.E.D. preparation, Rochester After School Program (RAP), School Age Child Care (SACC), and classes for adults with disabilities are also available. Contact Rochester Community Education and PAIIR at the Northrop Education Center, 201 8th Street NW, Rochester, MN 55901, (507) 285-8350, www.rochester.k12.mn.us/community-ed.

Chapter 21: Birthday Party Places

The following businesses, clubs, restaurants, and recreational venues offer either children's birthday party packages or welcome patrons to use their facility for parties with advance reservations. Birthday party packages typically include use of the facility/party area and an activity related to the venue. Some establishments require you to bring your own food, beverages, and decorations while others supply these items as part of the party package. Please contact the establishment of your choice for more information about age requirements, birthday party packages and cost.

Arcades

Machine Shed Arcade
Galleria Mall–Centerplace, Rochester, MN 55902, (507) 529-8438

Arts and Crafts

Color Me Mine
3160 Wellner Drive NE, #101, Rochester, MN 55906 (507) 252-0365,
www.rochester.colormemine.com

Michaels Arts and Crafts
60 25th Street SE, Rochester, MN 55904, (507) 285-5947, www.michaels.com

Nordic Gypsy Beads & Jewelry
20 3rd Street SW, Rochester, MN 55902, (507) 288-2258

Athletic Clubs/Gyms

Rochester Area Family YMCA
709 1st Avenue SW, Rochester, MN 55902, (507) 287-2260, www.rochfamy.org

Rochester Athletic Club
3100 19th Street NW, Rochester, MN 55901, (507) 282-6000, www.rochesterathleticclub.com

Rochester-Olmsted Recreation Center
21 Elton Hills Drive, Rochester, MN 55901, (507) 281-6167, www.ci.rochester.mn.us/park

Bowling

Colonial Lanes
1828 14th Street NW, Rochester, MN 55901, (507) 289-2341

Recreation Lanes
2810 North Broadway, Rochester, MN 55906, (507) 288-2601

Golf/Miniature Golf

Foxes Mini Golf
1030 Bailey Avenue, Wabasha, MN 55981, (651) 565-4330

Links of Byron
222 2nd Avenue, Byron, MN 55920, (507) 775-2004

Miniature Golf at the L.A.R.K.
P.O. Box 39, Lark Lane, Kellogg, MN 55945, (507) 767-3387, www.larktoys.com

Putter's Paradise at Recreation Lanes
2810 North Broadway, Rochester, MN 55906, (507) 288-2602

Rochester Indoor Golf Center
2700 West Country Club Road, Rochester, MN 55903, (507) 288-4851
Located 1 mile west of Saint Mary's Hospital.

Skyline Raceway
2250 40th Street SW, Rochester, MN 55902, (507) 287-6289

Gymnastics

Kathy's All-American Training Center
191 County Road 11 NW, Pine Island, MN 55963, (507) 356-8933, (507) 635-5446

Rochester Area Gymnastics Academy—RAGA
4430 19th Street NW, Rochester, MN 55901, (507) 285-9262, www.ragagym.org

Horseback/Pony Rides

Ironwood Springs Christian Ranch
7291 County Road 6 SW, Stewartville, MN 55976, (507) 533-9933 (stables), 888-533-4316 or
(507) 533-4315 (information and reservations), www.ironwoodsprings.com, e-mail: iscr2000@aol.com

Riverside Trails
Rock Dell, MN 55920, (507) 285-5223
Call for directions.

Ice Skating

Rochester-Olmsted Recreation Center
21 Elton Hills Drive, Rochester, MN 55901, (507) 281-6167, www.ci.rochester.mn.us/park

Nature Centers

Quarry Hill Park and Nature Center
701 Silver Creek Road NE, Rochester, MN 55906, (507) 281-6114,
www.rochester.k12.mn.us/quarryhill

Restaurants with Arcade or Play Areas

McDonald's Playplace
1306 Apache Drive SW, Rochester, MN 55902, (507) 288-2264

Mr. Pizza
1729 South Broadway, Rochester, MN 55902, (507) 288-1488

Rock Climbing

Prairie Walls Climbing Gym
4420 19th Street NW, Rochester, MN 55901, (507) 292-0511, www.prairiewalls.com

Roller Skating

Harmony Roller Rink
Hwy. 52 North, Harmony, MN 55939, (507) 886-4444

Owatonna Roller Rink
120 18th Street SW, Owatonna, MN 55060, (507) 451-9871, office: (507) 455-9731, www.owatonnarollerrink.com

United Skates Roller Skating Center
Corner of SE Market and SE Railway Streets, Brownsdale, MN 55918, (507) 567-2539

Snow Tubing

Ironwood Springs Christian Ranch
7291 County Road 6 SW, Stewartville, MN 55976, (507) 533-9933 (stables), 888-533-4316 or (507) 533-4315 (information and reservations), www.ironwoodsprings.com, e-mail: iscr2000@aol.com

Swimming

Rochester Area Family YMCA
709 1st Avenue SW, Rochester, MN 55902, (507) 287-2260, www.rochfamy.org

Rochester Athletic Club
3100 19th Street NW, Rochester, MN 55901, (507) 282-6000, www.rochesterathleticclub.com

Rochester-Olmsted Recreation Center
21 Elton Hills Drive, Rochester, MN 55901, (507) 281-6167, www.ci.rochester.mn.us/park

Tea Rooms

Victorian Lace Inn Tea Room
1512 Whitewater Avenue, St. Charles, MN 55972, (507) 932-4496

Tennis

Rochester Indoor Tennis Club
2700 West Country Club Road, Rochester, MN 55902, (507) 288-4851

Theaters

Chateau Theatres
971 East Circle Drive, Rochester, MN 55906, (507) 536-7469, www.chateautheatres.com

Toy Stores

The L.A.R.K. Toy Company
P.O. Box 39, Kellogg, MN 55945, (507) 767-3387, www.larktoys.com

Chapter 22: Health, Wellness & Spiritual Resources

ROCHESTER
Assisi Community Center
1001 14th Street NW, Suite 200, Rochester, MN 55901, (507) 280-2180, www.acomc.org

Assisi Community Center (ACC) is a nonprofit retreat and conference center located at the Assisi Heights Convent. The convent is situated on a 100-acre landscape of rolling hills overlooking the city of Rochester. The facilities and grounds provide an idyllic setting and supportive environment for ACC programs, retreats, and conferences. People of all faiths and social conditions are invited to come to ACC for quiet reflection, healing, and spiritual renewal. A diverse selection of one-day workshops, conferences, and overnight retreats are offered throughout the year as well as a Solitude Wing, Rustic Hermitage, and Meditation Center for personal retreats. Centering Prayer, Peacemaking, A Journey of Loss and Hope, Discovering Your Inner Treasures, Men's and Women's Retreats, Lenten Retreats, a Hilltop Retreat for Persons with Cancer, Yoga, Qi-Gong, Life Purpose, Simplicity and Solitude, and Intuition and Creativity for Spiritual Enhancement are just some of the workshops and retreats that have been offered. Additional on-site facilities and services include an outdoor Labyrinth walk, Integrative Therapies–a Spiritual Holistic Healing Center, the Assisi Creativity Center, Justice and Peace Network, and a library with spiritual resources and materials. Conference rooms, overnight facilities, and food service is also available. Please contact ACC for a calendar of events, conference planning and scheduling, or to make arrangements for a personal or group retreat.

Cost: varies by service
Hours: Monday–Friday, 8 a.m.–4:40 p.m. and by appointment

Calvary Episcopal Church
3rd Ave. & 2nd Street SW, Rochester, MN 55902, (507) 282-9429, www.calvary-rochester.org

Calvary Episcopal Church was originally built during the Civil War between 1862–1863. As Rochester's oldest church, it is now surrounded by the Mayo Clinic campus in the heart of downtown Rochester. In 1987, Calvary Episcopal began to view its presence as spiritual oasis amid the hustle and bustle of the city and started an outreach program, the Oasis Courtyard Series, for residents and visitors of the area. The Oasis Courtyard Series features two summer programs that take place outdoors in a lush grassy area surrounded by colorful gardens. Tuesdays in the Courtyard focus on a program of meditative arts and relaxation. Participants are provided with the opportunity to partake in meditative and relaxation exercises such as yoga, Qi-gong, Tai Chi, Rieke, and guided imagery. On Thursdays, the Courtyard series offers noontime vocal and instrumental concerts, storytelling, theatrical performances, poetry readings, and more. The program presents a wide variety of musical styles from folk to classical to jazz and everything in between. The summer programs are held in the Calvary Episcopal Church Courtyard on Tuesdays and Thursdays at noon. In the event of inclement weather, events are held inside the church. All programs are free and open to the public, and audience members are invited to bring a lunch. Please note that the church sanctuary is open daily from 8 a.m.–9 p.m. for meditation, prayer, rest, and reflection. Call the church or visit their website for a current schedule of programs.

Cost: free
Hours: sanctuary: open daily, 8 a.m.–9 p.m.
  oasis programs: Tuesdays and Thursdays, noon (summer only)

Integrative Therapies

1001 14th Street NW, Suite 250, Rochester, MN 55901, (507) 280-2191, www.integrative.org

Integrative Therapies is a nonprofit Spiritual Holistic Healing Center with the mission to "serve all who desire a holistic approach to life by affirming the value of all persons, supporting their quest for wholeness, and exemplifying love and healing." The center is located at Assisi Heights in northwest Rochester and is staffed by certified and/or licensed practitioners. Multi-disciplinary services available at Integrative Therapies include therapeutic massage, homeopathy, acupuncture, Rieki, healing touch, Chinese (Tui-Na) massage, transformational counseling, spiritual direction, and mediation counseling. Integrative Therapies also offers classes and workshops related to these healing arts through the Assisi Community Center. Please contact Integrative Therapies for more information or to schedule an appointment with a practitioner.

Cost: varies by service
Hours: Monday–Friday, 8:30 a.m.–5 p.m.; evening and Saturday appointments are
  available

Mayo Clinic Patient and Health Education Center

Mayo Medical Center, Siebens Building–Subway Level, 200 1st Street SW, Rochester, MN 55905, (507) 284-8140, (507) 284-2511, www.mayo.edu or www.mayoclinic.org

The Mayo Clinic Patient and Health Education Center is open to Mayo Clinic patients and their families, Rochester residents and visitors as well as Mayo Medical Center employees. Resources available at the center include a staff of health educators, library, health education classes, and medical exhibits and displays. The library is equipped with books (may be checked out), health-related journals, newsletters, magazines, educational pamphlets and brochures, videos, CD-ROMS, and multimedia programs for interactive patient education. Health education classes routinely scheduled at the center include Asthma, Breast Self-Examination, Care of the Back, Chronic Fatigue Syndrome, Fibromyalgia, Lifestyle for a Healthy Heart, How to Measure Your Blood Pressure, Hypertension, Managing Your Weight, Menopause, Preparing for Surgery, Rheumatoid Arthritis, Skills for Injecting Medication, Stress Management, Testicle Self-Examination, and Wise Exercise. Asthma and Preparing for Surgery classes are also available for children. Class registration is required. The Mayo Clinic Cancer Education Center, located in the Gonda Building, is an additional resource that is invaluable for those seeking information, education, and support for cancer-related diseases.

Cost: free, fee for classes
Hours: Health Education Center: Monday–Friday, 8:30 a.m.–5:30 p.m.
  Cancer Center: Monday–Friday, 8 a.m.–5 p.m.

The Mustard Seed Christian Center
Little Faith Ministries, P.O. Box 7032, Rochester, MN 55903, (507) 285-4851,
www.LittleFaithMinistries.org
The Mustard Seed is located off North Broadway Avenue at 11 9th Street NE in Rochester.

The Mustard Seed Christian Center, an outreach ministry of Little Faith Ministries, opened its doors to the Rochester community in February 2002. The Mustard Seed offers a wholesome gathering place with a Christian atmosphere for children, youth, and adults. Concerts, Family Nights, Single's Nights, seminars, Bible studies, and children's story times are some of the events featured on the Mustard Seed's monthly calendar. It's a great place to meet new friends, listen to music, play a game, share a snack, or just spend time together with family and friends. All are invited to join in the fun and fellowship at the Mustard Seed, and ideas for new events are always welcome. The Mustard Seed's 1,000-square-foot facility is available for use by groups and families on a first come, first served basis. Please call or visit the website for a current event schedule or to obtain more information about having your group event at the Mustard Seed.

Cost: by donation
Hours: call for a current schedule

FRONTENAC
Villa Maria Retreat and Conference Center
29847 County 2 Boulevard, Frontenac, MN 55026, (651) 345-4582, www.villamariaretreats.org

Villa Maria Retreat and Conference Center is situated on 169 acres of woods, prairies, and meadows in Old Frontenac with views of Lake Pepin and its surrounding bluffs. The interfaith retreat center is sponsored by the Ursuline Sisters "for the purpose of assisting people in their spiritual and personal search for God." In addition to offering its own programs and retreats, Villa Maria hosts retreats and meetings for visiting groups. Villa Maria's Marian and Ursuline Halls, a residential building and conference center, respectively, are modern facilities with a full range of amenities. Amenities at Marian Hall include overnight accommodations for up to 100 people, family-style meal service, a chapel, meeting rooms, library, gym, stage, and heated indoor pool. Ursuline Hall, an octagon shaped building with full surround windows and high wood-beamed ceilings, serves as the main conference center. Outdoor amenities include a Labyrinth and easy access to Frontenac State Park with opportunities for walking, hiking, cross-country skiing, birding, and more. This facility is fully equipped with modern audio-visual equipment, internet hookups, and teleconferencing capabilities along with an old-fashioned fireplace, piano, and patio with swings. In addition to this, Camp Villa Maria provides guests with the opportunity to choose a more rustic experience or less expensive option at the retreat center. Camp facilities include a lodge, one year-round cabin, and a three-season cabin. The Villa Maria Calendar of Retreats offers a wide variety of programs throughout the year. Individually directed retreats, A Taste of Contemplative Seeing, Lasting Peace, Art as a Spiritual Practice. Couples', Men's, and Journaling Retreats are a sample of the retreats that have been offered. Please call for a current retreat schedule or to obtain more information about having your event at Villa Maria.

Cost: varies by program
Hours: Monday–Friday, 9 a.m.–5 p.m.; Saturday–Sunday, by chance

JANESVILLE
Holy Spirit Retreat Center
3864 420th Avenue, Janesville, MN 56048, (507) 234-5712, www.acomc.org

Holy Spirit Retreat Center, an affiliate of Assisi Heights in Rochester, is sponsored and operated by the Sisters of the Saint Francis. The retreat center is situated on 30 wooded acres along the shores of Lake Elysian. The natural beauty of the area provides a nurturing environment for individuals and groups seeking spiritual growth and renewal. Facilities at Holy Spirit include a retreat center with a lounge, fully equipped kitchen, dining room, conference room, chapel, and overnight accommodations for up to 30 people. The Lower Level of the Sister's residence is available for small groups and has four bedrooms, a living room, kitchen, dining area, and bathroom. Holy Spirit also offers the La Foresta Hermitage for personal retreats and solitude. The one-room cabin with modern amenities has large, open windows with lake views and easy access to walking paths, bike and cross-country ski trails, and an outdoor labyrinth. Please note that individuals and groups using the retreat facilities for their own events must bring and prepare their own food. A wide variety of day and overnight retreats and conferences are available throughout the year. Retreat topics have included Forgiveness in an Unforgiving World, Journey with Women in Scripture, Living from the Heart of Prayer, Centering Prayer, Advent, and the Sacred Labyrinth. Please contact Holy Spirit Retreat Center for more information or to obtain a current schedule of retreats and conferences.

Cost: varies by program
Hours: weekday hours, by chance

SPRING VALLEY
Good Earth Village
Route 1, Box 258, Spring Valley, MN 55975, (507) 346-2494, www.goodearthvillage.org

Good Earth Village (GEV), a Christian outdoor ministry and camp, is owned and supported by approximately 130 church congregations in southeastern Minnesota. The mission of Good Earth Village is "to be a place where the body of Christ is strengthened as people bear witness to Christ, care for creation, and live and learn in an environment of God's Grace." The camp is situated on 500 acres among the rolling hills, prairies, and woodlands of rural Spring Valley, Minnesota. Barr Lodge, a modern facility with a rustic atmosphere, is the hub of GEV. The multi-purpose building has a fully equipped kitchen, meeting and dining space, a fireplace, piano, bathroom facilities, and a lounge area. GEV offers a variety of overnight accommodations including Hilltop cabins and a family campground with easy access to modern bathroom with showers as well as Old Town and the Covered Wagons, which have more primitive living quarters and outhouses. Outdoor chapels, hiking trails, a creek, small petting zoo, a craft shack and canteen area are some of the amenities located throughout GEV. The new Log Lodge at GEV will celebrate its grand opening during the summer of 2003. The fully modern lodge will provide comfortable overnight accommodations with handicapped accessibility for guests and visitors. In addition to providing an outdoor ministry with children and youth camps throughout the summer, GEV has a full schedule of year-round programs and events. These events have included Family Fall Festivals, Youth Blast, Quilter's Retreats, Youth Director's Getaways, Winter Fun Days, Christmas Cookie

Exchanges, Family Camps, Trout Fishing Retreats, and Confirmation Kick-Offs. GEV facilities and food services are also available for rental by visiting groups and organizations. Please contact GEV for more information or to obtain a schedule of camps, retreats, and programs.

Cost: varies by program
Hours: Monday–Friday, 8:30 a.m.–4 p.m.; Saturday–Sunday, by chance

STEWARTVILLE
Ironwood Springs Christian Ranch
7291 County Road 6 SW, Stewartville, MN 55976, (507) 533-9933 (stables), 888-533-4316 or (507) 533-4315 (information and reservations), www.ironwoodsprings.com, e-mail: iscr2000@aol.com

Ironwood Springs Christian Ranch, a nonprofit, nondenominational year-round camp, is located in rural Stewartville along the Root River on 200 rural, wooded acres. The camp's mission is "to provide an atmosphere and opportunity for adults and children to get to know themselves, others and God better. We strive to do this through our lives, words, and activities." Facilities at Ironwood Springs include the Main Lodge, cabins, a dormitory, Log Chapel, and a campground. Situated in a shady, wooded area west of the Main Lodge, the campground has 26 electric and 7 nonelectric sites. In addition to this, Edgewood Park, another area of the Ranch, has 12 open, electrical sites. The campground is equipped with flush toilets, hot showers, public phones, firewood (for sale), and a dump station. Recreational amenities at Ironwood Springs include a recreation center in the Main Lodge, an outdoor swimming pool, playgrounds, tennis courts, basketball courts, a miniature farm with animals, horse stables, and walking and hiking trails. Riverview Lodge is currently under construction at the Ranch and will be a modern, handicapped-accessible facility with extensive overnight accommodations, an indoor swimming pool and spa, and a large meeting room. Ironwood Springs offers horse-related summer camps for children and youth, the National Wheelchair Sports and Recreation Camp, Family Camps, S.O.A.R. (Spiritual Outdoor Adventure Retreat), an off-site camping experience for boys, and Camp Jornada for kids with cancer and their families. Saturday Nite Concerts performed by Christian musicians are also held at the Ranch from late May through Labor Day weekend at 7 p.m. in the Log Chapel. Other events held throughout the year include the Lumberjack Weekend, Quilter's Retreat, Annual Pancake Supper, Open Houses, a Benefit Auction and more. Ironwood Springs welcomes groups and organizations to rent their facilities. Call the camp to request a brochure or newsletter, obtain a current schedule of camps and programs, or make reservations for your special event.

Chapter 23: Special Interest Groups & Clubs

Archery

Rochester Archery Club
P.O. Box 6701, Rochester, MN 55903, www.rochesterarcheryclub.com

Arts and Crafts

Michaels Kid's Club
Michaels Arts and Crafts, 60 25th Street SE, Rochester, MN 55904, (507) 285-5947,
www.michaels.com
Located adjacent to Walmart Super Center in south Rochester.

Moon's Craft Shop
Miracle Mile Mini Mall, 104 16th Avenue NW, Rochester, MN 55901, (507) 288-2199

Automobiles

Antique Automobile Club of America
Rochester, MN 55901, (507) 281-1097, www.aaca.org/hiawatha

Birding

Hiawatha Valley Audubon Society
Winona, MN 55987, www.hvas.org or e-mail webmaster@hvas.org

Rochester Area Companion Bird Club
(507) 533-8440, e-mail: mikefrench@charter.net

Zumbro Valley Audubon Society
P.O. Box 6244, Rochester, MN 55903, www.zumbrovalleyaudubon.org

Boating

Lake City Yacht Club
Lake City Yacht Club Marina, Lake City, MN 55041, www.lakecityyachtclub.com

Book Clubs

Barnes & Noble Booksellers
15 1st Street SW, Rochester, MN 55902, (507) 288-3848, www.bn.com
Located by the Galleria Mall in downtown Rochester.

Barnes & Noble Booksellers
1425 Apache Mall, Rochester, MN 55902, (507) 281-7950, www.bn.com
Located at Rochester's Apache Mall.

Rochester Public Library
101 2nd Street SE, Rochester, MN 55904, (507) 285-8000; www.rochesterpubliclibrary.org

Bowling

Rochester Area Bowling Association
Rochester, MN, (507) 282-8314

Rochester Women's Bowling Association
Rochester, MN, (507) 287-6575, www.bowl.com

Bridge

Four Seasons Duplicate Bridge Club
Realife Cooperative Recreation Room, 875 Essex Parkway NW, Rochester, MN 55901, (507) 282-3736
Meets Wednesday afternoons at 12:30.

Rochester Duplicate Bridge Club
Comfort Inn, 1625 South Broadway Avenue, Rochester, MN 55904, (507) 288-0896, (507) 289-8421
Meets Mondays and Fridays.

Senior Citizen's Duplicate Bridge Club
Rochester Senior Citizen's Center, 121 North Broadway, Rochester, MN 55906, (507) 287-1404,
(507) 282-3736
Meets on Monday afternoons at 1 p.m.

Business

American Business Women's Association
P.O. Box 6903, Rochester, MN 55903, www.abwahq.org

Downtown Business Association
P.O. Box 416, Rochester, MN 55903, (507) 287-3577, (507) 285-8233

Service Corps of Retired Executives—SCORE
220 South Broadway, Suite 100, Rochester, MN 55904, (507) 288-1122, www.score.org

Canine Clubs

North American Versatile Hunting Dog Association—NAVHDA
(507) 775-7115, www.navhda.org

Rochester Dog Obedience Club
Rochester, MN, (507) 288-5050, (507) 289-9221, www.rdocmn.org

Rochester Minnesota Kennel Club
P.O. Box 5803, Rochester, MN 55903, (507) 282-0089, rmkc.8m.com

Rochester Retired Greyhounds as Pets—REGAP
Rochester, MN, (507) 287-0478

Ceramics

Color Me Mine
3160 Wellner Drive NE, #101, Rochester, MN 55906 (507) 252-0365,
www.rochester.colormemine.com

M & W Ceramics
3875 Collegeview Road East, Rochester, MN 55904, (507) 282-5663

Warehouse Ceramics
RR 1, Box 50A, Racine, MN 55967, (507) 378-2295

Chess

Rochester Chess Club
Peace United Church of Christ, 1503 2nd Avenue NE, Rochester, MN 55906, (507) 282-6117

Christian

Christian Women's Club of Rochester
Rochester, MN, (507) 367-2194, RochesterCWC@aol.com

Community Bible Study
Christ United Methodist Church, 400 5th Avenue SW, Rochester, MN 55902, (507) 289-4019
Located at the corner of 4th Avenue & 4th Street SW.

Interfaith Community Network
Mt. Olive Lutheran Church, 2830 18th Avenue NW, Rochester, MN 55901, (507) 281-3122,
(507) 288-1580

Little Faith Ministries
P.O. Box 7032, Rochester, MN 55903, (507) 285-4851, www.LittleFaithMinistries.org

Christian Youth

Camp Victory
RR1, Box 154, Zumbro Falls, MN 55903, (507) 843-2329, www.campvictory.com,
e-mail: info@campvictory.com

Good Earth Village
Route 1, Box 258, Spring Valley, MN 55975, (507) 346-2494, www.goodearthvillage.org

Ironwood Springs Christian Ranch
7291 County Road 6 SW, Stewartville, MN 55976, (507) 533-9933 (stables), 888-533-4316 or
(507) 533-4315 (information and reservations), www.ironwoodsprings.com, e-mail: iscr2000@aol.com

Rochester Area Youth for Christ
P.O. Box 1164, Rochester, MN 55903, (507) 288-4567

Young Life
12 Elton Hills Drive NW, Rochester, MN 55901, (507) 281-9797

Coin and Stamp Collecting

Rochester Area Coin and Stamp Club
P.O. Box 7323, Rochester, MN 55903, (507) 289-5280

Conservation and Sportsmen's Clubs

Byron Sportsmen & Conservation Club
Box 592, County Road 15, Byron, MN 55920, (507) 634-4577, www.geocities.com/byronsc_55920

Chatfield Fish & Game Club
Box 392, Chatfield, MN 55923

Ducks Unlimited
P.O. Box 475, Rochester, MN 55903, (507) 282-9968

Izaak Walton League
P.O. Box 43, Rochester, MN 55906, (507) 753-2718
Izaak Walton Cabin, 937 7th Avenue NE, Rochester, MN 55906

Pheasants Forever
877-773-2070, www.pheasantsforever.org

Pine Island White Pines Sportsman Club
Hwy. 52 North, Pine Island, MN 55963, (507) 356-4823

Southern Minnesota Sportsman's Club
6251 20th Street SE, Rochester, MN 55904, (507) 282-9808, www.smsclub.org

Stewartville Sportsman Club
County Road 6 West, Stewartville, MN 55976, (507) 533-6660

Cycling

Cycling Club of Rochester
1409 South Broadway, Rochester, MN 55904, (507) 281-5007, www.rasc-mn.org

Dance

Rochester Area Square and Round Dancing
Square Dance Federation of Minnesota, www.squaredanceminnesota.com

Southern Minnesota Chapter of the United States Amateur Ballroom Dancers Association—USABDA
P.O. Box 7354, Rochester, MN 55903, (507) 281-1034, www.usabda.org

Tango Society of Minnesota
www.mntango.org

Disabilities

Ironwood Springs Christian Ranch
7291 County Road 6 SW, Stewartville, MN 55976, (507) 533-9933 (stables), 888-533-4316 or (507) 533-4315 (information and reservations), www.ironwoodsprings.com, e-mail: iscr2000@aol.com

PossAbilities of Southern Minnesota
1808 3rd Avenue SE, Rochester, MN 55904, (507) 281-6116, www.possabilities.org

Rochester Adaptive Recreation Program
Rochester Park and Recreation Department, 201 4th Street SE, Room 150, Rochester, MN 55904, (507) 281-6160, (507) 287-7980, www.ci.rochester.mn.us/park

Rochester Area Disabled Athletics and Recreation—RADAR
539 North Broadway, Rochester, MN 55906, (507) 280-6995, http://radarsports.tripod.com

Rochester Area Special Olympics
Adaptive Recreation, Rochester Park and Recreation Department, 201 4th Street SE, Room 150, Rochester, MN 55904, (507) 287-7980, www.ci.rochester.mn.us/par

Diversity/Multicultural

Diversity Council
220 South Broadway, Suite 105, Rochester, MN 55904, (507) 282-9951, www.diversitycouncil.org

Intercultural Mutual Assistance Association
300 11th Avenue NW, Rochester, MN 55901, (507) 289-5960

NAACP
P.O. Box 6472, Rochester, MN 55903, (507) 288-5300

Rochester International Association
300 11th Avenue NW, Rochester, MN 55901, (507) 289-5960, ext. 24

Film

Rochester International Film Group—RIFG
(507) 288-8990, www.rifg.org
Rochester International Association, 300 11th Avenue NW, Rochester, MN 55901, (507) 289-5960, ext. 24

Fishing

Walleye Searchers of Minnesota
P.O. Box 661, Rochester, MN 55903, www.walleyesearchers.com

Flying

Civil Air Patrol
Rochester, MN, (507) 287-6197, www.cap.gov, www.mnwg.cap.gov

Experimental Aircraft Association
Rochester Chapter, Local #100,www.eaa.org or www.eaa100.org
Sponsors Young Eagles program, ages 8 and up.

Southeastern Minnesota Flying Club
Rochester, MN, (507) 288-2676, (507) 271-3402, www.flyingclub.com/rochester

Four Wheeling

Rochester Rough Riders
Rochester, MN. Contact information may be found on www.mn4wda.com under "Club Members."

Gardening

Rochester Garden and Flower Club
Southeast Service Cooperative Building, 210 Woodlake Drive SE, Rochester, MN 55904,
(507) 282-4265, www.dwebsite.com/gardenclub

Genealogy

Olmsted County Genealogical Society
P.O. Box 6411, Rochester, MN 55903, (507) 282-9447, www.olmstedhistory.com

Health and Human Services Resources & Referral

Community Net
903 West Center Street, Rochester, MN 55902, (507) 287-7877, www.c-net.org or dial 211

Hobby Shops

Hendy's Hobby Shop
Miracle Mile Mini Mall, 1601 1ˢᵗ Street NW, Rochester, MN 55901, (507) 281-8321

Southside Speedway and Hobby Shop
2241 Marion Road SE, Rochester, MN 55904, (507) 281-3233, www.southsideracing.com

Horseshoes

Rochester Horseshoe Club
Rochester, MN, (507) 281-2536, www.minnesotahorseshoes.com

Juggling

Rochester Juggling Club
Rochester, MN, (507) 281-6371, www.juggling.org/~RochesterMN, e-mail: RochesterMN@juggling.org

Keyboard

Rochester Area Keyboard Club
Schmitt Music, 1765 U.S. 52 North, Rochester, MN 55901, (507) 288-1960

Library

Friends of the Rochester Public Library
101 2nd Street SE, Rochester, MN 55904, (507) 285-8000, www.rochesterpubliclibrary.org

Magic

Rochester Mystic 13 Magic Club
Rochester, MN, (507) 288-6892, (507) 289-5155, (507) 287-6069
See page 24 for more information.

Metaphysical

Search
P.O. Box 6524, Rochester, MN 55903, www.rochestermn.com/community/search

Model Airplanes

Marion RC Flyers
P.O. Box 8036, Rochester, MN 55903, (507) 281-2678, www.marionrcflyers.org

Rochester Aero Model Society—RAMS
P.O. Box 1853, Rochester, MN 55903, http://members.tripod.com/~rams_mn

Model Trains

Winona Railroad Club
P.O. Box 30143, Winona, MN 55987, www.winonarailroadclub.org

Mothers

La Leche League
Good Shepherd Lutheran Church, Rochester, MN, (507) 289-1748, www.lalecheleague.org

Mothers & More
www.mothersandmore.org

Meets at:
St. Luke's Episcopal Church, 1884 22nd Street NW, Rochester, MN 55901, (507) 288-2469
Sylvan Learning Center, Barlow Plaza, 1129 6th Street NW, Rochester, MN 55901, (507) 292-9270

Mothers of Preschoolers—MOPS

Christ Community Church, 4400 55th Street NW, Rochester, MN 55901, (507) 282-5569,
www.cc-church.org
First Baptist Church, 415 16th Street SW, Rochester, MN 55902, (507) 288-8880, www.firstb.org

Parents Are Important in Rochester—PAIIR

Northrop Community Center, 201 8th Street NW, Rochester, MN 55901, (507) 285-8033,
www.rochester.k12.mn.us/paiir

Southern Minnesota Mothers of Multiples

www.geocities.com/mothersofmultiples or e-mail: se_mn_moms@hotmail.com

Neighborhood Associations

Rochester Neighborhood Resource Center

700 4th Avenue SE, Hawthorne Education Center, Room 301, Rochester, MN 55904, (507) 529-4150,
www.rneighbors.org

New Residents

Rochester Area Chamber of Commerce

220 South Broadway, Suite 100, Rochester, MN 55904, (507) 288-1122

Rochester Greeters

Rochester, MN, (507) 282-9970, www.rochestergreeters.com

Rochester Newcomer's Club

Rochester Area Chamber of Commerce, 220 South Broadway, Suite 100, Rochester, MN 55904,
(507) 288-1122

Parents

Child Care Resource and Referral

126 Woodlake Drive SE, Rochester, MN 55904, (507) 287-1499, 800-462-1660, www.c2r2.org

Crisis Nursery

126 Woodlake Drive SE, Rochester, MN 55904, (507) 287-2020, 800-462-1660, www.c2r2.org

Family Support Network

126 Woodlake Drive SE, Rochester, MN 55904, (507) 287-2020, 800-462-1660, www.c2r2.org

Parents Are Important in Rochester—PAIIR

Northrop Community Center, 201 8th Street NW, Rochester, MN 55901, (507) 285-8033,
www.rochester.k12.mn.us/paiir

Parent's Night Out

First Christian Church, 3108 Hwy. 52 North, Rochester, MN 55901, (507) 282-2126

Rochester Area Solo Parents & Singles

Rochester, MN, (507) 285-0143, (507) 289-6870

Rochester Association of Christian Home Educators
Rochester, MN, www.homeschoolmn.com

Quilting

Quality Sewing Machine Center
111 Civic Center Drive , Rochester, MN 55906, (507) 288-9051

Quilter's Sew-ciety Club
P.O. Box 6245, Rochester, MN 55903, (507) 252-1829, www.qs.freehomepage.com

Radio

Rochester Amateur Radio Club
P.O. Box 1, Rochester, MN 55903, (507) 289-8086, www.rarchams.org

Rowing

Rochester Rowing Club
Box 1072, Rochester, MN 55905, www.rrcmn.com, (507) 289-0989

Scuba & Snorkeling

Rochester Scuba and Snorkel Club
webpages/charter.net/rsouthwick/scubaclub
Call MDC Sports [(507) 288-8802] in Rochester for additional contact information.

Sea Kayaking

Rochester Sea Kayakers Club
Rochester, MN (507) 252-5705

Senior Citizens

Elder Network
1001 14th Street NW, Suite 700, Rochester, MN 55901, (507) 285-5272, www.elder-network.org

Learning Is Forever—LIFE
Elder Hostel Network/LIFE Office, Rochester Community and Technical College, 851 30th Avenue SE, Rochester, MN 55904, (507) 280-3157, (507) 285-7210, www.roch.edu or www.elderhostel.org

Rochester Senior Citizen Center
121 North Broadway, Rochester, MN 55906, (507) 287-1404, www.rochesterseniorcenter.org

Service Clubs

Elks Lodge 1091
917 15th Avenue SE, Rochester, MN 55904, (507) 282-6702

Knights of Columbus
2030 Hwy. 14 East, Rochester, MN 55904, (507) 288-1492

Masonic Lodge
2002 2nd Street SE, Rochester, MN 55904, (507) 282-1820, www.spacestar.net/users/glmn021

Optimist Club
P.O. Box 485, Rochester, MN 55903, (507) 281-0463, dwebsite.com/rochesteroptimistclub

Rochester Civitan
P.O. Box 392, Rochester, MN 55903, www.rochestermn.com/community/civitan, www.civitan.org

Rochester Eagles Club
409 1st Avenue SW, Rochester, MN 55902, (507) 289-5931

Rochester Jaycees
220 South Broadway, Suite 100, Rochester, MN 55904, www.rochesterjaycees.com,
www.MNJaycees.org

Rochester Kiwanis Clubs
Rochester, MN, www.rochesterusa.com/kiwanis, www.mndak-kiwanis.org/rochestergoldenk

Rochester Lions Clubs
Rochester, MN, www.rochester76lions.org, www2.isl.net

Rochester Moose Lodge
915 21st Avenue SE, Rochester, MN 55904, (507) 282-7552

Sertoma 700 Club of Rochester
P.O. Box 721, Rochester, MN 55903, www.rochestermn.com/community/sertoma700,
www.sertoma.org

Sertoma 1200 Club of Rochester
428 3rd Avenue SW, Rochester, MN 55902, www.rochestermn.com/community/sertoma1200,
www.sertoma.org

Sewing

Quality Sewing Machine Center
1111 Civic Center Drive NW, Rochester, MN 55901, (507) 288-9051

Shooting

See Conservation and Sportsmen's Clubs.

Singles' Clubs

Family of Caring Unique Singles—F.O.C.U.S.
Mustard Seed Christian Center, P.O. Box 7032, 11 9th Street NE, Rochester, MN 55903,
(507) 285-4851, www.LittleFaithMinistries.org

Rochester Area Solo Parents & Singles
Rochester, MN, (507) 285-0143

Singles in Agriculture
118 East Front Avenue, Stockton, IL 61085, (815) 947-3559, www.singlesinag.org
Contact the national office for information about the Northern Great Plains Chapter, which includes southern Minnesota.

Single Volunteers of Rochester
Rochester, MN, www.geocities.com/rochsing, e-mail: rochsing@yahoo.com

Skating

Professional Skater's Association
1821 2nd Street SW, Rochester, MN 55902, (507) 281-5122, www.skatepsa.com

Rochester Figure Skating Club
Rochester-Olmsted Recreation Center, 21 Elton Hills Drive, Rochester, MN 55901, (507) 288-7536, www.web-site.com/rfsc

Skiing & Sports Clubs

Rochester Active Sports Club—RASC
Rochester, MN, (507) 287-6358, www.rasc-mn.org

SKILINK™ Ski Club for Kids
Welch Village SKILINK™ Learning Center, Welch, MN 55089, (651) 258-4567
Bus transportation available from Tyrol Ski Shop, 1923 2nd Street SW, Rochester, MN 55902, (507) 288-1683

Traverski Ski & Sports Club
P.O. Box 7094, Rochester, MN 55903, www.isl.net/~feet1st, groups.yahoo.com/group/Traverski

Skydiving

Minnesota Skydiver's Club
Owatonna, MN 55060, (952) 431-1960, www.mnskydive.com

Sled Dog Club

Southern Minnesota Sled Dog Club
Zumbrota, MN 55992, (507) 732-4041, www.mushing.com/clubs.htm

Snowmobiling

Bluff Valley Riders Snowmobile Club
Harmony, MN 55939, (507) 886-2242

Byron Sno-Bears
P.O. Box 743, Byron, MN 55920, (507) 775-2497

Caledonia Sno-Gophers Snowmobile Club
Box 281, Brownsville, MN 55919, (507) 482-6212, (507) 725-SNOW (7669)

Houston Money Creek Snowriders
Money Creek Haven, Houston, MN 55943, (507) 894-4133, (507) 896-3544

La Crescent Snowmobile Club
P.O. Box 54, La Crescent, MN 55947, (507) 895-6363, (507) 895-8364

Spring Grove Snowmobile Club
Spring Grove, MN 55974, (507) 498-3415

Stewartville Driftskippers
Box 41, Stewartville, MN 55976, (507) 533-8168, (507) 533-8166

Trailbusters Snowmobile Club
Route 2, Box 28, Mabel, MN 55954, (507) 493-5369

Tri-County Trail Blazers
P.O. Box 214, Spring Valley, MN 55975

Valley Crest Riders Snowmobile Club
c/o M & M Lawn & Leisure, Rushford, MN 55971, (507) 864-7781

Square Dancing

Square Dance Federation of Minnesota
Rochester Area Square and Round Dance Club, www.squaredanceminnesota.com

Teen Dance—Nightclubs

Aquarius Club
1201 Eastgate Drive SE, Rochester, MN 55904, (507) 281-5229
Call for schedule of teen nights.

The Jungle Sports and Entertainment Complex
Steele County Road 45, Owatonna, MN 55060, (507) 444-9890, www.junglerocks.com
Call for schedule of teen nights.

Mantorville Social Club
421 Clay Street, Mantorville, MN 55955, (507) 635-5922
Call for schedule of teen nights.

Toastmasters (Public Speaking)

Several Toastmasters groups meet at different times and locations throughout Rochester. Please visit www.toastmasters.org to obtain contact information for local chapters.

Track

Rochester Track Club
P.O. Box 6711, Rochester, MN 55903, (507) 282-0451, www.rochestertrackclub.com

Treasure Hunters

Zumbro Valley Treasure Hunters
P.O. Box 6883, Rochester, MN 55903, (507) 288-6567,
www.rochestermn.com/community/treasurehunt

Vegetarian

Vegetarian Information Group of Rochester—V.I.G.O.R.
P.O. Box 253, Rochester, MN 55903, (507) 536-0227, (507) 289-9061, www.vigr.org

Volunteer

American Red Cross
Southeast Minnesota Chapter, 310 14th Street SE, Rochester, MN 55904, (507) 287-2200,
semn.redcross.org

Olmsted County Government Volunteer Opportunities
Olmsted County Government Center, 151 4th Street SE, Rochester, MN 55904, (507) 287-2220,
www.olmstedcounty.com/volunteer

Rochester Community Education
Northrop Community Center, 201 8th Street NW, Rochester, MN 55901, (507) 285-8033,
www.rochester.k12.mn.us/community-ed

Single Volunteers of Rochester
www.geocities.com/rochsing, e-mail: rochsing@yahoo.com

Southern Minnesota Youth Works
Rochester Area Americorps Program, 300 11th Avenue NW, Rochester, MN 55901, (507) 529-2710,
www.semif.org

Summer of Service—SOS
Northrop Community Center, 201 8th Street NW, Rochester, MN 55901, (507) 287-2135,
www.rochester.k12.mn.us/sos
This is a community service program for youth in grades 6–9.

Volunteer Connections
Community Net, 903 West Center Street, Rochester, MN 55902, (507) 287-7877, www.c-net.org

Volunteers in Education
Rochester Public Schools, 334 16th Street SE, Rochester, MN 55904, (507) 285-8551,
www.rochester.k12.mn.us/distr/vol

Walking

Walksport America
P.O. Box 16325, St. Paul, MN 55116, 800-757-WALK (9255), www.walksport.com
The Walksport program is held locally at Rochester's Apache Mall.

Waterskiing

Rochester Water Ski Club
Box 193, Oronoco, MN 55960, (507) 367-4485

Winemaking

Purplefoot Winemaker's Club
Rochester, MN, www.purplefootclub.com

Women

American Association of University Women
Rochester, MN, (507) 282-9447, www.rochestermn.com/community/aauw

American Business Women's Association
P.O. Box 6903, Rochester, MN 55903, www.abwahq.org

Daughters of the American Revolution
Rochester, MN, www.dar.org

Executive Women International
Rochester, MN, www.executivewomenmn.org

Rochester League of Women Voters
Rochester, MN, www.lwv.org

Women of Today
Rochester, MN, (507) 285-3177, rochestermn.com/community/womentoday or
e-mail: RochWT@hotmail.com

Writing

Magazine Writer's Group
Rochester, MN, (507) 289-3503

Rochester Public Library Writer's Groups
101 2nd Street SE, Rochester, MN 55904, (507) 285-8000, www.rochesterpubliclibrary.org

Root River Poetry Association
2819 34th Avenue SE, Rochester, MN 55904, (507) 289-6450

Rural America Writers' Center
412 West Broadway, Plainview, MN 55964, (507) 534-2900, www.jonhasslertheater.org

Writers of the Roundtable
618 23rd Street NE, Rochester, MN 55906, (507) 280-8956

Woodcarving

Rochester Woodcarver's Club
Rochester, MN, http://members.aol.com/RochCarve

Youth Clubs & Groups

4-H Clubs
Olmsted County Extension Office, 1421 3rd Avenue SE, Rochester, MN 55904, (507) 285-8251

Boy Scouts of America
Gamehaven Council, Scout Service Center, 1124 11½ Street SE, Rochester, MN 55904, (507) 287-1410, 800-524-3907, www.gamehavencouncil.org

Boys & Girls Club/Youth Employment Program—YEP
1026 East Center Street, Rochester, MN 55904, (507) 287-2300, www.bgca.org

Community Youth Outreach
Rochester, MN, (507) 281-6182

Edith Mayo Girl Scout Camp
4228 8th Street SW, Rochester, MN 55902, (507) 282-8459 (mid-June to mid-August only)

Gamehaven Boy Scout Reservation
5015 Simpson Road SE, Rochester, MN 55906, (507) 287-1517 (summer only)

Girl Scouts of America—River Trails Council
mailing address: P.O. Box 9338, Rochester, MN 55903
physical address: 4228 8th Street SW, Rochester, MN 55902, (507) 288-4703, 800-598-5516, www.rivertrails.org

Junior Achievement of Rochester
334 16th Street SE, Suite 12, Rochester, MN 55904, (507) 281-6156, www.ja.org

Order of DeMolay: Rochester Chapter
2002 2nd Street SW, Rochester, MN 55902, (507) 282-1820, www.demolay.org

Order of DeMolay: Winona Chapter
P.O. Box 92, Winona, MN 55987, (507) 932-5286, www.angelfire.com/mn/WinonaDeMolay

Police Athletic League
Rochester Police Department, 101 4th Street SE, Rochester, MN 55904, (507) 285-8300, (507) 285-8285, www.ci.rochester.mn.us/police

Rochester Area Family YMCA Youth Programs and Y–Mentors
709 1st Avenue SW, Rochester, MN 55902, (507) 287-2260, www.rochfamy.org

Southern Minnesota Youth Works—Americorps Program
RCTC Heintz Center, #58, Room C111, 851 30th Avenue SE, Rochester, MN 55904, (507) 292-1412, www.semif.org, www.americorps.gov

Summer of Service—SOS

Northrop Community Center, 201 8th Street NW, Rochester, MN 55901, (507) 285-8033,
www.rochester.k12.mn.us/community-ed
This is a community service program for youth in grades 6–9.

Y-Mentors

Rochester Area Family YMCA, 709 1st Avenue SW, Rochester, MN 55902, (507) 287-2260,
www.rochfamy.org

Youth Commission of Olmsted County

Northrop Education Center, 201 8th Street NW, Rochester, MN 55901, (507) 287-2135,
www.rochester.k12.mn.us/youthcommission

Chapter 24: Unique Shopping

ROCHESTER
Al's Farm Toys
Miracle Mile Shopping Center, 104 17ᵗʰ Avenue NW, Rochester, MN 55901, (507) 288-1616, 800-988-1615, wwww.alsfarmtoys.com

It shouldn't surprise anyone to find Al's Farm Toys in Rochester, a town surrounded by thousands of acres of southeastern Minnesota farmland. Al's features an outstanding selection of collectible farm toys as well as Breyer horses and animals, construction and farm toys, Thomas the Tank engine, Mary's Moo Moo's, Precious Moments, Corgi collectibles, Caterpillar toys, and more. Other farm-themed products available at the store include books, videos, prints, signs, shirts, hats, watches, bedding, games, weather vanes, and much more.

Cost: varies by purchase
Hours: Monday, Thursday, Friday, 9:30 a.m.–8:30 p.m.; Tuesday–Wednesday, 10 a.m.–6 p.m.; Saturday, 9:30 a.m.–6 p.m.; Sunday, noon–5 p.m.

Bernie's Lapidary Supply Company
1800 North Broadway, Rochester, MN 55906, (507) 282-3233, www.bernieslapidary.com

A fascinating collection of rocks, gemstones and fossils are available for viewing and purchase at Bernie's Lapidary Supply Company. Huge geodes, moon rocks, agate slices, loose gemstones and minerals are displayed at the store as well as an interesting selection of ornamental and decorative items created from these beautiful crystals, such as table lights and book ends. Bernie's also carries an excellent assortment of books, lapidary equipment and supplies, silversmith tools, and jewelry.

Cost: varies by purchase
Hours: Monday–Friday, 9 a.m.–5:30 p.m.; Saturday, 9 a.m.–4 p.m.

Bread Baker Company
Miracle Mile Shopping Center, 17ᵗʰ Avenue NW, Rochester, MN 55901, (507) 289-7052

A Rochester favorite, the Bread Baker Company is a take-out bread bakery that sells a variety of breads, sweet breads, rolls, and cookies. The Bread Baker grinds their own flour and makes all their breads from scratch at the bakery. Customers find the bakery's wheat mill, which is located in an enclosed area near the store's entrance, an interesting piece of equipment. Sample the breads of the day such as country French, rosemary red onion, zesty raisin orange, and outrageous rye before making your selections. Boxed lunches and a delicious assortment of gluten-free products are also available.

Cost: varies by purchase
Hours: Monday–Friday, 6:30 a.m.–6 p.m.; Saturday, 7 a.m.–5 p.m.; Sunday, closed

Bruegger's Bagels
1201 South Broadway, Rochester, MN 55904, (507) 287-0203 and
102 Elton Hills Drive NW, Rochester, MN 55901, (507) 287-6045

Bruegger's is a fun place to visit during the long winter months. Preschoolers love to watch the bagel bakers as they retrieve the boiled rings of dough and transfer them to the big revolving oven. Cozy up with a warm bagel and entertain the kids with the simple act of bagel baking.

Cost: varies by purchase
Hours: Broadway location: Monday–Friday, 6 a.m.–7 p.m.; Saturday, 7 a.m.–5 p.m.;
  Sunday, 7 a.m.–4 p.m.
  Elton Hills location: Monday–Thursday, 6 a.m.–7 p.m., Friday, 6 a.m.–6 p.m.;
  Saturday, 6:30 a.m.–4 p.m.; Sunday, 7 a.m.–2 p.m.

Extraordinary Booksellers
107 1st Avenue SW, Rochester, MN 55902, (507) 289-2407

Extraordinary Booksellers, located just down the block from the Peace Plaza in downtown Rochester, is like walking into an antique store for books. Comfortable chairs scattered throughout the bookstore invite customers to take their time as they browse through the incredible selection of used books and magazines. The store carries rare, leatherbound, and nostalgic books as well as ordinary hard cover and paperbacks in a variety of categories such as children's, religion, science, self-help, history, classics, and everything else imaginable.

Cost: varies by purchase
Hours: Monday–Saturday, 11 a.m.–8 p.m.

Friends of the Library Bookstore
Rochester Public Library, 101 2nd Street SE, Rochester, MN 55904, (507) 287-2612

Browse through the wide variety of used fiction and nonfiction books at this bookstore located adjacent to the Rochester Public Library. The books are organized by categories, and you will find exceptional bargain prices. The bookstore is staffed by volunteers, and all the funds from the store are used to support the Rochester Public Library.

Cost: varies by purchase
Hours: Monday, 11 a.m.–8:30 p.m.; Tuesday, Friday, & Saturday, noon–4 p.m.;
  Wednesday & Thursday, 10 a.m.–4 p.m.; Sunday, 1:30 p.m.–4:30 p.m.
  summer weekend hours: Saturday 9 a.m.–1 p.m.; Sunday; closed

Herold's Flags
2002 2nd Street SW, Rochester, MN 55902, (507) 288-1165, 888-288-1165

A kaleidoscope of color greets customers when they step into Herold's Flags. The specialty store stocks an extraordinary variety of flags representing more than 180 foreign countries and the United States as well as sports, seasonal, art, and advertising flags. In addition to flags, you will find home, commercial, and telescopic flag poles and other flag-related products such as windsocks, banners, books, flag pins, stickers, and display cases.

Cost: varies by purchase
Hours: Monday–Friday, 10 a.m.–6 p.m.; Saturday, 10 a.m.–5 p.m.; Sunday, closed

House of the Crafty Mouse
Miracle Mile Shopping Center, 716 17th Avenue NW, Rochester, MN 55901, (507) 282-7711, www.craftymouse.com

The House of the Crafty Mouse is considered to be "the" Rochester gift shop by local residents. The 12,000-square-foot store offers an extraordinary selection of home decor items, seasonal decorations, ornamental garden pieces, stamping and scrapbooking supplies, and the latest in giftware and collectibles.

After browsing at the House of the Crafty Mouse, it's easy to relax at one of the white gingerbread-style tables or high top tables at the Coffee Mouse Café, which adjoins the store. The café's country kitchen atmosphere offers "sugar and spice and everything mice." The Café features a House Mouse Coffee Blend, which, along with its other custom blends, is roasted daily. Other beverages on the menu include flavored coffees, lattes, espresso, cappuccino, mocha, a house tea latte, and the Mouse's special blends of hot chocolate and apple cider. In addition to assorted pastries, cookies, fudge, jumbo turtles, and English toffee, the Café serves its signature Heart pocket sandwich of the day, soups, a savory cheesy mouse muffin, and chicken or tuna salad sandwiches. Flavored waters, milk, juices, iced tea, and soda are also available.

Cost: varies by purchase; café: $
Hours: store: Monday–Friday, 10 a.m.–9 p.m.; Saturday, 10 a.m.–5 p.m.; Sunday,
1 p.m.–5 p.m.
café: Monday–Friday, 9:30 a.m.–8 p.m., Saturday, 9:30 a.m.–5 p.m.; Sunday,
11:30 a.m.–5 p.m.

Miracle Mile Shopping Center

115 16th Avenue NW, Rochester, MN 55901, (507) 288-2455

Miracle Mile Shopping Center was the first shopping mall in Minnesota located outside the Twin Cities. Rochester's first shopping center opened in October 1952 and was considered an innovative way to shop. Today, this strip mall is a popular neighborhood shopping center with quick and easy access to about 39 specialty stores and service shops. Its location is convenient for visitors since it is just three blocks from Saint Mary's Hospital and just off Highway 52 North at the 2nd Street exit. Many of the shops listed in this section are located in the Miracle Mile.

Toy Zone

Miracle Mile Shopping Center, 17th Avenue NW, Rochester, MN 55901, (507) 286-8440

There's something for little kids and big kids alike at the Toy Zone, which is not just an ordinary toy store, but a child's dream come true. The store maintains a huge inventory of high-quality, specialty toys including arts and crafts supplies, science and nature related toys, puzzles, dolls, stuffed toys, Playmobil® products, Thomas the Tank Engine® and Brio® train sets, educational materials, travel games, party favors and much more. Kids are welcome to play at the train tables and with Rokenbok® radio-controlled vehicles during their visit. You have to see the Toy Zone to believe it!

Cost: varies by purchase
Hours: Monday–Friday, 10 a.m.–8 p.m.; Saturday, 10 a.m.–5 p.m.; Sunday,
noon–5 p.m.

HARMONY
Austin's Angora Goats and Mohair Gifts

RR 2, Box 41B, Harmony, MN 55939, (507) 886-6731, www.bluffcountry.com/austins.htm,
e-mail: mohair@means.net

Ada and Jim Austin welcome you to visit their angora goat farm and gift shop. Ada is eager to introduce you to her babies in the "Kids Krib" and answer questions about their herd of 200 angora goats. Touch one of the baby angora goats at the "Kids Krib," and feel the luxurious hair that is the source of mohair wool. After learning about the goats, step into the gift shop where you may sample and/or purchase goat meat, cheese, milk, and fudge.

The gift shop also displays and sells handmade mohair-blend woolen products including sweaters, socks, blankets, coats, slippers, hats, capes, scarves, baby sweaters, and mittens. Eighty percent of the gift shop merchandise is handcrafted by approximately fifteen professional mothers who spin, card, and knit the wool. Some of the truly unique gifts that you will find at Austin's are the handcrafted Santas and Woodsmen with mohair beards. Other items for sale include angora hides, goat skulls, raw mohair, dyed mohair and mohair-blend yarns.

Picnic tables are available for use by visitors. Primitive camping facilities are also located on the property. Please see Amish Country Camping in Chapter 12 for more information on the campground.

Cost: free
Hours: call for hours

The Village Green
90–92 2ⁿᵈ Street NW, Harmony, MN 55939, (507) 886-2409, www.harmony.mn.us

A visit to Harmony wouldn't be complete without a stop at the Village Green, located adjacent to the Harmony Visitor's Center. The Village Green features a few gift shops located in the old Harmony Train Depot, a late 1800s Victorian home, and a turn of the century schoolhouse. The train depot houses a gift shop; the Sugar Plum House is an ice cream and sandwich shop located in the Victorian home, and handcrafted Amish quilts are displayed and sold at the schoolhouse. Take time to stroll through the village.

Cost: varies by purchase
Hours: Monday–Saturday, 10 a.m.–5 p.m.; Sunday, noon–5 p.m.

HOUSTON
VanGundy's Elk Farm & Antler Shed Gift Shop
3383 State Hwy. 76, Houston, MN 55943, (507) 896-2380

At VanGundy's, "if we're home, we're open." Visitors may stop by the farm by chance or call ahead for a tour. Larry and Patty VanGundy began raising Rocky Mountain Elk, once native to Minnesota, in 1993. Their private elk farm started with six heifers and one bull and currently has a total of 68 elk. The Antler Shed Gift Shop is a stunning gallery with an impressive variety of unique elk-related products from antlers to art work to medicinal supplements. VanGundy's sells "Vital-Ex" and other Velvet Antler products and supplements. Many scientific studies have indicated that these supplements increase energy, relieve arthritis symptoms, enhance mood and promote general wellness. While browsing through the gallery, take a few minutes to view the video of the "bugling bulls," which is both interesting and entertaining.

Cost: free
Hours: by chance or reservation

KELLOGG
The L.A.R.K. Toy Company
P.O. Box 39, Lark Lane, Kellogg, MN 55945, (507) 767-3387, www.larktoys.com

The L.A.R.K. Toy Company, which stands for Lost Arts Revival by Kreofsky, is a 31,000-square-foot complex that features an enchanting handcarved and hand-painted carousel. As one of the largest children's specialty toy stores in the United States, L.A.R.K. visitors can easily spend the day playing a round on the 18-hole miniature golf course, browsing through the toy museum and specialty toy stores, riding the carousel, and eating lunch at The Rocking Café. Explore all that the L.A.R.K. has to offer; you won't be disappointed!

Cost: $
Hours: Monday–Friday, 9 a.m.–5 p.m.; Saturday–Sunday, 10 a.m.–5 p.m.
  winter hours: open Friday–Sunday in January & February
  mini-golf season: May–mid-October during store hours; evening mini-golf is
  available from June–Labor Day (call for evening hours)

SVJ Creative Designs
191 Hwy. 42, Kellogg, MN 55945, (507) 767-3039, www.svjcreative.com, svj@wabasha.net

Just a few miles off the Great River Road (Highway 61) near Kellogg, you will find SVJ Creative Designs. This family-owned business manufactures wrought iron rail-ings, lawn and garden items, and is a retailer of concrete lawn ornaments. SVJ's iron products are handcrafted on the premises, and many of their original designs have been patented and copyrighted. Some of the items for sale include lawn furniture, metal silhouettes, plant and bird feeder hangars, sun catchers, gazing balls, clocks, weathervanes, windmills, and lighthouses. Browse through the huge outdoor display or indoor shopping area. Seeking something special? Estimates for custom work are available for homes and businesses.

Cost: varies by purchase
Hours: Monday–Saturday, 9:30 a.m.–5 p.m.; Sundays, noon–5 p.m.; call for weekend
  hours after the Christmas season

LAKE CITY
Treats and Treasures
108 East Lyon Avenue, Lake City, MN 55041, (651) 345-2882

Treats and Treasures is an old-fashioned gift shop with a variety of local and regional gifts, souvenirs, and collectibles including T-shirts, sweatshirts, nautical items, jewelry and beads, regional books and cookbooks, Watkin's spices, beads, audiotapes, CDs, Beanie Babies, kites, and other unique gift items. Sample the shop's homemade fudge, caramel corn, and coffee while you browse or purchase treats from the old-fashioned candy counter.

Cost: varies by purchase
Hours: February–April & November–December: Wednesday–Friday 10 a.m.–
  5:30 p.m.; Saturday, 9 a.m.–5 p.m.
  May–October: Monday–Friday, 10 a.m.–5:30 p.m.; Saturday, 9 a.m.–5 p.m.;
  Sunday, 11 a.m.–4 p.m.
  January: closed

OWATONNA
Cabela's
3900 Cabela Drive, Exit 45 on I-35, Owatonna, MN 55060, (507) 451-4545, www.cabelas.com

Cabela's, the "World's Foremost Outfitter" of fishing, hunting, and outdoor gear has a 150,000-square-foot showroom in Owatonna. The showroom is like a wildlife museum with hundreds of mounts from around the world, waterfowl hovering overhead, "A Tribute to Sportsman" majestic mountain display, and a 53,000 gallon aquarium filled with Minnesota gamefish. Trophy game animals on display include Rocky Mountain elk, bighorn sheep, Alaskan caribou, polar bears and more.

The store also features a gun library with high quality guns to buy, sell, or trade in addition to an indoor archery range. A restaurant deli on the upper level offers a variety of sandwiches from wild game such as smoked buffalo along with traditional deli fare. Of course, let's not forget Cabela's extensive selection of fishing, hunting, and camping gear as well as outdoor clothing and home decor available for purchase. A visit to Cabela's is not just a day at the mall type of shopping experience, it's an event.

Cost: varies by purchase
Hours: Monday–Saturday, 8 a.m.–9 p.m.; Sunday, 10 a.m.–6 p.m.

PINE ISLAND
Pine Cheese Mart and Von Klopp Brew Shop
51146 Hwy. 52 Boulevard, Pine Island, MN 55963, (507) 356-8336, 800-596-2739, www.makewineandbeer.com

Pine Cheese Mart and Von Klopp Brew Shop of Pine Island has served the area from its current location since 1969. The shop sells a savory selection of Wisconsin and imported cheeses, and owner Wally Van Klopp, an experienced brewer and award winning wine maker, maintains an extensive inventory of wine and beer making supplies for the home brewer and wine maker. A large selection of gift items is also available at the shop including beer steins, picnic baskets, Beanie Babies, John Deere collectibles, Norwegian memorabilia, specialty crackers, Swiss chocolates, and more. Take time to stop at Pine Cheese Mart; it's worth a visit.

Cost: varies by purchase
Hours: Monday–Saturday, 8 a.m.–6 p.m., Sunday & holidays, 9 a.m.–6 p.m.

RUSHFORD
Norsland Lefse
P.O. Box 692, 303 North Elm Street, Rushford, MN 55971, (507) 864-2323, 800-584-6777

Norsland Lefse of Rushford has been producing traditional lefse, a Norwegian bread made from potatoes, for more than 17 years. The lefse and other Scandinavian treats are made "the way grandma used to make it." If you're not able to stop by Norsland Lefse on your next trip to southeastern Minnesota, mail orders are available.

Cost: varies by purchase
Hours: Monday–Saturday, 8 a.m.–4 p.m.

SPRING VALLEY
The Treehouse

Hwy. 63 South, (507) 561-3785, www.bluffcountry.com/treehouse.htm
Located 12 miles south of Spring Valley.

The Treehouse is a gardener's dream come true. Browse among the beautifully land-scaped display gardens, which have a huge selection of annuals, perennials, evergreens, statuaries, planters, fountains, shrubs and shade trees. Novice gardeners will appreciate the Treehouse because all displays are well-labeled and divided into sun, part-sun or shade sections. Visitors are welcome to take free self-guided tours of the gardens and relax on one of the park benches while the kids play on the playground. The gift shop has a nice selection of nature-related and garden-themed gifts and accessories, such as indoor fountains, gazing balls, garden stones, flags, bird feeders, cards, trellises, decorative arches and more. Guided tours are available for groups. Please call for more information.

Hours: official opening of display gardens for the season: last Weekend in April;
April–June: Monday–Saturday, 9 a.m.–5:30 p.m.; Sunday, noon–5:30 p.m.;
July–December: Monday–Saturday, 9 a.m.–5 p.m.; Sunday, noon–5:30 p.m.

WYKOFF
The Bank Gift Haus and Tea Room

P.O. Box 205, 105 Gold Street, Wykoff, MN 55990, (507) 352-4205, www.bluffcountry.com

The oldest building in Wykoff, a former bank, is now home to The Bank Gift Haus and Tea Room. Constructed of brick, it was the only building to remain standing on the west side of Gold Street after a devastating fire in 1895. In fact, charred roof beams are still visible near a small section of the ceiling. The Bank Gift Haus and Tea Room commemorates its history as a bank with beautiful mahogany and marble teller windows where visitors purchase their gifts. An old safe, safety deposit boxes, and a wallpaper trimmer are among the interesting antiques to view while you browse the shop. You will be delighted to find a tasteful selection of seasonal home decor and gift items as well as crystal, china tea sets, Heritage Lace products, collectibles, inspirational books, garden flags, Ty Beanie Babies, and a large assortment of greeting cards. Wander downstairs to the Kinderhaus and year-round Christmas Shop, and you will discover a collection of high-quality children's toys, books, Gotz dolls as well as Christmas ornaments, giftware, candles, and decor. Homemade fudge, made on site, is also available for purchase.

The Bank Haus Tea Room is a quiet and relaxing place to enjoy conversation and company. Located in the back of the Gift Haus, it has a seating capacity of 20. The menu features a limited choice of homemade soups, salads and desserts that changes every day or two. Special entrees may occasionally be made. Reservations are strongly recommended. Groups are welcome, but advance notice is preferred.

Cost: $
Hours: tea room: 11:30 a.m.–4 p.m., closed Sundays
gift shop: Monday–Saturday, 10 a.m.–5 p.m.

Part VII:
Appendices

Appendix 1: Rochester City Map

Appendix 2: Rochester Downtown Map, Subway & Skyway

Appendix 3: Rochester Park & Recreation Map

Appendix 4: Seating Charts to Area Theaters & Arenas

Appendix 5: Chambers of Commerce

Appendix 6: Visitor Information & Tourist Centers

Appendix 7: Historical Societies

Index

Appendix 1: Rochester City Map

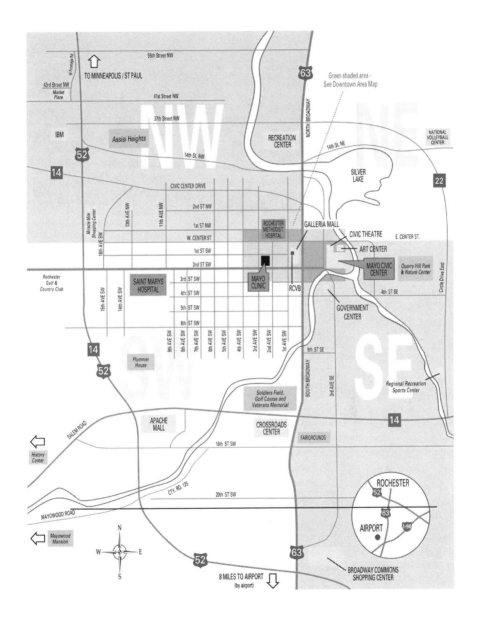

Appendix 2: Rochester Downtown Map, Subway & Skyway

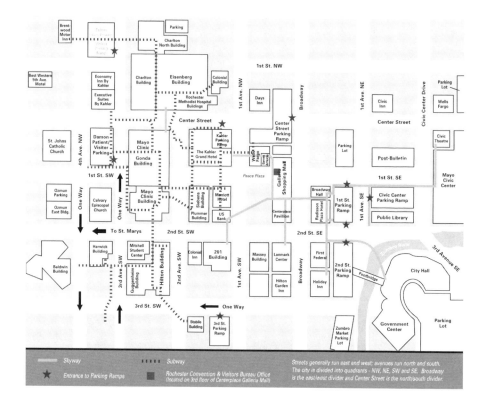

Brent-
wood
Motor
Inn

Parking

Charlton
North Building

Best Western
5th Ave.
Motel

1st St. NW

Economy
Inn By
Kahler

Charlton
Building

Eisenberg
Building

Colonial
Building

1st Ave. NW

Broadway

1st Ave. NE

Civic Center Drive

Parking
Lot

Executive
Suites
By Kahler

Rochester
Methodist Hospital
Buildings

Days
Inn

Civic
Inn

Wells
Fargo

St. Johns
Catholic
Church

4th Ave. NW

Damon
Patient/
Visitor
Parking

Mayo
Clinic

Center Street

Kahler
Parking
Ramp

Center
Street
Parking
Ramp

Center Street

Gonda
Building

The Kahler
Grand Hotel

Wells
Fargo

Parking
Lot

Post-Bulletin

Civic
Theatre

1st St. SW

Peace Plaza

Galleria Shopping Mall

1st St. SE

Mayo
Civic
Center

Ozmun
Parking

One Way

Calvary
Episcopal
Church

Mayo
Clinic
Building

Siebens
Building

Marriott
Hotel

Broadway
Hall

1st St.
Parking
Ramp

1st Ave. SE

Civic Center
Parking Ramp

Ozmun
East Bldg.

One Way

Plummer
Building

US
Bank

Centerplace
Pavilion

Radisson
Plaza Hotel

Public Library

To St. Marys

2nd St. SW

2nd St. SE

Harwick
Building

Mitchell
Student
Center

3rd Ave. SW

Hilton Building

Colonial
Inn

201
Building

1st Ave. SW

Massey
Building

Lanmark
Center

Broadway

First
Federal

2nd St.
Parking
Ramp

3rd Avenue SE

City Hall

Baldwin
Building

Guggenheim
Building

Hilton Building

2nd Ave. SW

Hilton
Garden
Inn

Holiday
Inn

Footbridge

3rd St. SW

One Way

Stabile
Building

3rd St.
Parking
Ramp

Zumbro
Market
Parking
Lot

Government
Center

Parking
Lot

Skyway

Subway

Entrance to Parking Ramps

Rochester Convention & Visitors Bureau Office
(located on 3rd floor of Centerplace Galleria Mall)

Streets generally run east and west; avenues run north and south.
The city is divided into quadrants - NW, NE, SW and SE. Broadway
is the east/west divider and Center Street is the north/south divider.

Appendix 3: Rochester Park and Recreation Map

ROCHESTER CIVIC CENTER ARENA

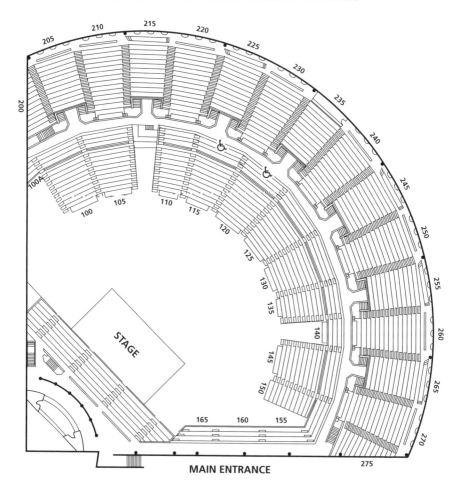

ROCHESTER CIVIC CENTER AUDITORIUM

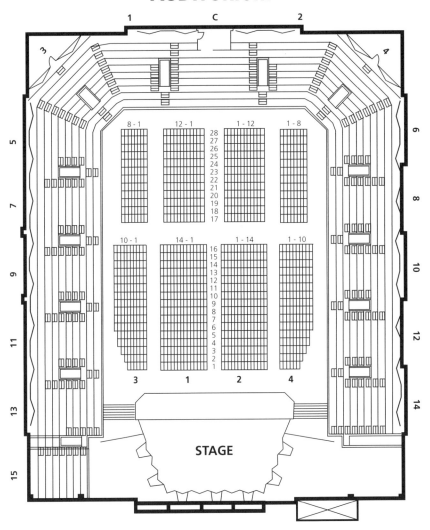

STAGE

ROCHESTER CIVIC CENTER
PRESENTATION HALL

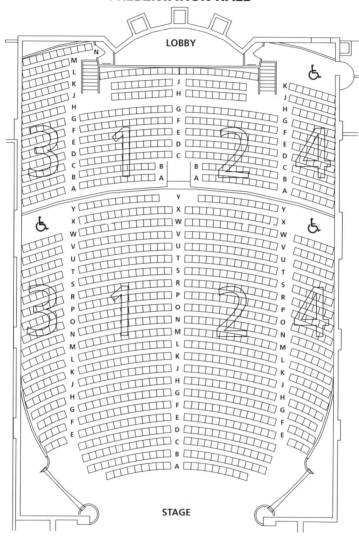

FLOOR PLAN OF ROCHESTER CIVIC THEATER AUDITORIUM

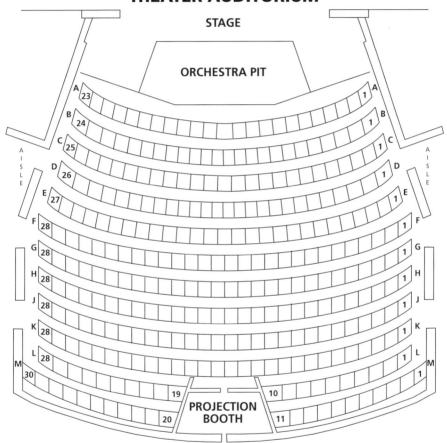

STAGE

ORCHESTRA PIT

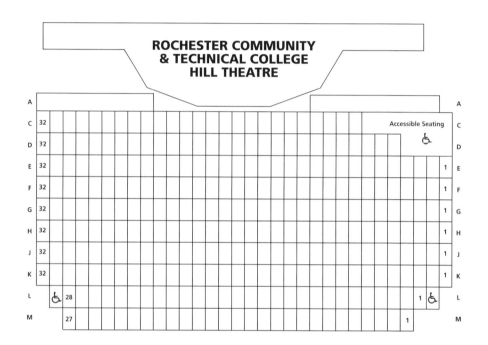

**ROCHESTER COMMUNITY
& TECHNICAL COLLEGE
HILL THEATRE**

Accessible Seating

ROCHESTER REPERTORY THEATER

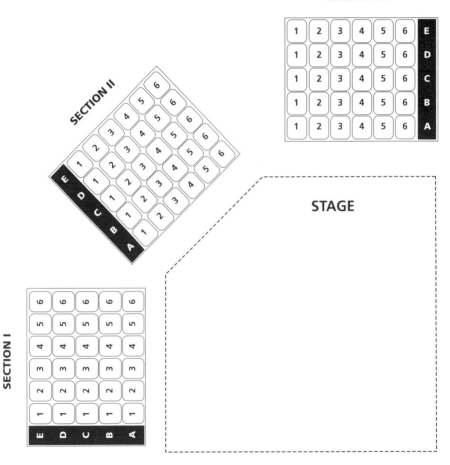

SECTION III

SECTION II

SECTION I

STAGE

STEWARTVILLE PERFORMING ARTS CENTER

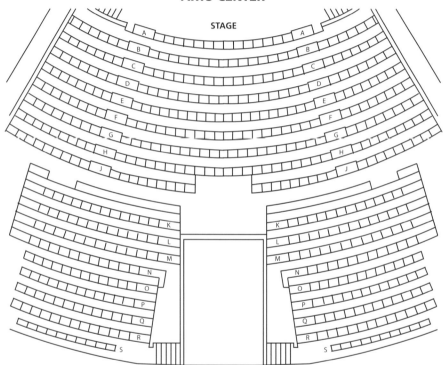

Appendix 5: Chambers of Commerce

Rochester Area Chamber of Commerce
220 South Broadway, Suite 100, Rochester, MN 55904, (507) 288-1122,
www.rochestermnchamber.com

Caledonia Area Chamber of Commerce
Box 24, Caledonia, MN 55921, (507) 725-5477, www.caledoniamn.com

Cannon Falls Area Chamber of Commerce
Box 2, 103 North 4th Street, Cannon Falls, MN 55009, (507) 263-2289, www.cannonfalls.org

Chatfield Commercial Club
Call the City Clerk (Thurber Community Center, 21 2nd Street SE, Chatfield, MN 55923,
(507) 867-3810, www.ci.chatfield.mn.us) for the Chatfield Commercial Club's current contact information.

Kasson Chamber of Commerce
P.O. Box 326, Kasson, MN 55944, (507) 634-2002, www.cityofkasson.com

La Crescent Chamber of Commerce
P.O. Box 132, 221 North 3rd Street, # 102, La Crescent, MN 55947, (507) 895-2800, 800-926-9480,
www.lacrescent.com

Lake City Chamber of Commerce
P.O. Box 150, 212 South Washington Street, Lake City, MN 55041, (651) 345-4123, 800-369-4123,
www.lakecity.org, www.lakecitymn.org

Mantorville Chamber of Commerce
Riverside Gifts, P.O. Box 358, 420 Main Street NE, Mantorville, MN 55955, (507) 635-5464,
www.mantorville.com

Owatonna Chamber of Commerce & Tourism
320 Hoffman Drive, Owatonna, MN 55060, (507) 451-7970, 800-423-6466, www.owatonna.org

Spring Valley Chamber of Commerce
P.O. Box 13, Spring Valley, MN 55975, (507) 346-7367, www.ci.spring-valley.mn.us

St. Charles, City of
830 Whitewater Avenue, St. Charles, MN 55972, (507) 932-3020, www.stcharlesmn.org

Stewartville Chamber of Commerce
P.O. Box 52, 200 South Main Street, Stewartville, MN 55976, (507) 533-6006,
www.stewartvillemn.com

Wabasha Area Chamber of Commerce
P.O. Box 105, 160 West Main Street, Wabasha, MN 55981, (651) 565-4158, 800-565-4158,
www.wabashamn.org

Winona Area Chamber of Commerce
P.O. Box 870, 67 Main Street, Winona, MN 55987, (507) 452-2272, www.winonachamber.com

Zumbrota Chamber of Commerce
P.O. Box 2, Zumbrota, MN 55992, (507) 732-4282, www.zumbrota.com

Rochester Convention & Visitor's Bureau
Galleria Mall, 111 South Broadway, Rochester, MN 55904, (507) 288-4331, 800-634-8277, www.rochestercvb.org

Chatfield Tourist Information Center
Center of City Park, Chatfield, MN 55923, (507) 867-3966, www.ci.chatfield.mn.us

Dresbach Information Center/Minnesota Travel Information Center
Route 2, Box 7A, La Crescent, MN 55947, (507) 895-2005, www.exploreminnesota.com

Fountain City Office
P.O. Box 115, 104 Main Street, Fountain, MN 55935, (507) 268-4923, www.bluffcountry.com/fountain.htm

Harmony Visitor's Center
P.O. Box 141, 15 2nd Street NW, Harmony, MN 55939, 800-247-6466, www.harmony.mn.us

Houston Tourist Information Center
Houston Nature Center, 215 Plum Street, Houston, MN 55943, (507) 896-4668, (507) 896-3234, www.houstonmn.com

Kellogg, City of
P.O. Box 147, Kellogg, MN 55945, (507) 767-4953, www.mississippi-river.org

Lake City Tourism Bureau
21 South Washington Street, Lake City, MN 55041, (651) 345-4123, 877-LAKE-CITY, www.lakecitymn.org

Lanesboro Area Tourism Association
P.O. Box 20, 100 Milwaukee Road, Lanesboro, MN 55949, (507) 467-2696, 800-944-2670, www.lanesboro.com

Mabel Information Center
P.O. Box 311, Mabel, MN 55954, (507) 493-5350, www.bluffcountry.com/mabel.htm

Mississippi Valley Partners
P.O. Box 334, Wabasha, MN 55981, 888-999-2619, www.mississippi-river.org
Includes the Mississippi River towns of Frontenac, Lake City, Camp LaCupolis, Reads Landing, Kellogg, and Wabasha.

Owatonna Convention and Visitor's Bureau
P.O. Box 331, Owatonna, MN 55060, (507) 451-7970, 800-423-6466, www.owatonna.org

Peterson, City of
Box 74, Peterson, MN 55962, (507) 875-2523, (507) 875-2267, www.peterson-mn.com, www.rushford.net

Pine Island, City of
P.O. Box 1000, 250 South Main Street, Pine Island, MN 55963, (507) 356-4591, www.pineislandmn.com

Preston Area Tourism Association
P.O. Box 657, 813 Hwy. 52 North, Preston, MN 55965, (507) 765-2100, 888-845-2100,
www.bluffcountry.com/preston.htm

Root River Trail Towns
P.O. Box 398, Lanesboro, MN 55949, (507) 467-2696, 800-944-2670, www.bluffcountry.com/rrtt.htm

Rushford Area Historic Depot Museum & Trail Center
401 South Elm Street, Rushford, MN 55971, (507) 864-7560, www.rushford.net

Southeastern Minnesota Historic
Bluff Country Visitor's Bureau
P.O. Box 609, 15 2nd Street NW, Harmony, MN 55939-0609, (507) 886-2230, 800-428-2030,
www.bluffcountry.com
Includes towns of Brownsville, Caledonia, Chatfield, Eitzen, Fountain, Harmony, Houston, La Crescent,
Lanesboro, Mabel, Preston, Peterson, Rochester, Rushford, St. Charles, Spring Grove, Spring Valley,
Winona, and Wykoff.

Spring Grove Area
P.O. Box 241, Spring Grove, MN 55974, (507) 498-5434, (507) 498-5221, www.springgrovemn.com

Spring Valley Tourist Information Center
P.O. Box 13, Spring Valley, MN 55975, (507) 346-1015, www.ci.spring-valley.mn.us
Located at the corner of Grant and North Broadway Streets.

St. Charles Tourist Information
830 Whitewater Avenue, St. Charles, MN 55972, (507) 932-3020, www.stcharlesmn.org

Wabasha Area Chamber of Commerce
& Tourist Information Center
P.O. Box 105, 160 West Main Street, Wabasha, MN 55981, (651) 565-4158, 800-565-4158,
www.wabashamn.org

Winona Convention and Visitor's Bureau
P.O. Box 870, 67 Main Street, Winona, MN 55987, (507) 452-2272, 800-657-4972, (24-hour
information line), www.visitwinona.com

Wykoff Tourist Information
P.O. Box 205, Wykoff, MN 55990, (507) 352-4205, www.bluffcountry.com

Appendix 7: Historical Societies

Contact information for southeastern Minnesota's historical societies is listed below. Many of these organizations also have a museum that features exhibits of local history and community memorabilia.

Please contact the historical societies for information about local museums. Additional information about Minnesota's historical sites may be obtained from the Minnesota Historical Society, 345 West Kellogg Boulevard, St. Paul, MN 55102, (651) 296-6126, www.mnhs.org

Cannon Falls Historical Society
P.O. Box 111, Cannon Falls, MN 55009, (507) 263-4080, (507) 263-4503

Chatfield Historical Society
Thurber Community Center, 21 2nd Street SE, Chatfield, MN 55923, (507) 867-3810, www.ci.chatfield.mn.us

Dodge County Historical Society
P.O. Box 433, Mantorville, MN 55955, (507) 635-5508, www.dodgecohistorical.addr.com

Fillmore County Historical Society
U.S. 52 & 202 County Road 8, Fountain, MN 55935, (507) 268-4449, www.rootsweb.com/~mnfillmo/society.htm

Goodhue Area Historical Society
P.O. Box, 141, Goodhue, MN 55027, www.ci.goodhue.mn.us/gahs

Goodhue County Historical Society
1166 Oak Street, Red Wing, MN 55066, (651) 388-6024, www.goodhuehistory.mus.mn.us

Hesper-Mabel Historical Society
P.O. Box 56, Mabel, MN 55954, (507) 493-5018

Houston County Historical Society
104 History Lane, Caledonia, MN 55921, (507) 725-3884, (507) 896-2291

Kenyon Area Historical Society
Gunderson House, Kenyon, MN 55946, (507) 789-5365

La Crescent Area Historical Society
171 Skunk Hollow Road, La Crescent, MN 55947

Lake City Historical Society
City Hall, Lake City, MN 55041, (651) 345-5836

Lanesboro Historical Society
P.O. Box 345, 105 Parkway South, Lanesboro, MN 55949, (507) 467-3439

Mantorville Restoration Association
P.O. Box 157, Mantorville, MN 55955, www.mantorville.com

Mower County Historical Society
P.O. Box 804, 12th Street and 6th Avenue SW, Austin, MN 55912, (507) 437-6082

Olmsted County Historical Society
1195 County Road 22 SW, Rochester, MN 55902, (507) 282-9447, www.olmstedhistory.com

Pine Island Historical Society
Pine Island, MN 55963, (507) 356-4056

Plainview History Association
Route 1, Box 209, Plainview, MN 55944, (507) 534-2670, www.mnhs.org

Preston Historical Society
Houston and Preston Streets, Preston, MN 55965, (507) 765-4555

Rushford Area Historical Organization
403 East North Street, Rushford, MN 55971, (507) 864-7223

Spring Valley Community Historical Society
112 South Washington Avenue, Spring Valley, MN 55975, (507) 346-2763

Steele County Historical Society
1448 Austin Road, Owatonna, MN 55060, (507) 451-1420

Stewartville Area Historical Society
P.O. Box 362, 305 North Main Street, Stewartville, MN 55976, (507) 533-8035

Wabasha County Historical Society
Read's Landing, MN 55968, (507) 282-4027

Wanamingo Historical Society
Wanamingo, MN 55983, (507) 824-2722

West Concord Historical Society
600 1st Street West, West Concord, MN 55985, (507) 527-2628

Winona County Historical Society
160 Johnson Street, Winona, MN 55987, (507) 454-2723

Wykoff Area Historical Society
Wykoff, MN 55994, (507) 352-5681

Index

City and Attraction

Adams
Adams Dairy Days .89
Cedar River Country Club 196

Altura
Carley State Park 159
Carriage Museum at Lazy D Campground . . .67
John A. Latsch State Park 160
Lazy D Campground & Trail Rides 114
Lazy D Trail Rides & Carriage
    Company 130, 132
Swimming Beach at Whitewater
    State Park 223
Whitewater State Park 157, 245, 255
Whitewater State Park Geological Center . . .134

Apple Valley
Cheer America Schools of Cheerleading,
    Pom Pom & Baton 231

Austin
Mower County Fair 100
Mower County Historical Society 304

Berne
Berne Swiss Fest 102

Brooklyn Park
Minnesota United Snowmobilers
    Association—MnUSA 256

Brownsdale
United Skates Roller Skating Center . . .212, 260

Brownsville
Caledonia Sno-Gophers Snowmobile Club . .278

Byron
Byron Lanes 183
Byron Sno-Bears 278
Byron Sportsmen & Conservation Club 270
Byron Swimming Pool 226
Christmas in the Country 75
Dodge County Speedway 239
Garten Marketplatz Perennial Farm 140
Good Neighbor Days 94
Great Southern Grass Drag Nationals
    & Swap Meet 106
Halloween Festival and Party at
    Oxbow Park .109

Links of Byron 191, 196, 259
Oxbow Park Annual Fun Fest and
    Art Show 87
Paddock School of Horsemanship 131
Red's Berries 142
Tweite's Pumpkin Patch 109, 132
Zollman Zoo at Oxbow Park and
    Nature Center 162

Caledonia
Beaver Creek Valley State Park 158
Caledonia Area Chamber of Commerce 301
Caledonia Swimming Pool 226
Camp Winnebago 115
Dunromin' Park Campground 115
Houston County Fair 100
Houston County Historical Society 304
Ma-Cal-Grove Country Club 197
Schech's Water Powered Mill 61
Starlite Bowling Center 183

Cannon Falls
Bluff Breeze Farm 51
Cabin Fever Days 77
Cannon Falls Area Chamber of Commerce . .301
Cannon Falls Campground 116
Cannon Falls Canoeing 185
Cannon Falls Historical Society 304
Cannon Valley Classic Sled Dog Races 77
Cannon Valley Fair 94
Voices of the Valley 91

Chatfield
Chatfield Brass Band and Chatfield Music
    Lending Library 31
Chatfield City Park 151
Chatfield Commercial Club 301
Chatfield Fish & Game Club 164, 270
Chatfield Historical Society 304
Chatfield Swimming Pool 226
Chatfield Tourist Information Center 302
Chatfield Trout Classic 85
Chatfield Western Days 103
Chatfield Wildlife Management Area 163
Chosen Valley Golf Club 197
Chosen Valley Lanes 183
Country Art Gallery 13
Friends of the Chatfield Public Library
    Garden Tour .139
Pease Wildlife Museum 67
William Pease Wildlife Management Area . .163

Dodge Center
Centerfest 89
Dodge Center Swimming Pool 226

Dodge Country Club 197
Land of a Thousand Winds 52

Elba
Country Heritage Adventures 51, 163
Crystal Springs State Fish Hatchery 164
Elba Fire Tower 51
Historic Marnach House 61
Lynnhaven Farm and Antiques 52
Wescott Orchard and Agriproducts 142

Elgin
Elgin Cheese Days .89

Eyota
Chester Woods Park
   (and Beach) 116, 131, 150
Eyota Days 94
Picket Fence Garden & Gifts 52

Fountain
Fillmore County Historical Society 304
Fountain City Office 302
Fountain Trail Days 89
Spruce Pine Tree Farm 145

Frontenac
Mount Frontenac Golf Course 197
Mount Frontenac Ski Area 249
Villa Maria Retreat and
   Conference Center 264

Goodhue
Goodhue Area Historical Society 304
Volksfest 89

Goodview
Goodview Days 89

Grand Meadow
Meadowfest 89

Hammond
Hammond Classic Car Show 96

Harmony
Amish Country Camping 117
Amish Country Tours 52
Austin's Angora Goats and Mohair Gifts . . .164
Bluff Country Bird Festival 86
Bluff Country Studio Art Tour 85
Bluff Valley Riders Snowmobile Club 277
Clover Art Gallery .13
Great Harmony Fourth of July 94
Harmony Golf Club 198
Harmony Municipal Campground 117

Harmony Roller Rink 212, 260
Harmony Toy Museum 67
Harmony Visitor's Center 302
Michel's Amish Tours 52
Minowa Carver's Annual Show & Sale 97
Niagara Cave 52
Root River Trail Wagon Ride 107
Slim's Woodshed Woodcarving Museum . . .68
Southeastern Minnesota Historic Bluff
   Country Visitor's Bureau 105, 303
Tom Jarland Carriage Service 133
Village Green 286

Hayfield
Hayfield Community Pool 226
Hey Days 94
Oaks Golf Club 198
Spare Time Lanes 183

Homer
Historic Bunnell House 62

Houston
Classcycle Bikes of Houston 179
Cushon's Peak Campground 117
Houston Hoedown 95
Houston Money Creek Snowriders 278
Houston Municipal Campground
   at South Park .118
Houston Nature Center 136
Houston Tourist Information Center 302
Money Creek Buffalo Ranch 165
Money Creek Haven 118
Money Creek Junction
   Bluegrass Festival 87, 103
Our Front Porch Gallery &
   Gathering Place 14
Valley High Country Club 198
VanGundy's Elk Farm & Antler
   Shed Gift Shop 165

Janesville
Holy Spirit Retreat Center 265

Kasson
Dodge County Fair 94
Festival in the Park 99
Four Seasons Arena 251
Kasson Ballet School 188
Kasson Chamber of Commerce 301
Kasson Swimming Pool 226
King's Orchard 143
Southeastern Winds Community Band 31
Turn Crest Stable 131

Kellogg
Ewe Name It Ranch 52
Kellogg, City of 302

L.A.R.K. Toy Company 261, 287
Midway Recreation Park 240
Miniature Golf at the L.A.R.K. 192, 259
Mountainland Timber Tree Farms 146
Nielsen Tree Farm 146
SVJ Creative Designs 287
Watermelon Days 105

Kenyon
Don Knopf Memorial Carriage and
   Cutter Parade .79
Kenyon Area Historical Society 304
Kenyon Country Club 199
Old-Fashioned Christmas at
   Gunderson House 76

La Crescent
Apple Blossom Scenic Drive 53
Apple Fest 105
Apple on Main Tea Room & Gifts 39
Dresbach Information Center/Minnesota
   Travel Information Center 302
La Crescent: Apple Capital of Minnesota . . .143
La Crescent Area Historical Society 304
La Crescent Chamber of Commerce 301
La Crescent Community Arena 251
La Crescent Snowmobile Club 278
La Crescent Swimming Pool 226
Mississippi River Lock & Dam #7 53
Pine Creek Golf Course 199

La Crosse
Great River Steamboat Company 54

Lake City
Camp Lacupolis Campground 119
Chickadee Cottage Tea Room
   and Restaurant 40
Earthen Path Farm 139
Frontenac State Park 158
Hok-Si-La Municipal Park 224, 246
Hok-Si-La Park and Campground 119, 152
Johnny Appleseed Days 105
Lake City Chamber of Commerce 301
Lake City Golf Club 199
Lake City Historical Society 304
Lake City Swimming Beach at
   Ohuta Park 224
Lake City Swimming Pool 226
Lake City Tourism Bureau 302
Lake City Yacht Club 267
Lake Pepin Campground & Trailer Court . . .119
Lake Pepin Golf Course 199
Lake Pepin Guide Service 188
Loren's Mississippi River Guide Service 188
McCahill Park 152
Oak Center General Store 40
Ohuta Park 152

Patton Park 153
Pepin Heights Orchard 143
Rhythm & Brew .41
Roshen Park 153
Sail Away of Lake City 182
Sailboats, Inc. 182
Treats and Treasures 287
Water Ski Days 91
Wild Wings Fall Festival 107
Wild Wings Gallery 14
Winter Fest 80

Lanesboro
Art in the Park 92
Avian Acres Native Bird Supply &
   Petting Zoo 166
Bluff Country Gathering 88
Buffalo Bill Days .99
Capron Hardware 179
Commonweal Theater Company
   & Lanesboro Radio Company at
   the Mane Theater 21
Cornucopia Art Center 14
Das Wurst Haus .54
Eagle Bluff Environmental
   Learning Center 80, 92, 136
Eagle Cliff Campground and Lodge 120
Eagle Cliff Canoe & Tube Rental 185
Fall Weekend Getaway at Eagle Bluff
   Environmental Learning Center 107
Highway 250 Campground 120
Historic Scanlan House Bed & Breakfast 179
Lanesboro Area Tourism Association 302
Lanesboro Canoe Rental 185
Lanesboro Golf Club 200
Lanesboro Historical Society 304
Lanesboro State Fish Hatchery 166
Little River General Store 179, 185
Old-Fashioned Barn Dance 88, 97
R & M Amish Touring 54
Riverview Campground 120
Root River Outfitters 179, 186
Root River Trail Towns 303
Scenic Valley Winery 55
Sojourner Café 41
Summer Weekend Getaway at
   Eagle Bluff Environmental Center 92
Sylvan Park 153
Sylvan Park Campground 121

LeRoy
Lake Louise State Park 158, 247, 255

Lewiston
Lewiston Country Club 200

Mabel
Brumm's Petting Zoo & Gifts 166

Hesper-Mabel Historical Society 304
Hesper-Mabel Steam Engine Days 107
Mabel Information Center 302
Mabel Steam Engine Museum 68
Meadowbrook Country Club 200
Steam Engine Park 153
Trailbusters Snowmobile Club 278

Mantorville
Dodge County Historical Society 304
Historic Mantorville 62
Mantorville Brewing Company 55
Mantorville Chamber of Commerce 301
Mantorville Restoration Association 304
Mantorville Social Club 278
Mantorville Theater Company 21
Marigold Days 105
Olde-Fashioned Christmas in Mantorville 76
Olde Tyme Days 89
Zumbro Valley Recreation Club 201

Mazeppa
Apple Ridge Orchard 51, 144
Hurricane Hills 240
O'Brien Christmas Wonderland 76
Ponderosa Campground 121
Run-n-Gun Paint Ball Sports 207
Steeplechase Ski & Snowboard Area 249

Millville
Spring Creek Motocross (MX) Park 240

North Mankato
Rochester Sports and Vacation Show 77

Oronoco
Oronoco Gold Rush Days 103
Oronoco Park 151
Oronoco Park Campground 121
Rochester Water Ski Club 92, 241, 280

Ostrander
Uff-Da Days 100

Owatonna
Brooktree Golf Course 201
Cabela's 288
Festival of the Arts 97
Great Serengeti Indoor Waterpark at
    the Holiday Inn & Suites 221
Havanna Hills 201
Hidden Creek Golf Club 201
Jungle Sports and Entertainment
    Complex 278
Minnesota Skydiver's Club 277
Minnesota State Orphanage Museum 68
Wells Fargo Bank .55

Owatonna Arts Center &
    Sculpture Garden 15
Owatonna Chamber of Commerce
    & Tourism 301
Owatonna Convention and
    Visitor's Bureau 302
Owatonna Country Club 202
Owatonna Extravaganza 97
Owatonna Roller Rink 213, 260
Owatonna Skate Park 217
Rice Lake State Park 159, 247, 255
Steele County Fair 100
Steele County Historical Society 305
Steele County Speedway 239
Village of Yesteryear 63

Peterson
1877 Peterson Station Museum 69
Geneva's 180, 186
Peterson, City of .302
Peterson Municipal Campground 122
Peterson State Fish Hatchery 167

Pickwick
Pickwick Mill 63

Pine Island
Kathy's All-American Training Center . .234, 258
Pine Cheese Mart and Von Klopp
    Brew Shop 288
Pine Island Cheese Festival 89
Pine Island, City of 302
Pine Island Golf Course 202
Pine Island Historical Society 305
Pine Island Lanes 183
Pine Island Swimming Pool 226
Pine Island White Pines
    Sportsman Club 270
RideAbility 171, 232
Wazionja Campground 122

Plainview
Corn on the Cob Festival 99
Dis & Dat Country Mall 51
Eastwood Park 147, 149, 154
Eckstein Athletic Field 154
Gopher Lanes 183
Jon Hassler Theater 21
Migrant Festival 92
Piper Hills Golf Club 202
Plainview Community Swimming Pool 226
Plainview History Association 305
Rebekah's 42
Rural America Writers' Center 280
Union Plainview Youth Center 210
Wedgewood Park 154

Preston

B & B Olympic Bowl 183
Brick House on Main Coffeehouse
   and Gift Shop 42, 179
Evening of Leisure 98, 103
Fillmore County Fair 94
Fillmore County Fairgrounds
   Campground 123
Forestville/Mystery Cave
   State Park 159, 248, 255
Hidden Valley Campground 123
Historic Forestville 63, 94
Independence Day at Historic
   Forestville 94
Maple Springs Campground 123
Mystery Cave at Forestville State Park 55
Old Barn Resort 123, 202
Pine Tree Orchards, Inc. 144
Preston Apple and Berry Farm 142, 144
Preston Area Tourism Association 303
Preston Golf and Country Club 203
Preston Historical Society 305
Preston Swimming Pool 226
Root River Outfitters at the
   Old Barn Resort 180
Trailhead Inn 180
Trout Days 88

Racine

B.E.A.R.C.A.T. Hollow 167
Buffalo Fest 98
Burr Oak Buffalo Ranch & Trading Post 168
Warehouse Ceramics 269

Read's Landing

Wabasha County Historical Society 305

Red Wing

Four Seasons Bike Rental & Sales 180
Goodhue County Historical Society 304
Outdoor Store 180

Regional

85-Mile Garage Sale 85
Beaver Creek Valley State Park 158, 255
Candlelight Ski 78, 80
Cannon Valley Trail 177, 214, 246
Carley State Park 159, 247, 254, 255
Douglas State Trail 131, 178, 213, 244
Forestville/Mystery
   Cave State Park 159, 248, 255
Frontenac State Park 158, 245, 254, 255
Great River Birding Festival 87
Great River Bluffs
   State Park 159, 248, 254, 255
Great River Ridge Trail 178, 214, 247
Harmony–Preston Valley
   State Trail 178, 214, 246

Hiawatha Senior Baseball League 176
John A. Latsch State Park 160, 255
Lake Louise State Park 158, 247, 255
Mystery Cave at Forestville
   State Park 55
Rice Lake State Park 159, 247, 255
Root River State Trail 179, 215, 247
Sweet Adelines 30
Whitewater State Park 157, 245, 255
Whitewater State Park Geological Center . . .134

Rock Dell

Riverside Trails 130, 133, 259

Rushford

Ferndale Country Club 203
Magelssen Bluff Park 154
Magic Kingdom Park 155
Nordic Lanes 183
Norsland Lefse 288
North End Park Campground 124
Rushford Aquatic Center 225
Rushford Area Historical Organization 305
Rushford Historic Depot Museum
   and Trail Center 69, 303
Rushford's Parade of Lights 76
Valley Crest Riders Snowmobile Club 278

Spring Grove

Ballard House 64
Spring Grove Area 303
Spring Grove Snowmobile Club 278
Spring Grove Swimming Pool 226
Supersaw Valley Campground 124
Syttende Mai Celebration 88
Trollskogen Park & Campground 125

Spring Valley

Antique Engine and Tractor Show 98
Brave Community Theater 22
Deer Creek Campground
   and Speedway 125, 239
Good Earth Village 265, 269
Hellrud's Christmas Trees 146
Methodist Church Museum:
   A Laura Ingalls Wilder Site 70
Root River Country Club 203
Spring Valley Chamber of Commerce 301
Spring Valley Community
   Historical Society 305
Spring Valley Swimming Pool 226
Spring Valley Tourist Information Center 303
Treehouse 289
Tri-County Trail Blazers 278
Valley Lanes 183
Washburn-Zittleman Historic House 70
Wilder Fest 100

St. Charles

Gladiolus Days 99
Legion Unity Lanes 183
Mel Brownell Family Aquatic Center 225
St. Charles, City of 301
St. Charles Golf Club 203
St. Charles Tourist Information 303
Victorian Lace Inn B & B, Tea Room
   & Gift Shop 42, 260
Winona County Fair 95

St. Paul

Minnesota Department of Natural
   Resources—DNR 245
Southeastern Minnesota Prairie Day 100
Walksport America 230, 280
Youth Firearms Safety and Adult
   Hunter Education 216

Stewartville

Bear Cave Park 147, 149, 155
Dairy Queen of Stewartville 192
Fireworks at Stewartville's Summerfest 94
Florence Park 155
Ironwood Springs Christian Ranch . . . .
   125, 130, 133, 254, 259, 260, 266, 269, 271
Ironwood Springs Christian Ranch—
   National Wheelchair Sports &
   Recreation Camp 171, 231
Riverview Greens Golf Course 204
Sears House 64
Snow Tubing at Ironwood Springs
   Christian Ranch 254, 260
Stewartville Area Historical Society 305
Stewartville Bowl 183
Stewartville Chamber of Commerce 301
Stewartville Community Band 32
Stewartville Community Pool 226
Stewartville Driftskippers 278
Stewartville Performing Arts Center 22, 300
Stewartville Sportsman Club 270
Summer Saturday Nite Concerts 93
Summerfest 95

Theilman

Many Hands Farm 139
Whippoorwill Ranch Kampground 126

Viola

Viola Gopher Count 89

Wabasha

Annual Soar with the Eagles Weekend 82
Arrowhead Bluffs Museum 70
Coffee Mill Golf & Country Club 204
Coffee Mill Ski Area 248
Delta Queen Steamboat Docking 56, 98, 99
Eagle Watch at Riverfront 78, 80, 83, 111

Eagle's Nest 43
Foxes Mini Golf 192, 259
Great River Houseboats 182
Grumpy Old Men Festival 81
Meet Me Under the Bridge Concerts 93
Mississippi Valley Partners 302
National Eagle Center and EagleWatch
   Observation Deck 137, 168
Nature Conservancy 138
Old-Fashioned Fourth of July 94
Pioneer Campsite Resort 127
Pioneer Lanes 183
Riverboat Days 99
Snowmobile Challenge Cup 256
Wabasha Area Chamber of Commerce
   & Tourist Information Center 301, 303
Wabasha County Fair 95
Wabasha Swimming Pool 226

Wanamingo

Wanamingo Historical Society 305
Wanamingo Swimming Pool 226

Welch

Hidden Valley Campground 128
SKILINK™ Ski Club for Kids 249, 277
Welch Mill Canoeing & Tubing 186
Welch Village Fall Festival and Ski
   & Snowboard Swap 109
Welch Village Ski and Snowboard Area 250

West Concord

Survival Days 95
West Concord Historical Society 305
West Concord Pool 226

Whalan

Aroma Pie Shop .193
Gator Greens Mini Golf 192

Winona

Acoustic Café 44
Arches Museum 71
Back 80 Paintball Sports 207
Blue Heron Coffeehouse 44
Bob Welch Aquatic Center 225
Bud King Ice Arena 251
Cathedral Studios 65
Cedar Valley 204
Center Gallery at Saint Mary's
   University of Minnesota 15
Conway Universal Studios 65
Delta Queen Steamboat Docking 56, 99
Downtown Winona Historic District 64
Garden Path Tour 140
Garvin Heights Park and Lookout 156
Great River Bluffs
   State Park 159, 248, 254, 255

Green Lantern Coffeehouse 44
Hiawatha Valley Audubon Society 267
Julius C. Wilkie Steamboat Center
   at Levee Park 57
Lake Park 156
Levee Park 156
Paul Watkin's Art Gallery 16
Pla-Mor Campground & Marina 126
Polish Cultural Institute 71
Prairie Island Campground 127
Prairie Island Nature Area 169
Rock Solid Youth Center 211
Steamboat Days Festival 93
Sugar Loaf Bluff 57
Theatre du Mississippi 22
Upper Mississippi National
   Wildlife and Fish Refuge 169
Watkins Museum .71
Westfield Golf Course 205
Westgate Bowl 184
Winona Area Chamber of Commerce 301
Winona Arts Center 16
Winona Bowl 184
Winona Convention and Visitor's Bureau . . .303
Winona Country Club 205
Winona County Historical Society 305
Winona Polish Apple Day—
   Smaczne Jabika 110
Winona Railroad Club 273
Winona's 4.8 Skate Park 217
Winona's Glorious Stained Glass Tour 65

Wykoff
Bank Gift Haus and Tea Room 45, 289
Ed's Museum 72
Historic Wykoff Jail Haus
   Bed & Breakfast 45, 57
Wykoff Area Historical Society 305
Wykoff Tourist Information 303

Zumbro Falls
Bluff Valley Campground 128
Bluff Valley Lights 110, 129
Windmill Haven .146
Zumbro Falls Golf Club 205
Zumbro Valley Canoe & Tube Rental 187
Zumbro Valley Sportsmen's Park 129

Zumbrota
Aromas 45
Covered Bridge Park 157
Crossings at Carnegie 16, 46
Ellison Sheep Farm 51
Evergreen Lanes .184
Goodhue County Fair 100
Shades of Sherwood 129
Southern Minnesota Sled Dog Club 277
Zumbrota Chamber of Commerce 301
Zumbrota Covered Bridge 65

Zumbrota Covered Bridge Music
   and Arts Festival 93, 157
Zumbrota Golf Club 205
Zumbrota Swimming Pool 227

Attractions

A
4-H Clubs 281
37th Street Billiards 180
85–Mile Garage Sale 85
1877 Peterson Station Museum 69
Acoustic Café 44
Adams Dairy Days 89
adaptive recreation 171
   see also: disabilities, groups; Rochester
    Adaptive Recreation Program
Al's Farm Toys 283
Aldrich Memorial Nursery School
   Annual Carnival 87
All-Breed Dog Show 105
All Star Magic Gala 23
Allegro School of Dance 187
Allendale Park 252
American Association of
   University Women 280
American Business Women's
   Association 268, 280
American Red Cross 279
American Red Cross Annual
   Neighbor Saver Saturday 82
AmericInn Hotel & Suites of Rochester 219
Amish Community of Southeastern
   Minnesota 52
Amish Country Camping 117
Amish Country Tours 52
Annual Butterfly Count 95, 100
annual garden tours 139
Annual Soar with the Eagles Weekend 82
Annual Spring Gardening Seminar 82, 140
Antique Automobile Club of America 267
Antique Engine and Tractor Show 98
Apple Blossom Scenic Drive 53
Apple Fest 105
Apple on Main Tea Room & Gifts 39
Apple Ridge Orchard 51, 144
Aquarius Club 278
arcades 172
archery 174
   clubs 267
Archery Headquarters 174
Arches Museum 71
Aroma Pie Shop .193
Aromas 45
Arrowhead Bluffs Museum 70
art centers 8
Art in the Park 92
Art in the Sky 8

Artistic Framers 8
arts and crafts 258
   clubs 267
   see also: ceramics; hobby shops;
   quilting; sewing; woodcarving
Arts on Fifth Avenue 24
Assisi Community Center 262
Assisi Heights Convent 58
Austin's Angora Goats and
   Mohair Gifts 164, 285
automobiles
   clubs 267
   racing 239
autumn in Historic Bluff Country 105
Autumn Woods RV Park 113
Avian Acres Native Bird Supply
   & Petting Zoo 166

B

B & B Olympic Bowl 183
B.E.A.R.C.A.T. Hollow 167
Back 80 Paintball Sports 207
Ballard House 64
Bank Gift Haus and Tea Room 45, 289
Barnes & Noble Booksellers 39, 47, 267
Barnes & Noble Booksellers at
   the Historic Chateau Theatre .39, 47, 50, 267
baseball 176
batting cages 176
Bear Cave Park .155
Bear Creek Farm 131
Bear Creek Pow Wow 83
Beaver Creek Valley State Park 158, 255
Berne Swiss Fest 102
Bernie's Lapidary Supply Company 283
berry picking 142
bike rentals 179
biking 177
   see also: cycling
billiards 180
bingo 181
birding
   clubs 267
   see also: Annual Soar with Eagles
   Weekend; Avian Acres Native Bird Supply
   & Petting Zoo; EagleWatch at Riverfront;
   Great River Birding Festival
Blue Heron Coffeehouse 44
Blues Fest 100
Bluff Breeze Farm 51
Bluff Country Bird Festival 86
Bluff Country Gathering 88
Bluff Country Studio Art Tour 85
Bluff Valley Campground 128
Bluff Valley Lights 110, 129
Bluff Valley Riders Snowmobile Club 277
Board to Death Sports—Madrone
   Family Indoor Skate Park 217
boating
   canoes 184

club 267
rentals 181
see also: fishing guides; Rochester
Rowing Club; sea kayaking
Bob Miller Comedy Magic 23
Bob Welch Aquatic Center 225
bowling 182
   associations .268
boxing 184
Boy Scouts of America 281
Boys and Girls Club of America 209
Boys & Girls Club/Youth Employment
   Program—YEP 281
Brave Community Theater 22
Bravo Espresso and Gourmet Coffee 36
Bread Baker Company 283
Brent W. Coggins—Magic by Sin'gee' 23
Brick House on Main Coffeehouse
   and Gift Shop 42, 179
bridge clubs 268
Brooktree Golf Course 201
Bruegger's Bagels 283
Brumm's Petting Zoo & Gifts 166
Bud King Ice Arena 251
Buffalo Bill Days 99
Buffalo Fest 98
Burr Oak Buffalo Ranch & Trading Post 168
business associations 268
   see also: women
Byron Lanes 183
Byron Sno-Bears 278
Byron Sportsmen & Conservation Club 270
Byron Swimming Pool 226

C

Cabela's 288
Cabin Fever Days 77
Caledonia Area Chamber of Commerce 301
Caledonia Sno-Gophers Snowmobile Club . .278
Caledonia Swimming Pool 226
Callaway Gallery .8
Calvary Episcopal Church 262
Camp Lacupolis Campground 119
Camp Victory .269
Camp Winnebago 115
campgrounds .113
Canada Geese at Silver Lake Park 161
Candlelight Ski 78, 80
canine clubs 268
   see also: sled dog club; Carl
   and Jean Frank Canine Park
Cannon Falls Area Chamber of Commerce . .301
Cannon Falls Campground 116
Cannon Falls Canoeing 185
Cannon Falls Historical Society 304
Cannon Valley Classic Sled Dog Races 77
Cannon Valley Fair 94
Cannon Valley Trail 177, 214, 246
canoeing .184-187
   see also: boating

Capron Hardware .179
Caribou Coffee 36
Carillon Christmas Concert 74
Carl and Jean Frank Canine Park 150
Carley State Park 159, 247, 254, 255
Carriage Museum at the Lazy D
  Campground 67
Cathedral Studios .65
Cedar River Country Club 196
Cedar Valley 204
Celebration of Lights 74
Cemetery Walk 90
Center Gallery at Saint Mary's
  University of Minnesota 15
Centerfest 89
Central Park 147, 148
ceramics 269
Chateau Theatres 173, 261
Chatfield Brass Band and Chatfield
  Music Lending Library 31
Chatfield City Park 151
Chatfield Commercial Club 301
Chatfield Fish & Game Club 164, 270
Chatfield Historical Society 304
Chatfield Swimming Pool 226
Chatfield Tourist Information Center 302
Chatfield Trout Classic 85
Chatfield Western Days 103
Chatfield Wildlife Management Area 163
Cheer America—Schools of Cheerleading,
  Pom Pom & Baton 231
chess 269
Chester Berry Farm 142
Chester Woods Park
  (and Beach) . . .116, 131, 150, 223, 244, 254
Chickadee Cottage Tea Room
  and Restaurant .40
Child Care Resource and Referral 274
Children's Dance Theater 18
children's music events & organizations 32
Choose and Cut Fraser Firs 145
Choral Arts Ensemble of Rochester 25
Chosen Valley Golf Club 197
Chosen Valley Lanes 183
Chris Manahan Tree Farm 145
Christian organizations 269
Christian Women's Club of Rochester 269
Christian youth organizations 269
Christmas in the Country 75
Christmas tree farms 145
Circus World Bingo 181
Civil Air Patrol 271
Classcycle Bikes of Houston 179
Classic Car Rally .90
Clover Art Gallery .13
Coffee Mill Golf & Country Club 204
Coffee Mill Ski Area 248
Coffee Mouse Café at the House of
  the Crafty Mouse 36

coffeehouses 36
  see also: tea rooms
coin collecting 270
Colonial Lanes 173, 182, 236, 258
Color Me Mine 258, 269
Commonweal Theater Company
  & Lanesboro Radio Company at
  the St. Mane Theater 21
Community Bible Study 269
Community Net .272
Community Supported Agriculture 139
Community Youth Outreach 281
Conoco Kids' Classic 229
conservation and sportsmen's clubs 270
Conway Universal Studios 65
Cooke Park 147, 148, 150, 252
Corn on the Cob Festival 99
Cornucopia Art Center 14
Country Art Gallery 13
Country Heritage Adventures 51, 163
Covered Bridge Park 157
Crisis Nursery 274
Crossings at Carnegie 16, 46
Crystal Springs State Fish Hatchery 164
Cushon's Peak Campground 117
cycling 270
  see also: biking
Cycling Club of Rochester 270

D
D & R Star 180
Dairy Queen of Stewartville 192
dance
  ballroom 175, 270
  children's 18
  instruction 187
  organizations .270
  square and round 219, 270, 278
  teen 278
Dance Dana & Company 187
Das Wurst Haus 54
Daube's Bakery 37
Daube's Konditorei & German Restaurant . . .37
Daube's Pastry Pavilion 37
Daughters of the American Revolution 280
Days of Yesteryear 101
Deer Creek Campground and
  Speedway 125, 239
Delta Queen Steamboat Docking 56, 98, 99
Dis & Dat Country Mall 51
disabilities, groups 271
  see also: adaptive recreation;
    Rochester Adaptive Recreation Program
Diversity Council 271
diversity/multicultural organizations 271
Dodge Center Swimming Pool 226
Dodge Country Club 197
Dodge County Fair 94
Dodge County Historical Society 304

Dodge County Speedway 239
Don Knopf Memorial Carriage and
  Cutter Parade 79
Douglas State Trail 131, 178, 213, 244
Down by the Riverside Concerts 28, 95
Downtown Business Association 268
Downtown Rochester Farmers' Market 139
Downtown Winona Historic District 64
Dresbach Information Center/Minnesota
  Travel Information Center 302
Ducks Unlimited .270
Dunromin' Park Campground 115

E

Eagle Bluff Environmental
  Learning Center 80, 92, 136, 216
Eagle Cliff Campground and Lodge 120
Eagle Cliff Canoe & Tube Rental 185
Eagle Watch at Riverfront 78, 80, 83, 111
Eagle's Nest 43
Earthen Path Farm 139
East Park 147, 149
Eastwood Golf Course 194, 245, 253
Eastwood Park 147, 149, 154
Eckstein Athletic Field 154
Ed's Museum 72
Edith Mayo Girl Scout Camp 281
Elba Fire Tower 51
Elder Network 275
Elgin Cheese Days 89
Elks Lodge 1091 . . . . .181, 276
Ellison Sheep Farm 51
Essex Park 147, 148, 150, 174, 245, 253
Evening of Leisure 98, 103
Evergreen Lanes .184
Ewe Name It Ranch 52
Executive Women International 280
Experimental Aircraft Association 272
Extraordinary Booksellers 284
Eyota Days 94

F

Fall Festival at Sunrise Cottages 108
Fall Weekend Getaway at Eagle Bluff
  Environmental Learning Center 107
Family Fun Night 83
Family of Caring Unique Singles—F.O.C.U.S. 276
Family Support Network 274
Fantasy of Wreaths 110
farm tours 51, 163
farmers' markets .139
Ferndale Country Club 203
Festival in the Park 99
Festival of Music Series 25
Festival of the Arts 97
Festival of Trees: A Celebration of Giving . . .110
Fillmore County Fair 94
Fillmore County Fairgrounds Campground . .123
Fillmore County Historical Society 304

film group 271
Fire Prevention Week 108
Fireworks at Stewartville's Summerfest 94
fishing club 271
  see also: boating
fishing guides 188
fitness clubs 188
Florence Park 155
flying organizations 271
football 190, 236
Forestville/Mystery Cave
  State Park 159, 248, 255
Forever Christmas 74
Foster-Arend Lake and Beach 221
Foster-Arend Park 147, 148, 150
Fountain City Office 302
Fountain Trail Days 89
Four Seasons Arena 251
Four Seasons Bike Rental & Sales 180
Four Seasons Duplicate Bridge Club 268
four wheeling 272
Fourth Street Youth Boxing Gym 184
Foxes Mini Golf 192, 259
Fred Astaire Dance Studio 175
Friends of the Chatfield Public
  Library Garden Tour 139
Friends of the Library Bookstore 284
Friends of the Rochester Public Library 273
Frontenac State Park 158, 246, 254, 255

G

galleries, art 8, 85
Gamehaven Boy Scout Reservation 281
Garden Path Tour 140
gardening 139
  clubs 272
Garten Marketplatz Perennial Farm 140
Garvin Heights Park and Lookout 156
Gator Greens Mini Golf 192
Geneva's 180, 186
genealogy society 272
Gilded Star Gallery 8
Girl Scouts of America—River Trails Council .281
Gladiolus Days 99
go-karts 190
Golden Generation Show 106
golf
  indoor 193
  miniature courses 191
  outdoor courses 194
Golf Equipment Swap Meet 111
Golf Headquarters 193
Good Earth Village 265, 269
Good Neighbor Days 94
Goodhue Area Historical Society 304
Goodhue County Fair 100
Goodhue County Historical Society 304
Goodview Days 89
Goose Poop Art .161
Gopher Lanes 183

Graham Park and Arena at the
  Olmsted County Fairgrounds 150
Great Harmony Fourth of July 94
Great River Birding Festival 87
Great River Bluffs
  State Park 159, 248, 254, 255
Great River Houseboats 182
Great River Ridge Trail 178, 214, 247
Great River Steamboat Company 54
Great Serengeti Indoor Waterpark
  at the Holiday Inn & Suites 221
Great Southern Grass Drag Nationals
  & Swap Meet .106
Greater Rochester Grower's Market, Inc. . . .139
Greek Festival 101
Green Lantern Coffeehouse 44
Grumpy Old Men Festival 81
gymnastics .234, 259

H

Hadley Valley Enterprises 51
Halloween at Charter House 108
Halloween Festival and Party at
  Oxbow Park 109
Hammond Classic Car Show 96
Harmony for Mayo Concerts 25
Harmony Golf Club 198
Harmony Municipal Campground 117
Harmony–Preston Valley
  State Trail 178, 214, 246
Harmony Roller Rink 212, 260
Harmony Toy Museum 67
Harmony Visitor's Center 302
Havanna Hills 201
Hawthorn Hills Golf Learning Center . .194, 245
  Golf Etiquette Classes for Juniors 193
Hayfield Community Pool 226
hayrides 132
health and human services resources 272
health and wellness resources 262, 272
Hellrud's Christmas Trees 146
Hendy's Hobby Shop 272
Heritage House 58
Herold's Flags 284
Herring Art and Frame 9
Hesper–Mabel Historical Society 304
Hesper–Mabel Steam Engine Days 107
Hey Days 94
Hiawatha Senior Baseball League 176
Hiawatha Valley Audubon Society 267
Hidden Creek Golf Club 201
Hidden Valley Campground
  Preston 123
  Welch 128
high school sports tournaments 75
Highway 250 Campground 120
hiking 206
Hill Theater at Rochester Community
  & Technical College—RCTC 18, 298
Historic Bunnell House 62

Historic Chateau Theatre
  Barnes & Noble 39, 47, 50
Historic Forestville 63, 94
Historic Mantorville 62
Historic Marnach House 61
Historic Scanlan House Bed & Breakfast 179
historic sites 58
Historic Wykoff Jail Haus Bed
  & Breakfast .45, 57
hobby shops 272
hockey rinks 252
Hok-Si-La Park and Campground 119, 152
Hok-Si-La Municipal Park 224, 246
Holiday Homes Tour 74
Holiday Inn South 219
Holy Spirit Retreat Center 265
HoNK*SQuEAK*ScRaTcH*BOOM! 32
Honors Choirs of Southeastern Minnesota . . .32
horseshoe club 272
hot air balloon rides 206
horseback riding .130
  lessons 131
  Minnesota Horse Trails and
    Campgrounds 132
  trails 130
  Trails and Campgrounds in Southeastern
    Minnesota State Parks 132
House of the Crafty Mouse 284
Houston County Fair 100
Houston County Historical Society 304
Houston Hoedown 95
Houston Money Creek Snowriders 278
Houston Municipal Campground at
  South Park 118
Houston Nature Center 136
Houston Tourist Information Center 302
Hurricane Hills 240

I

Independence Day at Historic Forestville 94
Integrative Therapies 263
Intercultural Mutual Assistance Association . .271
Interfaith Community Network 269
Ironwood Springs Christian Ranch . . . .
  . . . .125, 130, 133, 259, 260, 266, 269, 271
Ironwood Springs Christian Ranch—
  National Wheelchair Sports &
  Recreation Camp 171, 231
Izaak Walton Cabin 270
Izaak Walton League 270

J

Jake and Jenny Outdoor Day 96
James Krom Natural Images 9
Janet Lang Dance Studio 187
Java Café and Salad Brothers 38
Java Café Coffee and Espresso 38
Jerry's Billiards 180
John A. Latsch State Park 160, 255
Johnny Appleseed Days 105

Jon Hassler Theater 21
Judd Park 253
juggling club 272
Julius C. Wilkie Steamboat Center
    at Levee Park 57
Jungle Sports and Entertainment
    Complex 278
Junior Achievement of Rochester 281
Junior Gym at the Rochester Area
    Family YMCA .209
Junior Gym at the Rochester
    Athletic Club .209
Just for Kix 188

K
Kahler Grand Hotel 220
Kasson Ballet School 188
Kasson Chamber of Commerce 301
Kasson Swimming Pool 226
Kathy's All-American Training
    Center .234, 259
Kellogg, City of .302
Kennellamas 161
Kenyon Area Historical Society 304
Kenyon Country Club 199
keyboard club 273
Kid Fest 78
Kids' Gym at Rochester Family YMCA 207
Kids' Gym at the Rochester Athletic Club . . .207
Kids' Sports Expo .84
King's Marina 181
King's Orchard 143
Knights of Columbus 276
Knights of Columbus Bingo 181
KROC Home and Vacation Show 82
KROC Women's Fall Expo 108
Kutzky Park 147, 148, 150

L
L.A.R.K. Toy Company 261, 287
L'Atelier 9
La Crescent: Apple Capital of Minnesota . . .143
La Crescent Area Historical Society 304
La Crescent Chamber of Commerce 301
La Crescent Community Arena 251
La Crescent Snowmobile Club 278
La Crescent Swimming Pool 226
Lake City Chamber of Commerce 301
Lake City Golf Club 199
Lake City Historical Society 304
Lake City Swimming Beach at
    Ohuta Park .224
Lake City Swimming Pool 226
Lake City Tourism Bureau 302
Lake City Yacht Club 267
Lake Louise State Park 158, 247, 255
Lake Park 156
Lake Pepin Campground & Trailer Court . . .119
Lake Pepin Golf Course 199
Lake Pepin Guide Service 188

La Leche League .273
Land of a Thousand Winds 52
Lanesboro Area Tourism Association 302
Lanesboro Canoe Rental 185
Lanesboro Golf Club 200
Lanesboro Historical Society 304
Lanesboro State Fish Hatchery 166
Lazy D Campground & Trail Rides 114
Lazy D Trail Rides & Carriage
    Company 130, 132
Learning Is Forever—LIFE 275
Legion Unity Lanes 183
Levee Park 156
Lewiston Country Club 200
library organizations 273
Lifeguard Olympics 102
Links of Byron 191, 196, 259
Little Faith Ministries 269
Little River General Store 179, 185
Live Nativity Drive-Through 75
Loren's Mississippi River Guide Service 188
Loveugly Cabaret Bar & Coffee Lounge 38
Lynnhaven Farm and Antiques 52
Lyra Concert Baroque Orchestra 26

M
M & W Ceramics 269
Ma-Cal-Grove Country Club 197
Mabel Information Center 302
Mabel Steam Engine Museum 68
Machine Shed Arcade 173, 258
Magazine Writer's Group 280
Magelssen Bluff Park 154
magic club 273
Magic Kingdom Park 155
Magical Entertainer—Alan Skogerbo 23
magical shows 23
magicians 23
Manor Park 252
Mantorville Brewing Company 55
Mantorville Chamber of Commerce 301
Mantorville Restoration Association 304
Mantorville Social Club 278
Mantorville Theater Company 21
Many Hands Farm 139
Maple Springs Campground 123
Maple Valley Golf and Country Club 194
Marcelli's Espresso and Gourmet Coffee 38
Marigold Days 105
Marion RC Flyers .273
martial arts 206
Martial Arts Fitness Center 206
Martin Luther King Junior Celebration 76
Masonic Lodge 276
Masque Youth Theatre and School, Inc. 18
Mayo Clinic Art & Architectural Tour 58
Mayo Clinic Bike Safety Fair 86
Mayo Clinic Chamber Symphony 26
Mayo Clinic Community Safety Fair 108
Mayo Clinic General Tour 59

Mayo Clinic Patient and Health
    Education Center .263
Mayo Clinic Peregrine Falcon Program 162
Mayo High School 252, 253
Mayo Historical Suite 66
Mayo Medical Center Art Collection 10
Mayo Stage Door Drama Club 19
Mayowood Mansion 59
Mayowood Garden Tour and Private
    Garden Tour 90, 140
Mayowood Mansion Holiday Tours 111
McCahill Park 152
McDonald's Playplace 207, 260
Meadow Lakes Golf Club 194
Meadowbrook Country Club 200
Meadowfest 89
Med-City Aquatics Champion Swim
    School & Club 231
Med-City Marathon and Relays 229
Meet Me Under the Bridge Concerts 93
Mel Brownell Family Aquatic Center 225
metaphysical organization 273
Methodist Church Museum:
    A Laura Ingalls Wilder Site 70
Michaels Arts and Crafts 258
Michaels Kid's Club 267
Michel's Amish Tours 52
Middle School Sports Program 232
Midway Recreation Park 240
Midwest Lumberjack Show and
    Championships .90
Migrant Festival 92
Miniature Golf at the L.A.R.K. 192, 259
Minnesota Bike Trails & Rides 179
Minnesota Chill—Women's Professional
    Volleyball 242
Minnesota Department of Natural
    Resources—DNR 245
Minnesota Master Gardener Program 141
Minnesota Skydiver's Club 277
Minnesota State Orphanage Museum 68
Minnesota United Snowmobilers
    Association—MnUSA 256
Minowa Carver's Annual Show & Sale 97
Miracle Mile Shopping Center 285
Mississippi River Lock & Dam #7 53
Mississippi Valley Partners 302
model airplane clubs 273
model train club 273
Money Creek Buffalo Ranch 165
Money Creek Haven 118
Money Creek Junction Bluegrass
    Festival 87, 103
Moon's Craft Shop 267
mothers 273
    see also: parents; women
Mothers & More .273
Mothers of Preschoolers—MOPS 274
motorcross racing 240
Mount Frontenac Golf Course 197

Mount Frontenac Ski Area 249
Mountainland Timber Tree Farms 146
Moving Waters Guide Service 188
Mower County Fair 100
Mower County Historical Society 304
Mr. & Mrs. Magic—Magical Michael
    & Terri McKay .24
Mr. Pizza .173, 260
museums 66
music 24
Music Together 33
Music with Connie Jelatis Hoke 33
Mustard Seed Christian Center 264
Mystery Cave at Forestville State Park 55
Mystic 13 Magic Club 24, 273

N
NAACP 271
Nachreiner Park 252
National Eagle Center and EagleWatch
    Observation Deck 137, 168
National Karate and Kickboxing 206
National Night Out 101
National Volleyball Center 229
nature centers 134
Nature Conservancy 138
Niagara Cave 52
Nielsen Tree Farm 146
Nordic Gypsy Beads & Jewelry 258
Nordic Lanes 183
Norsland Lefse 288
North American Versatile Hunting Dog
    Association—NAVHDA 268
North End Park Campground 124
Northern Heights Park 253
Northern Hills Golf Course 195, 245
Northgate Health Club 188
Nutcracker Ballet .75

O
Oak Center General Store 40
Oak Summit Golf Course 195
Oaks Golf Club .198
Oasis Courtyard Programs at Calvary
    Episcopal Church 26
O'Brien Christmas Wonderland 76
Ohuta Park 152
Old Barn Resort 123, 202
Old-Fashioned Barn Dance 88, 97
Old-Fashioned Christmas at
    Gunderson House 76
Old-Fashioned Fourth of July 94
Olde-Fashioned Christmas in Mantorville 76
Olde Tyme Days 89
Olmsted County Fair 95
Olmsted County Genealogical Society 272
Olmsted County Gold
    Rush Days 86, 101, 106
Olmsted County Government Volunteer
    Opportunities .279

Olmsted County Historical Society
  (& Museum) 66, 305
Optimist Club 276
orchards 142
Order of DeMolay 281
Oronoco Gold Rush Days 103
Oronoco Park 151
Oronoco Park Campground 121
Our Front Porch Gallery & Gathering Place . . .14
Outdoor Store .180
Owatonna Arts Center & Sculpture
  Garden 15
Owatonna Chamber of Commerce
  & Tourism 301
Owatonna Convention and
  Visitor's Bureau 302
Owatonna Country Club 202
Owatonna Extravaganza 97
Owatonna Roller Rink 213, 260
Owatonna Skate Park 217
Oxbow Park 114, 255
  and Zollmann Zoo 151, 244
  Nature Center 135
Oxbow Park Annual Fun Fest
  and Art Show 87

P

Paddock School of Horsemanship 131
paintball 207
Panera Bread 39
parents 257, 274
  see also: mothers
Parents Are Important in Rochester—
  PAIIR 257, 274
Parent's Night Out 274
Park Institute 206
park system chart 148
Patton Park 153
Paul Watkin's Art Gallery 16
Peace Fountain and Charles
  Eugene Gagnon 10
Peace Lantern Ceremony 102
Peace Plaza 50
Pease Wildlife Museum 67
Pepin Heights Orchard 143
performing arts .18
  see also: music; theater
Peterson, City of 302
Peterson Municipal Campground 122
Peterson State Fish Hatchery 167
Pheasants Forever 270
Picket Fence Garden & Gifts 52
Pickwick Mill 63
picnic shelters .147
Pied Piper Children's Books & Music 47
Pine Cheese Mart and Von Klopp
  Brew Shop 288
Pine Creek Golf Course 199
Pine Island Cheese Festival 89
Pine Island, City of 302

Pine Island Golf Course 202
Pine Island Historical Society 305
Pine Island Lanes 183
Pine Island Swimming Pool 226
Pine Island White Pines Sportsman Club 270
Pine Tree Orchards, Inc. 144
Pioneer Campsite Resort 127
Pioneer Lanes .183
Piper Hills Golf Club 202
Pipsqueaks Indoor Play Zone 208
Pla-Mor Ballroom 175
Pla-Mor Campground & Marina 126
Plainview Community Swimming Pool 226
Plainview History Association 305
play centers, indoor 207
Plummer House of Arts and Gardens 60
points of interest 50
Police Athletic League 281
Polish Cultural Institute 71
Ponderosa Campground 121
PossAbilities of Southern Minnesota 271
PossAbilities Youth Recreation
  Program 171, 232
Prairie Island Campground 127
Prairie Island Nature Area 169
Prairie Walls Climbing Gym 210, 211, 260
Preston Apple and Berry Farm 142, 144
Preston Area Tourism Association 303
Preston Golf and Country Club 203
Preston Historical Society 305
Preston Swimming Pool 226
Professional Skater's Association 252, 277
public speaking 278
Purplefoot Winemaker's Club 280
Putter's Paradise at Recreation Lanes . . .191, 259
Pyramid Theater Alliance 19

Q

Quality Sewing Machine Center 275, 276
Quarry Hill Nature Center Fall
  Harvest Festival 106
Quarry Hill Park and Nature Center . . .134, 147,
  149, 245, 259
Quilter's Sew-ciety Club 275
quilting 275
  see also: arts and crafts; sewing

R

R & M Amish Touring 54
radio-controlled NASCAR racing 208
Rebekah's 42
recreation centers 209
Recreation Lanes 176, 182, 191, 236, 258
Red's Berries 142
Rescue of Santa 111
Rhythm & Brew .41
Rice Lake State Park 159, 247, 255
Ricochets Gymnastics Club 234
RideAbility 171, 232

Riverboat Days 99
Riverside Trails 130, 133, 259
Riverview Campground 120
Riverview Greens Golf Course 204
Rochester Active Sports Club—RASC 277
Rochester Adaptive Recreation
  Program 171, 232, 271
Rochester Adopt-a-Park Program 150
Rochester Aero Model Society—RAMS 273
Rochester All-Stars Youth Cheerleading 233
Rochester Amateur Radio Club 275
Rochester Amateur Sports Commission 242
Rochester American Legion Baseball 233
Rochester Archery Club 174, 267
Rochester Area Bowling Association 268
Rochester Area Builders' Home and
  Garden Show 79
Rochester Area Chamber of
  Commerce 274, 301
Rochester Area Club Lacrosse—RACLX 233
Rochester Area Coin and Stamp Club 270
Rochester Area Companion Bird Club 267
Rochester Area Disabled Athletics
  and Recreation, Inc.—
  RADAR 172, 233, 271
Rochester Area Family
  YMCA 188, 206, 219, 231, 258, 260
Rochester Area Family YMCA—
  Dolphins Swim Team 234
Rochester Area Family YMCA
  Youth Programs and Y-Mentors 281
Rochester Area Girls' Choir 34
Rochester Area Gymnastics Academy—
  RAGA 234, 259
Rochester Area Keyboard Club 273
Rochester Area Solo Parents
  & Singles .274, 277
Rochester Area Special
  Olympics 172, 234, 271
Rochester Area Square and
  Round Dancing 270
Rochester Area Youth for Christ 269
Rochester Aria Group 27
Rochester Art Center 11
Rochester Association of Christian
  Home Educators 275
Rochester Athletic Club . . . .
  177, 189, 207, 220, 222, 227, 228, 231, 258,
  260
Rochester Balloon Company 206
Rochester Bike Trails 177
Rochester Boychoir .34
Rochester Carillon 27, 60
Rochester Chess Club 269
Rochester Civic Music 27
  Rochester Civic Music Community Band . . .28
  Rochester Civic Music Concert Band 28
  Rochester Civic Music Concert Choir 28
Rochester Civic Theater 19
Rochester Civitan 276

Rochester Community and
  Technical College 231
Rochester Community Education 231, 279
Rochester Community Youth
  Basketball Association—RCYBA 234
Rochester Convention & Visitor's Bureau . . .302
Rochester Diving Club 235
Rochester Dog Obedience Club 268
Rochester Duplicate Bridge Club 268
Rochester Eagles Club 276
Rochester Figure Skating Club . . .235, 252, 277
Rochester Figure Skating Club
  Annual Ice Show 84, 241
Rochester Garden and Flower Club . . .141, 272
  tour 140
Rochester Giants 190
Rochester Golf and Country Club 195
Rochester Greeters 274
Rochester Honkers Baseball Club 243
Rochester Horseshoe Club 272
Rochester Indoor Golf Center 193, 259
Rochester Indoor Tennis Club 227, 261
Rochester International Association 271
Rochester International Film Festival 84
Rochester International Film Group—
  RIFG 271
Rochester Jaycees .276
Rochester Juggling Club 272
Rochester Kiwanis Clubs 276
Rochester League of Women Voters 280
Rochester Lions Clubs 276
Rochester Male Chorus 29
Rochester/Marion KOA Kampgrounds 113
Rochester Matmen—Youth
  Wrestling Club .235
Rochester Methodist Hospital 50
Rochester Minnesota Kennel Club 268
Rochester Moose Lodge 276
Rochester Music Guild 29
Rochester Music Men 30
Rochester Mystic 13 Magic Club 24, 273
Rochester Neighborhood
  Resource Center 274
Rochester Newcomer's Club 274
Rochester-Olmsted Recreation Center . . . .
  . . . . .148, 190, 220, 250, 258, 259, 260
Rochester Orchestra and Chorale 30
Rochester Outdoor Tennis Center 228
Rochester Park and Recreation Department . . . .
  147, 148, 206, 218, 228, 230, 231, 244, 252,
  253, 254
Rochester Public Library 47, 268
  special performances at 20
  visitor privileges at 48
Rochester Public Library Writer's Groups 280
Rochester Radio Theater Guild 20
Rochester Repertory Theater Company 20
Rochester Retired Greyhounds as Pets—
  REGAP 268
Rochester Roadrunners 176

Rochester Rogues Rugby Football Club 216
Rochester Roosters Old Time
  Baseball 90, 102, 243
Rochester Rough Riders 272
Rochester Rowing Club 215, 275
Rochester Royals Baseball 176
Rochester Scuba and Snorkel Club 275
Rochester Sea Kayakers Club 275
Rochester Senior Citizen Center 275
Rochester skating trails 213
Rochester Soccer Club 218
Rochester Sports and Vacation Show 77
Rochester Swim Club Orcas and
  Olympic Swim School 235
Rochester Track Club 229, 279
Rochester Water Ski Club 92, 241, 280
Rochester Women's Bowling Association . . .268
Rochester Woodcarver's Club 281
Rochester World Festival 84
Rochester Youth Baseball Association—
  RYBA 236
Rochester youth bowling 236
Rochester Youth Cheerleading
  Association—RYCA 236
Rochester Youth Fastpitch Softball
  Association 236
Rochester Youth Football Association—
  RYFA 236
Rochester Youth Hockey Association—
  RYHA 237
Rochester Youth Soccer Association—
  RYSA 172, 237
Rochester Youth Softball—Girl's
  Slow Pitch 237
Rochester Youth Volleyball Association—
  RYVA 237
Rochester Youth Wrestling Association—
  RYWA 237
RochesterFest 90
Rochester's Fourth of July Fireworks and
  Community Concert 94
Rochester's Municipal Garden Plots 141
rock climbing 211, 260
Rock Solid Youth Center 211
Root River Country Club 203
Root River Outfitters 179, 186
Root River Outfitters at the
  Old Barn Resort 180
Root River Poetry Association 280
Root River State Trail 179, 215, 247
Root River Trail Towns 303
Root River Trail Wagon Ride 107
Roshen Park 153
rowing 215, 275
  see also: boating; canoes; sea kayaking
rugby 216
Run-n-Gun Paint Ball Sports 207
Rural America Writers' Center 280
Rushford Aquatic Center 225
Rushford Area Historical Organization 305

Rushford Area Historic Depot Museum
  and Trail Center 69, 303
Rushford's Parade of Lights 76

S

Sail Away of Lake City 182
Sailboats, Inc. 182
Saint Mary's Hospital 50
Sandtrap 193
Scenic Valley Winery 55
Schech's Water Powered Mill 61
Schulz Christmas Trees 145
Screwball Balloons 206
scuba & snorkeling club 275
Search 273
Sears House 64
Sekapp Orchard and Farms 52, 142
SEMVA—Southeastern Minnesota
  Visual Artists Gallery 12
Senior Citizen's Duplicate Bridge Club 268
senior citizens organizations 275
Sertoma 700 Club of Rochester 276
Sertoma 1200 Club of Rochester 276
service clubs 275
  see also: volunteer organizations
Service Corps of Retired Executives—
  SCORE 268
sewing 276
  see also: arts and crafts; quilting
Shades of Sherwood 129
shooting sports 216, 270
Silver Lake Canoe & Paddle Boats 185
Silver Lake Gym .184
Silver Lake Municipal Pool 222
Silver Lake Park 149, 150, 161
  East 147
  Three Links 147
  West 147
Silver Lake RV Park 113
Silver Lake Skate Park 217
Silver Pear at the Fast Frame Gallery 12
Single Volunteers of Rochester 277, 279
singles' clubs 276
Singles in Agriculture 277
skateboard parks 217
skating
  clubs 252, 277
  figure 241
  ice .206, 250, 259
  inline 212
  rinks 250, 252, 253, 260
  roller 212, 260
  trails 213
  see also: hockey rinks; skateboard parks
Ski Swap 109
skiing
  clubs 277
  cross-country .244
  downhill 248
  trails 244

see also: Water Ski Days; Water Ski Shows;
  waterskiing club
SKILINK™ Ski Club for Kids 249, 277
skydiving club 277
Skyline Raceway 190, 191, 259
Skyline Raceway (waterslide only) 222
Skyway Golf Classic 79
Slatterly Park 147, 149, 150
sledding 253
sled dog club 277
  see also: canine club
sleigh rides .132
Slim's Woodshed Woodcarving Museum 68
Snow Tubing at Ironwood Springs
  Christian Ranch 254, 260
Snowmobile Challenge Cup 256
snowmobiling 256, 277
snowshoeing 254
Socrates Youth Futbol Club 238
Sojourner Café 41
Soldiers Field Golf Course 196, 245
Soldiers Field Memorial Park 147, 149, 150
Soldiers Field Municipal Pool 223
Soldiers Field Veterans' Memorial 61
Southeastern Minnesota Flying Club 272
Southeastern Minnesota Historic
  Bluff Country Visitor's Bureau 303
Southeastern Minnesota Prairie Day 100
Southeastern Minnesota Suzuki
  Association—SEMSA 34
Southeastern Minnesota Youth
  Orchestra—SEMYO 35
Southeastern Winds Community Band 31
Southern Minnesota Adult Soccer
  Association—SMASA 218
Southern Minnesota Chapter of the
  U.S. Amateur Ballroom Dancers
  Association—USABDA 175, 270
Southern Minnesota Mothers of Multiples . .274
Southern Minnesota Sled Dog Club 277
Southern Minnesota Sportsman's Club 270
Southern Minnesota Youth Works 279
Southern Minnesota Youth Works—
  Americorps Program 281
Southside Speedway and Hobby
  Shop .208, 272
Spare Time Lanes 183
Special Performances at Rochester
  Public Library 20
spiritual resources 262
sports leagues for adults 218
sports teams 242
sportsmen's clubs 216
Spring Creek Motocross (MX) Park 240
Spring Grove Area 303
Spring Grove Snowmobile Club 278
Spring Grove Swimming Pool 226
Spring Valley Chamber of Commerce 301
Spring Valley Community Historical
  Society 305

Spring Valley Swimming Pool 226
Spring Valley Tourist Information Center 303
Spruce Pine Tree Farms 145
Square Dance Federation of
  Minnesota 219, 278
St. Charles, City of 301
St. Charles Golf Club 203
St. Charles Tourist Information 303
stamp collecting 270
Starbucks at Barnes & Noble 39
Starbucks at Barnes & Noble—
  Historic Chateau Theatre 39, 50
Starlite Bowling Center 183
state parks 157
  campgrounds 113
Steam Engine Park 153
Steamboat Days Festival 93
Steele County Fair 100
Steele County Historical Society 305
Steele County Speedway 239
Steeplechase Ski & Snowboard Area 249
Sterling Berry Farm 142
Stewartville Area Historical Society 305
Stewartville Bowl 183
Stewartville Chamber of Commerce 301
Stewartville Community Band 32
Stewartville Community Pool 226
Stewartville Driftskippers 278
Stewartville Performing Arts Center 22, 300
Stewartville Sportsman Club 270
story telling 47
Studio Academy Gallery 12
Sugar Loaf Bluff 57
Summer of Service—SOS 279, 282
Summer Saturday Nite Concerts 93
Summer Weekend Getaway at
  Eagle Bluff Environmental Center 92
Summerfest
  LeRoy 95
  Stewartville 95
Supersaw Valley Campground 124
Survival Days .95
SVJ Creative Designs 287
Sweet Adelines 30
swimming 219, 260
  indoor pools and waterparks 219
  lessons 227
  outdoor pools and swimming areas 221
Swimming Beach at Whitewater State Park . .223
Sylvan Park 153
Sylvan Park Campground 121
Syttende Mai Celebration 88

T
Tango Society of Minnesota 270
tea rooms 36
teen dance—nightclubs 278
tennis 227
theater(s) 18
Theatre du Mississippi 22

toastmasters groups 278
Tom Jarland Carriage Service 133
Town Bell Clock and Alarm 61
Toy Zone 285
track 229
   club 279
Trailbusters Snowmobile Club 278
Trailhead Inn 180
Transportation Fair .86
Traverski Ski & Sports Club 277
treasure hunters 279
Treats and Treasures 287
Treehouse 289
Tri-County Trail Blazers 278
Trollskogen Park & Campground 125
Trombones Anonymous 31
Trout Days 88
tubing 184
Turn Crest Stable 131
Tweite's Pumpkin Patch 109, 132

U

Uff-Da Days 100
Union—Plainview Youth Center 210
United Skates Roller Skating Center . . .212, 260
University Center Art Gallery 12
Upper Mississippi National Wildlife
   and Fish Refuge .169

V

Val Webb Gallery 13
Valley Crest Riders Snowmobile Club 278
Valley High Country Club 198
Valley Lanes 183
Valley Street Machines Annual Car
   and Truck Show & Swap Meet 96
VanGundy's Elk Farm & Antler Shed
   Gift Shop 165, 286
Vegetarian Information Group of
   Rochester—V.I.G.O.R 279
Vertigo Theatre Factory 20
Victorian Lace Inn B & B, Tea Room
   & Gift Shop .42, 260
Viking Park 253
Villa Maria Retreat and Conference Center . .264
Village Green 286
Village of Yesteryear 63
Viola Gopher Count 89
Voices of the Valley .91
Volksfest 89
volleyball 229
Volunteer Connections 279
volunteer organizations 279
   see also: service clubs
Volunteers in Education 279

W–X

Wabasha Area Chamber of Commerce
   & Tourist Information Center 301, 303

Wabasha County Fair 95
Wabasha County Historical Society 305
Wabasha Swimming Pool 226
walking 230, 281
Walksport America 230, 280
Walleye Searchers of Minnesota 271
Wanamingo Historical Society 305
Wanamingo Swimming Pool 226
Warehouse Ceramics 269
Washburn-Zittleman Historic House 70
Water Ski Days 91
Water Ski Shows 241
waterskiing club 280
Watercolors for Lita's Children 13
Watermelon Days .105
Waterpark at the Hawthorn Suites 221
Watkins Museum 71
Wazionja Campground 122
Wedding Extravaganza 77
Wedgewood Park .154
Welch Mill Canoeing & Tubing 186
Welch Village Fall Festival and Ski
   & Snowboard Swap 109
Welch Village Ski and Snowboard Area 250
Wells Fargo Bank 55
Wescott Orchard and Agriproducts 142
West Concord Historical Society 305
West Concord Pool 226
Westfield Golf Course 205
Westgate Bowl 184
Whippoorwill Ranch Kampground 126
Whitewater State Park 157, 245, 255
Whitewater State Park Geological Center . . .134
Wild Wings Fall Festival 107
Wild Wings Gallery 14
Wilder Fest 100
wildlife 161
   see also: nature centers; zoos
William Pease Wildlife Management Area . .163
Willow Creek Campground 114
Willow Creek Golf Course & Little Willow
   Executive 9-Hole Course 196
Windmill Haven 146
Windrider Ballooning 206
winemaking 280
Winona Area Chamber of Commerce 301
Winona Arts Center 16
Winona Bowl 184
Winona Convention and Visitor's Bureau . . .303
Winona Country Club 205
Winona County Fair 95
Winona County Historical Society 305
Winona Polish Apple Day—
   Smaczne Jabika 110
Winona Railroad Club 273
Winona's 4.8 Skate Park 217
Winona's Glorious Stained Glass Tour 65
Winter Fest 80
Winter Weekend Getaway at Eagle Bluff
   Environmental Learning Center 80

women 280
  see also: mothers
Women of Today 280
woodcarving 68, 97, 281
Woodruff's Llamas 162
Writers of the Roundtable 281
writing 280
Wykoff Area Historical Society 305
Wykoff Tourist Information 303

Y
Young Life 269
youth clubs and groups 281
Youth Commission of Olmsted County 282
Youth Firearms Safety and Adult Hunter
  Education 216
Youth Ice Fishing Contest 79
youth sports camps 230
youth sports organizations 231
Yulefest 75

Z
Zephyr Skate Tours and Vacations 213
Zollman Zoo at Oxbow Park and
  Nature Center .162
zoos 161
  see also: nature centers; wildlife
Zumbro Falls Golf Club 205
Zumbro Park South 253
Zumbro Valley Audubon Society 267
Zumbro Valley Canoe & Tube Rental 187
Zumbro Valley Recreation Club 201
Zumbro Valley Sportsmen's Park 129
Zumbro Valley Treasure Hunters 279
Zumbrota Chamber of Commerce 301
Zumbrota Covered Bridge 65
Zumbrota Covered Bridge Music and
  Arts Festival 93, 157
Zumbrota Golf Club 205
Zumbrota Swimming Pool 227

About the Autor

Nicole O. Hansen, a 15-year resident of Rochester, is also a wife, mother, family manager, writer, occupational therapist, and community volunteer. Her educational background includes a master's degree in occupational therapy from Texas Woman's University and a bachelor's degree in psychology from West Virginia Wesleyan College. Prior to her profession as a full-time mother, Nicole was employed as an occupational therapist by the Mayo Clinic in Rochester, Minnesota. As a writer, Nicole has had the privilege of studying under the guidance of Minnesota author, Carol Bly, and has taken writing workshops at The Loft in Minneapolis. *Out & About in Rochester & Southeastern Minnesota* is her first book.

Please feel free to write to the author with feedback and/or updated information for the second edition of *Out & About in Rochester & Southeastern Minnesota* at the following address:

Nicole O. Hansen
P.O. Box 7236
Rochester, MN 55903

www.outandaboutinrochester.com
e-mail: nicole@outandaboutinrochester.com

Photo Credit: copyright Hart Photography, Rochester, MN 55902

Notes